The

WRITERS
STUDIO

at

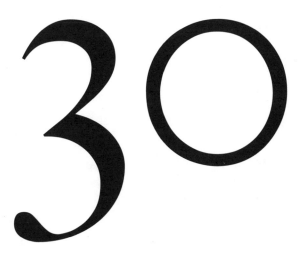

Fiction and poetry from the first 30 years of the
landmark school of creative writing and thinking

FOREWORD BY PULITZER PRIZE-WINNING POET
AND THE WRITERS STUDIO FOUNDER AND DIRECTOR, PHILIP SCHULTZ

EDITOR, ODETTE HEIDEMAN / POETRY EDITORS, LISA BELLAMY AND PETER KRASS

EPIPHANY EDITIONS

ISBN: 978-0-692-86066-3

Epiphany Editions
71 Bedford Street
New York, NY
10014

CONTENTS

A FEW WORDS ABOUT THE WRITERS STUDIO 12
Philip Schultz

THE ADVENTURES OF 78 CHARLES STREET 15
Philip Schultz

I

THE WRITERS STUDIO
ADVISORY BOARD AND FRIENDS

THE LUCKY ONES 19
Jill Bialosky

THE GOD WHO LOVES YOU 20
Carl Dennis

BAD DREAM 22
Cornelius Eady

ONE PIECE 23
Jennifer Egan

ATTAINABLE FELICITY 35
Julia Glass

THE WATCH 46
Edward Hirsch

ISSUES I DEALT WITH IN THERAPY 47
  Matthew Klam

THE INCALCULABLE LIFE GESTURE 62
  James Lasdun

IN THE COMA... 72
  Robert Pinsky

PRAYER 73
  Grace Schulman

THE SWEET RED AWAKENING OF BRUCE ALLEN DeSILVA 75
  Patricia Smith

COTILLION PHOTO 77
  Rosanna Warren

II

THE WRITERS STUDIO
TEACHERS AND STUDENTS

MIDDLE SCHOOL GARDENING CLUB...................................... 80
  Laurel Ingraham Aquadro

HARVEST 82
  L.L. Babb

MACAROONS: THE LAST DAYS 93
  Lisa Badner

THE ENGLISH DEGREE 95
  J. Banerjee

Forgetting 98
  Cécile Barlier

Monkey Spinning a Prayer Wheel.................................. 105
  Lisa Bellamy

One of Them 106
  Sylvie Bertrand

Best of the Boy Stuff 120
  Reneé Bibby

Why I Fly-fish 130
  Julianne Bond

Overboard... 131
  Robley Browne

Old Dog... 134
  Christina Perez Brubaker

No Lie 148
  Erica Bryant

wind 149
  Ross Bryant

Love Me Two Times 150
  Sarah Carriger

Hellion 161
  Doris Cheng

Then One Day You Give A Guy Your Legs 169
  Jennafer D'Alvia

Road Trip with a Dead Therapist 177
    Isabelle Deconinck

The Old Economy Husband 190
    Lesley Dormen

Chekhov Said 203
    Therese Eiben

First Girl 208
    Elizabeth England

She-Monster Gets Fired 213
    Kim Farrar

Thank You For Making Today Beautiful 215
    Patricia Follert

Painter Hung Liu introduced herself saying 217
    Gail Ford

First Kill 219
    Janet Franklin

Judy Garland Gets Dressed 220
    Christina Frei

In the Concession 222
    Annette Frost

The Good Wife 223
    Rebecca Gee

Product Recall 224
    Judy Gerbin

DOOR OPEN! 226
James Gibbs

EAT, EAT, EAT 232
Sherine Gilmour

PATRIMONY 235
Nancy Green

KEEP MOVING 242
Patrick Hansel

A ROOM THAT HAS LIZZY IN IT 243
Michele Herman

PERSONS IN NEED OF SUPERVISION 253
Joel Hinman

CALL AND RESPONSE 265
Lucinda Holt

A DRIP 272
Carey Ann Hunt

WILDING 273
Scott Hunter

PROBABLY LAST MEETING OF BLUEBELL RIDGE II HOMEOWNERS
ASSOCIATION 283
Philip Ivory

CLEAVED 286
Kathie Jacobson

THE BOAT AND THE WATER 293
Elizabeth Kandall

Echo Lake..295
Timur Karaca

Eve 302
Jennifer Kearns

Apple Pie 304
Eleanor Kedney

El Camino...306
Robert Kendrick

Uprising 307
Maggie Kennedy

Satellites 311
Hani Omar Khalil

I watch him, my husband..313
Jay Kidd

Trust...314
Liz Kingsley

All Dressed in Green..315
Peter Krass

Domino 316
Cori Kresge

Implausible 317
Iris Lee

Anyone Crazier Than You 318
Andrée Lockwood

STILL 324
Ann Lovett

PLAYBOY.. 325
Lela Scott MacNeil

GRAFFITI DREAMS 332
Marnie Maguire

BACK... 334
Andrea Marcusa

ETCHINGS.. 336
Nancy Matsunaga

PURPLE HEAD... 345
Sarah McElwain

ON THE AMERICAN PLAN 353
Joanne Naiman

THE WORLD OUTSIDE MY BELLY........................... 365
Rachael Lynn Nevins

DANCERS 366
Mark Fenlon Peterson

BETHPAGE BLACK 374
Jean Pfeffer

THE CLOSET.. 375
Whitney Porter

SHIP OUT ON THE SEA 378
Máire T. Robinson

GRIEF 380
Joyce Roschinger

THE LEGACY 381
Desiree Rucker

PIECE OF MY HEART...383
Elliot Satsky

A LESSON IN COLORS, PARTS 1 & 2 394
Rosalia Scalia

THE RED BIRD 399
J.D. Serling

ASTRONAUTS..410
Christopher X. Shade

A PRICE FOR LITERACY..413
R. A. Shockley

HOW YOU LEARN YOUR EX IS DATING AN APPLE RETAIL SPECIALIST
ALSO THE DJ ALSO A TRANSMAN &HOW YOU LEARN TO PRAY,
REALIZING YOU WANT HER BACK...416
Tristan Silverman

ACROBAT 418
Patricia Solari

STILL. LIFE...419
Mara Sonnenschein

SKIN 428
Douglas Sovern

FOUR DECKHANDS..437
Sean Sutherland

THE SWANS...438
   Anamyn Turowski

THE FATE OF ANTON K —..441
   Santian Vataj

THUGS 450
   Iromie Weeramantry

BOYFRIENDS 454
   Cynthia Weiner

HOMECOMING..468
   Abigail Wender

KNITTING AIR...470
   Carol White

LOU GEHRIG'S ARMY 471
   Catherine Wolf

CONTRIBUTORS NOTES..472

PREVIOUS PUBLICATION CREDITS 495

A Few Words About
The Writers Studio

RECENTLY, ON A FLIGHT TO MANTUA, ITALY, the Italian man seated next to me asked me what I did for a living. It's a question I usually dread because telling someone I'm a poet usually makes him or her self-conscious, and can end even a casual conversation. It's as if they suddenly see their sentences being diagrammed on a blackboard by Mrs. Hildebrand, their fourth grade teacher. Some look at you as if they can't understand how they misjudged you so completely. Poets, after all, are wounded, forlorn, self-absorbed creatures and I looked so normal and nice. But we were about to land in Milan and I'd been up half the night listening to his sometimes-fascinating saga about raising goats and sheep on the organic farm he'd started in the Hudson Valley, and I was too tired to lie. So I told him straight out, regretting it immediately. He sat back and looked confused, and a little curious, and said, "But that's so impractical." Yes, this from someone who raises sheep and sells goat cheese for a living. And then, after we landed and I was getting my bag, he added, "Yes, okay, but what do you *do* for a living?"

I told him I directed the small school for creative writing that I founded some thirty years ago and, smiling now, he laughed, "Well, that's even more impractical. Without a doubt you do the two most impractical things I can imagine."

Why this anecdote by way of an introduction to an anthology of work gathered to celebrate and maybe verify the existence of an idea that's somehow stretched over the past thirty years, an idea that's become a school of highly valuable and intriguing students and teachers, who have all, in their own unique ways, managed to both inspire and enrich my life for so long?

Without doubt the desire to write imaginatively and seriously is indeed an impractical thing to do; impractical, risky and provocative. And perhaps somewhat magical, too. Many who grew up with me in the immigrant streets of Rochester, NY in the fifties would probably call it crazy. Why bother to educate myself if I would throw it all away on such a whimsical notion? And what to make of all my students over all these years, how to understand what it is they were all asking of themselves, and of me? In many cases they've had to give up valuable time and money to pursue something others see as byzantine and arcane. Even the ones who finally quit trying to be writers encountered something in themselves they hadn't known was there before, a seriousness of purpose perhaps, or an identity that gives much more than it takes: the gift of purpose and self-appreciation, of satisfaction. A synonym for the word impractical is unusable, or useless. Was this goat farmer really asking me why I was doing something so useless? He at least produced food, sustained the lives of essential animals, not to mention his own. What was I sustaining, I and so many like me?

Most serious literary writing gathers a rather small audience compared to its more commercial relations, and the audience for poetry has probably grown smaller since you began reading this. Yet to most writers this isn't a source of complaint, but of pride. Yes, we want to be read but we want something else much more. We want to say something only we can say, demonstrate something essential that others, complete strangers, can acknowledge and perhaps even feel some sympathy for; to go on record as having felt this and believed that during this particular time. And we know that in order to accomplish this we must not ask for more, though more may come, more can't be allowed to infringe on or blur the goal. In other words, we can't allow ourselves to wonder if such a curious, preposterous and splendid a process is practical, or especially useful.

As my wife, Monica Banks, who has enabled this school to perform at its highest level for many years, often reminds me, I'm a lucky man. Lucky to have been entrusted with the well-being of so many precious imaginations, for the opportunity of teaching and the friendships and affection it has engendered over all these years. No one does anything alone, of course. This anthology isn't so much a sampler of achievements, although the stories and poems gathered here do indeed represent achievement. It's an offering of thanks and a show of indebtedness. Often enough, the school seems to own a life of its own, to have come about according to its own mysterious means, in the way, say, a poem seems to own its jurisprudence, its own special environment. But The Writers Studio didn't just appear out of nowhere early one spring morning; it was imagined and cobbled together, idea by idea, mistake by mistake, and its main idea—that of persona writing, borrowing another writer's narrator, his or her personality, attitude, and disarray and filtering it through the generous bravado of a Walt Whitman and Ernest Hemingway, or the childlike, lusty wonder of an Isaac Babel narrator — evolved out of my early love of the first-person narrators that allowed me to immerse myself in the colorfully beguiling imaginations of such engaging storytellers. The school first appeared in the form of a business license I got in the fall of 1987 at City Hall in New York City, when I started to refer to my small (tiny, some would say) one-bedroom apartment at 78 Charles Street, in the heart of the West Village, as headquarters. Little did I understand what I was starting, certainly not why.

The blame for which can be spread among many amazing friends and students, among them Marc Frons, Elliot Figman, Abby Wender, Frazier Russell, Harold Marcus, Lisa Kaufman, Amy Dana, and especially Eleanor Kedney, Mark Peterson, Therese Eiben and Nancy Matsunaga who extended the idea to San Francisco, Tucson, Amsterdam and the Hudson Valley; and those who make the school function: Cynthia Weiner, our Assistant Director, Lesley Dormen, our Associate Director, Liz Kingsley, our Administrative Director, Reneé Bibby, our Branches Director, and Lisa Bellamy, who teaches so many essential classes and, along with Peter Krass, read the poetry submissions for this anthology, as well as Andrée Lockwood, who helped with the fiction, Lucinda Holt, who runs our online program, Rebecca Gee, who runs our KidsWrite non-profit branch, and Isabelle Deconinck, who runs our reading series and provides invaluable support. I especially want to thank Willard Cook, Odette Heideman and Moss Turpan of *Epiphany*, who offered so much guidance and expertise in putting this anthology together. And for the friendship, advice and inspiration of our Advisory Board: Jill Bialosky, Kathryn Court, Carl Dennis, Jennifer Egan, Julia Glass, Marc Frons, Bill Henderson, Edward Hirsch, Matt Klam, Robert Pinsky, Grace Schulman, and Rosanna Warren. Most of all I want to thank my wife, Monica Banks, who came up with the idea for this anthology of student and teacher work and without whose wisdom and guidance this strange endeavor never would've occurred. A window then into the kind of thing we teach and encourage. Enjoy then this rich assortment of impractical and willful voices. They know, I truly believe, whereof they speak.

— Philip Schultz

The Adventures of 78 Charles Street

Philip Schultz

(From *Failure* / Originally published in *The New Yorker*)

For thirty-two years Patricia Parmelee's yellow light
has burned all night
in her kitchen down the hall in 2E.
Patricia — I love to say her name — Par-me-lee!
knows where, across the street,
Hart Crane wrote "The Bridge,"
the attic Saul Bellow holed up in
furiously scribbling *The Adventures of Augie March,*
the rooftop Bing Crosby yodeled off,
dreaming of Broadway, the knotty,
epicene secrets of each born-again town house.
Indeed, we, Patricia and me, reminisce
about tiny Lizzie and Joe Pasquinnucci,
one deaf, the other near-blind,
waddling hand-in-hand down the hall,
up the stairs, in and out of doors,
remembering sweetening Sicilian peaches,
ever-blooming daylilies, a combined one hundred
and seventy years of fuming sentence fragments,
elastic stockings, living and out-living
everyone on the south side of Charles Street.

How Millie Kelterborn, a powerhouse
of contemptuous capillaries inflamed
with memories of rude awakenings,
wrapped herself in black chiffon
when her knocked-up daughter Kate married a Mafia son
and screamed "Nixon, blow me!"

out her fifth-floor window,
then dropped dead face first
into her gin-spiked oatmeal.
How overnight Sharon in 4E
became a bell-ringing Buddhist
explaining cat litter, America, pleurisy, multiple orgasms,
why I couldn't love anyone who loved me.

And Archie McGee in 5W, one silver cross earring,
a tidal wave of dyed black hair,
jingling motorcycle boots, Jesus boogying
on each enraged oiled bicep, screaming
four flights down at me for asking
the opera singer across the courtyard to pack it in,
"This is NYC, shithead, where fat people sing while fucking!"
Archie, whom Millie attacked with pliers
and Lizzie fell over, drunk on the stairs, angry
if you nodded or didn't, from whom, hearing his boots,
I hid shaking under the stairwell,
until I found him trembling outside my door,
"Scram, Zorro, I'll be peachy in the morning."
In a year three others here were dead of AIDS,
everyone wearing black
but in the West Village everyone did
every day anyway.

Patricia says, The Righteous Brothers and I
moved in Thanksgiving, 1977,
and immediately began looking for
that ever loving feeling, rejoicing
at being a citizen of the ever-clanging future,
all of us walking up Perry Street,
down West Tenth, around Bleecker,
along the Hudson, with dogs, girlfriends
and hangovers, stoned and insanely sober,
arm in arm and solo, under the big skyline,
traffic whizzing by, through

indefatigable sunshine, snow and rain,
listening to The Stones, Monk, Springsteen and Beethoven,
one buoyant foot after the other, nodding hello
good morning happy birthday adieu adios auf wiedersehen!
before anyone went co-op, renovated,
thought about being sick or dying,
when we all had hair and writhed on the floor
because someone didn't love us anymore,
when nobody got up before noon, wore a suit
or joined anything, before there was hygiene,
confetti, a salary, cholesterol,
or a list of names to invite to a funeral ...

Yes, the adventures of a street in a city of everlasting hubris,
and Patricia's yellow light
when I can't sleep and come to the kitchen
to watch its puny precious speck stretch
so quietly so full of reverence
into the enormous darkness,
and I, overcome with love for everything so quickly fading,
my head stuck out the window
breathing the intoxicating melody
of our shouldered-and-cemented-in little island,
here, now, in the tenement of this moment,
dear Patricia's light,
night after night,
burning with all the others,
on 78 Charles Street.

I

THE WRITERS STUDIO
ADVISORY BOARD
AND FRIENDS

THE LUCKY ONES

Jill Bialosky

(from *The Players*)

Our labor realized in the crowns
of marigolds, blue eyes of the hydrangeas,
smell of lavender and late bloom of the hosta's
erect purple flower with its marvel of thick
green leaves. In our twilight
every year we trimmed back and the garden grew
more lustrous and untamable as if the eternal woods
and animals asleep at night in its beds were claiming it back.
The water in the pool shimmered an icy Tuscan blue.

When we arrived we swam
until the stress from the grueling
life in the city released our bodies. Later
we sat under the umbrella and watched a garter snake
slip into the water, careful not to startle
its flight-or-fight response. Its barbed-wire
coil. Comet of danger, serpent of the water,
how long we had thwarted the venom of its secret
lures and seductions.
It swam by arching then releasing
its slithery mercurial form.
Through the lanky trees
we heard the excited cries

of the neighbor's children—ours, the boy of our late youth,
of our happiness and our struggles, the boy who made us whole
and broken, was in his room perhaps dreaming
of a girl and sleeping the long, tangled sleep of a teenager.

It was a miracle, our ignorance. It was grace
incarnate, how we never knew.

THE GOD WHO LOVES YOU

Carl Dennis

(From *Practical Gods*)

It must be troubling for the god who loves you
To ponder how much happier you'd be today
Had you been able to glimpse your many futures.
It must be painful for him to watch you on Friday evenings
Driving home from the office, content with your week—
Three fine houses sold to deserving families—
Knowing as he does exactly what would have happened
Had you gone to your second choice for college,
Knowing the roommate you'd have been allotted
Whose ardent opinions on painting and music
Would have kindled in you a lifelong passion.
A life thirty points above the life you're living
On any scale of satisfaction. And every point
A thorn in the side of the god who loves you.
You don't want that, a large-souled man like you
Who tries to withhold from your wife the day's disappointments
So she can save her empathy for the children.
And would you want this god to compare your wife
With the woman you were destined to meet on the other campus?
It hurts you to think of him ranking the conversation
You'd have enjoyed over there higher in insight
Than the conversation you're used to.
And think how this loving god would feel
Knowing that the man next in line for your wife
Would have pleased her more than you ever will
Even on your best days, when you really try.
Can you sleep at night believing a god like that
Is pacing his cloudy bedroom, harassed by alternatives
You're spared by ignorance? The difference between what is

And what could have been will remain alive for him
Even after you cease existing, after you catch a chill
Running out in the snow for the morning paper,
Losing eleven years that the god who loves you
Will feel compelled to imagine scene by scene
Unless you come to the rescue by imagining him
No wiser than you are, no god at all, only a friend
No closer than the actual friend you made at college,
The one you haven't written in months. Sit down tonight
And write him about the life you can talk about
With a claim to authority, the life you've witnessed,
Which for all you know is the life you've chosen.

Bad Dream

Cornelius Eady

(From *Transition: Poems in the Aftermath*)

It's like waking up, but not waking up
The things of this world
A film in your mouth,
Milk in the fridge a bit
Too long, you know
That flavor,

You're walking in a thrift shop
— how did you get there?
And the thought occurs
As you check the price tags
That everything you see

Once had a glory
Before the rust sat in,
Was once connected
To something bigger
Whose story

Is now gone. Forever.

Then you wake up
But you don't wake up
And you walk to a coffee shop

What happened?
Everyone there shivers and sips
Sips and shivers.

How did you all land in a coffee shop?
How come this coffee doesn't work?

The bad taste in the cup.

ONE PIECE

Jennifer Egan

(From *Emerald City and Other Stories* /
Originally published in *North American Review*)

My brother builds models for a hobby. From plastic pieces he makes ships and airplanes, racing cars, those see-through human bodies where you put in the heart and stomach and things. I arrange the pieces for him. For years we've had the same quiet days: lawn mower sounds, children laughing on our neighbors' lawns, faint noises of TV from where Dad sits alone in his study watching a game. Every year the models get more complicated.

Six years ago, when Bradley was ten years old and I was seven, our mother started the car to take us shopping. After backing out of the garage, she remembered her grocery coupons. We stayed in the car, engine running, while she went inside to get them. It was a hot day, one of those afternoons when bits of white fluff fill up the air and under everything you hear beating locusts. That's how I think of it now, anyway.

Bradley sat in front. While our mother was gone, he slid over and started fooling around at the wheel, making believe he was driving. The electric door to the garage was shut. When our mother came back with her coupon book, she walked through the space between the garage door and the front of the car to get to her side. She was in a hurry. She had on a straw hat, and her hair flopped out the front. Maybe because of that hat she couldn't see Bradley. Maybe she saw him and thought it was safe to walk there.

The car jerked forward and hit the door. You wouldn't think a person could be so hurt from a thing like that, but they said she had bleeding inside her. Sometimes I stare at those plastic human models in Bradley's room with all their different parts and wonder which parts of her bled.

I remember my mother like you remember a good, long dream you had. I see a beautiful shadow leaning down, maybe over the edge of my crib. I remember her singing a lot, silly songs when she dried me after a bath about friendly vegetables and farm animals speaking in rhyme. She was in the church choir, and we would walk there together through the snow on mornings when the sun was so bright I had to keep my eyes closed. I held her hand, and she guided me over the ice.

There's one time I remember most, like that part of a dream that keeps coming back. She was leaving for the airport, dressed up in nice shoes and panty hose, and I was riding my trike. I must have been four years old. As she walked toward the car, I rode behind her, pedaling faster and faster until I hit her ankle and tore the stocking and made her bleed. It wasn't an accident. I knew what would happen; but I couldn't believe it. I kept pedaling.

I remember the look on her face when she turned and saw me behind her. Her mouth opened, and she stood touching her hair for a minute. Then she leaned down and put her hand on the bloody cut. I cried like I'd been hit myself. When I think of that now, I still want to.

With Bradley in the car, maybe it was like that. I think about it.

*

BRADLEY LIKES DOING THINGS that are dangerous. Stunts, I mean. He's raced motorcycles and jumped from a plane in a parachute. He's run along the top of a train, hang-glided, sailed alone on Lake Michigan when a storm was due. I watched all of it. There's a secret we don't need to say out loud: having me there keeps him safe. I keep my eyes on Brad no matter how far away he goes, and I hold him in place. It's a talent of mine, I guess. A kind of magic. When our mother walked through that space, maybe I looked the wrong way.

*

THE BELSONS ARE COMING to our house for a barbecue, and I'm making a pie with Peggy, our stepmother since last year. Outside the kitchen window Bradley pushes my stepsisters, Sheila and Meg, on the tire swing. Peggy keeps looking out there like she's nervous. Dad's beside her, chopping onions for burgers.

"He's pushing them awfully hard," Peggy says.

Dad looks out and so do I. Sheila and Meg are six and seven years old, Peggy's daughters from her first marriage. Dad smiles. "Brad's good with kids," he says, kneading the chopped meat.

"That's not what I said."

Dad is quiet. I stare at my blob of crust. "What do you want me to do?" he says.

Peggy laughs. "Nothing, I guess." She dumps her flour and sugar mix over a pile of apple slices. "If I have to tell you, then nothing."

She sticks her hands in the bowl and starts tossing the ingredients. Her wedding ring cracks against the glass. Dad's hands are still, covered with bits of meat. He's watching Brad. "I trust his judgment," he says, but he sounds sad.

"Me, too," I add.

Peggy looks from one of us to the other and then out the window again. She shakes her head. I hate her at that moment.

As I roll out the pie dough, I hear that heavy thump of a person's whole weight falling. Sheila lies on the ground under the tire swing. Meg is still holding on to it, looking stunned. Nothing moves for a second but the tire, which sails back and forth, creaking on its rope. Then Peggy runs outside, scattering butter and juice, and bends down over Sheila.

Dad runs after her. He's a big man, gentle most of the time. But today his face goes red and his eyes look small and fierce as an elephant's. He takes Brad by the shoulders and shakes him hard. "Godammit!" he says. "When Peggy trusts you with those kids ..."

"Stop it!" I shout from the kitchen.

Dad looks helpless and clumsy inside his body. He gives Brad a shove that knocks him backward onto the grass. Then Dad pauses, like he doesn't know what to do. As Bradley gets to his feet, Dad reaches down to help, but stops halfway. He comes back to the kitchen and pounds both his fists into the hamburger meat.

Sheila sits on the counter, sniffling, while her mother wipes Bactine on her skinned knee. Dad shakes his head. "It was an accident, okay?"

Peggy doesn't answer. She leans close to Sheila's knee and swabs it with a cotton ball.

"I'm saying he didn't mean it," Dad says.

"Of course he didn't."

Dad watches her and Sheila, like something is still not settled.

"I just saw it coming," Peggy says.

*

SHEILA PARADES HER SKINNED KNEE with its bandage and orange stain for the Belson girls, who are close to her age. Peggy lays our pie in the oven, and Dad puts on his goofy chef's hat as soon as the coals are hot enough for grilling. He and Neil Belson each sip a Beck's and argue over whether the Cubs will make it to the World Series.

I lean against Dad's arm. He has big, solid arms that make you safe when he hugs you, like you're inside a house with its front and back doors locked. "Well, look at you, miss," he says, pressing a spatula down on the spitting meat. "This one's got my heart," he tells Neil Belson, raising his Beck's. "Forever and always."

They both laugh. "Who could blame you?" Mr. Belson says. I pretend to rub smoke from my eyes, embarrassed.

Sometimes I feel like the simplest things I do—chew gum, cartwheel across the lawn, even bite my nails, which I'm trying to quit—fill Dad up with happiness. His eyes get soft, and I know no matter what I ask, he'll say yes in a minute.

"Do me a favor, baby?" he says. "Use your magic to cheer up your big brother?"

I try to. I offer Bradley my pickle and bites of my burger, even though he already has one. I tell him a few dead baby jokes, which are the only kind I can remember. But he bites his lips and stares at his hands like he's trying to figure something out.

"Is Bradley feeling okay?" Celia Belson asks Peggy during lunch. Peggy leans over and whispers to her. They give each other a look that surprises me, like they both know something they don't need to talk about.

"How about a game of softball?" Dad says, wrapping his arms around me from behind and speaking to the group. He has a good, warm smell of beer and bread. Dad likes games: football, soccer, Parcheesi. Tic-tac-toe if there's nothing else. Our mom did, too, and when she was alive they'd play gin rummy late into the night.

Brad says he'll sit out.

"C'mon, Brad," Dad coaxes. "We need your power hitting." He wants to make up but doesn't know how. His hands hang at his sides.

"No thanks," Bradley says. "Really."

I catch another fast look between Peggy and Celia. Brad sees it, too.

I sit out with him. I watch the rest of them play, and Bradley tears blades of grass in two and piles the pieces at his feet. Everything is wrong: Dad's shoulders droop as he stands at first base. Peggy scowls while waiting her turn to bat. Celia Belson keeps glancing over at us. I stare at each one of them the way I stare at Brad when he's doing a stunt. But nothing improves.

Sometimes I have these thoughts. I imagine walking onto a battlefield where men are shooting at each other, and making them stop. Just by walking out there, just by looking at them a certain way and holding my arms up. I imagine how quiet it would be, like a scene from a movie where something happens to hundreds of people at once. In my scene the soldiers drop their guns and slap each other on the back the way men do when they're glad about something. They look at me in awe.

"I'll get the pie," I tell Bradley.

I run back to the house and open the oven. The pie looks delicious, sugar bubbling along its edges. The dish is hot. I hold it with the oven mitts and sniff the steam coming out of the top. It's just what we need, I think.

I hurry back up the lawn. Sun shines in my eyes, and I blink a few times because it looks like Brad is at bat. I keep walking, holding the pie without noticing where I'm headed. He looks mad as hell. His jaw moves as he grinds his teeth, and I wonder what they said to make him play.

Dad is pitching, his back to me. Only after he throws the ball do I realize where I'm standing. Everyone sees it at once. It happens both slow and fast, slow because there's enough time after Dad pitches for parents and children to shout, "Bradley, wait!" and there's enough time for Brad to get the most awful look on his face, like he's seeing the worst thing on earth and he can't avoid it. Like he's the one about to get hit.

I just stand there, holding the pie. I know what will happen, like I've already seen it.

Then Bradley is shaking me hard, so my head bumps the grass. "Stand up," he hollers. "You're getting everyone scared."

I'm dizzy. I smell baked apples and sugar glaze. I hear people shouting, "Leave her alone for God's sake!" But Bradley keeps shaking my arm so it tugs in the socket.

I stand up and push the hair out of my face. Bradley puts his arm around me. "See? She's fine," he declares in a thin voice. "F-I-N-E. Fine."

The group stands in a quiet circle around us.

Brad takes my hand and pulls me. "C'mon," he says. "You need some water."

I try walking but something doesn't work right. My feet aren't attached to my body.

"Come on!" Bradley urges, pulling my arm. I look at his face and see how his lips shake, how wide and scared his eyes are, and I try my best to follow. But the next time he pulls I fall onto the grass and then I hear more shouting, Dad's voice louder than the rest. "You get the hell away from her!" he bellows, and that's the last thing I hear.

*

I HAVE A MINOR CONCUSSION, which is mainly just a greenish bruise near my temple and a bad headache. I stay in bed for a week, and every day Bradley comes to the doorway and stands there looking at me.

"I'm fine," I say the second I see him. "Completely fine." He nods and looks at me like there's something he wants to say but can't figure out how.

One day he comes in. He sits on the edge of my bed and stares at my face. "How well do you remember Mom?" he says.

It's the first time he's ever asked me that. I tell him about the shadow bending over, the singing. I want to tell him how I hurt her with my tricycle wheel, but for some reason I don't.

"She was beautiful," he says. "Like an angel." Then he leans back on his elbows, looking tired. "Know something?"

"What?"

"Dad's probably told you. Probably a hundred times. But I never did."

"Told me what?"

"You look the same. Like she did."

He's staring at me. There is a bluish color around his mouth, and his eyes have that spooked look you get when you stare in a mirror late at night. I watch the sheets. "No," I say. "Dad never told me that."

I think of pictures I've seen of our mother and try to compare us. But I can't remember what I look like.

"You're the same," he says. "No joke."

I twist the edge of my sheet, shaping it into the head of a rabbit. Brad clears his throat. "Dad says I should stay away from you," he says. "He ordered me. Grabbed my shirt in front of everyone. Like this." He leans forward and grips the top of my nightgown, pulling me toward him. I must look shocked, because he lets go instantly. "Shit!" he cries, shaking his hand like he doesn't know who it belongs to. "Christ Almighty!"

"It's okay," I tell him, leaning back against the pillows. But my heart is beating fast.

Brad pulls a miniature rowboat out of his pocket and bounces it in his palm. He takes a small, crinkled tube of glue and dabs some on two plastic oars. "Look, Holly," he says. "I'm sorry for that."

He carefully glues the oars onto the boat. I wish he would go away.

After a while Bradley looks up at me. "You were there," he says.

"Where?"

He's staring at me in a desperate way. And then I know where he means: in that car, six years ago.

"What happened?" he says. "I want you to tell me."

"I don't know. I can't remember it."

Brad narrows his eyes. "I think you do. I think you're afraid to say."

"Well, I don't." It frightens me to talk about it. I keep trying to catch my breath, and it makes me dizzy. Brad looks more scared than I am.

"You saw," he says. "You know the truth about it."

I know I should tell about the thing with my tricycle. I should say how the worst things happen sometimes on purpose but they're not your fault. I should say the truth wouldn't matter even if I knew what it was.

Instead, I just lie there.

After that day Brad makes sure we stay apart.

*

THERE'S A WALL BETWEEN MY brother's room and mine. If I listen I can tell exactly where he is, standing up or sitting down, whether he's building something or lying on his bed, looking at the ceiling. When he walks I feel the floor shake under me. I can almost see him, I guess the way blind people do. Sometimes I see him so well I forget what else I'm doing.

My friends call. There are swimming parties, tennis games, all the summer things. I hardly go. I stay in my room and listen to Bradley, the same as I used to watch him. When I don't know where he is, I start to worry.

One time I knock and go in. He's working on a model of the *Apollo 13*, building the launchpad. I start arranging pieces by their codes, E's with E's, G's with G's, different piles for small and big. I know how he likes them.

"That's nice," I say, looking at the spaceship.

Bradley shrugs. I look around at the planes and boats covered in shiny paint, the racing cars and station wagons. They hang from the ceiling by strings. "They're all nice," I tell him.

Brad frowns. I remember going with him parachuting a couple of months ago. It was windy, and I stood by the side of the runway with long dry grass whipping my legs. Bradley waved to me from the plane before they shut the door, and his expression reminded me of astronauts I'd seen on the news, just before they went into space. You could tell they knew they'd be heroes if they ever made it back. So when Brad came staggering toward me through the long grass, dragging the parachute behind him, I started clapping. He had a streak of dirt on his face and was limping. He stood there smiling at me like he hardly ever smiles, and I think for a minute he felt like he'd been to the moon and back.

"You know, I do this stuff?" he says, looking up from the launchpad. "And I have no idea why? It's like it's all broken, and my job is to fix it." He laughs like it isn't funny, just weird.

"I know what you mean."

And I do. But Brad shakes his head like I'm just saying that to cheer him up. He goes back to his glueing.

*

THE BELSONS HAVE A SUMMER HOUSE. It's right on Lake Michigan, with a dock and a little beach and lots of tall trees that stick out over the sand. If you climb high enough in one of those trees, you see a whole new shore with houses bigger than the Belsons' on it. Brad taught me climbing three years ago, before it got too easy for him.

"I'd rather stay here alone," he tells Dad the day before we're supposed to visit them. I'm listening from the kitchen.

The leather in Dad's chair squeaks. "Brad, let's have a talk," he says. "I think it's time."

"If it's about Holly, you can save it," Brad says. "She comes in my room, I can't lock her out, okay? There's limits."

"Not about Holly."

"I'm following orders," Brad continues, more loudly. "Keeping away like you said." He lets out two hoots of laughter. I stare out the kitchen window at the tire swing hanging in the heat.

"You think I'm dangerous," Bradley says.

"Now you're talking crazy."

"You think I'm one of those people who causes disasters."

"Bradley," Dad pleads. "Son, don't say things like that."

"And what if you're right? What if I am?" His voice is thin and high, a crying voice. "I walk in the room and Peggy flinches like I might hit her, and you know what? I want to! I want to beat the shit out of her, I'm so mad. Maybe it's true!"

"Brad, stop. Stop, Brad, this is nonsense." I hear Dad getting out of his chair. "We're spooked a little, all of us. God knows why." His voice is wheezy. "I want you to come with us to Lake Michigan," he says. "We need to straighten this out. Clear it right up."

Brad doesn't answer, but I know he'll be there.

*

DURING THE RIDE WE PLAY twenty questions and license plate bingo, Dad starts a contest counting gas stations, and Brad wins it. When I look at Dad's face in the mirror, I see him smiling.

After three hours of driving we park along a shady road and cross the soft ground to the Belsons'. Bradley helps Dad unload the groceries and sleeping bags from the car and bring them to the kitchen, then says he'll go take a swim before lunch. Sheila and Meg want to swim, too.

"I can't take you now," Peggy says, chopping an onion for Celia Belson's chicken salad. "Brad, would you mind—" She breaks off, and the room goes quiet. Even the kids stop talking. Peggy stares at that onion, blinking at her wet hands. The screen door snaps shut as Brad runs outside.

"—taking them with you?" Peggy finishes, like nothing happened.

I'm so mad at Peggy I bite my own tongue. I stare at the knife she's holding and want to take a swipe at her arm with it. But when she looks at Dad, I see she's mad at herself, madder than I am, afraid of what he'll say.

"I'm sorry," she whispers. There are tears on her face, but it might be the onion. Neil and Celia Belson work hard at gathering their trash into a bigger bag. Dad comes over and rubs Peggy's neck. He tells the girls he'll take them swimming after lunch.

I follow Brad. Between the house and the beach are dunes covered with tough reeds that scratch your legs when they brush you. Brad runs over those dunes, letting the reeds whip his calves. He splashes into the lake and starts swimming.

He goes straight out. I keep my eyes on him until he's so small I wouldn't know it was a person if I wasn't already watching.

"Turn around," I say out loud.

But he keeps going. In a hurry I run to a tree we used to climb, a tall one that sticks out over the sand and has a few boards nailed to the trunk. Bark flakes in my hands, but once I reach the first limb, the climbing gets easier. I see him again, moving out there like a spider on a big gray web. The higher I go, the better I see him, and I climb so high that the ground looks miles away. The branches are soft up here, and I hear lots of creaking. I straddle a branch and lean back against the trunk. I keep my eyes on Bradley, holding him up.

Then I see Dad below me on the beach. He goes to the water's edge and looks out. After a while Peggy comes out and stands beside him. She's brought him something in a napkin, but Dad takes a bite and drops it on the sand when she isn't looking. They just stand there, watching the lake.

I let them worry. They deserve it.

Brad is floating now, staring up at the sky. I glance up, too, just for a minute, at the thin clouds overhead. When I look back at Brad, he's disappeared. I stare at the spot where I last saw him and hold my breath, letting the seconds pass until I'm gasping. Finally Bradley splashes back to the surface—a big splash, like he's gone a long way down. He starts swimming in.

When Brad leaves the water, we're waiting for him. He keeps his head down. Dad gives his wet back a clumsy slap, then glances at his watch. "You've been gone almost an hour," he says.

"I floated a lot."

"We saved you some lunch," Peggy says.

In the kitchen I pull Brad aside, where no one can hear us. "They were scared to death," I tell him.

"Were you?"

I shake my head. "I watched you from the tree."

Bradley smiles a little, brushes some sand off my face. "I knew there was a reason I kept on floating," he says.

*

THAT NIGHT, NEIL BELSON makes a bonfire. He gathers sticks and branches and dry grass in a pile on the sand. His girls drag over what they can, and he thanks them loudly and makes a point of adding it. Celia brings out the potatoes in their foil and special pointed sticks for roasting.

All of us gather around to watch it burn. Fire wraps the sticks and leaves and crunches them to nothing. It makes a sound like laughing. Mr. Belson puts one arm around each of his girls, and Peggy holds on to Sheila and Meg. She touches her palms to their hot faces. I lean against my dad. "Look at Bradley," he says, shaking his head.

Brad is on the other side of the fire, sitting alone. Heat twists the air between us, so it looks like water running. Dad stares over the flames and smiles hard at Bradley, telling him with his face to come over, that he's welcome with the rest of us.

Say it, I want to order Dad. Call over to him.

But Dad just keeps smiling, and when Bradley doesn't move, Dad looks down and smiles in that direction, like he and the sand are sharing a sad joke. Meg wanders over, and he pulls her hair hack and wipes the sweat off her upper lip.

I stand up. So many things are wrong I can't sit there. I feel crazy, like worms have crawled inside my bones. I go to the water and let it soak my shoes. Then I stomp through the sand so it sticks to my feet and turns them into blocks. I look up at where firelight smears the branches of the tree I climbed today. I stare at that tree a long time. Then I walk toward the house, double back, and start climbing it from the side no one can see. I want to look down from above. I want to keep my eye on Bradley.

The first long limb is high above the flames and a little to one side. On my belly I slither along to its end and look down. No one sees me. Smoke floats past in a column. Bradley doesn't watch the fire, he keeps his eyes on Dad and Peggy and the Belson family.

Sweat drips down my face, and I feel it running inside my clothes. The fire makes a panting sound, but it looks smaller from above. Watching Bradley and the rest, I think to myself: How can I fix it? I remember what he said about the models, how they're broken and it's his job to repair them. One right piece, I think, and everything will turn good, like the soldiers dropping their guns on the battlefield. Just one piece. But what is it?

Then Bradley looks up. Maybe he felt me watching him. He doesn't say a thing, we just look at each other a long time, neither one of us moving. Fire lights his face and makes his eyes look hollow. The only sound is wood cracking in the fire.

I rise halfway to my feet and jump. I stay calm until the second my shoes leave the branch and I see the bonfire coming at me like a giant orange mouth. People are screaming. I hear the crash I make, and there's wild, rippling heat in my hair and clothes. Then I'm on the beach, rolled and pounded by a weight that is Bradley, pushing me into the cool sand, smothering flames with his body.

*

Everyone tells the story, how he pulled me out so fast the fire barely touched me. Like he knew I would fall, and was waiting to catch me.

"A premonition," Peggy calls it, narrowing her eyes with respect.

"Reflexes," Dad insists.

Bradley's stomach got scorched. Not badly enough for the skin to be grafted, but red and blistered where he put out the flames in my clothes. At Lakeside Memorial Hospital they wrapped him in white bandages and told him to rest. They said the scars might last. I think Bradley hopes so.

My hair got burned, nothing else. It's short now, and when I lie in bed at night, I think I can still smell the smoke in it.

Bradley has to stay in bed. I sit in a chair right near him. We don't say much. It's peaceful in his room, with the cars and planes and trucks twisting quietly over our heads.

"What'll you make next?" I ask him.

He looks up, taking in all the years of projects. "I might quit for a while," he says. "Try something new."

"A stunt?"

"That's old," he says.

I glance at the door and see Dad watching us, holding a deck of cards. I realize Bradley's talking to Dad more than me.

I have the oddest feeling then. I feel like our mother is there, like the four of us are together again in that room for the first time in years. As Dad deals out the hands, I see her, like she's sitting beside me: her dark waves of hair, the thin gold coin she wore around her neck, her cigarettes that smelled like mint. I remember her warm hands and sliver of wedding ring.

What I notice most, though, is how different I look. My hair is pale and straight. My skin is darker than hers, and a little shiny. I have freckles on my arms, and when I try to sing, I hit every wrong note.

I lean over to say this to Bradley. You were wrong, I want to tell him, you imagined that part. But there's a peacefulness in his face that I haven't seen since before the accident. He feels her, too, I think, and he knows she's not inside me. She's gone forever. But she would want us to be happy.

ATTAINABLE FELICITY

Julia Glass

(From *The Washington Post Magazine*)

T he whales are wearing party hats. "Let's be precise: the curators have adorned the cetacean skeletons to look *as if* they're wearing party hats," Zeke would say, only half joking, if he were here and not in the hospital bed that's supplanted the couch in their living room back in Vermont—though if Zeke were capable of being here, Lucinda wouldn't have been invited. She would never have found herself sitting through—she steals a glance at the book in Jonathan's lap—ninety-one chapters of *Moby-Dick*, read aloud in ten-minute morsels by a parade of earnest devotees, many of them motley in appearance and less than brilliant in their delivery. (Again, Zeke would have pointed out that she did *not* sit through the two or three dozen chapters read overnight, while she slept at the hotel, showered, and ate a hasty breakfast before returning to the museum.)

Without pretending to ask her out of anything more than pity, Jonathan insisted she join him and Cyril for the readathon. ("Mom, you'll go bonkers if you have to play Florence Nightingale twenty-four-seven.") She flew down on Friday from Burlington to Boston, her flight timed to arrive an hour after their plane from California. They'd already picked up the rental car when they met her at baggage claim. Both Jonathan and Cyril, the man she is now accustomed to thinking of as her second son-in-law, hugged her more firmly than usual. (Was this a covert assessment of how much weight she'd lost since Zeke's stroke in November?) "Now you will see a world you never dreamed of, the world of Melville geeks," said Cyril, grinning as if deranged.

"I call them Dickheads," Jonathan said. "But you'll have fun, I promise.

Cyril had to drag me by the ears, the first time I came along. Now I'm hooked."

"Correction: harpooned."

Nudging each other, they shared the laughter of the happily married—or of couples who know how to look as if they are. Lucinda, veteran of her husband's many political campaigns, is a virtuoso at that.

They arrived in New Bedford late Friday night and checked into their hotel. The reading was to begin at noon on Saturday. Cyril was also scheduled to be on a morning panel called "Stump the Scholars"—after which, Jonathan explained, he would remain for the entire reading. "Takes just over twenty-four hours. But you and I have permission to beg off at night."

Last night it snowed, just a sifting, enough so that even New Bedford—a town Lucinda remembers from years ago as dilapidated in the extreme, the anti-Nantucket—looks crisp and quaint, rooftops and pavements smooth and radiant as newly pressed linens. The sun is barely up, yet the atrium gleams with the eggshell luster of reflected snow. An aisle bisects two groups of folding chairs set in rows. This is how it would look if you held a wedding here, but these guests are divided into Readers and Listeners, not Bride and Groom (or Groom One and Groom Two). Though she wouldn't be caught dead reading aloud from *Moby-Dick* in front of a crowd (and a "webcam," according to Cyril), Lucinda sits with the Readers. Jonathan and Cyril wear numbered stickers on their left shoulders, indicating their place in the order.

The skeletons, massive as moving vans, hang at the summit of the atrium to appear as if they are swimming overhead. After staring at them for several seconds, Lucinda feels the visceral illusion of standing at the bottom of the sea. Two of the whales wear large cardboard top hats; the third wears an explosion of colorful, curly ribbon. And now Lucinda notices the little one—the baby—its smaller skull sporting a pirate's hat trimmed with glitter, more Halloween than New Year's.

At one of two podiums standing before the glass wall at the back of the atrium, a man in a plaid flannel shirt with a shaggy ashen beard is reading about one more high-seas encounter between the *Pequod* and another ship. He looks as if he's taking a break from splitting wood. Clustered at the other podium, waiting to read next, are a trio of antsy teenagers, identified in the program as "Students from Sacred Heart High, Fall River." Good Catholics from the town whose name always makes Lucinda shudder. A daughter butchering her parents with an ax. In the worst shouting matches she had long ago with her own teenage daughter, did Christina ever have fantasies so violent?

The woodsplitter reads well enough until he gets to the dialogue between the sailors of the two ships, which he performs in ludicrous accents. His misplaced conceit is embarrassing to witness.

Lucinda chides herself for being so judgmental. She doesn't go for confession too much anymore; if she did, she'd already be composing her recitation for Father Jess. She'd have to confess, as well, her inability to feel thoroughly proud of Jonathan and the life he's made. He and Cyril are professors at Berkeley: Jonathan in Gender Studies, Cyril in American Literature. (Their two most recent books — *Sexual Identity in Firstborn Children* and *The Fine Hammered Steel of Woe: Ecclesiastes and Melville's Ambivalent Soul* — sit on her bedside table, beneath others she is far more likely to read.) They have been living together for five years. For so many years before that, Jonathan's "mating status," as she once heard him call it, was so fluid — and his world so literally distant from hers — that when Lucinda found herself giving advice about the wedding, what disoriented her was not that her son would be marrying a man but that he would be settling down in any conventional sense.

"I'm going to stretch my legs," she whispers to Jonathan.

He whispers back, "Cyril should be up in about ten minutes," implying that her worst sin might be to miss his sliver of the reading. Jonathan read yesterday afternoon, the scene in which Ahab makes his brooding entrance. But Jonathan is just the sidekick. This is Cyril's show. Last year, when his book was published, the museum people let him read twice, once near the beginning, once near the end. Only Melville's great-great-grandson, a rumpled yet regal outdoorsy-looking man, is allowed that privilege year after year. Lucinda knows all this only because Jonathan keeps her eagerly informed.

She climbs the stairs to the mezzanine, where she stands almost level with the skeletons. Beyond the engineering feat that makes them appear to be swimming aloft, how did the museum obtain them in the first place? She locates the placards on the wall. "Excuse me," she says to a spectator leaning against them. "If I could just ..."

He steps aside, frowning slightly: how rude she is to let her attention wander from Melville's relentlessly magnificent language. The book is funnier than she remembers from college, and it is breathtakingly poetic in places, but in others it is inexcusably ponderous. Last night, she was drifting to sleep during that notoriously skimmed chapter, "The Whiteness of the Whale," when she was jolted awake by a passage describing a Vermont colt frightened by the scent of a buffalo hide. Vermont? How had Vermont crept into the story?

Just a metaphor, she realized, but she was awake, thinking of home. Was Zeke asleep? Had he eaten his dinner? Earlier that week, she made his favorite dish for New Year's Eve: smoked salmon lasagne. He ate a few forkfuls. Lucinda and the hired aide drank champagne while Zeke sipped mournfully at his carbonated cider, clutching the glass with both hands. Zeke was sleeping by ten; Lucinda stayed up till three in the morning, working on a quilt for Jonathan and Cyril. The traditional wedding quilt: white on white. She'll finish it by their first anniversary, next summer.

Now she learns that while one of these whales washed up dead on a beach, two others were killed when they collided with ships; one died because a fin was sheared off by the ship's propeller. That one was pregnant, her calf still in utero—and here it is, suspended beneath the false shelter of the mother's rib cage. Some of its skeleton hadn't quite formed; a diagram shows which bones were synthesized to make it anatomically whole.

Lucinda turns away from the wall, distressed to know these facts. When she looks over the mezzanine rail, she sees Jonathan looking up at her, beckoning. As he turns back, she spots the odd, shiny coin on his scalp; like her father, he's going bald from the middle out. (Mal would have celebrated his sixtieth birthday this year. Would he, too, be losing his hair by now?) Obediently, she goes back down. Cyril heads to the podium to wait his turn.

"If we calculated right, he's getting one of his favorite passages," Jonathan whispers urgently. He shifts toward her so that their thighs are touching and the open book rests half in his lap, half in hers.

Why does the work to which she gave so much of her life follow her everywhere? Pregnancy in its human form, not to mention mothers who look alarmingly young, are commonplace—but pregnant whales? She knows that Father Jess believes her faith foundered in the wake of Mal's death. *How could God create a scourge like* AIDS? *How could He allow the son of such a devout Catholic woman to end his own life?* (*How, for that matter, could God give her two gay sons?*) Lucinda knows this is the line of logic the young priest follows, and though he is dead wrong, she would never confess to him, casually or formally, the true source of the blow. She does not care if he thinks her so selfish or fragile.

Though fragile she has become, more fragile in spirit than body. Here it is Sunday morning, and she feels not an inkling of guilt that she is missing church.

Cyril begins in his low, elegant voice. It's easy to see how popular he must be with students. He is a short but handsome man, with the Devonshire cream complexion of his English mother (Mother of the Other Groom), the thick dark curls of his father (who, lacking Zeke's senatorial veneer, looked utterly at sea by comparison, his toast at the rehearsal dinner brief and somewhat baffled).

Jonathan leans against her shoulder. "This is *it*." On his left hand, which anchors the open book between them, a thick wedding band refracts his devotion. She felt this identical pride, if not perhaps the same degree of love, when she accompanied Zeke on his first junkets through Vermont — back when it was a state of struggling dairy farms, before ski condos and faux farmstead houses began to devour the slopes of the Green Mountains.

She is lucky to have such a good son, lucky that his father is open-minded enough to agree, lucky that he was not claimed early as well by the disease that killed his older brother twenty-two years ago.

Listening now, Lucinda wonders how on earth Cyril could have wished to read aloud about "squeezing sperm." Is this a terrible joke? She feels her blood rush to her face. And then, again, Jonathan presses against her shoulder.

Cyril pauses to survey his audience. " 'For now, since by many prolonged, repeated experiences, I have perceived that in all cases man must eventually lower, or at least shift, his conceit of *attainable felicity*' " — this he enunciates gracefully — " 'not placing it anywhere in the intellect or fancy; but in the wife, the heart, the bed, the table, the saddle, the fire-side, the country.' "

Felicity. Oh, Felicity.

When Cyril returns to his chair, Jonathan gives him a one-armed hug, shifting his legs away from his mother toward his husband. "Babe, you rock," she hears Jonathan whisper.

She gets up again, this time without excusing herself. The elevator will take her to exhibits away from the reading, away from the skeletons. What is a whaling museum, really, but a shrine to a peculiar type of butchery? Or, seen through the eyes of most people here, a cautionary tale. People who come to museums like this one feel a safe distance by virtue of what they believe to be enlightenment. But Lucinda sees no moralizing, no eternal damnation of the men behind the historic voyages portrayed in room after room. It's just history, that's all. Here's what happened, and here are the objects that prove it. Judge if you must, but times were different. The actions of your time, too, will be judged in ways you can't possibly know. Your very own actions might even be singled out.

On the top floor, she finds a show of contemporary watercolors, scenes of New Bedford. She only pretends to see them. The passage Cyril read reminded her of Felicity, Mal's beloved parrot, his only constant companion for the last few years of his life in New York. It took Lucinda a while to feel comfortable around this gorgeous but unpredictable creature. A close friend of Mal's—the friend who helped him take his life—lives with Felicity now. For several years he sent Christmas cards including pictures of the bird, who will certainly outlive Lucinda.

Mal, with his astringent wit, made genial fun of her work with all those far too young mothers, but he admired her for it. She knew that without his ever telling her so. The work, and her imagining his continued approval, is what kept her sane, what got her out of bed, after his death. Some nights, she'd end up staying in her office at The House, her teenage protégées sleeping in the upstairs rooms. She felt armored by the illusion that her presence could protect them. She started programs that trained them in culinary techniques, online publishing, administrative know-how. She raised money for a daycare center at The House, for scholarships. Professionally, Zeke enjoyed the reflected glory of her efforts, but he worried she'd collapse from exhaustion.

"If I weren't exhausted," she told him, "I'd collapse from grief." All idle moments filled instantly with grief, like sand absorbing rain. Since Zeke's stroke in November, she is slipping into this perilous state all over again.

After Mal's funeral, when most friends drifted away toward tending their own concerns, she paid frequent visits to Father Tom. Older but less conservative than Father Jess, he assured her (in private) that God had made her two sons the way they were, that Mal and Jonathan would be welcomed into the kingdom of heaven so long as they fully embraced Jesus Christ as their Savior.

Of the two, Mal had been the less attentive to her, but he had been honest. He told Lucinda he was gay over Thanksgiving break in his first year of college. Jonathan waited until a month after Mal's funeral, two decades later. Surely he'd known for most of that time, never mind the girls he'd clearly enlisted as decoys. What about Mal? she asked Jonathan, holding her anger at bay. Had he known? "I think he suspected," Jonathan told her. "But I figured you and Dad couldn't take it—two of us ... you know. I didn't want Mal to carry that secret around."

But, she protested, once his brother was ill and then dying *because* he was gay—a decline that went on for years—wouldn't the closer kinship have been a comfort? Hadn't Jonathan thought of that?

"Mom, I'm negative. I don't think that would have helped him at all. I think he'd only have felt more alone."

Lucinda was stunned. In the short time she'd known the truth about Jonathan, it hadn't occurred to her that he might also be ill, might also die young of this plague.

She threw herself into work at The House, into her girls and their babies. She gave interviews to feminist journalists who praised her for taking a sane approach to the "pro-life cause." She was called pro-motherhood, pro-sisterhood, pro-family, the "right kind of Catholic." She refused to discuss abortion. She became, in the eyes of too many people (even her grown daughter), a saint. And saints, like tyrants, fall hard. Saints are merely tyrants in the kingdom of virtue.

Abandoning the watercolors, she stands by a window with a movie-screen view of New Bedford. The snow has melted, returning the city to its grizzled, grubby old self. "Stop this," she scolds herself: out loud, since she is the only person in the room.

Heading down the nearest stairwell, she enters a vaulted gallery containing a slightly scaled-down version of a whaling ship. One can climb onto the deck and roam around, touch the riggings, the brass fittings, the wheel with which a scaled-down captain would steer the vessel toward a smaller version of the open sea. She is alone here.

Five years ago, she was in Montpelier, heading to meet her husband for lunch. An overweight, angry-looking young woman was walking toward her. Lucinda felt only the safe, unpleasantly instinctive pity of the affluent. Mentally, she had already passed the woman—but then, when they were about to pass, the woman stopped and blocked Lucinda's path. "You."

"Me?" said Lucinda, insipidly.

"Yeah. You. You ruined my life, you know." The woman's face went from menacing to contemptuous. "You and your fucking—oh, wait, your *mother-fucking* mission. To fill the world with babies. Jesus." She pursed her mouth as if to spit on Lucinda, and Lucinda flinched, blocking her face with a hand.

The woman did not spit. She laughed. "Bet I'm not the only one." Then she passed Lucinda, knocking her slightly with a shoulder, setting her off balance. Unable to move, Lucinda stood on the sidewalk for some time before navigating the last half block. At the restaurant (Zeke was, as always, as expected, late), she went into the ladies' room and sobbed for ten minutes.

Since then, any poorly dressed or hostile-looking youngish woman heading in her direction makes Lucinda's heart race, makes her cross the street or turn aside, pretending to look in a shop window or hunt for a phantom object in her purse.

"Mom! I thought we'd lost you."

"My legs cramp up if I sit for too long." She looks down at her son over the side of the ship, as if she's about to depart on a voyage. "Forgive me," she says more gently. "Cyril was terrific."

Jonathan beams. "Wasn't he?" He climbs the stairs to the deck, and she knows this is a concession. He came to reel her back to the reading. "Are you feeling all right? You look awfully tired."

"I don't sleep well in hotels."

"I thought you were a pro at that — traveling with Dad. The rubber-chicken circuit."

"Yes, I was. Was." She doesn't bother to tell him that even then, her recurrent insomnia kept her up, just as it did at home. Mal was the one who inherited that trait from her. They laughed at how productive you could be. It was a gift, said Mal, if you were a music critic for a newspaper, overnight deadlines a piece of cake. Lucinda, wide awake while her household slept, quilted. She can still do trapunto at four in the morning, her stitches tight and steady.

"Are you worried about Dad?" Jonathan asks.

"Depends what time frame you're talking about, sweetheart."

"Well. Today, I guess."

"Today I'm sure he's fine. By which I mean no different from yesterday or the day before." Zeke is lucid enough to be despondent about his diminished prospects; a mere two months ago, one reporter called him an "inspiringly vigorous octagenarian." He was struck down in the middle of a tennis game with colleagues from the State House. The doctor tells her that his prolonged silences may be his choice, that once it became clear he would not return to "one hundred percent," he may have given up. "My all-or-nothing patients are the hardest ones," he said, as if she might offer him sympathy.

"Let's get back to the reading," she says to Jonathan.

"Yes, absolutely!"

They pass paintings of carnage in exotic places, a case of Asian porcelain vessels, a doorway flanked by a pair of whale ribs six feet long. Jonathan opts for the elevator. "We'll go out for a great lunch after it's over. Cyril knows this amazing Portuguese place. Prepare to stuff yourself."

What *doesn't* Cyril know? Lucinda thinks unkindly.

They descend in silence, disembark, and head toward the crowded atrium. Most of the chairs are now filled; many people show up just for the drama of the climax, Jonathan told her with vague disdain. Approaching them from twenty or thirty feet away is a woman with free-flowing auburn hair. She wears wide beaded hoops in her ears and, around her neck, a cumbersome-looking camera. Though she does not appear impoverished or bereft, Lucinda realizes, panicked, that she looks distantly familiar. The worst kind of familiar.

She backs away, though there is nowhere to go but the coat room, and besides, it's too late. "Jonathan," she whispers — though what can Jonathan do?

"Mom?" He looks back at her, perplexed.

The woman is right there now, just beyond Jonathan. "I'm sorry," she says to him, "but I saw you earlier and I recognized you. I know it's been years, but I recognized you from Malachy's memorial in New York. You're his brother, aren't you?"

Jonathan's face brightens and he reaches for the woman's outstretched hand with both of his. Lucinda feels feverish, mired between a numb relief and a fear of losing her composure. The woman, Vera, is telling Jonathan that she was a junior colleague of Mal's at the newspaper, that she's now on staff at the book review. "We still talk about him," she's saying. "Still miss his wicked, delicious take on the world."

She turns to Lucinda. "Mrs. Burns, you look great. But what are you guys doing here?"

Lucinda waits for Jonathan to embrace his role as Cyril's cheerleader. Instead, he says, "You knew Mal?"

"Pretty well. I mean, as office friendships go."

"You knew my brother."

She laughs nervously. "We helped start that music scholarship. In his name."

"Wow, that's right," says Jonathan. He is still grasping Vera's right hand between his. "I miss him all the time. Like, every day."

"He was one of a kind."

"He was my big brother. I thought we'd have all the time in the world."

Vera nods. "He talked about you."

Lucinda can see that this is probably not true. This woman may even regret that she spoke to them.

Lucinda focuses on Jonathan now. His eyes glisten, but he is beaming. All of a sudden, he hugs Vera tightly and thanks her.

"You're welcome," she says. "Well, back to my assignment." She points toward the atrium, awkward in her attempt to break free.

"Wow," Jonathan says again, looking after Vera. "My God."

Why doesn't Lucinda share Jonathan's happiness at this encounter? Is she jealous that others have memories of her son that she will never know? Mal was her most difficult baby; she came to feel, in meeting his demands, that she owned him more than she'd owned Christina or, later, Jonathan. After Mal died, she wished that she could gather up and possess his entire life. She had a hard time parting with any of his belongings.

She waits for Jonathan to lead her back to the reading, though they can hear the narrative loud and clear from where they stand.

"Maybe you don't think I loved him enough, but I did." Jonathan stands utterly still beside her, not facing her. "He was hard to love, you know. Maybe not to you, but to just about everyone else. It didn't make him less wonderful."

Lucinda tries to remember when she started loving Mal more than her other children. She wants to believe it's when she learned he was ill, but that would be easy.

"Did you hear what I said, Mom?"

"Yes," she says. "I'm just a little in shock, sweetheart. I know you loved Mal. I know he loved you. How grown children love one another isn't for a parent to witness. All you can do is hope that they will."

Jonathan looks teary and wounded. He starts toward the reading. She reaches forward and grabs his arm. "Jonathan," she says. "We never speak about him anymore. Sometimes I forget that you lost him, too."

"I speak about him *often*," Jonathan says. "To Cyril."

She lags behind, ashamed. At Jonathan's wedding—which took place on a grassy hillside with a dizzying view of San Francisco Bay—Lucinda remembers, more than anything else, what she felt when she watched Jonathan and Cyril proceed (radiant with glee, nearly romping) back up the aisle after their vows. Zeke squeezed her arm. She felt the profound relief of a mother seeing her child engulfed by joy, but she understood, too, exactly why she couldn't quite join in. She wished that it were Malachy's wedding. She wished that Mal could be the one standing there in the field with his true love: Mal in the white suit, Mal against the white sky and the sunstruck surface of the bay, Mal in the blanching flashes of camera after camera sealing the moment to hold it far into the future. There must have been three hundred wedding guests, so happy for Jonathan and Cyril that several of them cheered, as if the two men had won a competition, not solemnly promised to be together forever. They were loved by so many people.

After Mal's death, Lucinda was told by numerous friends and fellow church-goers that she must learn to "let him go." They might mean that she should let him go to God, let him be released from his pain, or relinquish her possessive grief. What it meant to her, however, was that beyond accepting his death, she had to understand that from then on he would belong as much to others as he did to her. She had loved him too much, perhaps, more the way she ought to have loved his father. And God forgive her if, in helping all those girls have those unexpected babies, learn to be mothers far younger than they should have, she'd been trying to undo that death.

She threads her way through the crowd to find Jonathan again. He's saved her a seat amid the thickening crowd. Once she sits beside him, he puts one arm around Cyril's back and the other around hers. "Here it comes, the big photo finish," he whispers.

Lucinda tries to remember the end. The white whale escapes, of course, but does everyone go down with the ship, down into that dark, violent vortex? Are they all doomed? No; how silly of her. Ishmael remains behind on the surface. He's the one who lives to tell the extraordinary tale. And that's the thing about surviving: you get to tell the story, don't you? You get to be the keeper of the artifacts, the curator, the museum itself. You get to throw the parties and celebrate the weddings.

Cyril leans forward to look at Lucinda across Jonathan's lap. His smile is surprisingly shy. He winks. The three of them turn their attention to the latest reader at the podium, one of the very last. Jonathan has closed the book. From now on, they'll listen without reading along, to get the full effect.

THE WATCH

Edward Hirsch

(From *American Poetry Review*)

I threw a watch into Lake Michigan
In honor of eternity I'd do anything
To make her laugh on the jagged rocks

It started to rain at Evanston Beach
Her sadness was like a great cloud
In a suburb north of the city

We used to neck in her parents' kitchen
I remember the heat of our bodies
Against the refrigerator

One Sunday morning
I went to church with her family
And stood up when everyone else knelt down

She believed the voice of the Lord God walked
In the garden in the cool of the day
But I heard thunderstorms

I recall the lightning between us
The night we broke up in a small red car
In a parking lot near the beach

We sobbed for hours and hours
And lied on the phone in the morning
I felt too young to rescue her

The watch was waterproof
I wish I could dive under the rocks
And find it down there pulsing again

ISSUES I DEALT WITH IN THERAPY

Matthew Klam

(From *Sam The Cat and Other Stories* /
Originally published in *The New Yorker*)

We were on a preppy East Coast resort island, in the middle of summer, we just flew in for the wedding of my incredible friend Bob. We were here on vacation, away from the hot city; I was so glad to be out of that fucking house. The simple fact that it's a plane trip away and you're staying in a hotel on this fake, preppy island, and because you're not married and yet you're at a wedding together, because you're too cheap to go on decent vacations, because your own day-to-day life could use some tuning up and like any sane person you've already effortlessly erected an invisible barrier between yourself and that life back there and you're now pretending that it isn't real, and because Bob had become this big deal, your most skyrocketing friend, and Bob's wedding weekend finally arrived—well, it's a new beginning and I was feeling the excitement.

We got to the hotel and parked the rental car and walked down to the water in our street clothes. People passed by with beach umbrellas and L. L. Bean canvas tote bags, floating in the heat; kids ran happily in the wet patch left by the outgoing tide. We walked back up through the mushy sand to the steps of the parking lot of the hotel, Phylida's long white translucent sundress blowing in front of me. We passed the advance team for Gore, fifteen blond-haired women in their early twenties, wearing hairbands, talking on cell phones on the little patch of grass bordering some brown split-wood railings in front of the hotel.

I was looking at everything: the people getting out of the rental cars, the bracelets on the women, the sunshine brightly beaming. It was Bob's sunshine, you were on his island now. I looked back at Phylida; she smiled. The wind lifted her dress all the way up in the front, before she could catch it. A guy struggled to pull out his golf clubs from the trunk and a valet half his age whisked the bag away like a feather. The wife laughed. Who were they? I think every room in the hotel was rented to the four hundred people invited to the wedding.

It was an old wooden hotel, the charming kind, creaking stairway, crooked floors. Our room was small, antique crap in it, a jingling glass lampshade on a side table, a queen-size bed raised to an enormous height, a frilly cover, a cheap, modern glass door on sliders leading out to a wooden balcony that gave you splinters and, as promised, looked out on a downwind stretch of the same beach where Bob and Niloo would be getting married, a mile away.

They'd been hyping us with stuff in the mail for six months: the "Set this date aside" card; the letter that began, "Tell us exactly what you eat," with rows of boxes to check off ("Are you dairy tolerant?" "Do you like sushi or do you eat it to be polite?" "Our chef will not cook with peanuts"). The six-piece engraved invitation. Lists of the island's golf courses, a note about where they were registered ("Sheetmaker to the Earl of Windsor"), a special mailing to the lady guests — "We hope you'll start shopping for that perfect full-length formal summer gown to wear to our summer wedding on the shore." Another list for me because I was an usher, what kind of tux shirt collar they (Bob) wanted us to get, suggested books for preparing your toast. A fact sheet on the island, how it played a part in the Revolutionary War, how the something of democracy was born here, Bob wrote this — "to help free our nation of tyranny evermore and make America the most wonderful country in the world."

The freak-show element of the wedding was like a side thing: Madeleine Albright would be here tomorrow; Ruth Bader Ginsburg insisted on performing the ceremony; that advance team for Gore trying to figure out whether the rain would hold off so Al could helicopter in for an appearance.

What was I doing here?

Bob and I met during graduate school at a food drive for torture victims of repressive regimes; Bob was in charge of cans. He was silly and fun, a goofy guy in a baseball hat. He studied civil-rights law. He said he wanted to help black people straighten out the mess. I was getting a master's in international relations. Our friendship was based on leaving each other messages in fake Spanish accents, discussing girls' private areas. The next semester we became roommates. He came home at eleven o'clock and inhaled vats of popcorn.

We graduated. Bob moved out to be closer to the Justice Department. He worked in civil rights; he desegregated a poor school district in Mississippi that was secretly being run by the Klan. Bob jailed them. I sort of worshipped him. I thought he was Superman. They won a big case and he got to go on the televised press conference. He sat up tall and straight. He'd cut his hair short for it. Every answer out of his mouth was like a perfectly fired javelin. He'd starved himself on those long trips to Mississippi and now, with no hair, he looked like an astronaut.

Soon he was having chats with Janet Reno. He'd moved up. "It's titular." What's titular? "We do planning." They had some sticky problems in Immigration and Naturalization: they were trying to figure out how to throw Haitians back in the water. When I phoned him at work he could only whisper. He went to events at the White House, standing in for the Attorney General. "After Memorial Day," he explained, "you wear the white dinner jacket."

Time passed. He met everybody. He called Barbara Walters at home. He had four thousand names in his handheld electronic Rolodex. I swung by his apartment. He stuck handwritten notes from King Hussein on his refrigerator, photos of himself coming down the steps of Air Force One, looking pale and tired. He'd become important and I gladly took what he handed me, a box of candy, an opened bottle of peach schnapps, outpourings of guilt he felt at the sight of me.

He quit Justice and went to work on a guy's campaign. He ran it and won. You saw Bob on TV on Election Night, dancing in a hat made out of a dinner napkin. Alone, just the two of us, he entertained me with stories; he went in and out of remembering I was there.

He bought a nice house. He got a smaller cell phone, a full-time squirrelly assistant cutting into our lunches to tell Bob he had to go. He went to work for Senator Sheslow, whose wife just had a stroke, she was an invalid; Sheslow thought he might run for President. Bob was flying to Dallas and Japan, talking to folks. "It's like fund-raising." And Al Gore was calling to consider him for a job. These jobs didn't have names anymore. "I'll be the youngest member of Gore's top guys," he told me in his monotone robotic rambling into the speakerphone as he drove alone somewhere, exhausted. "It'll be utterly outstanding," he said.

He had other distinctions. A booming voice, big hands, thick fingers, brown-colored dents on his car from backing into trees, a colossal memory, he could produce anything ever said in passing, the name of my childhood pet turtle, how Sheslow voted on a tax bill fifteen years before, it all sat front row on his mind, it was all immediate. He knew Bill Bradley's weak spots, the trajectory of Chinese rocketry.

He had constant weight problems. He shrunk and ballooned and went on diets. He was hungry. He kept popcorn in a lunch bag in his suit-coat pocket. He bit his fingernails till they bled like they'd been shoved inside a sink disposal. I'd wonder, What's he gonna do next? Why did he like me? Why was Bill Clinton calling this guy for advice when he couldn't park his car without hanging two wheels on the curb?

The way he spoke now had changed, he used the word "outstanding," the word "sequentially." The last time I saw him was at this brunch fund-raiser he made me go to, he'd been bingeing on wheatgrass pills for four days and had stomach cramps and diarrhea but he said he felt "fantastic." Seeing him, the rare times I now got together with him, passing by his office at the Capitol, stopping at his house to be yawned at, or snored at, was like visiting his grave. Niloo would watch his snoring nostrils, he looked like a gorilla, and go, "He flies pretty high, doesn't he?" or "Guess who phoned us last night." In the old days I could get up and go home. Now I had to listen to his bullshit from her, too, swallow it twice.

Phylida and I stepped out onto the balcony. White wicker chairs with cushions, a table, warped by weather, resting on three legs. Two guys stood on the balcony next to ours, doing what we were doing, feeling the air. They were Italians, friends of Bob and Niloo's, also just arrived. Both guys were tan, had facial hair, wore mirrored lenses. They'd changed into swimming stuff and were ready to go down to the beach. They looked like a couple. One guy wore a very fine loosely woven shiny multicolor sweater in the zillion-degree sun. He fingered his webbed beach purse. The other guy had clean-shaven legs that were flawless and brown. The guy with the purse said, "We met them vacationing at a place like this in Lisbon." I had a panicky urge to figure out when Bob and Niloo had been to Lisbon, but I couldn't picture what continent Lisbon was on, so I said, "What kind of place was that?" Both guys smiled at once. I'd been holding Phylida's hand, and brought it up and kissed it.

On the balcony on the other side a woman sat alone having a beer. Her name was Sebastian. She had a long washed-out-green dress unwrinkling on a hanger and the ocean breeze kept tipping it into her face as she sat, looking pale and basically dead, squinting into the hot sun reflecting off the ocean. Phylida leaned across the railing and asked, "Did you and Niloo grow up together in New Jersey?" She offered Phylida a beer. I went back inside and hung up my suit.

I lay down on the bed and listened to the women chat. Phylida was leaning on the balcony divider, moving her weight back and forth, her butt aimed at the opening in the doorway at my feet. Phylida's butt had become the focal point of our life together. It was soft and circular and amazing. I got comfort knowing it was there. I shut my eyes and began twitching, conking out like the overworked dead person with bad breath who I'd become.

After a while Phylida came in and closed the sliding glass door and the see-through curtain, and lay down next to me and explained that Sebastian hadn't rented a car and wanted to ride over with us to the rehearsal dinner. Then she fell asleep. She hadn't slept all week. She hadn't slept in seven months and four years. Medical residents are sleep deprived. On call for three surgical rotations this week, she slept through her beeper one night, what they call a "no-hitter," got clobbered with huge repair jobs the next two nights, came home in a black cloud, unable to talk.

I said, "Are you asleep?" She didn't move. "How can somebody name a girl Sebastian?"

Phylida and I never fought. We also never saw each other. Our life consisted of lengths of days, with nothing fun in the middle. We got together and listed what had happened since the last time we spoke, became sad, and fell asleep. I kissed her canted hipbone through the cotton of the dress. I said, "Should I let you sleep?"

She said, "Did I sleep on the plane?" I said yes. She turned toward me exhaling. "This'll be us someday."

"What?"

"You and me."

Phylida and I were on the verge of something. Picture us picturing ourselves as next in line for our own wedding weekend. (We'd already talked about what kind of ring I would get her—the stone, the setting.) Picture us wondering: Why does this feel like nothing? Picture us thinking the same thing separately and not talking about it and coming up empty. She was trying to be nice, waiting for that fucking ring now for months and months, she did her perfect imitation of a good girlfriend, holding my Coke in the car, but it made her furious and we both wanted to get this over with.

I went for her chest, unbuttoning as fast as I could, pulling off her dress, opening up her bra. She looked in my eyes and waited.

I ran my hands all over her body. Phylida let out a breath and smiled. Her flaxen hair fell across a pillow. I kissed her nipples. She liked that. She did a noise with her tongue against her teeth—"tchk"—as I moved my hands around her silky cream mountains. I'd always been attracted to her, although sometimes she walked down the street like John Wayne with his dungarees shoved up his ass in "Stagecoach."

"They're yours," she said.

"What is?"

"This is the last pair of tits you'll ever squeeze," she said, and giggled.

"Why do you have to talk as if you just got out of an insane asylum?" I said. She smiled.

I licked her ribs. She had a perfect face. She had a single blond hair coming out of her chin I never saw before. She wore old blue cotton panties with just a slight fume of musk and salt. She let me pull them all the way down. She had a cunt. It was pink and cunt-shaped and smelled like roses. What else? She had a mother and a father. She made a bubble noise in her sleep. She lived for running late; she drove fast, ran people over in crosswalks. She smelled like saddle soap.

"I like that," she said, pulling at me.

It terrified me when she acted like a slut. I said, "Let me get unbuckled."

Bob's fantastic wedding weekend, plane ride from Boston, dry in-flight peanuts, mysterious hotel on the ocean, the grooved tracks of nauseating similarities between us and every other person in this hotel, in the world. I stared at her. I wanted to get married, too. I wanted to be swept away. Phylida and I had talked about our whole lives, where to live, how to live, we met the other's family, everybody loved everybody, yabba blabba—the only thing left was, like, pull the trigger, get that ring!

She said, "Your winky is starting to get a little small." She said this in a bright voice. She held it at the base, the outline of her lips was white, and blew me a little.

I could feel myself spiraling away from sex. I looked down at Phylida, beautifully pumping away, and the face of Steven Spielberg floated into my mind, expressionless, bearded, dumbfounded. I thought of how much money he had. He had a private jet with customized woodwork interior, two daybeds, and a cup-holder by every window. A friend of Bob's, some jackass named Dan who helped me plan the order of the toasts this weekend, also had a private jet. Shares of Dan's amazing start-up company cost twenty-six cents two years ago. This morning they were worth forty-seven dollars. Some of the other invitees were in on Dan's first stock offering. They had names like Lafayette and Sky. I didn't have enough money to be showing my face around this crowd. Sometimes when I traveled for work I pretended I was a foreign spy. I wasn't a spy.

Dan would be arriving in his jet today; in a half hour, in fact. I knew all this because Bob suggested I offer Dan my personal chauffeuring services but I actually wouldn't be able to because Dan could go fuck himself.

Happiness. Half penis. I didn't have the slightest interest in fooling around.

I pushed Phylida off me. She looked up, smiling, trying to keep the mood upbeat. Her red mouth, her beautiful face. I would've liked to chop my dick off and fling it from the balcony. "It's not gonna work," I said.

"Don't get hysterical."

"It happened last week. That's twice in a row."

"It happens to you every time we try to have sex away from home." She touched her lips. Her eyelashes were like a foot long.

I said, "I fucked you in Mexico."

"You fucked me in Mexico."

"Right."

"Don't get all penis-focused."

"Could we not talk about it and make me feel even worse?"

"You're thinking about getting married, our life together. You're worried about eternity."

"Oh Christ."

"I'm trying to help."

I stood, wearing just my underwear, and walked to the bathroom.

"You're rushing. You're tired."

"Thank you."

"Um ... You have a wedgie."

*

I DROVE AS PHYLIDA READ the directions through town to the restaurant. Every inch of street was jammed with traffic and sunburned people in salmon-colored shorts. Sebastian talked nonstop: "I wonder if Bibbity Blob is coming." She was nervous. When we pulled in line for the car valet Sebastian asked if I had a tissue and cleared her throat and served up a little morsel of vomit. "I hate this kind of thing," she said.

The women walked behind me as I strode through the restaurant, trying to think of a way to tell people I'd been to London twice for work in the last six months. There was a patio where people stood drinking. The dining area was out back under a tent. Phylida looked around and said, "At my wedding the bridesmaids will wear metallic scarves, very little makeup, full-length illusion skirts."

Phylida and Sebastian moved off to find food. A man with a foreign accent came up to me and said I was not to worry: even though he'd lost ten million dollars when he consolidated his businesses, the former premier of France was on his new executive board. He then drank his drink, said nothing, and stared at me. Another man joined us, holding a cigarette. His face had fine lines like an apple going soft. He said he thought the island was beautiful. People chatted. Candles were being lit inside the tent. I picked up the scent of pipe tobacco and gardenias. The moon came out. I spotted Bob in a blue tie and a red silk pocket square and a straw-colored jacket that was already damply dark under the arms from sweat. The last time I spoke to him was three months earlier when he left me waiting at a Thai restaurant until I gave up, because on the way over Sheslow beeped him. "Well," he said. The deep voice. "Come with me."

I wondered if Bob was taking me aside to explain why he'd chosen me as an usher. I wondered if maybe he was flipping out and needed now to talk seriously about marrying Niloo. He pulled out a set of keys. The sky was dusky and you could see fireflies.

He said, "My father-in-law brought some wine in his car. Would you just give me a hand?"

As we looked for the car in an open field beside the patio I reminded Bob that we hadn't spoken in months. He tried to remember our last talk. "I'm at a loss," he said, smiling.

"Where do you go for your honeymoon?" I asked.

"A tiny island nation near Sri Lanka." He said he knew the king.

As we got to the trunk of Mr. Niyangoda's black Mercedes I noticed that Bob's sweat stains had spread up his chest.

How was work?

"Fantastic." This was the most incredible week of his life. He put his finger in my face. "Sheslow will be the next President of the United States. I have no doubt." They'd just been tacitly endorsed by this one slob, things were zooming. "We will make our nation strong and safe and ethnic violence will be eradicated by prosperity." He was going on C-span on Monday. His shirt collar pinched his neck just slightly, so an arc of flesh hung from his chin. "We're bringing slot machines to highway rest stops."

I said, "How does C-span decide—"

He checked his beeper and called in to work while I listened to the tones of his tiny flip phone, waiting.

No word yet from Gore. "If he comes tomorrow," he said, "I've got the job."

"What about the Senator's Presidency?" I asked.

"Staying where I am would be a lateral move." He thought more and said, "In my heart I know he's a freak."

I said, "Bob, you're going to the White House."

He said, "I can't believe my life!"

In the trunk there were four cases of wine. The cases were made of wood. He said, "Do you know about *premier cru*?" He gave it his disgusting French accent. He lifted up one and read the name off the box. "Stuff like this goes right to the collectors," he said. He slid the case toward me along the lip of the trunk and sighed, grinning widely as the light from the restaurant caught the sheen on his temples, and whispered, "I feel like a god right now, you know?"—he was having a kind of galaxial moment—as the case began falling between us like some terrible tipped boulder and we both lunged for it, trying to stop it with our knees, and failing, as it slipped down the bumper, and there was a miserable gnashing of sound, the unmistakable sound, of glass breaking.

Bob came up with his teeth set across his open mouth. I froze. "Are you crazy?" he said.

I said, "You had it."

He called me an idiot, in the voice he used—well, pretty often, come to think of it. He tore a panel off the top of the crate and very carefully checked each bottle, setting them neatly on the grass. The neck of one was cracked beneath the foil and the top came off when he touched it, gushing wine. "Convenient twist-off," he said, staring at me insanely, and poured the rest on the grass in front of me and turned and fired the bottle out of sight. It went through some trees and smashed.

"That's five hundred dollars," he said. "That's a lot of money for a guy like you to be wasting."

I pointed to the red stain on his blazer. I couldn't help myself.

"My God," he said. "Look at my—look at my coat! ... My Cole Haan, you got it on my shoe!" We both reached down at the same time to wipe the wine off his *leche*-colored shoe and banged heads. He stood up, insane now, and in the split second in which he appeared to be deciding whether to punch me out or laugh he suddenly poked me in the forehead with his nail-hard poking finger and said, "That's using the old noggin!" He went on, now trying to be as lighthearted and fun as possible. "Your brain," he said, and paused, searching for something clever, "is like the surface of Mars, a red rocky place where scientists believe there is life" (he kept going, poke, poke), "but there is no life, right?" They had not yet found life on Mars, yes, I had to agree. Then he laughed and shook me as though we both knew the whole thing was a joke. "You almost wasted a case worth six thousand dollars!" I laughed, too. I try to laugh as much as possible.

When I got back to the tent, I spotted Phylida waving a seating card at me. The banquet had been divided into sections named after the countries of antiquity. We were in Flanders. Next over was Gaul, then Mesopotamia.

Phylida's face was flushed deep bluish red as she gestured toward Sebastian. "We've been glugging too much." Sleep deprivation combined with the many substances that swam inside her—she'd self-prescribed medications for everything from dry inner-eyelid-lining to mood swings to clenched jaw muscles—along with drinking a gallon of wine made her brain tilt slightly, causing her to combine or invent words. Sebastian held a stricken catlike pose. Then she left, having been assigned to Bavaria.

Appetizers arrived. The first speech, from Bob's dad, began, and I felt a funny gurgle down inside me like a warm gastric balloon rising. From that moment on, each time someone stood up I experienced a slight cramping gut, kind of needing to poop, while assembling and abandoning thoughts for the toast I was about to give; I'd feel in my pocket for the notes I'd made on the plane in case my speech flopped.

I said to Phylida, "Can you see a mark on my forehead?" She shrugged, but I felt it; it stung where he'd doinked me.

She said, "I'm sunburned." She touched her neck. "Ouch!"

Bob's brother made a toast.

A bird flew into the tent and got trapped. I seemed to be the only one who noticed. My colon felt distended. Dan, the guy with his own private jet, was now standing at the microphone, his glass raised. "They are today's dream, tomorrow's hope." It sounded like an illiterate campaign speech. I racked my brain to think of something to say. Phylida pulled both shoulder straps of her dress down and put some ice from the butter dish on her neck. When I asked what was going on she said, "My wine's completely dranken. Drinken." She had a selective intelligence. She looked around. "We need the guy." I waved at him. Maybe it was simply the release after so much hard work at the hospital. Without the support of the shoulder straps, her tits suddenly fell down. "Hello," my girlfriend-slash-fiancée-slash-bulbheaded alien then said to the folks across from us. "I already got a hangover."

Why was everything starting to suck?

I studied Wayne's face, Bob's closest longtime buddy, as he carefully picked his way along Bob's first kiss in summer camp, their car accident in driver's ed, how glad but also sorry he was to see Bob getting hitched. Phylida was now sweating. I said, "What's wrong with you?"

She said, "When is this gonna end?" She said she'd slept four hours total since Wednesday (though that didn't count drooling all down her blouse on the airplane) and started telling me about the last patient she'd admitted this morning, a homeless guy. There's a certain kind of fungus that only grows on a person's anus, she said, and he had it. It eats skin. She gave me her saintly look of pain.

I said, "You knew this would be a late night," and she started to cry. She put her hand up to her throat and took her pulse and put the other hand in the middle of her chest.

She said, "I'm having an arrhythmic palpitation." She had a heart murmur. She started tapping her cheek.

"What are you doing?"

"It's a test for hypocalcemia."

I said, "Call a taxi. Just go." She said she had to wait until I made my toast.

Niles was solemnly reading the exact figures of the landslide election Bob won running for seventh-grade class president when a woman at the table next to me looked over and sighed. I smiled back. I was next. At the far end of the tent guys were talking very loudly, smoking cigarettes. It was almost eleven. People were croaking. The woman introduced herself. She sat in Gaul and had to lean over because of the gap between tables.

I hadn't seen her before. I said, "You're a friend of Niloo's?" She said no. Her name was Anne. I said, "How do you know Bob?"

"He's a new friend."

"What does that mean?"

Leaning toward me caused the front of her dress to fall open. The tops of her tits were tanned and between her white satin bra cups was a tiny miniature bow the size of a snowflake, and I wondered if some person had tied that bow by hand. "Actually, I work for Gore."

I said, "Oh." She nodded. I said, "Is Al coming tomorrow?" She didn't know. Across the tent Niles was winding up. My gut bubbled. I said, "Are you going to hire Bob?"

She said, "We think he's amazing."

People had been saying that all night. I still couldn't figure out what they meant. "What do people see that makes him amazing?"

"His intelligence, his loyalty, his experience, his values." She had the serious determination of a nine-year-old girl burning army ants with a match.

"Yeah?"

"We admire his belief system."

Belief system? Based on what—liking people with money? The belief system in which he gorged himself on chicken tikka masala and then stood in the restaurant parking lot and stuck his finger down his throat and puked between the headlights of my car? The belief system that let him zip money into a certain fund during his last campaign from this other giant account out of which he paid himself?

"Oh," I said. "What belief system?"

Phylida, meanwhile, had woken up. I'm not sure how long she'd been staring at me. My future soulmate-slash-fever blister-slash-sleeping beauty had a string bean imprinted on her cheek. With her giant eyes and her pink face she looked like an unborn squirrel.

I said, "This is Anne."

Phylida said, "Did you enjoy looking down her dress?"

People cheered. Niles was done.

I took forever pushing between chairs to get to the spot with the mike. My legs felt like two thick rusty chains. I tested the microphone. There was now an audience, staring.

I took out the note in my pocket and silently read it. The night Bob phoned, in tears, about leading the polls. Hmm. I paused solemnly. Bob rose up in his chair. He had that stupid set to his eyes and mouth—picture Donald Trump—of always waiting to be looked at. I gazed over the crowd. What was I going to say? "Well—" The skin of my face felt like it had been stretched on a coat hanger in front of an oven. The next line on the piece of paper said, "Story about landlady." I thought for a second. It was something about a pizza box catching fire on the stove.

I cleared my throat. My legs: heavy. My face: hot. I thought of F.D.R., the onset of polio. I sputtered. "You've had a lot of jobs, Bob." I really should've read this over on the plane.

"Quite a few." I couldn't speak. "Big jobs." There's no funny or clever metaphor for what I was failing to do up here. I was dying. I should've figured I'd flip out and written down every word. I wanted to sit. I clenched my ass up and tried to go forward. "You're smart." I couldn't breathe. "Very smart." My small lungs shot puffs of white gas—performance anxiety. "An incredible guy." The people closest to me looked at me as if an asteroid was coming over my shoulder and was about to crush them. "Unfortunately I'm blanking on some of your successes." A couple of the smokers were laughing. Well, wouldn't you? "I'm sure they'll come to me in a moment." I reached down and quietly drank an entire glass of water. "Why couldn't I have been at some loser's wedding now?" I said to myself, out loud, into the microphone. "I wouldn't have to remember so much." Bob's head looked like a fire engine, his nostrils flaring. Niloo was grinning. "Can't you stop and give somebody else a chance, for Christ's sake?" I put the glass down and gripped the mike stand. I'm going to faint, I thought. No. I'm going to explode from my bowels. And then I'll faint.

It began as a queasy chuckle or two, and suddenly became a wave. The entire room erupted in laughter. In fact they'd been laughing for a while. All night everyone had been dying just to crack a smile—the natural tendency is to want to laugh at events like this—but no one had given them a chance. Now they had me: the buffoon. What the hell?

"Anyway, standing up here talking to you," I said, feeling a little more confident suddenly, "is actually the most time we've spent together in a year and a half, you big pain in the ass." They roared like a beer-hall crowd and I found myself remembering Bob's working his cell phone earlier in the night, and I pictured shoving it down his throat with a toilet plunger. The smokers had joined in, they were yelling at Bob now, one called him a pain in the ass. I stepped forward, trying to keep the momentum. "After Bob moves to the Oval Office," I said, pointing at them, "he'll send you guys some interns." More yucks, far out of proportion to the dopiness of the joke. I raised my right hand and in a lame Clinton drawl said, "I, Bob, solemnly swear to set aside interns who can suck a bowling ball through a crazy straw for my dearest former roommate." Niloo had leaned into Bob's shoulder, her face was twisted frozen as she cracked up. I made one of those fists politicians use when they're trying to be emphatic. Niloo couldn't control herself. I said, "Is this funny to you, Niloo? Do you know what you're in for?" Her face was crimped and she was sort of nodding. "Never stand directly in front of him after he's eaten a large meal. It's very dangerous." I made a puking, retching motion. "I don't know if anybody told you, Bob, vomiting and diarrhea are not the best answer to weight gain." One guy slipped out of his chair and a waiter had to dodge him. Bob was staring at me, immobile, his large mind turning.

Bob wasn't going to be introducing me to Al Gore tomorrow.

Back in Flanders, Phylida bent over and the people seated by her suddenly jumped backward out of their chairs. Phylida, I realized, had either just thrown up or had knocked something over or had fallen comatose onto the ground. That's my woman. I was marrying Drankenstein. I was the Bride of Drankenstein. What a wonderful couple we'd make. How pleasing to the eye and ear. What a future we had. Phylida reared her head after a moment, eyeballs rolling high into her forehead, with her sweaty brown-rooted old hair plastered against it, and I imagined my being up here again—next year? the summer after?—toasting her at our own wedding, and I thought: I might as well kill myself. "Bob," I said, and waited for his expression to change. No change. He was looking at me like I was a stain on your carpet that you scrubbed and it got worse. Ah, what the hell. I raised my empty glass and the place got silent. "How come you never call me back anymore, you fat, pusillanimous, popcorn-eating, obsequious, spermy, ass-licking, whoring, curry-barfing lackey?"

Had I gone too far?

"That," Phylida said, looking up at me when I returned to the table, her face gaunt and sculpted, "was a disaster."

I said, "It was fine. We can go now."

Back at the hotel, Phylida pulled her dress up over her head and threw it in the corner under the desk, kicked her shoes off and pulled down her nylons and sat on the edge of the bed in her underwear, groaning. Even hunched over like that, there wasn't a blip of fat on her. She put on her little spaghetti-strap camisole. I stared at her: narrow torso, strong shoulders, long neck. She looked like she was made out of rubber. I waited for her to look at me. "Are you gonna go right to sleep?" I said.

I was trying to be nice, trying not to want her. The night's debacle had left me charged. Why was her arm skin so soft? We were here together in this perfect glimpse of unreal time in a fancy hotel. I looked at her and she yawned. "I'm going to bed." My dick, of course, was hard. Not like that egg-yolk dick from earlier today. It now lay in my pants like a stunned fish.

I loved her so much I couldn't think. I loved her because I was horny. I was horny because I was sad, because the night could not have been more awful, because it was almost over. I thought back to that shocked look on Bob's face during my toast, the crowd laughing all around him.

She lay on her side, the table lamp on beside her. I saw that damned chin hair still, and the curving line down to her hollow waist and up the bump over her hip that's so unbelievably beautiful. I kissed her bare white inner forearm again and again.

"Please," she said, "I just want to go to bed." I said I could understand that. She thanked me sweetly. I realized that she was exactly what I wanted in a woman: sparkling eyes, springy hindquarters, the ability to save her own life. I felt for her then what I feel now, and knew without thinking anymore that we'd made it. Her nude hip was staring me in the face. I touched her unburned parts and she smiled. How could she stand me after tonight? We struggled to find a way I could hold her, and then it seemed we both were breathing harder.

I was unclothed and her skin burned against me. With her burns and loveliness and all, she pulled me in. I felt like a giant fishhook and I had her on the line and we were both rocking. She'd got ridden down into the bedspread and it must've felt like sandpaper against her burns but she said nothing, making sweet painful noises and lying low and going with it.

Afterward we ate the apples we'd brought for the plane. We found a movie on TV about a princess riding a motorcycle. The next morning we checked out of that place and drove across the island to a motel—it had a Jacuzzi in the kitchen. I knew I would miss this great event, with no way of predicting who might've flown in by now. Bibi Netanyahu? Marlon Brando riding a llama? I didn't feel like I should be at one place or the other. It didn't feel like a lateral move. It felt good. We ordered crab sandwiches from town and had them delivered to the room. We had a party.

THE INCALCULABLE LIFE GESTURE

James Lasdun

(From *It's Beginning to Hurt*)

Richard Timmerman, principal of an elementary school in the town of Aurelia, noticed a swelling under his chin one morning. Ignoring it (he assumed he was just fighting off some virus) he shaved and went to work. It was still there a week later, but he continued to ignore it. He had a busy job, a family, and plenty of other things to think about.

Among the latter was a problem that had been troubling him for several weeks now. His parents, who had died within months of each other the previous year, had left their house to him and his sister. Ellen, the sister, had moved in with them a few years earlier, ostensibly to help take care of their ailing father, but in reality (as everyone knew who knew the family) because she couldn't afford to buy or rent a place of her own. She had been a reckless spirit when she was young, traveling with a theater troupe in Europe, then living on ashrams in India, and had hit middle age with a crash: twice divorced, with a small son, large debts and no prospects of making a decent living. Now she was refusing to move out of the house.

It wasn't a big house, but Richard certainly could have used his share of whatever it was worth. He would have hired a lawyer to deal with the matter, but he had qualms about evicting his own sister, and was also a little afraid of how this might affect his reputation in the small community where they lived. Being put in this position, of having to be either a victim of Ellen's selfish stubbornness or else a bully, further upset him. Above all, he disliked how the problem, with all the childish feelings it aroused, seemed to have taken over his mind, vexing him whenever he lay in bed or drove to work. Whether he was inwardly fuming at Ellen or trying to force himself to feel more charitable toward her than he did, he could think of nothing else. He considered himself an idealistic person, above this sort of pettiness, but there it was, filling him with its tedious drone every time he had a moment's peace. If she'd had the decency to express guilt or even just some regret about depriving him of what he was owed, he might have found it easier to make allowances for her. But she seemed to think she had every right to stay put, and instead of asking him nicely to be generous or patient, had taken a position of self-righteous hostility, as if he were the one in the wrong. Furthermore, even as she made him feel vaguely criminal for being so much better off than she was (as if siblings somehow had a natural right to equal shares of whatever the world had to offer) she had a way of conveying lofty contempt for precisely the comforts—a decent car, occasional vacations, enough money to shop at the all-organic store in town rather than having to hunt for bargains in the Wal-Mart produce aisles—that distinguished his life from hers. Their phone conversations had become icy in the extreme.

Three weeks after he'd noticed it, the swelling still hadn't gone down. At his wife's urging, he made an appointment to see Doctor Taubman, the family physician, in East Deerfield.

The doctor was a small, trim, dapper man with a neatly shaped goatee and a pair of sparkling half-moon glasses. Largely on the basis of the latter, Richard had formed an idea of him as a person of intellectual leanings, like himself, though also like himself more interested in the nurturing of others (their bodies in his case, while in Richard's it was their young minds) than in the selfish pursuit of learning for its own sake. He felt an affinity with him, and although their conversations had never gone very far he sensed that an unspoken mutual respect existed between them.

Doctor Taubman picked up a silver pen after examining the lump. He was silent for a moment, then he cleared his throat.

"I don't want to say this is anything like lymphoma," he said, swiveling the pen in his fingers. "It could be perfectly benign, just a swollen lymph node from an infection, as you suggested. But at this point you need to have a specialist take a look at it and I think you should probably have it removed."

Richard blinked, momentarily too stunned to speak.

"You mean surgically?" he asked.

"Oh yes."

Smiling oddly, the doctor told Richard to schedule a CAT scan as soon as possible and to make an appointment to see an ear, nose and throat specialist for a biopsy. As if foreseeing that Richard would attempt to stave off the fear mounting inside him with the hope that these tests might turn out negative, he cautioned him that some tumors were not radio-opaque and would therefore not show up on the scan. He added that the specialist would probably opt for surgery regardless of the biopsy result since these, also, were not entirely reliable.

Recommending a local colleague, he stood up, still smiling and clearly expecting Richard to observe some unwritten clinic protocol in which it was agreed to behave as if a diagnosis of probable cancer were nothing out of the ordinary and certainly nothing to get upset about, at least not in his office. Considering his high regard for the man, Richard couldn't help feeling that he was being dealt with rather brusquely. He stumbled out into the parking lot with a sense of having been sent on his way with an armful of enormous, unwieldy objects that had been pressed on him against his wishes and for which he had no conceivable use.

He had intended running some errands in East Deerfield after the appointment, but he drove home instead, his hands slippery on the cold plastic of the steering wheel.

In the driveway, he stood for a moment, feeling dizzy. The white clapboard and blue trim of the house gleamed in the spring sunshine. Beyond, spaced across the broad lawn, were the shade trees that had outlasted several generations of humans: the weeping willow, the giant and festive blue spruce, the sugar maple and horse chestnut standing close to each other, their branches interlaced. All just as he had left them an hour and a half earlier, and yet charged with an air of circumspection now, as if the news had already reached them.

Sara, his wife, appeared from around the back of the house in her gardening gloves, her short, graying hair clinging in damp wisps to her face.

"What did the doctor say?"

She nodded silently as he told her. A stranger observing might have imagined her oddly unconcerned by the news. But this subdued reaction was simply her manner: the manifestation of a slow but scrupulous way she had of registering important matters. It was she who insisted that Richard go down to New York for both the scan and the biopsy, rather than have them done locally, and it was she, in her unobtrusively efficient way, who made the arrangements.

A week later, he took the train to New York and entered a building on the Upper West Side. He had barely slept since his visit to Doctor Taubmann. Some over-the-counter pills had given him a few hours of light oblivion each night, after which the feeling of dread they had held in precarious abeyance spilled back, filling his mind with a cold, pulsating wakefulness for the rest of the night. It happened to be a busy week at his school—a meeting with trustees, a planning session for a new science building, the monthly assembly for the "Tribes" program that he had recently introduced—and the effort of trying to conduct himself in his usual genial manner compounded the stress, leaving him with a muffled, torpid, leaden sensation that was somehow at the same time one of weightlessness and raw-nerved exposure.

Utter silence filled the elevator: it seemed not to move at all, so that when the doors opened it was as if the lobby had merely transformed itself into a corridor with a glass sign etched with the words *Lifestream Radiology.*

He went into the waiting room, feeling the fear inside him glow a little brighter. Was it death itself that frightened him? Not exactly. Nonexistence had never seemed a particularly disturbing concept, and he had often wondered why people made such a fuss about it. More upsetting was the prospect of being reassigned in the minds of others from the category of the living to that of the dying, which appeared to him a kind of sudden ruin: an abrupt calamitous coming down in the world, with all the disgrace and shame that accompany such a circumstance. And then beyond that there was the process, terrifying to contemplate, of being slowly, forcibly, painfully torn from one's own existence. Already, it seemed to him, the process had begun: a fissure had opened between him and the life he had made for himself—the wife and children he loved, the home in which their happiness had flourished, his demanding but inexhaustibly satisfying job. The fissure was still invisible, but like an ice floe that had cracked, it was only a matter of time before the two sides began to move apart from each other.

After twenty minutes his name was called and he was shown to a room where the radiologist, a woman with straggling gray hair and a wooden cross at her neck, prepared him for the scan.

"I'll be giving you a power surge injection of iodine for radiographic contrast," she said with a strained, bulging-eyed look, "after which you may become nauseous or feel the need for a bowel movement. But it's important that you lie completely still, and try not to swallow as that can affect the image."

He hung his head, restraining a childlike desire to sob.

"We'll go on in if you're ready ..."

The walls of the scanning room were windowless, hung with huge, glowing, photographic panels depicting sapphire waterfalls and emerald green alpine meadows. In the center stood the monumental white ring of the scanner with the gurney projecting below. From pictures he had seen of these machines, Richard had noted their strange fusion of the space-age with the primeval, but even so the vast size and eerie fluorescence of the instrument startled him. He lay down on the narrow dais. The woman plunged a needle into his arm. A tingling, pressurized heat surged into him. Not painful exactly, but shocking. The word "insult," in its medical sense, came to him as the substance raced through his veins. Something in him seemed to flinch in corresponding outrage or mortification. Was he going to throw up? Were his bowels going to betray him? Two lit faces suspended in darkness watched from behind a glass partition. The scanner began to hum. Above him the radiologist stood with her slight aghast expression, her stringy hair blueish in the light from the machine. She pressed a switch and the gurney slid his prone body slowly under the machine's arching panel of dials and sensors. By nature a respecter of limits and thresholds, he stared up at the great circular gateway towering over him, with a feeling of horror.

He swallowed suddenly; the reflex too strong to control.

"Sorry!"

"It's alright. I think we have what we're looking for."

Before he could fully absorb these words the woman had retreated behind the glass partition, conferring inaudibly with the two figures stationed there. A few minutes later she reemerged, carrying a large envelope. The wooden cross gleamed dully at her throat. She handed him the envelope, speaking slowly:

"This is what you're going to bring with you to your specialist."

He thanked her, putting on his jacket. On his way out he turned back, hearing himself ask in a thick voice:

"Did you—did you see something?"

She looked away from him, facing the machine.

"Oh, I don't really read the scans."

She had seen something! She was religious and even a small lie made her uncomfortable. He left, staggering out into the cool spring sunlight. The specialist's office was in Midtown. He walked, moving in the same daze of fear as before, only more deeply interred in its cause. Here was Broadway: billboards and scaffolding and more billboards over the scaffolding. A truck, turning, belched soot across a pool of white tulips. Why had this happened to him? He wondered. Had he committed some transgression without knowing it? Violated some fundamental law governing his life? He had been brought up in a churchgoing household, and although he no longer believed in a god or an afterlife, the habit of looking for meaning in the events that befell him was second nature. He carried with him a sense of having discovered at a certain point the precise terms on which existence was prepared to nourish his particular qualities as a human being, and of having abided by these terms as conscientiously as he could. He had been interested in many things: folk music, mathematics, philosophy, design; he had thought of becoming an academic, another time considered a career in engineering. But always at the point of embarking along one of these paths some stubborn element in his makeup had protested that although these professions might be fascinating, they lacked a particular radiance without which his own nature was not going to fulfill itself. This was the radiance of active virtue: direct, self-sacrificing involvement in the upward-aspiring efforts of his fellow humans. How this had become such a vital necessity to him he had not thought necessary to investigate, but there it was: in him like a compass needle, and he had followed it faithfully as it led him into the field of education, guiding him within that field to the progressive theories that articulated his own instincts; pointing the way forward at every juncture in his career.... Educators, he had read in an essay that had inscribed itself on his memory, were "the life-priests of the new era." They were "adepts" (he knew the passage as he had once known the Nicene Creed) "in the dark mystery of living, fearing nothing but life itself, and subject to nothing but their own reverence for the incalculable life-gesture ...."

The incalculable life gesture ... And yet here was death growing in his throat! He remembered a visit he and Sara had made to a relative of Sara's in Minneapolis. They had walked down the Nicolette Mall to the river and come to a place called Cancer Survivor's Park. The name, in stenciled metal letters over the gate, had shocked him. Its brazen literalness where some poetic euphemism might have been expected, gave its summons to celebrate the afflicted an aggressive thrust that had made him want to do just the opposite: to recoil from the very thought of such ghoulish beings. And yet now his best hope was to become one of them!

"Spare a dollar, mister?"

A beggar had intruded an empty coffee cup into his field of vision. Richard dropped some change into the cup. The man's eyes went straight to the coins; counting them. He turned away without a word of thanks.

A familiar stung sensation flared in Richard, reminding him how much he had come to dislike the city. He had found it exhilarating in the days when he lived here, but now, increasingly, he felt himself at odds with it. Every time he came down it seemed harder, cruder, more mercantile, the people thronging its streets crazier and more grotesque. On his last visit he had seen a woman in stiletto heels leading a muzzled raccoon on a leash. He didn't think of himself as censorious, let alone a prude, but the place seemed to bring forth some puritanical layer of his personality. A steady stream of disapproving observations would flow through him, unbidden. Even now he found himself grimly taking note of new depths of folly; new kinds of utterly unnecessary things—gadgets, clothes, jewelry, services, entertainments—publicized on every available surface in newly unpleasant ways, the ads caught up in their own logic of escalating tawdriness. One for a dating website outside a subway showed a near-naked couple grinning in post-coital bliss. Two intertwined hearts glowed above them, but it might just as well have been genitalia. The ideal state of affairs, things seemed to imply, was a continual orgy. If you weren't desirable then dye your hair, spend the day in a tanning salon, sign up at one of these gyms that flaunted its robotic, Lycra-clad members at passersby through vast street-level windows. Turn the inside of your head into your own private rock stadium ... The steady convergence of mainstream commerce with what had once been marginal or underground, was peculiarly dismaying. In the past, when you grew sick of one of these worlds, you could shift, mentally, into the other, but now they had consolidated and there was nowhere to escape. The whole world, as he had read somewhere, was an underworld. If you described New York to even a liberal-minded person of fifty years ago they would tell you the apocalypse must have come ....

But in the thick of these thoughts a sudden bewilderment seized him. Where did they come from? What was the basis, within him, for this indignation? On what rock of conviction was it founded? If you didn't believe in god or the soul or the hereafter then what was a human being if not merely living meat? And if that was so then surely it was natural to want to be healthy, nubile, muscular, lusty .... Better that than *tainted* meat, as he had become! It was he himself who was grotesque, surely, with this little death-kernel growing in his throat.

The specialist's offices were in a grandiose corner building. Granite steps led from the tree-lined street to a revolving door. Behind it was a dim lobby with a uniformed doorman who sent Richard up to the seventh floor. The offices themselves were sleekly modern: furbished in brushed steel and blond wood. The young woman receptionist was dressed like a model, with a pink puff of chiffon at her throat. There were no files or papers of any kind on her desk. Occasionally she spoke into thin air, answering an invisible, inaudible telephone.

The specialist, a Doctor Jameson, was much younger than Richard had expected: mid-thirties, with thick, fair hair and large freckles on his boyish face. Long ginger eyelashes gave him a sleepy, hedonistic look.

"Come on in, Mr, uh, Timmerman," he said, glancing at some papers.

He sat Richard in a contraption like a dentist's chair while he read through the referral papers, apparently for the first time. "Huh," he said neutrally. With a light toss he dropped the papers onto the desk.

"Let's take a look."

He leaned in over Richard, probing with strong, well-manicured fingers into the soft tissue under Richard's chin. He wore a watch that appeared to have neither numerals nor hands and he smelled faintly of vanilla.

Another laconic "huh" was his only comment after the examination. He stepped back over to the desk and picked up the envelope that Richard had brought, taking out the CAT scan images. He examined them for a long, silent interval.

"This is upstate somewhere, this, uh, East Deerfield?"

"Yes." Richard could hear the tremor in his own voice. Evidently he was about to be advised to move closer to some urban area with access to state-of-the-art treatment facilities. In which case it was all over.

"Why?" He asked.

"No reason. I just ..."

The doctor yawned.

"Excuse me. Sorry. You have a stone in your saliva gland. A small calcium deposit. Sialolithiasis is the technical term. If it becomes uncomfortable you can have it removed surgically, maybe broken up with ultrasound. Otherwise it'll probably work its own way out. Either way it's not a big deal."

Richard felt as if he were levitating out of the chair.

"You mean there's no ... there's no lymphoma?"

"No."

Only as he took the elevator back down did he pick up the note of faint scorn in the question about East Deerfield: the amused disdain of the cosmopolitan practitioner for his colleague out in the sticks. A smile rose on his lips. With it, clarified by the strong joy of the moment, came the memory of his obscure sense of having been too hastily dismissed by Doctor Taubman, as if the man had been afraid he was going to start visibly decaying right there in his office and scare away the other patients. He would have liked to strut into Taubman's office, not so much to berate him for his mistake as to flaunt his freshly certified health in the man's face ....

It was still sunny outside. He walked slowly toward the train station, conscious of how rare it was to be able to savor, so undistractedly, the pure pleasure of being alive. Everything he looked at, every face he passed, seemed a part of this pleasure; a fiery splendor suffusing even the most mundane things. A delivery man bustled by, wheeling stacks of clear-topped containers in which the vivid colors of cold cuts and raw vegetables, each partitioned in their own segment, glowed—it seemed to Richard—like the panels of a rose window in some ancient cathedral. In a parking lot behind a row of blossoming trees a shiny crimson car was being lifted effortlessly into the air by a hydraulic steel arm. Glorious! As he passed by, Richard realized he hadn't thought of his quarrel with his sister for days; not since his visit to Doctor Taubman. How trivial that whole business seemed. How absurd to have let it upset him as much as it had. In his exhilarated state the solution appeared obvious: he must call Ellen right away, tell her she could stay in the house for as long as she wanted. In his heart of hearts he had always known this was the right thing to do; he simply hadn't been able to summon, with any conviction, the feeling of largesse such a gesture would require. Now, however, he felt it in abundance. True, he had been counting on his share of the sale to put something substantial aside for his children's college fund; perhaps also build a screened-in porch so that they could eat outside in summer. But so what? He had a life—in every sense!—whereas Ellen had nothing. If it meant so much to her to go on living in the family home, then let her. Let her! The decision further boosted his sense of euphoria. As he took out his phone he seemed to glimpse some large, resplendent state of existence opening itself up to him.

He dialed her number.

"What?" Came the familiar voice.

"Ellen, it's me, Richard."

"I know. What do you want?"

"I just—" He broke off. Her hostile tone, though no different from the usual way she'd been talking to him since their quarrel began, presented an unexpected obstacle. It seemed necessary to bring her into his exuberant state of mind before he could reveal his momentous decision.

"I'm in New York. Our doctor thought I had lymphoma because of a lump under my chin, and I've spent the last week thinking I was going to die. But I'm not. I've just come out of a specialist's office and he says I'm fine. It was just a stone!"

He paused. Ellen said nothing.

"I thought I'd call you, you know ..." He trailed off, unnerved by the silence at the other end.

"I see," she said finally. "Well, I'm happy for you Richard. I'm glad you're not going to die. But now I'm afraid I have to go out. Since my car's broken down again, Scott and I have to start walking to the post office so I can pay my bills before it closes. Otherwise I'm sure I'd have time to chat."

The martyred tone was a specialty of hers. He tried not to let it provoke him.

"Listen. Ellen. I want to talk about the house."

"Ah. I thought so."

God, she was impossible! She knew him well enough to have an idea where he was trying to go with this. But was she going to be gracious about it? No! She was going to make it as unpleasant as possible. Already he could feel the old rankling annoyance mounting inside him. How easy it would be to succumb: lash out at her for making others pay the price for her hapless way of living; present her with some stark, inflexible ultimatum ... But he resisted it. He was damned if he was going to let her stop him making his great gesture of magnanimity. He would do it for his own sake, if not hers.

"What I want to tell you," he said, forcing out the words, "is that I've decided to let you stay on in the house for as long as you need to. That's all."

There was a long pause.

"Well that's awfully charitable of you Richard, and I'm glad you won't be trying to have me and Scott evicted from our home. But since I had no intention of leaving anyway it doesn't really change anything, does it? Now if it's okay with you, I have to run."

She hung up.

He moved on down Seventh Avenue, stunned. He told himself that he'd said what he wanted to say, and that was all that mattered; that however she took it, he'd acquitted himself with dignity and compassion. Furthermore, he'd brought an end to their tedious, unseemly quarrel, and now, finally, he would be able to turn his mind to loftier things again.

But all the earlier expansiveness had gone from him; in its place a drab, ashen sensation, as if the bitterness of his sister's dismal existence had flowed into him through the phone.

And for a moment he felt as if he hadn't yet had his appointment with Doctor Jameson after all: as if he were still waiting, frightened and uncertain, for his diagnosis.

In the Coma

Robert Pinsky

(From *At The Foundling Hospital* / Originally published in *Poetry*)

My friend was in a coma, so I dove
Deep into his brain to word him back. I tried

To sing Hallelujah, I Just Love Her So in
Ray Charles' voice. Of course the silence grew.

I couldn't sing the alphabet song. My voice
Couldn't say words I knew: Because I Could
Not Stop For Death, He Kindly Stopped For Me.

I couldn't remember the Dodgers and the Giants.

I tried to tell the stories that he and I
Studied when we were young. It was confused,
The Invisible Man was laughing at how a man
Felt History jump out of his thick fair head
And beat him half to death, as being the nightmare
Out of which Isaac Babel tried to awake.

The quiet. Next time won't you sing with me.
Those great diminished chords: A girl I know.

The cold of the coma, lightless. The ocean floor.
I struggled to tell things back from decades gone.
The mournful American soldier testifying
About My Lai: I shot the older lady.

Viola Liuzzo, Spiro Agnew, Jim Jones.

And by the time I count from one to four
I hear her knocking. Quiet of the deep,
Our mouths are open but we cannot sing

PRAYER

Grace Schulman

(From *The Paintings of Our Lives* / Originally published in *Poetry*)

Yom Kippur: wearing a bride's dress bought in Jerusalem,
I peer through swamp reeds, my thought in Jerusalem.

Velvet on grass. Odd, but I learned young to keep this day
just as I can, if not as I ought, in Jerusalem.

Like sleep or love, prayer may surprise the woman
who laughs by a stream, or the child distraught in Jerusalem.

My Arab dress has blue-green-yellow threads
the shades of mosaics hand-wrought in Jerusalem

that both peoples prize, like the blue-yellow Dome of the Rock,
like strung beads-and-cloves, said to ward off the drought in Jerusalem.

Both savor things that grow wild—coreopsis in April,
the rose that buds late, like an afterthought, in Jerusalem.

While car bombs flared, an Arab poet translated
Hebrew verses whose flame caught in Jerusalem.

Now Shahid sails Judah Halevi's sea as I,
on Ghalib's, course like an Argonaut in Jerusalem.

Stone lions pace the sultan's gate while almonds bloom
into images, Hebrew and Arabic, wrought in Jerusalem.

No words, no metaphors, for knives that gore flesh
on streets where the people have fought in Jerusalem.

As this spider weaves a web in silence,
may Hebrew and Arabic be woven taut in Jerusalem.

Here at the bay, I see my face in the shallows
and plumb for the true self our Abraham sought in Jerusalem.

Open the gates to rainbow-colored words
of outlanders, their sounds untaught in Jerusalem.

My name is Grace, Chana in Hebrew—and in Arabic.
May its meaning, "God's love," at last be taught in Jerusalem.

THE SWEET RED AWAKENING OF BRUCE ALLEN DESILVA

Patricia Smith

(From *Able Muse Review*)

His mother cranked out meals of gray cotton—
smoked shoulders, beaten beef or steel-hued ham,
stringy with fat, circling a mutant pig's thighbone.
There always seemed to be something dying
on top or inside of the oven. Stunned vegetables
clung dryly to the sides of saucepans, as if they
had tried to crawl free of their torrid little hell,
the relentless heat rising beneath them, sucking
their sweet souls free of water. And potatoes
were everywhere—squashed and scissored and
always somehow wounded, wearing their bruises
and burns with a certain shame that drove them
to the shadowy back edge of dinner plates.

She detested spices, believing that her square meals
were their own poetry, simple and sinless foods
that God Himself would have slurped from holy fingers.
Sauces, with their mysterious swirling and inevitable
redness, flustered her and spoiled the perfect white
line of her family at rest. Her two boys would grow
square and strong on what she placed before them.
Her husband always ate crouched in the middle of
a huge silence, loving her obviously and savoring
the daily feast, the broad bland muscle of his meal.

Her son felt as if he were chewing less than air. Years of
hot bland flesh sliced evenly onto flowered china, of
stews cooked to mud, of his mother's festive punch,

which consisted of a dash of every liquid she could
snatch from the Frigidaire, years of the little boulder
he lugged in his gut, the artful pushing of things around
and around on his plate, after all that belching up the
air of his mother's overdone love, he discovered ketchup
and was so happy he died a little. From that moment
he doused her meals with this brand-name blood, buried
it all beneath tomato and sugar, ignored the wringing of
her hands. When she wasn't looking, he would tip
the bottle to his mouth and give it a swift suck, letting
the scarlet wash bathe his throat in something that
hinted of a glorious sin one step beyond 1955, beyond,
Dighton, Massachusetts, and beyond his mother and
her carefully smoked shoulders. He had found his
own sin, and it was wild and bloody and went down
like something the devil had given him, and life began.

COTILLION PHOTO

Rosanna Warren

(from *The New Yorker*)

These young women will last forever, posed like greyhounds,
trapped in the silver crust of the frame.
You can't tell one from another, the breed is so pure.
They will never run. Each one aloft
on a frozen wave of white cotillion lace
to resemble marriage, to resemble fate.
I remember July sun pouring down
in a prickly meadow, and a garter-snake skin
laid out like fairy lingerie on a stone wall.
This was Connecticut, there would be a stone wall.
Crickets were scraping marrow from the day.
I was young; I'd been alone for weeks.
I painted the meadow morning and afternoon
trying to capture the crackling sound with my brush.
I was reading *Oedipus Rex*.
I understood neither the snake skin nor the play.
"Your life is one long night," said Oedipus
to the prophet, Oedipus, who saw nothing.
Oak trees rustled in drought. In saffron grass
small creatures skittered. There came a day
when I said to myself, "I should prefer to sleep."
Small planets tasted dry and bitter on my tongue.
And two days later I woke. Alone in the creaking barn
at dusk, not knowing what day, what month, what year,
but feeling the haul of earth rolling on its way.
"It is not your fate that I should be your ruin,"
the prophet said. I moved my arms,
my legs, I unclenched my hands,
and stood up dizzy from the cot. What was to come

would come in its own good time
outside the frame. The moon was rising
above the hill, a shy wind gathered force,
and trees, in their black silhouettes, linked arms.

II

THE WRITERS STUDIO
TEACHERS AND STUDENTS

MIDDLE SCHOOL GARDENING CLUB

Laurel Ingraham Aquadro

it's too painful, my student said
(carrying trays of seedlings frozen from frost)
to throw out the just sprouted then dead

and to curse the hours spent
dump hair-like roots into the moss
it's too painful, the eighth grader said

to never be able to mend
that which is planted, ungrown, and lost
and to waste what's just sprouted and dead

as her teacher, I am meant to correct,
support, explain, and end
any confusion that grows in her head

older, I know how so often we're rent
apart by little things lost
lovers barely known or met
vacancy, though the pain is gone

instead I told her the hours we'd spent
(dirt under our nails and feet sunken in rocks —
only to bury what's now dead)

was not a loss and was not wrecked
because, though frozen, we'd found on a roof
sun in a city of cement

our garden club saw that sunlight bends
to reach into corners to light up the dark,
disappears for months, but emerges again

so we stayed, uprooting aborted attempts
at spinach, tomatoes, lettuce, and squash
even though it's painful, we mend
and we learn to let go of the sprouted, and dead.

HARVEST

L.L. Babb

(From *The MacGuffin*)

It usually happens when I'm not at home. I'll return from work midafternoon and notice the hills are a blank green wash, broken only by clusters of scrub oak and fence lines. Once or twice, it has occurred on a Saturday or one of the weekdays when school is out. Then I've watched from my back porch, sipping coffee—the dogs slinking through the tall grass, sinewy and low, and the men, usually Hispanics culled from the day labor center in town, waving their hats or running bent forward with their arms open, as if begging for a hug from the recalcitrant earth. It takes most of the day to herd the sheep and their bouncy lambs down from the hills into the ravine, then across to my neighbor's ranch. In the week that follows, I'll pull on my rubber boots and trudge around the fence perimeter, looking for broken posts or downed wire where the ewes leaned heavily to reach for a scruff of vegetation. The property and fences are mine but the sheep are my neighbor's and he pays me a good rate to lease my twenty acres. Carl Wilson and I have had the same arrangement for fifteen years, ever since my father passed away.

The sheep come back shorn minus their lambs, which are auctioned in downtown Petaluma and carted away to slaughterhouses in central California. When I was child and my family owned its own flock, I used to look for something in the sheep's eyes when they returned without their lambs, grief perhaps or anger, but there was never anything there that I could see. When I got too close to their dull faces, they simply veered off in a tight bunch, presenting me with their shit-encrusted backsides.

Still, it is soothing to look out and see them there in the distance, dotting the hills with white. I've had offers to sell the land from a neighbor or two, but more often from developers who want to put up mini-estates on the crests that overlook town. My sister, who has not been on the property for more than two consecutive hours since she left home, would love to sell. I give her the entire amount from the pasture lease, which usually keeps her mollified and unheard from for a good nine months out of every year.

Then last winter, right after the lease was renewed, my sister appeared to collect the check and left without taking her son with her. She said she was running to town to pick up a few things, then called me from her cell phone an hour later to tell me that she needed some time to "get her head together." I knew there wasn't enough time in the world for my sister to get her head together, but I naïvely thought she meant a few days, a week maybe.

I've never had any children myself but I am not unfamiliar with teenagers. I work at the high school, filling out the attendance reports and calling parents to check on kids who've been skipping classes. I know what children that age are capable of. I suppose there are a few good ones, smart kids who have something going for them. But for the most part, they are as interchangeable as sheep. They arrive at school, muddle through four years, and depart with a lot of fanfare, shoving their sad little yearbooks in front of me to write something memorable when in truth I can't think of anything nice to say. I usually just sign my name over my face in the office group photo.

My nephew had just turned fifteen, quite possibly the worst age to deal with in my experience. In the brief period before I discovered Rian would be staying with me indefinitely, he had trampled down my broccoli, tracked sheep dung across the living room carpet, and lost the remote for the television.

After my sister's call, Rian and I sized each other up. I know what he saw—a plus-sized forty-two-year-old spinster with chapped lips and a self-inflicted haircut. What I saw was the evolution of a mustache gasping for breath on the bank of his upper lip, the tangle of greasy black hair barely concealing a swath of acne across his forehead, and a musty pea coat covered with some kind of pet hair. I hoped I didn't look quite as horrified as he did.

I've always been a person who takes care of what's in front of her. I figured out long ago that wishing and hoping and long-term plans lead nowhere. My sister had pipe dreams and practiced "creative visualization," and she never actually managed to accomplish one practical thing in her life. I had this boy, this teenager, in my care and I would do what needed to be done.

This was in January. The next morning, I drove him to the high school, deposited him in a chair beside my desk, and registered him for classes. My sister had left a paper sack of his clothes on the front porch, but of course I didn't have any of the required documents: no transfer records, no proof of immunization, no birth certificate. I wasn't even sure what grade to put him in. Apparently, my sister had been home-schooling him for the past couple of years because he'd been expelled from junior high.

"Why were you expelled?" I asked.

"Some bullshit," he mumbled. He slouched in the chair, his lips and chin covered by the collar of his hairy jacket. He spoke, he moved, as if everything required a few extra moments of thought. He was either slow-witted or working toward being insolent but too cowardly not to answer at all.

"I say you're a freshman," I said.

The ten-second pause. "Whatever," he said.

I could see from the get-go nobody was going to warm to him.

We fell into an uneasy pattern. Weekday mornings, we drove to the school, arriving at 7:30. There, we were quick to part company. I usually ate lunch in my car but if I passed through the cafeteria at lunchtime, I would see Rian hunched at the end of one of the long tables, alone. At three in the afternoon we drove home. After picking at whatever I served for dinner, he went up to his room, my sister's old room, and stayed there. He didn't play music or ask to talk on the phone. As far as I knew he never even removed that pea coat. He was perpetually ready to leave at a moment's notice. I sat in my chair by the fireplace, reading or doing a crossword puzzle, and I imagined him lying on the bed directly over me, fully dressed, staring at the ceiling, the way my sister did when she was a teenager, aching to be anywhere but where she was. You could feel the muted unhappiness seeping down through the floorboards and floating like a dingy cloud just below the ceiling. To tell the truth, it made me a little anxious, all that weighty quiet over my head but I tried to ignore it. He had a roof over his head, three meals a day, and he was going to school. My sister would be back, and he would be gone, and that would be that.

In late January, the flock moved down closer to the house and the lambs started to appear. It was cold and dry, and the babies slid out of their mothers in steaming gray lumps. They were up on their feet, nursing, within hours. Over the next week, the property came alive with lambs in various stages of development.

That weekend I took a walk along the property line. At the top of the hill, out of sight of the house, a section of barbed wire dipped to the ground. The posts on either side were nearly horizontal. Something large had pushed down the wire. A section of my property backed onto a regional park and it wasn't uncommon for hikers to trespass onto my land, holding down the barbed wire with a heavy boot to get in. Each time I found the fence like this, it felt like someone had trampled me down, took a little bit away from me, exposed me and the sheep under my care to danger.

I trotted back down to the house, opened the back door, and stuck my head in. The kitchen clocked ticked; the refrigerator motor sputtered and went quiet.

"Rian?" I called.

There was the long moment of nothing then a groan of floorboards on the landing in the hall. After a full minute, his impassive, expressionless face appeared at the entrance from the dining room. Everything about him made me suddenly, inexplicably angry. It may well have been his big foot that ruined the fence, sneaking furtively around the edges of my life, making me uneasy and off kilter.

"Time to make yourself useful," I snapped. "Get outside."

He looked startled for one moment but immediately the blank mask slipped down over his face again. He shuffled forward and followed me outside.

I grabbed a wheelbarrow, two small bags of cement, and a shovel from the barn. "Fill those buckets with water and follow me," I told Rian. I pushed the loaded wheelbarrow down into the ravine and started up the hill. I didn't look back until I got to the top.

Rian had filled the buckets and started after me. But now he stood halfway up the hill as if transfixed. He was staring at the lambs. They were everywhere, running up as close to him as they dared and darting away, dancing lightly on their feet, bawling, butting heads with each other, kicking up their heels, and leaping in the air like kittens. The look on his face was almost comical—goofy, stunned, and enchanted.

I had seen that expression before, mostly on tourists driving past the farm on their way out to Point Reyes. City-its, my dad used to call them. They'd get out of their cars to snap pictures, or coax the babies close to the fence with fistfuls of whatever they had in the car; I'd seen them hold out a handful of red licorice or they'd tear up a clump of long grass and shake it at the lambs as if no one had noticed the pasture full of the same exact grass on the other side of the fence. Once, a couple of years ago, a man with two little blonde-haired girls came to the front door to see if he could buy a lamb to take home as a pet. Money, he said, was no object. There was a lady with a bright scarf and big sunglasses waiting in a BMW convertible in the driveway. She smiled and waved at me. The man was ruddy-faced and overweight—he looked like the kind of person who didn't like to be told he couldn't have something. I wondered if he thought he would just put the lamb in the back seat with the girls. I considered telling him he was a nincompoop. Instead I sent them round to Wilson's. The lambs weren't mine to sell. I never heard what happened after that. He might have done some serious thinking but I was not optimistic.

"Come on," I shouted down to Rian. "Get a move on."

At that he sprinted up the hill, the water sloshing out of the buckets. He stopped in front of me, panting. The buckets were less than half full and the bottoms of his jeans and his black boots were soaking wet.

"What ... where did they all come from?" he gasped.

I wasn't in the mood for explaining the birds and the bees. "Oh, for Christ's sake, Rian," I said, dumping the meager contents of the buckets into the wheelbarrow. "Go back down, fill those buckets, and try to keep some water in them on the way back up here."

Rian's gaze darted from the lambs, to me, over to the downed fence posts and the barbed wire lying on the ground, then back to the lambs, and then something seemed to click behind his eyes. He took off, clumping down the hill, the empty buckets banging against his legs.

He was back in no time with two nearly full buckets of water. He poured while I mixed the cement in the wheelbarrow with the shovel until we had a pretty good consistency. Then he helped dig out one of the holes a bit wider and held the post steady as I ladled in the cement.

"Who knocked down the fence?" he asked, glancing around as if the culprits were hiding nearby.

I shrugged my shoulders. "Trespassers," I said, "hikers, maybe, or a mountain lion."

"Mountain lion," he repeated.

"Ten minutes," I said. "Hold that still for ten minutes." I started to work on the other posthole.

"I used to have a cat," Rian said.

Ah-ha, I thought, the animal hair on his coat identified.

"In Denver," Rian said.

"What?"

"In Denver. That's where I had a cat. It wasn't my cat really. It was my mom's boyfriend's kids' cat but it liked me the best. It only slept with me at night."

I looked up to see if this was the same boy I'd been living with for a month. He had actually strung together a few sentences in a row.

"All this property," he said. "You and my mom must have had lots of pets."

I put my head down and concentrated on digging. We had always had working dogs, a border collie or heeler mix or another kind of mutt when my parents were still working the farm. My dad wouldn't let us give them names—they were all just "Dog." And barn cats had prowled around the property all the time. They were good for keeping the rodents out of the feed but their numbers occasionally became unruly. My dad had periodically trapped the kittens and the less wily adults. Once, when I was five or six years old, I came around the corner of the barn and found him drowning a kitten in the cement water trough. It was a tiny gray tabby that I had foolishly taught to come to me when called. My father held it underwater and watched the sweep of the second hand on his Timex like a housewife timing a soft-boiled egg.

I knew from past experience not to relate those kinds of details. Farm kids had a different relationship with animals than other kids did.

"Nope," I said. "No pets."

"Well," he said, "you had the sheep. The lambs."

I stopped chipping at the posthole and stared at him for a few seconds.

"Don't be ridiculous," I said. I sounded just like my dad.

Rian spent the rest of the day outside on the hill. He suddenly seemed to think it was his responsibility to watch over the flock, the same flock that had been doing just fine before he got here.

I diced onions, carrots, and potatoes for stew and watched out the kitchen window as he traversed back and forth, in and out of eyesight, shooing lambs away from the fence, and staring off into the horizon for invaders. He was undoubtedly stepping into all kinds of shit out there and I knew I'd have to head him off before he came back into the house.

Around four, I yelled up to him to come down for dinner. He came, reluctantly. He kept looking back up at the hill. At one point, he actually walked backward for a few yards until he tripped over something hidden in the tall grass.

"Leave those boots outside," I called when he finally came to the door.

He did as he was told. Without the boots, he seemed smaller. He looked a bit like the happy toddler my sister used to bring with her to pick up her money.

I plopped a bowl of stew in front of him.

"Do farmers have shepherds anymore?" he asked.

"Not that I know of," I said. Good Lord. Now that his power of speech button had switched on, was I going to have to constantly interact with him?

"This is really good," Rian said, pointing to the bowl with his spoon. "What is it?"

"Lamb stew," I said, keeping my head down.

He put his spoon down. "You mean like the sheep out there?" he said.

"I mean like the lambs out there."

"The babies?"

"Nobody eats sheep. Meat's too tough." Maybe that would shut him up for a while. But when I glanced up, the stricken look on his face wasn't as satisfying as I'd hoped.

"I think," he said, pushing the bowl away, "I think I'm a vegetarian."

Fine by me, I thought, and for the next couple of days Rian picked out whatever he could from the meals I served. On Thursday, my regular library day, I checked out a vegetarian cookbook, just to look at. It would be like my sister to come back and accuse me of neglecting her child by not meeting his nutritional needs. Some of the recipes didn't sound too bad. I supposed it wouldn't hurt to make a couple of them. I figured Rian would burn out on the lambs and the vegetarian stuff soon enough. Teenagers lack the conviction and self-discipline to stick with anything very long.

Then about a week after Rian discovered the lambs I got up at three AM to use the bathroom and noticed a light on in the barn. There was nothing in the barn that needed illumination; there hadn't been a working bulb in the light fixture for five years or so. Over the years mice had cleared out every stitch of hay and now the barn was completely empty except for an old tractor that didn't run, some rusty tools, and the bald dirt floor.

Except that night. There was Rian with a flashlight. And a lamb. And my grandmother's hand-stitched quilt spread out beneath the both of them like they were on a picnic.

Rian jumped to his feet when he saw me. "He's hurt," he said. "I couldn't find his mother."

The lamb bleated woefully as if seconding Rian's statement. It turned its head to look at me and I could see one of its eyes was gone. A trail of dried blood dribbled onto the white snow of its face like the exaggerated tear of a clown.

"Get it out of here," I said.

"But it's hurt," Rian said.

"Rian," I said, keeping my voice level and enunciating each word, "that quilt has been in my family for almost ninety years."

"Something," Rian intoned, using the same level of gravitas in his voice as I had, "something ripped his eye out."

I glared at him and he glared back. For the first time I recognized my little sister's stubborn features in his face.

"It happens all the time," I said.

"Not to him. It doesn't happen to him all the time."

Why hadn't I seen this coming? "It's an animal," I said.

Rian sat back down on the quilt, hard. A poof of dust squirted out into the dim light. "I'm not leaving him."

I squared my shoulders. This was the time to make my dad's speech — the one about how animals weren't people, that they didn't feel pain like we did or have emotions or thoughts of mortality or fear. That people who thought that way were fools and softies. They were fools who didn't understand where their dinner came from, that meat didn't fall from the sky in shrink-wrapped Styrofoam trays. They didn't understand that animals were put on earth for us to use, not to love.

It was the speech that let me live in this world and forced my sister to run away from it.

I opened my mouth to begin and the lamb called for its mother, a long drawn-out bawl, a croaky human-sounding "Maaaaaaa." Rian threw his arms around the lamb and burst into tears.

I'm not stupid. I realized that there was more going on at that moment than an injured lamb but damned if I knew what to do about it. I stood there for a few minutes trying to figure out what to say and staring at this funny little cowlick on the back of Rian's head that I'd never noticed before. It bobbed up and down as his shoulders shook.

Finally, I said, "You'll freeze out here. You need another blanket."

"I'm okay," Rian mumbled into the lamb's neck.

I went back inside. I got back in bed and lay there looking up at the ceiling. Just when Rian's "visit" had begun to feel, if not welcome, at least not horrible, now he'd got himself attached to one of the lambs. I was going to kill my sister when she finally showed up. If she ever came back.

The following morning Rian was up early and rooting around the screened-in porch looking for some rope to take the lamb for a walk. There was no way that was ever going to work but Rian stuck with it, coaxing the animal forward until it would walk beside him. And then Rian wanted to drag my dad's old recliner out to the barn and use my mother's willowware bowl for a water dish. I compromised by giving him the cushions from an old sofa in the basement and a dented metal saucepan that I used to catch drips when the attic sprung a leak. Rian named the lamb Tom Shanks, which I thought was incredibly clever, but of course I didn't let Rian know that. He already was feeling pretty full of himself that he'd got that lamb to walk on a leash.

And then, I'll be the first to admit it, things began to slowly slip a little sideways. I was at Cooper's Pharmacy when I spotted a black eye patch in the Visine aisle and, for some reason, call it a temporary insanity, it made sense to buy it for Tom Shanks. It wouldn't stay on, of course, until I bought a packet of elastic and sewed on another piece that went around Tom's chin. Then, it was embarrassing to watch Rian out walking the lamb up and down the road looking a little bit too much like Mary with her little lamb, so I bought one of those spiked dog collars from Western Feed. And after Tom rubbed his head against a post in the barn until he was bald, Rian fashioned what he called a "do rag" from one of my dad's old shirts that stayed on with the help of the elastic from the eye patch.

There was a now a cot and a little table and a space heater in the barn, which all seemed almost reasonable at the time, but when Rian asked if we could get an extra television and a cable box out there, I put my foot down. That's when Rian came up with the idea of putting adult diapers on Tom so he could come into the house for a couple hours in the evening.

So that's where we were in early April, eating dinner in front of the television—me in my favorite chair, Rian sprawled out in Dad's recliner, and Tom on a blanket in front of us, chewing a plateful of alfalfa with his jaws moving from side to side, looking for all the world like a geriatric pirate with a continence problem and loose dentures—when my sister walked into the house.

She came in without knocking, a flurry of cold air and patchouli oil and swirling scarves. Rian didn't have a chance to get up from his chair before his head disappeared into a tornado of fluttering fabric and bangle bracelets.

"Oh," she said, releasing him to pat his cheeks and stare into his eyes. "I missed you. You haven't changed at all. Thank goodness." She hugged Rian's head again, then plopped down on the arm of the recliner, shedding scarves and dropping them on the floor.

"I bet you two are glad to see me," she said. She leaned toward Rian. "Guess what? I met someone. You're going to love him. He lives in Flagstaff, Arizona. It's a sixteen-hour drive so we have to be up early and get out of here first thing in the morning." She peered into Rian's bowl. "What is that?"

"It's vegetarian chili," I said. "Your son is a vegetarian."

"Really?" she said. "That is so cool." She gazed benignly around the living room. It spoke volumes about my sister that a lamb with an eye patch and diapers watching television in the living room wasn't even worth commenting on.

Rian looked from Tom to me and back to Tom, then that mask of indifference, the one I hadn't seen in weeks, flattened the features of his face.

They left before sunrise the next morning. When there's a man involved, my sister can be very motivated. From my bedroom window, I watched the light in the barn come on. Then I heard Rian at the back door and my sister's footsteps on the stairs. They didn't bother to say good-bye or thank you. Maybe they thought I was still asleep. Maybe they thought I didn't want to be bothered. The front door closed. A car engine started. There was the receding sound of tires on the gravel driveway then silence for what seemed like an eternity. When the gas heater banged on automatically at six AM, I nearly jumped out of my skin.

Well, that, apparently, was that. I had my home and my life back again.

Which I was grateful for, don't get me wrong. Right away I set Tom back in the pasture. Without all the paraphernalia he looked like any other lamb with one eye gone. He butted the gate and bawled miserably, but he wasn't my problem anymore. Wilson would be harvesting the lambs soon. I went about setting my house to right. I opened all the upstairs windows to air out the smell of my sister's hippy perfume and stripped the bed where she'd slept. I turned on the radio, threw a load of laundry in the washer, scrubbed the bathroom, mopped the kitchen, and vacuumed all the rugs. Rian and the lamb had wreaked havoc on the hardwood floors. All the while Tom kept bleating. I could hear him no matter how much I tried to drown out the sound.

Tom stopped bawling sometime in the early afternoon. I crept to the kitchen to peek out the window and see if he had finally wandered off to join the rest of the flock up the hill but no, there he was, leaning against the gate, exhausted. Every couple of minutes he would look woefully up into the sky. I wondered if Tom remembered the bird that must have swooped down and taken his eye. Perhaps the lamb thought that's what had happened to Rian, that something terrible and dark had come and taken Rian away, that he'd lost another irreplaceable piece of himself. Right here was living proof of the folly of forming attachments. My dad had been so right. Once you were caught up in all that nonsense, you were doomed to a life of heartache. It made a person feel a little weepy if you thought about it too long.

I leaned over the kitchen sink and splashed some cold water on my face. Outside, Tom Shanks bleated once, his voice breaking. Then there was nothing but the sound of the kitchen clock and my own breathing.

And then a thought came to me that only vaguely surprised me, as if I'd been thinking about it all along. What would be the harm if the lamb were still here when Rian came back with my sister next year? Tom certainly wouldn't be a cute little lamb anymore; he'd be an adult ram, stinky and randy and unpredictable. Rian could see for himself how stupid it had been to become attached. It could be a teaching moment, a real life lesson.

I started to warm to the idea. I could hold on to the lamb for a little longer if there was a goddamned point to it.

So I went out to the gate, put the collar and leash on Tom Shanks, and started walking toward Wilson's ranch. I would have to pay Wilson for the lamb and he was going to think I'd lost all my marbles. But I was already past that. I was thinking there was no way I was going to start changing diapers at this point in my life, especially on an animal, and I certainly wasn't going to take up sleeping in the barn or listening to a lamb bawl night and day. What I was going to do was stop by the library after work on Monday, pick up a book on dog training, and set about housebreaking a sheep.

MACAROONS: THE LAST DAYS

Lisa Badner

(From *The Cape Rock*)

The shop steward shows me her frozen toes.
Your father turned the heat off, again.

Cold is a state of mind, my father says.
In shorts and a muscle tank.

More complaints come in: a chemical taste.
Hard as a rock. Spoiled. Soapy.

Saponification: when coconut turns to soap.
A mystery, dad says.

My husband thinks I tried to poison him with your product,
a customer writes. *Please, tell him it's the coconut.*

Maybe you should, my father replies,
poison him.

Dad's knee is busted.
Doctors are fucking assholes, he says.

The other leg gives out.
He falls down the stairs.

The bookkeeper's skin is a greenish tint.
Lungs filled with fluid. Just got another stent.

Phone message from Exterminator: Let your rats run wild,
Macaroon King, I don't work for free.

My father bolts the door,
so the Rabbis can't get in.

We watch them buzz on the new
security TV. Purchased

after Jesus the mechanic
stole the computers.

THE ENGLISH DEGREE

J. Banerjee

My mother lived in the forest. Though she might be sitting at a table of people or watching the news or folding the laundry, some cell of her, a strand of her hair, the bend of her elbow, pointed to the forest beyond our house, where she spent the hours not loaned to us. Under maple and oak, her face wetted by dogwood when she brushed past, down to the marsh a mile or so out, where the cat-eyed dragonflies zipped and hovered and the wood snake sunned itself on a mossy rock that the stream cupped. She knew what a woman raised in a fourth-floor Calcutta apartment should not: that hundreds of titmice gather in a treetop at dusk to chatter, that the jewelweed growing next to poison ivy is its antidote. She brought the jewelweed leaves home and drowned them in the birdbath to show us their iridescence, and as the shadow of her hand passed from them, they would wink back the mottled sky. She knew that woodpeckers would drum in riffs of sevens, nines and elevens. She knew that hummingbirds drank no water but what stayed in flowers. The forest wasn't fairy tale: she opened wider with a stick the unstrung chest of a mourning dove that the hawk had gotten to first, the dove's wings splayed like a rent gown; she washed the blood from the cat's head and mangled paw after its monthly fights with raccoons and possums. In the months she was away from home, she saw what crueler things people did to one another, first in Bangladesh before we were born, then in Lebanon, then from the low bowl of Sarajevo into the rocky hills deeper into Bosnia, finally in Chechnya. In the months she was at home, she walked and walked through the Connecticut woods, with and without us, quiet for so long that all of us, including her, waited for her voice to come back, to crack open like a bud. In the months away, she wrote for the newspaper, for someone's breakfast perusal 7,543 miles away, that this village in the Bengal delta had been burned to the ground and that an eighteen-month-old boy dressed only in a shirt screamed in the middle of it for his mother. In the months away, she rode from the Druze to the Shiite zone in Beirut only to have her friend who was driving shot and killed by a sniper. The blood freckled the left side of her face and darkened her sunglasses. She brought the car to a halt, turned it around and drove him to the hospital and wrote a story for the paper that night that ran somewhere deep inside the front section next to an ad for Bendel's. In the months away, she walked past an outdoor pump in Sarajevo two minutes before the women and children gathering water there were shelled. She made herself turn and go back because that is what reporters do. In the months away, in one of those thousands of minutes away, she opened the gate to a factory yard in Grozny and saw dogs gnawing on the corpse of a young Russian conscript.

Eventually, she spoke of what she did on a given day, not what she had seen when she was away. She gave things names: the bird whose song started with the first three notes of Beethoven's Ninth was the chickadee, the caterpillars falling from the trees would turn to northern blues, the green stalks at the base of the sugar maples were wild ramps. She found things that came before us and that would outlast us: the stones striped by the glaciers, the arrowheads blunted from too many hunts, the children's buckets of raspberries and blackberries, her fingers red with juice and cuts, the lacy skull of a skunk. These were spread on the kitchen counter, as dinners or afternoon coffee grew cold on the table. At night, she read journals from the town archives of local farmers long dead, monographs about the local geology, books on Connecticut history, the Audubon field guides to birds of New England. She listened to tapes of birdsong, while the birds slept outside. The world she found in the forest did not need her. It went on without her voice. It meant her no ill will. It had its own rules that she was not obligated to understand, as she was those of her fellow men. She knew she could never be a part of it. She was always the outsider and she had parlayed that into a map that led her out of a life in India that seemed her destiny: work as a schoolteacher perhaps, an arranged marriage to a man who would have been just as disappointed with her as she with him. She took her universally acknowledged useless degree in English from Calcutta University, for she could not be doctor or engineer with it, and went to write about the war raging in Bangladesh, first for Indian papers and then for the Brits and Americans. She had no accent when she wrote, she went where she was told, and she said nothing of how the varieties of violence surprised her even when she became an old woman. She married an editor who had grown up in Connecticut and moved to a landscape that she thought looked like the one in the Enid Blyton novels she had read as a girl. She left her children to do her work. We were not work. We were easy to her. She came back with funny stories set in cities and airports and restaurants, with toys and books from Heathrow or Charles de Gaulle, and nothing from the places she had really been.

We never tugged on those doors of hers. Once, she returned from a long walk on a bright fall day, and the knees of her khaki pants were wet. I said nothing, but I knew, as I had years ago when I had followed her into the forest one morning, that she had fallen to her knees under a stand of oak, without sound or prayer, rocking gently in the fallen leaves, because she could no longer bear to stand in such a world as she had come to know.

FORGETTING

Cécile Barlier

(From *The Lindenwold Review*)

I forgot my son on the Col des Aravis.
This is how I recall it happened:
At one o'clock in the afternoon on August 23, 1983, six of us sit in two cars following each other on the winding road to the Col. In the head car, I'm driving and my father sits next to me, my window down one inch, letting in spiky surges of Alpine air. My eight-year-old son lies across the seats in the back. He's sleeping; he's slept from the start. The oily green of the slopes and my son's shallow breathing have left us wordless, silent all the way, feeling solemn for no reason. Or maybe my son is not sleeping, maybe he's faking it to avoid conversation, and the two of us in the front pretend we don't know his act, respecting his childish truce, causing in each other unspoken gusts of tenderness. Looking in the rearview mirror, I can see the second car right behind us. It's close enough to see the facial expression of my mother driving, lifting one hand from the steering wheel to point her finger at the mountaintops on the left side of the road. She's in control of the vehicle and its surroundings; been there before, this is her childhood territory, now playing tour guide for us visiting family. My teenage daughter is in that car nestling her head against my prehistoric grandmother.

In the protective bubble of the car, I feel part of this lineage of Nordic dreamers, somehow stuck between generational aspirations, with enough vision to pursue scientific research and play Bach's sonatas, but lacking the boldness to ever become an astronaut or sing opera under the morning shower. I am the kind satisfied with my own shyness, never imagining the terror that will follow. A large section of my memory of that moment hinges on the rearview mirror. I look back and I look back. I see my son sleeping, my mother driving, and at the bottom of it all: I see my eyes looking.

When we get to the Col, we have to drive to the end of the main road to find two parking spots, one on each end of the gravel-covered lot. My father makes me maneuver until the nose of the car faces out, ready to leave. It's tricky, for the spot is tight and a number of cars enter the lot at that time. I grumble and joke about my father's obsessive disorder on the subject of the art of parking; it's an old story between us, as old as my driver's license. My son is still asleep despite the commotion and the slamming of the front doors.

Then I say: Wake up, Mousse, you can't stay in the car, my love. Let's go take a look at the shops, maybe we'll find a souvenir for Daddy.

I don't remember him answering. I just see my right hand pushing the red button to unleash the seatbelt, and then his small body unwinding from his cradle position. I take his hand to extract him from the rented car.

Outside it looks like a postcard from *The Sound of Music*: the part where Julie Andrews spreads her arms open and her skirt twirls around her and the lush fields and the snow-covered blue mountains belong to her as much as she belongs to them. I take a big gulp of air and squeeze my son's hand and the three of us head down to the other car. I decide to ignore the uneasiness I always feel when stuck at the bottom of a slope. Here there's not one but two green slopes sliding toward us; it's grandiose like two oversized waves of land forming an arrowhead.

When we approach, my mother's loud, too loud for a normal conversation.

She says it's too late and at first I'm wondering what it is too late for.

My grandmother stays in the car and her window is down. She cannot get out of the car on her own and now I'm guessing that she really doesn't want to. Her face is inscrutable with a hint of violence. Or perhaps it is silent resignation, or regret, or something along the line of: It was awful, but now I've said it. She's the one to whom my mother keeps saying it's too late. Too late to apologize, that is. That much is said.

A horn blows somewhere in the parking lot. My mother breaks away from us and heads for the souvenir shops or the small chapel at the end of the road or whatever lies as far as possible from the car. I watch myself looking at my mother's back, and I'm envious of my own composure. It may be the excess of oxygen at that altitude. Or the habit of their drama.

In any case I do not know what's coming, because this is *before*.

There's no wind. The air is stagnant yet completely clear. My father makes a small hand salute and lights up a cigarette. I think I smell the smoke. I think I try to breathe it in. It makes me bend my neck. That smoke is another thing that gets me high, blurry on the edges.

It's OK, I say. Then I watch myself tapping lightly on my grandmother's shoulder and asking if she'll be fine, if she needs anything while we take a short walk. Oh, you know ... she says, and I nod in agreement. I really do know, but I cannot put that knowledge into words. I am the sort that can only focus on one thing at a time. That one thing right now is my son's shirt. He put it on backward. The care label is sticking out. I hadn't noticed before; I should have noticed. The way it works, or the way it's supposed to work: I notice my son's shirt, which is inside out, and I correct it. Or I plan to correct it. It's the thought that counts. In a moment or so I will take my son to a public bathroom and I will have him take his shirt off and put it back on the right way, with the label scratching the skin between his shoulder blades. He will fuss and I will insist that we take care of that now because it matters to me that he look good. He will say that I am not the boss of him and I will deprive him of that childish illusion. Oh yes, I will say, I am very much the boss of you.

In that one minute I don't think I have any doubt, I don't think I wonder whether this bossiness is something I have to put on, like a nightgown, in order not to feel naked.

And maybe I feel I can manage all the nurturing, for all of them. Maybe I don't even have to think about it. It's as natural as the warmth produced by a lightbulb. Maybe I would only be flipping through a photo album now, if things weren't about to go the way they go. But in that moment in the bathroom, I make the mistake of looking at myself in the mirror. I see my mother's purple eyes in my own, her sorry-dog look that she carries with elegance. They look at me, those eyes, and they don't get it.

And I imagine my grandmother in the car picking her nose where the ingrown hair has grown—and I rush out of the bathroom, only to see my mother's back again, my mother with her raven hair and her dark blouse, making a phantasmal shadow puppet. She's hunched up like a six-year-old and I can no longer deny my own part in this play or how inadequate my slowness is as I look left and right, as I cross the road back to where she's standing near the parking lot. I will not shout, Mom, just forgive your mother's sloppiness and move on. And it's not easy not to say it. Or maybe it's easy.

At any rate she's buying something from one of the stalls, my mother. I stay behind. Perhaps ten or fifteen meters from her, I watch the snow on the ridge. I notice the passage of clouds beyond Mont Blanc, perhaps I feel the wind rising. There's so much time there. A preposterous pack of seconds. But there's something else, too: the promise of fear, as if the air had turned solid. Only it's gone by the time my father walks up to me and asks to please take my mother with me in the car. He will drive the second car. My mother will have the cathartic talk with me. He does say *cathartic*. I see myself nodding again. The lot is packed now.

We leave fast because my car is parked right and ready to go. The first thirty-five kilometers are quiet, the inside of the car crammed with our breaths. I think I'm thankful to my mother for not talking, to my daughter in the back for reading despite the turns. My father's car is the one two cars down behind us. I see he's behind us. I see bits of his car in both wing mirrors. The bits outside my peripheral vision, in my blind spot.

Kilometer 42 is when the beginning of a question first crosses my mind. I know because we're arriving close to Thones and the one embranchment where I don't know which way to go. There's a kilometer marker marked 42, white and yellow and trite. Which way do I turn? I ask. Left, my mother says. Wait..., she says. We could take the old route, too; it's longer and there's a short section of highway, but it's worth it—so picturesque. Which? I say, and it sounds as if I'm annoyed. Right, she says, make a right.

I make a right and after a minute or so I check whether my father's car is still behind. And it isn't. Now the doubt that surfaced at marker 42 grows out of its own limbo. Insistent. Hitting in my head like a small hard ball on a squash tennis court. Is Mousse in the car with my father? Do I know for a fact that my son got in my father's car? Did I see Mousse in the parking lot after I left the bathroom? Did I officially ask my father to take him in? Did my father assume I would take Mousse with me? Does everyone just assume Mousse is in the other car? I see myself tightening my grip on the wheel, scratching my knee. My armpits start itching. But wait: I saw the top of his head in the mirror. I did. Him sitting in the back in the center, snug behind the two of them up front. The top of him barely making it in the reflection. Positive. A puff of my son's hair is imprinted in my short-term memory in an active and accessible way. I watch myself dismissing my instinct, thinking it's absurd. I watch myself not sharing any of this with my mother or my daughter.

There is a toll ahead. We're about to enter the short section of highway. I will need the pass, which is in the glove compartment. I ask for it and my mother cries out. It makes me jump and swerve off to the emergency lane. Her hand pulls out something sticky: a half-sucked lollipop. Mousse left it there yesterday or the day before. For an instant, the red lollipop seems like another shot at salvation—because of its brightness, or the sweetness, or because it conjures my son's sugared lips. I see my mother lifting it up in the sun, and I see myself wanting to ask her and my daughter whether they saw him get in the car, or if they looked back and saw him once we were driving. Just to make sure. Then I have to lower my window because the pass is not working and I have to pay with cash after all.

Hello. Nice day. Here's your change.

And my mother reaches over. She tries to toss the lollipop into a trashcan next to the toll booth. She misses and the red candy crashes into the pavement. After that I think I don't want to talk. I think I'm paralyzed. I have this idea that if I ask the question, it will make Mousse disappear from my father's car, where he is for sure, taking the second half of his pretend nap.

I want to get to Annecy and see them. My mother seems to have forgotten all about her altercation with her own mother. She does not have the cathartic talk. Maybe mercy is in the slowness of the scenery or in the palm of my daughter on her shoulder. When she starts speaking, I listen to her comments with only half an ear; she names each mountain, each unsigned village. She talks about family friends I don't think I've ever met. Her chatter has this anesthetic effect, the kind I loved as a child. And now I think it terrifies me, this numbing. I drive faster. I want to beat the traffic.

*

At one o'clock in the morning, I sit in the inspector's office at the central police station. The inspector is telling me that my son's disappearance is the sort that happens all the time, with a peak in August and in the places with the most tourists. The inspector is good-looking. I see myself encumbered by her beauty. Maybe I shouldn't look at her when she talks; maybe it would help to look at the ground. She's explaining to me what they do when a child goes missing. She's saying that the law mandates that they respond immediately, that they enter the child's information in the National Missing Children database, that they contact INTERPOL. She stops and asks if I understand. I must have said I understand because that triggers a series of questions and instructions.

She asks me to please look in all the rooms of my grandmother's house.

She asks me to please check the backyard if there is one. I keep saying I have forgotten him on the Col des Aravis, in the bathroom. Maybe I just imagine I say that, maybe I don't talk. She asks me where my husband is. This I tell her because she asks me to please check whether Mousse is with his father in Paris. When we're done, when I stand up to leave, when we shake hands, when she taps on my shoulder with her free hand, she says it isn't rare to find a child asleep in a hiding place or in a closet.

*

FOR THE THIRD TIME IN TWELVE HOURS, I drive back to the Col. This time I'm alone. Maybe they let me go. Maybe I didn't tell them and I slipped out. I decide to stay there in the car in the parking lot next to the bathroom. At night, there's no one. It's packed with a few things that glow. The snow on the ridge glows. The bell on the chapel glows. The rented car glows when I get out of it to check the bathroom—once again—just in case. I open the door to the stall where Mousse was earlier. He isn't there. Someone hasn't flushed and the smell of urine is pungent like after eating asparagus. I get out before I get sick.

I have brought the posters with his picture, and I watch myself nailing them to the wooden lampposts, using thumbtacks. There's no hammer sound other than in my head. I look at Mousse and his missing front incisor; I touch the hole every time I move on to the next lamppost. Not a very recent photo. My husband is the one who takes all of them and he's in Paris or on the first train to Annecy.

By morning, my car is out of gas from idling, but I have one full can in the trunk. The shops reopen at nine. I question all the shopkeepers and they are supportive, even though none of them seem to recall Mousse. They say this has happened before on the Col. One of them gives me the number for a specialized association called 16,000 Missing Children. I try to call the association from a booth but it is Sunday and I have to leave a message. On the recording, I say I forgot my son on the Col des Aravis. His name is Mousse. I say I was trying to get his shirt back on the right way and then I got distracted and I left him there. I say I am on the Col, waiting. I try to say more but the recording doesn't take messages over one minute long and it cuts me off mid-sentence.

Later my husband and someone from the association come to get me. They say Mousse is back at my grandmother's house. Somebody has taken him there. They don't know who.

My husband says that earlier that morning when he gets there, my grand-mother's door is pushed open, blowing a summer wind in the hallway, the sort that rattles around in corridors between mountains, lifting the pages of the phone book left open on the writing cabinet. He sees Mousse there, disheveled by the gusts, squatting in the frame like a china boy and hungry for breakfast.

If I am the kind of woman to have forgotten her son in a public bathroom, this is the sort of image I will latch on to: the sort of recounted memory I will build for myself as if I had been there in the hallway instead of waiting for him in the wrong place. I will hang on to that moment precisely because I will not have been there in it, with an embrace that my son won't ask for — because I myself won't know for sure whether I'm still capable of a squeeze—because somewhere at the bottom I will carry this atrocious doubt. And all I will have is the memory of a squeeze, the memory of love. Not the thing itself. Not my son.

MONKEY SPINNING A PRAYER WHEEL

Lisa Bellamy

(From *Nectar* / originally published in *The Massachusetts Review*)

I staggered out of the theater after *Waiting for Godot.*
Jeez, I griped to Peter, *that's it? We're all just wind and gristle?*
Yep, he said after a minute, and I knew he was trying to remember
whether he'd stuck the parking ticket in his wallet or pocket.
He rather gallantly takes the notion of a meaningless universe in stride,
while I feel like a bewildered monkey spinning a prayer wheel
when I attempt to contemplate the so-called larger questions.
At the Tibetan Buddhist center downtown, we recite the Heart Sutra:
Perceiving that personality is inherently empty saves beings from suffering,
as monks, red cheeks puffed out like twenty Dizzy Gillespies, accompany us,
blowing long horns, strident heralds announcing ego's apocalypse,
and I'm thinking, *What?* What are we *talking* about here?
I recite daily my version of Marvin Gaye's mantra as fast as I can:
What's going on, what's going on, what's really going on?
Oh God, send me someone wise and shimmering,
send me the archangel who carries the sword that cuts through confusion
or, if there's no archangel handy, send me a soothing, jazzy brunch voice
and an arm pulling me onto the raft as I thrash in the river of *dukkha,*
in my memory of chipping my tooth on the granite rock in our backyard,
and me wailing as my mother ran from her chaise lounge
where she'd been sunbathing and reading Leon Uris, her freckled arms
and the smell of her suntan oil—where is she? Where is she?

ONE OF THEM

Sylvie Bertrand

(From *Epiphany*)

The only thing one needs to know before doing something big is whether one is ready to die for it or not.

Not that Julie is about to die or to do anything big. All she's done for now is take small sips of the coffee this man has prepared for her. She listens while he speaks. She doesn't know yet whether she can like this man or not; she doesn't know whether coming up to his apartment was a mistake or not; all she knows is that he likes his coffee dark and strong, stronger than any coffee she's tasted before.

Got any milk?

No, the man says, no milk, sorry. He moves from the kitchen counter toward his coat, which hangs off a stool.

I can go and get you some if you want.

No, no, Julie says. She takes another small sip, winces and smiles.

It should have been a little scary, terrifying even, going into this man's apartment, a man she'd just met, a man twice her age, a man who once did something big, years ago, some kind of terrorist act that involved kidnapping and murdering a political figure; a man who was caught, judged, and went to jail for it.

He just wrote a book about it all, but she hasn't read it yet.

But she isn't afraid. She believes she can recognize a violent man when she sees one, because she grew up surrounded by angry, violent men. She feels reassured by this man's gentle voice, the concern in his eyes, the softness of his smile.

Nothing has happened with this man yet. Nothing may happen. Her own agenda is unclear, his unknown.

But even before coming up to his apartment, the idea of meeting him again had already changed her. She began to notice things more now, simple things like the way older people in the bus hung on to their grocery bags even when nobody sat next to them; or the white ring that salt, mixed with melted snow, left at the tip of her new leather boots; or how she always knew, before people like bus drivers even spoke to her, whether they were English speakers or French speakers. She noticed that bus drivers were *always* French speakers.

It was a week ago that she and the man had made this plan: she would meet him at lunchtime on Friday, after her math and French classes, before art and history. They would go to the diner at the corner of Decarie and Jean-Talon and have coffee. She took the bus. He was waiting for her at the bus stop when she arrived. He wore a hat even though it was a mild winter day. He reminded her of a nerd disguised as a hippie for one of those cheesy school-sponsored theme parties, the kind of guy who tries to look cool but never does. You could feel it, some kind of innate eagerness barely hidden under false layers of aloofness. Just a bit taller than her; blondish beard cropped close to his skin; his hair, medium length, wavy with bangs pushed to one side; a pair of aviator glasses, gold-rimmed; a beige leather jacket with white fake fur on the collar. And of course, that hat—a knitted, close-fitting, wool hat, the ultimate in *uncoolness*, even (or especially?) in a town as cold as Montreal.

He smiled at her and lifted his hand in a slow wave as she got off the bus. She found him more handsome than she remembered. They walked a few blocks, straining to hear each other over the parkway's noise. He asked her a few questions; she answered each without expanding on any. As they were waiting for the light to change before crossing to reach the northeast corner, where the diner was, he said he had coffee at home, which was right there, around the corner.

Wanna come up?

Why not? They had talked already enough to make her feel that nothing terrible was going to happen. She is sixteen and trusts her instincts. Of course she would have never been able to explain this to anyone, and for that reason, among many others, she hasn't told anyone about meeting him.

Okay, she'd said.

And this is how she is here now, sitting next to him on his bed because the only other furniture in the flat is a desk and one chair. The sun is hitting the hardwood floor in sharp angles. There is one radiator hissing loudly. So this is how it works: a man invites you for coffee, you think, why not, and next thing you know you are sitting at the edge of a bed, his bed, talking about what is worth dying for and what isn't.

People ask me, was it worth it? It depends, the man is saying. It depends whether what you believe in is worth dying for or not.

He is talking; she is listening. All she really knows from him, she read from the blurb at the back of his book: he was one of those terrorists who kidnapped and killed the vice-premier of Quebec during the October Crisis. But that was all in the past, old stuff no one takes seriously anymore, stuff like this ideological battle he is talking about now, about how the French speakers have been colonized by the English, how the Catholic church has been used to keep them in their place, and how everyone has been corrupted by the power of people with big money (he always uses the English words for that, never the French ones: "big money," "cheap labor," "bosses"). And this is how it happened, how it bubbled up, this whole crisis that blew up one day in late October in 1969, which might as well be a million years ago, with makeshift bombs exploding in wealthy neighborhoods and how he, just twenty years old, a member of the South Shore gang, ended up with that kidnapped vice-premier in his aunt's suburban living room, and when the Canadian government declared martial law (*Martial* law! Can you imagine? he asks her, sending the *Canadian* army, into the streets of Montreal!), well, they, he and his three cell members, did the only thing they could do.

He talks and talks; she stays silent, doesn't nod, doesn't smile, doesn't say what she thinks, which is that she can't imagine, that it is impossible for her to envision what it would take to become so serious about something like language. French. English. Words. Really?

Still, this is certainly something different, something that has never happened to any of her girlfriends at school; something she won't talk about, not right away, but it won't matter, because the experience itself will hang around her like an aura, and people will know.

He stops speaking, looks at her sheepishly, and says, I am speaking too much, sorry. I've been lonely for too long.

This confession surprises and rattles Julie, and she feels she must say something, make amends somehow.

It's just that I didn't have a chance to read your book yet, she says. But I have it with me, she says. She takes his book out of her schoolbag.

He smiles and says, It's okay, people your age don't care about all this.

He moves his hand flat on the bed behind her back, not touching it, not touching her, his own torso leaning slightly closer.

Julie may not know much about armed revolution and terrorist tactics or even the history of oppression her own people have endured, but she knows that when a man you barely know gets closer to you, it is up to you to move back, to keep your distance, lest you give the wrong signal, send the wrong message.

She doesn't move.

*

THEY MET TWO WEEKS AGO, at the Francophone Book Fair that takes place every year in downtown Montreal. Her friend Sandrine had mentioned that her uncle, who ran a small publishing company, was looking for someone to mind the booth in the evening. Julie, whose father's disappearance just a year before had left her mother scrambling to support Julie and her siblings, had jumped at the opportunity: six dollars an hour, four hours a night for ten consecutive days. She took a bus and then the subway downtown every day after school; the uncle drove her back late at night.

Most evenings she was left alone at the booth, while the uncle went around the convention center to network. The man's booth was right across from hers. He too was alone most of the night. His booth wasn't really a booth, just one long table, and on that table, piles of his book, a small yellowish paperback. He sat behind that table for five days before she even noticed him, or his booth. There was something different about that day too; day one, day two, day three, day four, the same; then, on day five, she had felt it, his gaze hovering like a knife over her neck. So she'd looked up and seen him. At the end of her shift, she'd crossed the aisle, picked a copy of his book, and looked inside. He watched her as she read the little blurb about him, his life, his arrest, conviction, jail time, and now, parole.

He told her she looked familiar. She laughed.

I'm too young, she said. Was barely born when all of this—*this*, she shrugged as she pointed at the pile of books on the table—happened. He smiled and asked her how old she was. She lied and answered eighteen.

Would you like me to sign a book for you?

Oh no, she said, I have to go back to work. She looked at her own booth, but no one was there. Still, she quickly put the book back on the table.

I don't have the money, she said.

He took a book, opened it, picked up his pen.

If you want one, I'll give it to you.

Sure, thanks, she said. With her attitude, she was trying to convey indifference, but inside she was excited about getting the book signed by the author himself. She might even read it.

She stared at him while he applied himself to writing something on the first page of the book. His hair was thin and looked soft, almost like a baby's. His hands too, delicate, beautiful, not the hands of a madman or nutcase.

In the book, he wrote: *You know nothing of snow until you've lived under the bark of frost.*

And then he had asked her if she would meet him for coffee.

*

HE GETS UP, SEARCHES THROUGH the pockets of his coat, comes back with a pouch of tobacco and rolling papers.

You see, he tells her now, carefully laying tobacco and the papers on a magazine, things were different back then. *Back then*; back then, he keeps saying those words, *back then in my time*. He is trying to take her back then in time, but it is so hard for her to imagine it, *his time*, back then, some, what, thirteen, fourteen years ago!

His time: cafés bursting out with young people like her, everywhere and at all times, like in early spring, when winter's grayness has finally lifted, when the banks of black snow lining the curbs have melted away. People's bodies are opening up, defenses dissolving, skins touching each other by chance—except that this time, in *his* time, it felt as if winter would never come back, as if spring was eternal. Even the smoke rising from the polluting stacks on the South Shore seemed lighter, purer. Hope floating about like colorful balloons against the blue sky. Ideological discussions spreading around like fresh gossip. Under the political clamors and cultural ferment, it seemed as if each individual was establishing a secret but exciting connection with the world. One could almost hear it, the little people and the whole wide world, whispering like two new lovers.

He smokes, and she wants to smoke too. Just as she is about to ask him to roll a cigarette for her, he stops talking abruptly, gets up again, picks up something from his table, comes back to the bed with an envelope in his hands.

I feel so *ancient*, he says. Look at me, a thirty-two-year-old man, talking about the old days. He rolls his eyes. You must think I'm boring, he says.

It's fine, she says. But now she knows his age. She thought he was younger. Here, look, he says.

He shows her a picture: him back then, some twelve years ago, standing in front of a lake, summertime, hands on hips, smiling. In black and white, he looks really handsome. Tanned, trim, already bearded, but with longer hair. More hair. Yes, a handsome young man: she would have definitely liked him, if she too had lived back then.

Another picture: him with other young men, their wrists raised in the air, the big blue and white nationalist flag with the four fleurs-de-lis in the background.

She is interested in those pictures more than his words. Sensing this, he shows her more pictures, his left hand holding one after the other, his body leaning on his right arm, his right hand right behind her buttocks. Her long thick hair falls down like a curtain over her face; through the curtain, she stares at each picture intently, as if she was an investigator looking for some clue in a crime scene.

He kisses her through her hair, little kisses aiming for her cheekbone. She likes the way he smells. Clean, neutral. The beard is soft. She turns her head, lets his lips find hers. I'm kissing an old guy, she thinks to herself. Interesting, although not exciting, not exactly. A tang of tobacco and black coffee; something unidentified that tastes sweet. She holds on to the image in her head, that first black and white picture of a young man just a few years older than her. She gets into the kiss, kisses back. She reminds herself: this man is a writer. In his time (back then!) a revolutionary fighter. Now, some kind of historical figure, whose hands, hands that once murdered someone, some politician, some minister, are gently but confidently reaching under her sweater, lifting it up.

But she pushes him away, and he doesn't insist, not yet, not at that moment. She looks away. She doesn't know what she wants from him, but she is afraid of what he wants from her. Sex, of course. Does she want to have sex with him? She has no idea, partly, well, mainly, because she is still a virgin. She isn't even sure what it really means, to have sex. It is still abstract, almost as abstract as his political talk over something that happened fifteen years ago.

They are lying on the bed on top of the blankets, with their clothes on. He puts his arm around her waist. Under his glasses, his eyes are closed. It seems that he has fallen asleep. She turns away from him and looks outside the window of the small studio apartment. It is snowing lightly. Out there, across the parkway, is the only world she knows, and in that instant she hates it for being so small, so limited, so easily known. She can hear the traffic from the highway that cuts the neighborhood in half; she imagines, up a few bus stops, her high school building, where all the good girls like her, bright young girls like her, are all dressed in the same uniform of quilted skirt and off-white shirt and forest green blazer with matching socks; they, unlike her, are now heading back to the afternoon classes, walking up the long and narrow tree-lined slope that leads to the main building, austere under the dark and low-hanging branches, its massive stone entrance thickened from age, its walls layered with centuries of cold and wetness, of humidity and heat, of shadows and light and anything alive that has ever brushed its surface.

What a difference it makes, to be here on a bed with a man twice her age, and not there.

If she were among them, this is what she would do: she and her girlfriends (her gang: the cool ones, a self-selected club that excludes hippies, preppies, and nerds) would change their clothes, as they always do before and after leaving the school. As a general rule, she and her friends wear black at all times, black being the anti-color protecting them against the angst-inducing colors of the early '80s: that royal blue, that oversaturated eggplant, neither mauve nor burgundy, and that awful, *awful* forest green. As a general rule, these friends stick together and deride everything and anybody they encounter that isn't, well, one of them.

She likes to think that she is one of them. She works at being one of them. But is she? She wouldn't think of telling them about the fact that her father has disappeared, about her mother's financial struggles, about the fact that the only reason Julie is still in that same school is because her mother went to the school's director, Mother Superior herself, and asked her for free tuition, which she received, allowing Julie to stay on as the school's sole charity case.

And now, there is *this*, whatever this is, a date, the beginning of an affair? With this man, of all people. She can't even imagine bringing it up with any of her friends. Weird, she can hear them scream already, *weird! You're so weird!* Not the fact that he is older: there are a few, not many, but a few other girls who have older boyfriends, affairs going on with men almost twice their age. Not that it is something you go around school telling everyone about. More like something you tell on a late night, in one of those intoxicated tell-all sessions with one or two of your closest friends. But this, she can't imagine telling anyone. An apartment in a building overlooking the highway. This guy, this man, who can't stop speaking of politics, injustice, oppression, independence. This man who's been convicted of terrorism, kidnapping, murder, and has spent years in jail.

She looks around her: an apartment that belongs to an adult who isn't a relative. A bed, a coffee table, an armchair in a corner, a television set in the other. Books just about everywhere. A place like she might move into in a couple of years. She has just jumped into the future, her own future now coming into focus, taking the shape of a small, simple apartment like this one, nothing fancy, just an *adult's place.*

He moves, turns around, puts a hand on her belly. He looks at her but she looks away. She is afraid he will want more from her *right now.* So she asks him.

Tell me about those thirty-six hours you spent with the vice-premier before killing him.

*

I can't say, This is me, I did that. I can't. It still feels like it happened to someone else, like it wasn't me, but someone else.

She is still lying in bed. He is standing now, and stares down at her.

You had to be there to really understand. Now I know that the whole thing seems rather hard to believe. We didn't want to kill the vice-premier, not at all. We kidnapped him. When you want to kill someone, you just kill him, shoot him or something, I don't know. We never hurt anyone before, not even during our bank robberies.

What we really wanted was—

He stops. He sits next to her on the bed. Her stomach grumbles loudly, and she laughs nervously.

You're hungry.

In a second he is in the kitchenette, opening the fridge's door and peering in: a few cans of beer, a forgotten piece of hard cheese, that orange baking soda box on the bottom shelf.

I'm going to order in. Do you like Chinese food?

It's my favorite, she says.

They eat Chinese takeout on the bed, picnic style: crispy egg rolls, chicken balls in that bright orange-red sweet and sour sauce, slippery lo mein noodles, baby spareribs smothered in a thick, dark brown sauce. She eats like a ravished animal. He eats slowly, chewing with his eyes closed, then staring at her, watching her eat before picking up the next bite.

We took good care of the vice-premier, you know, while we waited, he says. Made sure he was comfortable. Even ordered some food in once, when we ran out of spaghetti. We asked him what he'd like; he said BBQ chicken. We were all so starved that when the delivery guy arrived, we didn't even care if we got caught.

She swallows her last bite, nods. It seems obvious to her that the man facing her would do such a thing, be considerate to his prisoner. Like he'd been considerate to her, not forcing himself upon her, being gentle, not insisting on having sex, not right away.

Once they are done eating, he piles up the emptied Styrofoam containers and takes the whole mess to the kitchen area and dumps it in a garbage can under the sink.

I should get going, she says.

After a pause, he says, Okay, I will walk you back to the bus.

But instead of getting up, she pulls the magazine with the tobacco and rolling papers toward her and begins rolling a cigarette.

He looks at her, silent. He sees her book, his book, on the floor, picks it up, places it on top of her schoolbag.

She takes the cigarette to her mouth but it is too loose; tobacco falls off, the paper burns too quickly.

Here, he says, let me show you.

As he rolls he begins another story. It's about the history of our people, he says, centuries of it, before even he was born. There are a few facts she already knew about, if only vaguely, things she learned just last year in her national history class. There was a battle at that place called the Plains of Abraham, which the French lost, ceding the territory to the British. Soon after, there were those other rebels, soon to be Americans, fighting for independence in the south against the British. They came up north to stir trouble and gather more support, which could have changed a lot of things if it had worked, but it didn't. Then, those who eventually lost the battle in the south, the former British loyalists, came north to establish themselves among the former French colonists. Then, still later, maybe a century or so later, there were those first guys, the French-speaking ones, who named themselves the Patriots and who led their own rebellion and tried to get rid of the British, but that also didn't work.

Okay, bummer of a national history, if you'd ask her! Terribly unlucky. Maybe unfair, even. But wasn't it the same everywhere? The same story repeating itself over and over, painted with different hues or colors on a slightly altered canvas—a bit tighter here, a bit looser there—but at the end, if you look close, what you've got is a frame, four right angles, with a mess of reds and blues and greens and blacks and a bunch of uneven lines and strokes, and some empty spaces too, where the brush should have been but isn't, and instead of a country, you have a blank, ill-defined, barely noticeable. At the end of the day, it's not like things were better elsewhere, in Africa, in India. And what about the USSR?

At the end, though, all she says is this: It is so hard to believe, that there could ever be a revolution right here, in Quebec. Elsewhere, yes. But here? I don't know.

He squints back at her, as if trying to read her mind.

To want a country, when you have none, is always a revolutionary act. There is no way around it.

She stares at the cigarette he is smoking, the cigarette that was meant for her, a tiny rolled-up one. She inhales the smell of the pungent and musky dark tobacco. She hears his voice ask:

Don't you want to live in your own country?

Now that the question has been asked, she realizes that for as long as she can remember, she has known that she would live elsewhere.

I don't know, she says. Maybe not.

Really? And where would you go?

She shrugs. New York, or France. I don't know.

I see, he says.

She stares as the smoke comes out of his mouth, shape shifting in the afternoon light before melting off in the dry, overheated air; white fog, gray clouds, and then a dubious, purple haze.

It feels good but embarrassing too, to have said it, something she may want, something different.

Hey, she says, give me a puff of that. He hands her the cigarette. She keeps it.

Do you speak English?

Yes, she says, which is not true, her English being bad, terrible in fact, much poorer than her classmates', who have grown up in the English-speaking neighborhood where the school is, but where Julie and her family just moved last year, after her father's disappearance.

A bilingual girl, he says. He shakes his head, gets up and goes behind the kitchen counter to make a fresh pot of coffee from his drip machine. She lies back on the bed, carefully taking puffs from the cigarette, listening to the sound of coffee percolating. She can't tell how long it has been since she's been in this man's apartment. The day seems to stretch like a dream, no beginning or end, just a muddy, unclear middle. The usual markers of her day are unavailable in this unknown and new space, but she did try to keep track anyway: first period, math, long gone; second period, French, just before lunch. Then lunch: she imagines her friends lining up at the cafeteria, trays in hand, their chatter louder than the sound of utensils and glasses and metal plates; then the line breaking into small groups, well-defined tribes who head back to their respective tables, solidly demarked territories, as stately as any country.

This is the big battle of her generation, the war over coolness. Her tribe: the punk girls from the neighborhood, the artsy style. At her table: girls with black or purple or bleached hair, girls like her who, in the morning, wore their ripped jeans and torn checkered tweed jackets and long scarves and funky men's hats all the way to the locker room. The rebels among the good girls who wore their uniform to school: like black crows among white sheep, except that at the end everyone comes out alive, pinky cheeks, bright futures looming with husbands from good families, healthy kids, and a house in the suburb.

Not exactly the kind of stuff he was fighting for back then, in his time. Not what you think of when you talk about a revolution.

Then she hears the sound of young schoolchildren shouting as they come off a bus and she realizes that it is actually much later than she thought, three in the afternoon already, lunch break long over, and she has now officially skipped an entire day at school. Wednesday's fourth period of class just about to end, with Sister Justine, her short curly white hair and her ancient thick, black, square glasses and her long hands extolling nature's colors, feverishly trying to open her students' eyes to their beauty—*Look at these trees outside, the deep burned orange in the trunks, the lavender mixed in the gray of the bare branches, and the tiny, tiny buds, the variety of their whites and yellows, sprouting dots from an infinite spectrum already shaping the full potentiality of greens to come once spring is finally here!*

The students would be staring at Sister Justine while she talked, her pale, skinny fingers flapping by her head like moths around a lightbulb; then, bending their heads in front of the blank paper before them, they would draw thick-skinned trees with brown trunks and dark green leaves.

They just couldn't help it.

She is surprised to find that she wishes she hadn't missed her art class. She is Sister Justine's favorite, and wonders if her absence has been noticed.

He comes back with the coffee, pours her another cup.

I know what will happen to you, he says.

What?

You will be one of those who leave and never come back. You will become one of those who speak French with a French accent, or worse, you'll become an American. Your children will speak English, and everything we did—

He shakes his head, makes a gesture with his hands that means: it will be all over; it is already over.

The way he does that scares her, because she understands that it is true, and that he already hates her for it.

*

Yes, at the end, they had to kill him, the vice-premier. Once the manifesto they wrote was read live on the radio, once the Canadian government declared martial law and sent in the army, once they heard that another cell on the north shore had surrendered, it became obvious that they would get nothing in exchange for releasing him except, perhaps, a flight to Cuba as political exiles. Exile, or jail, these were the only options. But you see, at the end it was a matter of life and death, not just for them, not just for the vice-premier, but for an entire people. He—the vice-premier—was a good man. He was a family man. He pleaded with them. He believed they would do the right thing. He believed the *government* would do the right thing. When it became clear that the government wouldn't negotiate, he, the vice-premier, lost it. He threw himself, still blindfolded, through a window. But he didn't make it through. The window was narrow, too narrow for an adult body to go through. All he did was to cut his forehead on the broken glass.

He could have taken the blindfold off. He had already managed to untie his wrists. But he didn't even try. Bloodied, he sat on the floor in the middle of their living room, his eyes closed, his head hanging low against his chest.

He was already dead inside.

Claude, Francis, Joseph, they didn't want to do it, but they did it anyway. It was never courage; it was about will.

It was about being ready to die for what you believe in.

Only he, Emile, wasn't ready for it. Once the body was disposed, it was Emile's turn to lose it. He fell to his knees in the middle of the living room and cried like a baby.

That's what his book was about.

*

THEY ARE NAKED UNDER the thin blanket, lying side by side on their backs, staring at the ceiling.

And so this will be the story she will tell later: they didn't have sex, not really, that time she went up with him to his flat; that's what she would say in a few years to her girlfriends when asked when was her first time. *Was he your first? Not really.* It depends what you mean by having sex. She was about to leave, and they kissed again, and then he guided her back to the bed. He undressed her. She didn't help him, didn't resist; she let him do it. They had lain naked in bed for what seemed like an eternity, her body as light as a sheet of silk paper, his as solid as a rock—paper, rock, she'd thought she was the winner, but who was holding the scissors?

Then he had kissed her, on the lips, on her breasts, her stomach, and the whole time she watched herself from above, as if she was having one of those near-death experiences they talk about in magazines. She was floating above her body, and she watched as he kissed her down her belly, then licking with his tongue, reaching down lower, and continuing, his tongue striking her, non-stop for, what, at least ten minutes if not more and the whole time she was watching from above, knowing that this was a big moment for sure but not able to feel anything, not really; not really, like she'd said later.

He stopped and asked her if she enjoyed it. She said she didn't mind, it was okay, she said.

Oh huh, he'd said, and he said he was sorry, and he truly looked sorry, even though she kept saying it was okay. And she meant it too: what was there to be sorry about, when she was the one who had no idea how to react, not even in the most basic way, as in: yes, no. She had felt the same way she'd felt in the science lab after dissecting a frog. Behind a mask, wearing gloves, once she observed the entrails through the microscope, she'd found that she felt nothing for the frog, no pity, no fear, no disgust, nothing at all.

It is as if it all happened to someone else.

Now he has rolled over and is lying on his stomach, his face between his crossed arms. She sits at the very edge of the bed, covering herself with her sweatshirt. Soon, the room goes dark, streetlights piercing through the bare trees and the half-shut blinds. The apartment is completely silent, except for the soft sound of his snoring.

She gets up quietly. She gets dressed quickly, walks out of the apartment, shutting the door behind her carefully.

The winter sky, as it does just before snowfall, has turned into concentric shades of purple, as if illuminated from behind. The temperature has dropped; her breath is visible. She lifts the hoodie of her coat over her head and walks toward the bus stop. But once there she doesn't stop to look if a bus is coming. She continues to walk, and all the way home she can feel his book tucked in her schoolbag like a small explosive device, ready to explode.

Best of the Boy Stuff

Reneé Bibby

(From *Third Point Press*)

ousey is growing a beard. Her sister grew boobs. Rousey is growing a beard. She first noticed it two weeks into the school year, looking in the mirror and debating a face wash. Bristles of darker hair sparsely distributed across her jawline and chin. She tugged at them with her fingernails. They didn't pull out. She admired the way they pushed out longer than the other soft fur of her face. They'd shown gumption, appearing like that, resisting her casual efforts to remove them. She decided to let them stay. See where it might go.

It occurs to her that if something like this has been inside of her all this time that there may be other things. Other surprises. Unknown strengths waiting to emerge. Not actual superhero powers. Ordinary powers, but *more than*. Better.

All that face gazing didn't even make her late for breakfast. And breakfast is important—she sees that now. Food will fuel all that is growing inside her. Hoa has already put Rousey's breakfast plate together. Hoa is technically the housekeeper, but she is basically what keeps the family going. Today it's just slide ride into her chair and start eating.

At the table, her sister, who has spent her life inside an iPhone, chooses this day to look up at Rousey and say, "Eew, what is going on with your face?"

"Nothing, butt-munch."

"For real, you have fur growing on your face."

"It's a beard." Rousey punches her sister on the arm.

"Ever heard of tweezers?" Rousey's sister backhands her on the forehead. Didn't even drop her iPhone to do it.

"Yeah, right." Rousey swings a leg under the table and gets her sister in the calf. "I don't want to end up with *chola* eyebrows, like you."

Rousey's sister puts down the iPhone and puts Rousey in a headlock. Rousey thumps her in the ribs.

"Girls," Hoa admonishes.

"Cut it out." Their dad looks up from his tablet. That is not usually enough to make them stop, but today he also adds, "Rousey, what's going on with your face?"

Released from the headlock Rousey tells them all, "It's my beard."

Her sister laughs. "You can't call face pubes a beard."

"Leave me alone!"

Her dad asks her sister, "Why can't you help her with this stuff?"

"It's not my job to fix this freak," at the same time Rousey yells, "She's not the boss of me."

Their father covers his eyes. "Jesus. I dunno what the hell—your mother—"

"Don't you bring her up!" Rousey warns.

Even her sister *tsks* in distaste and picks up her phone again. Hoa flutters forward waving a hand, dispelling the evocation.

*

AT LUNCH, SHE MEETS UP with her only friend, Oscar. "Hey, check it out." She juts out her chin for him to look. He leans in very close and leans back out.

"Ooh, on fleek, girl," he yells. "I'm totes jelly beans."

She knew he would be jealous. His four older brothers call him "sister" and a show of manliness like this would certainly help his cause.

He turns her face one way then the other, exclaiming over and over.

The other kids who also sit outside of the lunch hall on the grassy hill notice the commotion. On the hill, Oscar and Rousey have the territory under the cottonwood. Another group of all girls sits by the oleander. And a third group of boys play hacky sack as if lunch was something they didn't need, anyways. Groups don't cross over into each other's spots, but Oscar is loud, and eventually Oleander Group ambles closer. Oscar exclaims to them, "Doesn't her beard look like *gold* against her skin? It's, like, jewelry."

Rousey knows each girl's name. She's been in class with them since sixth grade, but wouldn't bank on them knowing hers. She's been a ghost. Just a girl even the other losers look through. Mousey Rousey.

"Is that ... face hair?" Melissa asks.

"Hell *yeah* it is," Oscar affirms.

"Is it real?"

"Yeah, feel it!" Oscar orders. And Rousey holds her chin out for a few of the braver girls to run their fingers across her jaw. Their fingers are soft and quick like a breath across the face. The girls giggle.

"So, are you turning into a boy?" Olivia asks.

Rousey contemplates the idea. Decides, "No, I'm just taking the best of the boy stuff."

"Their face hair?"

"Yeah, a beard will keep my face warm. And protect me from sunburns."

"What happens when you grow boobs?" Sascha says.

"Duh. I'll have boobs and a beard."

"That'll be so ... interesting?" Olivia says.

"Yeah, I mean, nobody else at school will look like me. Or maybe even in the world."

"What about bearded ladies at the circus?" Olivia says.

"Those weren't really women. They were just men pretending to be women," Rousey says.

"Ooh, so do you think in, like, olden times you would have been considered a witch? Or, maybe a shaman for Native Americans?" Caroline asks.

"Probably, yeah." They murmur about this. They've never met a shaman before.

Rousey tells them, "I think I'm going to P.E. today."

"No *way*," Oscar yells. "We haven't gone *all* year."

"I'm going, but I'm not playing," Caroline says. "It's dodgeball."

"Those balls are gross," Olivia says.

"They *hurt*," Sascha says.

"Yeah, I'm going. *And*, I'm not going to be the first person out."

"No way," Oscar yells.

"You going to hit Jacob Calgary in the face?"

Jacob Calgary is tall, blond, and moves like a jaguar. There's no way she's hitting him in the face. Even if he was the first to call the kids who eat outside on the hill "the Turd Herd."

"No," Rousey says. "I'm not going to hit anyone. I'm just not going to get out. That's why it's called *dodge*ball."

"That plan is not going to work," Oscar says. "At some point even if you dodge *all* the balls it would just be you and one person at the end trying to get you out."

She considers. "Fine. I'll hit Derek Loope."

*

AND SHE DOES. She plonks him right in the face with a half-deflated red ball.

He stares at her in wonderment. He gets hit twice more before Lydia, an eighth grader on his own team, yells at him to get off the freaking court.

*

HER FATHER CLEARS HIS THROAT eight times. Says, "They e-mailed me your mid-semester grades. Your teachers say—your teachers say … that you are doing well. You're finally turning in all your homework and doing well on quizzes. They said if you keep it up you might actually be able to bring up your grades and pass your classes."

"Yep," she agrees.

"Honey." Her dad is bright red. "Did you want … this thing with your, uh, beard?"

She isn't sure exactly what he is getting at and the only choice she has is to wait it out. She'd sensed this conversation coming. Her dad popping in to her bedroom for "Good night, love," and then lingering before she dismissed him, "*Good night*, Dad." Putting his tablet down in the morning, picking it back up, turning down the TV, clearing his throat. But he hadn't managed to get it out without Hoa as backup. So there is Hoa, actually sitting still at the table with them, instead of bustling around the kitchen.

Her dad continues to clear his throat. He's alarmingly red-faced. "Dad, don't have a stroke."

"Right. Okay, I just want to say—ask—did you want—maybe … a doctor … or …"

"A doctor?"

"Yeah, I mean, if you wanted this … thing cleared up."

"Oh, Dad." She puts a hand on his arm. He knows so little about what it's like to be a girl. "I'm good."

"You know that if you ever need anything you can talk to me, right? Or, Hoa." And Hoa bobs her head in a deep nod.

"I know."

More throat clearing, and a look between the two of them. There's only one way out of this, and if she doesn't make it sound sincere he might keel over. "If something ever comes up, I'll totally come to you. Probably Hoa first, but then you too, okay?"

He kind of laughs. "Okay. Good, good, good. Well, I'm glad you're doing well. At school. I knew you always had it in you. You know. Maybe we should all go out soon? For dinner, at the pizza place like we used to? Hoa, you should come, too."

Hoa flaps her hand at Rousey's dad in a way that suggests he's being ridiculous.

"Yes! Hoa, you have to come, please!" She drags out the word *please* very long. Hoa slaps the table, closing out her sitting-down duties, and is up and starting on the kitchen cleaning. Rousey follows Hoa and leans into her, so that Hoa has to work around Rousey to clean all the counters she's already cleaned. "Come to pizza! Come to pizza! Come to pizza!"

Hoa grumbles. "I'm busy. Cleaning up after you girls." Then she sighs very deeply. Which means yes.

*

HER BEARD IS SHORT, but full, almost all across her jaw. At school, as her beard grows, so grows her friend ranks. A girl on each side and even more following behind every time she walks down the hall. Rousey is the bubble gum at the center of a Blow Pop.

United now by her shamanism, the kids on the hill are not the Turd Herd anymore. They sit inside the lunchroom. At a table. They don't scurry along the edge of hallways or use the bathrooms during class because the coast will be clear. Sure, there are whispers and laughs as they walk past. But they walk instead of slinking. That's new.

And Derek Loope stares at her during math. Lots of kids stare, but they do it quickly and if she looks back, they look away. But not him. He rumbles about the halls and basically stops in his tracks if she's coming his way. Since the second grade, she's been watching the way he flips his hair, twirls his pens, writes awkwardly left-handed. And now Derek Loope looks at her.

She's thrilled when two girls come up to her at the end of lunch. They're average girls. Brown hair, skinny, plain, and part of Derek's circle. They pass her a note in a moment when her new friends are distracted dumping their own lunch trays.

The note says:

Will you meet Derek L under the bleachers at fourth period?

☐ *Yes* ☐ *No*

Rousey doesn't know what happens under the bleachers, but she's always wondered. The bleachers are eighth-grader territory. Above the bleachers are the cool eighth graders, and below the bleachers is the territory of *hip* eighth graders. The ones who wear T-shirts with bacon jokes or mustaches. Who get good grades but aren't into cheesy activities like cheerleading or football. Of course she's going.

*

SHE GETS THERE EARLY to scope the place out. Cigarette butts litter the dirt. She is not going to take up smoking even if that's what it takes to get invited back down here.

Derek comes up behind her. "Hey."

"Hey," she says.

"What class are you missing?"

"Spanish."

"World History."

He leans against one of the poles. She leans against one, too.

"Your hair looks nice." But even as he says it, his eyes are on her beard. It's like his eyes are fingers and he's digging in. Not just looking, but combing through. It's weird, to be felt up without being touched. She wants to step away, just a foot left into the shadows of the bleacher seats. But even a month before she would have never been brave enough to come down into eighth-grade territory. She tosses her ponytail and says, "Thanks."

"You want to make out?"

"Sure," she says.

He moves closer. He is breathing hard. She stands straight, not sure if she should do something, too. He puts his hand on her hip, so she puts a hand on his. He closes his eyes. She closes hers. His breath blows across her face in a firm way she likes. If it was just this: his hand on her hip, breathing hard, it would be about the best thing she could imagine. But what would be the point of sneaking under the bleachers to do this? Surely, there's more to it. She squeezes her eyes tight and waits for the next cue.

He shoves her away. Jolts her eyes open. "I can't do it. It's too gross."

"What?"

"It's—it's—you look like a boy." He has his hand over his mouth like he might throw up.

The other day she felt the bumps of breast on her chest. Her hair is long and golden. Yesterday, her sister showed her how to put on mascara. She's a girl who gets to be a boy, too. Wasn't that her appeal? Confused she asks, "Then, don't you kind of want of kiss a boy?"

"No way, you fucking freak." He is far away, but spittle flies from his mouth and lands on her. She knows objectively it's just spit, but the droplets feel like hot wax across her face. She has to blink really fast.

"Why did you—why did you ask me here?"

"It was just a dare. Someone ..."

But his eyes on her face. The look of awe during dodgeball. "No, but you—"

"You're disgusting. Nobody will ever want to kiss you. Who will ever want to have sex with you? Someone would have to be a freak, like you."

She feels like a stepped-on grape. She didn't know it was possible to feel this way. Like all of her insides spilled out into the cigarette dust.

But, how is it that he's the one crying? His eyes, bright with tears, still search her face.

"You're a liar," she insists to him. "And I never wanted to kiss you, anyway."

*

SHE RUNS AWAY.

She runs to the janitor closet. The place where she used to hang out when she skipped P.E. She knows that the cinderblock slop sink is the perfect size to fit in.

She's crying, which is fine. Everybody cries.

Her mom never liked crying. "All you do is cry. Such a *sensitive* child." Never mind that Rousey didn't make a sound that night when their mom, tugging her sister along, woke Rousey. Took them from their warm beds into the really cold car. Never mind she half-slept quiet as a turtle in the back seat as the night changed to morning. She didn't start crying until they got into the motel room—Mom forgot to bring Bunny. Mom forgot a lot of things; there were no suitcases, just them in pajamas. But to leave Bunny?

Her mom, so bleary—her moist red eyes and lipstick smeared beyond the lips—said, "Don't make me regret bringing you. It's just a *toy*."

No clothes or shoes or socks or anything, but Mom had all her jewelry, the big bangles of silver and looping chains of pearls, but not Bunny. Dear sweet Bunny. No, Rousey shouldn't be so *attached* to something. Rousey needed to grow up, for god's sake.

Just the three of them in that small room—no school, no change of clothes, just the constant TV and sometimes the utter quiet of Mom sleeping—and if they so much as sniffled? Into the bathroom, *sit in the white tub!* Until they were done feeling sorry for themselves. Until they could come out and act like *grown-ups*. They could come out and watch TV with the *other* grown-ups.

Both Rousey and her sister had to go to the tub, more than once. They choked hard sobs into their cupped hands, stifling the noise, and used the rough white towels to wipe their faces. Coming back out, red-eyed but not crying. The other sister tucked under Mom's arm on the wide queen bed, looking nothing like a grown-up. Looking like the little wet lamb they'd seen born fresh at the petting zoo.

But by night with the dark easing into the room it could feel special. Pizza every day, delivered right up to their motel door like it was their house and then it felt fun. An adventure. Eating the pizza on the bed.

On the sixth day, after staying up to watch David Letterman, they popped out of bed to see her rumpled sheets on the other bed, still shaped in her body, but no Mom. Maybe she'd gone to get bagels? A decent breakfast. Never mind her suitcase was gone. Surely she would be back, remembering that she'd left something very important at the motel.

When that night darkness crept into the room they didn't feel at all like grown-ups. Still, they did their best. Put up the "Do Not Disturb" sign when they left the room, peered out the door at housekeeping and said their mother was sleeping. To buy food at the vending machines, they scrounged up coins from cushions and counters where their mother had tossed them. They ate pizza crust from the trash, and then they sucked on ice just to pretend they were eating something.

Two weeks later, a few counties over their mother ran out of cash and finally used a credit card. A private detective their dad had hired tracked backward to the motel in Florida. Their dad spent a lot of money on the guy, who was *absolutely* worth it. But it was Hoa who knew to open the closet where they hid. Where their mother had told them to hide if they heard anyone besides housekeeping at the door, because if some bad men ever found them ... "They would eat you two up. Such tasty fucking morsels. You have no idea how the world is out there. What the world is going to do to you."

Just an empty narrow closet to protect them from bad men. Just the two of them with their arms around each other's necks.

"Girls." Hoa sighed.

And they all cried then. Even their dad.

*

Rousey runs her fingers through her beard. She feels the sensation in her fingertips and she feels the sensation on her face. It's like being petted and petting something, like being both inside and outside her body at the same time. It's different than brushing her hair, scratching an itch. A beard is more intense—the rub of stubble beard under her fingertips, the bristles shifting deep in the hair shafts of skin of her face—back and forth: hair, finger, skin, molecules, atoms; a frisson of two sensations reverberating in ascending scales of intensity until she magics herself—transports to calmness. It's a place she gets to.

A great wide field of grass with a big bowl of sky overhead. It's a place she's seen, maybe on TV or in a movie. A place with soft sounds of nature, wind and rustling of grass. Grass moving like waves and the sky agape, forcing her to take big breaths.

She hears the crunch of footsteps and swish of breaking stems ahead of her, and though she can't see them, she feels her sister, her father, Hoa, walking just ahead of her. The shape of them reflects in a flare of light and she knows she is walking with them, forward, and how they will always be there, across a row of grass, close so that she can call to them, move near if she needs comfort. There is the low tone of other people, future peoples that she has yet to meet and she begins to see that as she continues into the broader world that the beard will bring its own type of heartache. Vitriol and harshness. Hate. But it will bring her interesting people, conversations with strangers, love, and so it will bring her great joys, too.

When she glances back, she sees the trail of bent stems of grass and a clouded sky. And there is her mother, a dark scarecrow behind, getting smaller and smaller as she moves. There's Derek Loope, too, a burned circle in the grass. Something she gets to leave behind.

She rubbed the lamp of her beard and it reminded her: she's okay. She's *good*.

And a boy? Her mother? They will not end her.

She stirs out of the calmness, shifting her butt on the tiles of the sink. She isn't crying, anymore.

Mrs. Lauren opens the closet door. A light shaft blinds Rousey.

"Rousey," Mrs. Lauren said. "I thought I heard crying? What—? What are you doing in here? Are you okay?"

Rousey stands up in the slop sink and comes to the door. "Yeah, I'm fine."

"Are you sure? I can call your dad."

"*Tsk,* Mrs. Lauren. I'm *fine.*"

"Well, school's out. You may have missed the bus ..."

"I don't ride the bus, Mrs. L, I walk home."

Mrs. Lauren keeps talking as they walk to the front of the school. Rousey can see her sister walking over from the High School to pick her up for pizza night.

Her sister yells, "Hurry up, fart-face, Dad wants us home, *pronto.*"

Rousey steps down the stairs of the school into the perfect beam of sunlight. She yells back, "Don't rush me, butt-nugget!"

Tonight they will go out and eat as a family—which means Hoa will be there with them. She and her sister will fight, then later they will probably watch *Clueless.* Their dad will fall asleep on the couch and Hoa will scoop them ice cream and also fall asleep on the couch. Her sister will trap Rousey under the blankets and hotbox her farts until Hoa and their dad wake up with all the yelling and they will be sent to bed.

But as she's about to go down the stairs to join her sister, all of that potential is ahead of her and she knows the measure of what is behind her. Right now—it's like a freaking perfect moment.

Why I Fly-fish

Julianne Bond

Because my husband left and the bed is cold
Because I call him and hang up after too much red wine
Because my hands shake and I've stopped painting
Because at this point, outsmarting an old trout with some string and yarn
seems like a big accomplishment
Because no one talks for hours, which is a relief because all words have left me,
though sometimes it's lonely without voices
Because of frayed mesh vests with lamb's wool pocket squares,
on which nesting bead-eyed mayflies plot new ways of luring fish
Because I long for a river, cold and clean,
my felted boots slipping and sliding on current-worn stones
Because the rushing water, cold against my legs, feels like flying
Because in waders I won't feel the fish bite me
Because I'm afraid of trout, of their eyes, black and glassy,
looking straight into my soul and stealing it
Because despite this, I love how their silver tails roll and catch the light,
like the tinkling antique bracelets I bought from a one-eyed, honest man in the Kasbah
Because wandering along the tree-shadowed banks
and discovering sun-bleached bones pocked with tiny ant holes filled with sand
is the highlight of my day
Because only then can I forget my husband's voice on the phone that day,
so far away in New York
His voice on the line, soft and fading, like he was already gone
Because as I listened to the quiet hum of his voice
I pressed my cheek against the cool window overlooking our garden of white flowers
and traced a fish with my fingertips
Because I belong to no one

OVERBOARD

Robley Browne

(From *Knee-Jerk*)

The mother was in the back of the raft attempting to control things with her paddle when the girl in the red bikini passed by them again. She watched the father turn his head, lift his paddle inexplicably, and then lay it across the bow of the vessel. The inviting pastoral river had suddenly given way to wild, unpredictable rapids and before she could think to yell out to him she felt the raft dipping down a precipice and turning sideways, her picnic basket filled with carefully wrapped sandwiches, homemade brownies, bottled water, and a Thermos of piping hot coffee toppling out across the floor of the rented craft, the four of them tipping into the froth, the daughter letting out a scream as the family tumbled out into the river, and then the raft capsizing above them, blocking out the hazy sunshine, the gurgle of cold water against her eardrums, feeling herself sinking, sinking into the seemingly bottomless river until she glided to a stop and began swimming back toward the surface; bursting out with a gasp as she looked around and before she had caught her breath she had taken the scene in in its entirety: the overturned raft cascading away over white water, the daughter shivering on a boulder hugging her knees in front of her, the father with his arm about the low branch of a tree near the bank, his hand above his eyes looking pointlessly up and down the river calling their son's name over the roaring rapids, the mother taking a deep breath and diving back under, that mysterious place inside her knowing instinctively that the boy was somewhere still down there, not yet sure of what she would do if she found him, eyes not yet adjusted to the murky water of the river, then seeing the bright white midriff of his belly poking out from under a rippling T-shirt, grabbing his limp body and pulling it up to the surface where her first priority was to try and get him over to a rock, which to her amazement she was able to do, as a shirtless man holding a beer and a woman in a sun hat glided by laughing, and there on the rock she saw for the first time how blue her son was, his eyelids closed and his bowl haircut matted across his dripping forehead, his top lip gone purple like a slug, and she tapped the side of his freckled cheek calling out his name, which caused the daughter to begin shouting it as well, as did the husband who was still clinging to the tree downstream, and the mother kept saying it's all right sweetie, it's all right just hang on, and seeing no sign of breathing she pulled up his wet T-shirt and began pushing down hard on his chest, counting thirty, the picnic basket empty of its contents and upside down now lodged against the bottom of the rock the mother and son were on, and tilting his head back the mother pinched his nose and gave two breaths to the boy, waiting for some kind of reaction, any kind of reaction, and seeing none she began pushing on his chest again, knowing it was supposed to be thirty but losing count and then sitting back on her heels she looked up and began shouting obscenities at the celestial sphere for not giving her the foresight to insist that her husky young son put on his too-orange lifejacket, thinking the son would be trading splashes with his cackling older sister right now were it not for that brunette in the red bikini and then the boy began coughing up bits of plant matter and bubbling water across the fractured rock, the look of him returning to that of a normal boy, for now at least, the two of them looking out at the bone-chilling river until something sloshed up behind them and seeing her husband's dripping hand come forward she thrust it away, somehow lifting the boy up and carrying him over the bank of the river, gnashing her teeth as she tried to imagine herself living the rest of her life with that horrible sinking feeling she had to endure, as though the river was somehow in cahoots with the father, whisking everything—and everyone—conveniently away, her stomach in knots as she keeps replaying over and over again that moment when she took her eyes off the son, though later on after they get home what she can't stop thinking about is how she was too weak to take the wheel when the father climbed in and wrestled it away from her, pushing her over to the passenger side with his hip, weaving their wood panel station wagon through the Sunday drivers, the family picnic basket lost behind them to the wild river, having drifted away and disappeared somewhere in the rapids, making the mother unwilling to just go with the flow, at least where the father was concerned, and when he wouldn't change and she couldn't make him, the mother moved out into a second-hand RV, where she found herself to be quite capable in the driver's seat, and even as she was moving away from something, she kept telling herself she must also be moving toward something, exchanging glances through the windows of the other cars, following a pickup full of shimmering young swimmers for a time, looking so much like her own, just a spectator among spectators now, her mind focused on them drifting away, attempting to capture them forever like a camera.

OLD DOG

Christina Perez Brubaker

Marilyn Olsen sat on her front porch waiting for her son Mikey to arrive. RJ, her Great Dane, was at her feet, his front legs crossed at the joint, his tongue hanging from his mouth like a wet washcloth. Recently she'd caught a chill she couldn't shake so she was enjoying the late September heat. She wore a silk tunic and a matching headscarf she'd bought at Saks with a credit card she never intended on paying off. Marilyn was dying. Not in the same slow way as the rest of us. She'd been given an expiration date.

"Tell me when it's a quarter after," she said when her caretaker, Isabel, appeared on the porch holding a large bowl of water. "I'm not gonna sit here all day if they're gonna be late."

The girl agreed with a grunt. Placed the metal bowl down and pushed it toward RJ with her foot, water sloshing over the sides in little tidal waves. Standing beside Marilyn's chair, she rested her round body against the doorframe. Together they watched RJ's long tongue turn the bowl from clear liquid to murky spit.

"He's bringing his husband all the way from Boston. Can you believe it?" Marilyn rubbed her dog's pointy ears. "How do you say homosexual in Mexican?"

She knew Isabel was Puerto Rican. She'd corrected her a dozen times but Marilyn didn't see the difference. Plus she liked watching the girl wrestle with her temper.

"We say pato." She pursed her lips. "Queer like a duck. Or maricón, but it isn't nice."

Marilyn thought of her late husband, Ralph. He said things like faggot and fairy. The last time she saw him he lay in a satin-lined coffin, hollow cheeks smeared with rouge. She'd spent ten years wondering if they would've gotten married had she not been pregnant, only to realize—while staring at his corpse—that she loved him deeply. The possibility of seeing him again was the only good thing about getting sick. A single speck of light in an otherwise dull black hole.

She closed her eyes and Ralph—a smudged silhouette—took her by the hand, swung her across the porch. Gin breath sweet like pine needles. His beard rough against her cheek.

"When was the last time you saw him?"

Marilyn twisted in her seat. "Saw who?" she snapped.

"Your son. How long's it been since you seen your son?"

On the lawn two crows picking at a piece of trash squawked loudly. Marilyn covered her ears. "Damn birds."

"What's the use of having a dog that don't bark at birds?"

"Can't hear like he used to. Besides, what's the use of paying *you* if all you do is yap?" She kicked off one slipper to stroke RJ's fur with her toes.

"Do you want me to wait with you or not?"

"Not."

*

IN THE KITCHEN ISABEL PRAYED for patience. Her relationship with the old lady, which had evolved into something more—part arrangement, part pact—was like a shaken soda can ready to burst from the pressure. A dozen spats a day alleviated the strain slowly; a steady leak instead of an explosion, but the friction was draining.

That morning she'd ordered Isabel to make dinner. For my son, that beans, rice, and steak mess you make. She hadn't eaten anything more than corn chips and mango yogurt in weeks, but it hadn't stopped Isabel from using the kitchen. Now she found comfort in the smell of cilantro and sizzling onions. She opened the oven and cut a small slit in the steak, revealing its insides. Pink juices spilled into a bloody puddle.

When her aunt, who was more like a mother, succumbed to kidney failure the doctors gave Isabel a brochure. Signs the end was near. So she wasn't surprised the never-mentioned son was coming for a visit. Number four on the list referred to the patient tying up loose ends.

On the radio next to the toaster she turned the volume up. Salsa, she'd said the first time she played it, purposefully exaggerating her s's like a snake. The old lady had made a face, but that was before the cancer had moved from her pancreas to her liver, and from her liver, to her lungs. Now she didn't seem to care what music Isabel played. Moving her arms and hips in opposite directions she danced on the balls of her feet. Licking the knife she'd used to cut the steak—salt and fat sweetened by onions and vinegar—before tossing it into the sink. It's almost over, she reminded herself. Bang. Boom. Clank.

*

Michael Olsen-Smith and his husband, James, drove from their hotel—a drab Courtyard Marriott that had looked decent online—to his mother's home. James was behind the wheel. Michael sat slouched in the passenger seat. He knew he was being a sullen pain in the ass, but he couldn't help it. His mother had wreaked havoc on his insides. He hadn't had a proper bowel movement since she'd called with the news.

Mikey, she'd said. I'm dying.

Now James pointed at the row of Craftsman-style homes and the canopy of leaves that covered the street. "Who knew the City of Orange was so quaint?"

It was an obvious effort to lighten the mood but it only irritated Michael more. "That's it," he said, tapping on the window at his childhood home. "James, I said, this is it."

"I heard you," he said, pulling their rental car alongside the empty curb.

The house, tan siding with a faded green trim, looked smaller than Michael remembered. On the wraparound porch in an oversized wicker chair sat his mother. She wore a dress—swirled pinks and gray—that hung on her like a trash bag, a matching scarf tied around her head like a helmet.

"Is that her?" said James without moving his lips.

She waved.

"Yup. That's Marilyn."

"She's not what I expected."

"Just wait."

Lying in front of her like a rug was a giant black dog.

"Oh my god," James gasped. "RJ. In the flesh."

"Wonderful. He's even uglier in person."

"And bigger. Way bigger than I expected."

Michael was living in New York when he found out his mother—who'd refused him any pets—had adopted a dog. He was living on the Lower East

Side. Sharing an apartment with three other guys. It was a reckless time. After a particularly long weekend of partying he left his mother a message. Said the upcoming holidays had him feeling down, layering each word with what he hoped was a subliminal plea for money. What he got in return was an invitation in the form of a holiday postcard, a gold banner—The Season of Joy—across a photo of a massive dog sitting on his mother's lawn. On the back, in her crooked cursive:

Come home. We'd love to have you.
XO, Mom and Ralph Junior

SHE'S LOADED, he'd complained to his friends. Couldn't send me a fucking dime.

With the next year came another card. This time a photo of RJ on his back in front of Marilyn's fake Christmas tree. His giant black balls on display. A-maz-ing! James, Michael's then boyfriend, had said before attaching it to the refrigerator with a magnet for everyone to see. Michael played along with the joke. What will Ralph Junior do this year? But really, for some inexplicable reason, he despised his mother's dog.

Now, as he climbed the porch steps—James a few feet behind him—he stared RJ down.

"Mikey." His mother clapped then held out her arms.

She'd always been a lean woman, lean but sturdy. She was built like an athlete—a runner, or a cyclist—though he'd never known her to break a sweat. Now, her once ruddy skin was a translucent shade of yellow that sagged from her limbs.

"Mother," he said, unexpectedly hoarse. When he bent down to embrace her, RJ scrambled to his feet. Butting his head between them he sniffed Michael, first his pockets, then his crotch. Forceful nudges accompanied by two loud snorts Michael tried to block with a swift knee.

"Ralphy," she laughed. "Are you saying hi to your brother?"

He rolled his eyes at James. Then pulled him to his side. He was about to introduce his husband to his mother but stopped abruptly when a girl appeared in the doorway. She was barely five feet tall. She had a young, fat face, clear olive skin, and round, syrup-colored eyes. Her hair—black and frizzy—was wrapped in a knot on top of her head. She wore a faded pink tanktop and cut-off denim shorts, both too tight for her egg-like frame.

"Mikey," Marilyn said. "I'd like you to meet Isabel."

"Hi." The girl smiled, a brief grin that didn't touch her eyes. She held out a plump arm his mother—a woman who referred to the men who trimmed her trees as beaners and wetbacks—took with surprising familiarity.

"Take me inside," she instructed.

Bewildered, Michael watched the mismatched duo walk toward the door with careful movements.

"You coming?" his mother said.

James nudged Michael forward. *Go!* he mouthed.

They moved into the wake of the girl's perfume, vanilla and coconut. Once in the darkened hallway Michael turned and hissed at James, "Who the fuck is this?"

"I told you," his mother hollered over her shoulder. "Her name's Isabel. She's been taking care of me. I'm sick, not deaf."

*

IN THE LIVING ROOM James filled the tense silence with small talk: lovely home, beautiful antiques, such unique taste. While the girl served drinks from a silver tray.

"Your favorite," Marilyn said.

Scotch was her favorite, but Michael was too anxious to point it out. Thankful for something to calm his nerves he took a long sip that tasted like tape while hers sat untouched on the table beside her, ice cracking.

On an oval piece of lace in the center of the coffee table sat an appetizer platter: deviled eggs, red peppers and carrots, crudités with no dip. Unnerved by the strange sound of Latin music coming from the kitchen, Michael—who sat beside James on the sofa—selected a deviled egg only to discover the rubbery membrane hadn't been removed. His mother watched him from his father's favorite recliner. RJ stood beside her like a gargoyle. He chewed and chewed, taking inventory of his parents' home. The smell of wood and musty furniture was familiar, the onions and faint canine odor were new. He looked at RJ looking at him—a piece of eye snot draped over his left eye—and wrinkled his face in disgust.

Somehow James had steered the conversation to his sister's battle with cancer. When he called her a survivor for the third time—nervous, cottonmouth clicks—Marilyn interrupted by raising her hand, a gesture that in another situation might have been mistaken for a low high five. "Glad to hear all she lost was her tits."

"Mom!"

"What? It's the truth. I'd gladly lop mine off if it meant I got to live."

"I'm sorry," James stuttered. "I didn't mean—"

"No need to apologize. It's not your fault I got it in the pancreas. Breast cancer's the pink nursery yard of this disease. Your sister—"

"So there's nothing else they can do?" Michael blurted, afraid of what she'd say next.

"Keep me comfortable. That's their grand plan."

"Shouldn't you be in a hospital?"

"You know I hate hospitals. Remember your father? We spent a week there before his bunk heart finally gave out."

"I was nine. I remember sleeping in a chair."

"Well, it was awful, those demeaning gowns and all that bodily fluid. If I'm gonna die, I want to do it here. At home."

Die. The word hung in the air between them.

"Did they say how long?" Michael asked, pausing between every few words.

"That's the kicker. They can't say for sure. It could be weeks. Could be months. That's why I got Isabel."

Michael moved to the edge of the cushion until a knee pressed against the coffee table. "She doesn't look like a nurse," he whispered.

"Do you have any idea how much home care costs?" she barked. "My doctor and some social worker in a cheap suit said five to six thousand a month. Sometimes more. I told them they could go straight to hell." She was almost to her car when the dark-skinned woman who scheduled her appointments caught up with her. "Nearly gave me a heart attack, I thought I was getting mugged. But she said she knew someone who'd do it for cheaper."

Michael stabbed a thumb at the kitchen. "So she's a complete stranger?"

"No, she's related to that lady somehow. It started out with her driving me to treatments, but it was just plain easier to have her move in. She's been here over a month."

"I thought Dad sold his shipping business to the highest bidder."

"He did. Poor man. He was planning an early retirement. We were going to travel. Take you to Europe, instead he took a dirt nap."

James flinched. "So you can afford legitimate help."

"The girl's all I need."

As if on cue Isabel—who was listening from the kitchen while eating olives out of a jar—appeared in the arched entryway of the living room.

"Time to eat," Marilyn announced, though the girl hadn't said a word.

In the dining room they sat at one end of a long mahogany table, Marilyn at the head, RJ to her left, his chest equal with the tabletop. Michael and James across from each other.

As Isabel served the food—a fruit smoothie for Marilyn and two plates piled high with thin slices of meat on a bed of red beans and rice—Michael eyeballed her feet, blue toenails and cheetah-print flip-flops. When his gaze returned to her face he found her glaring at him.

"Enjoy." She smiled wide, revealing two gold molars, before disappearing into the kitchen.

"Mother," he whispered. "People are known to take advantage of these types of situations."

"And what type of situation is that? A woman dying *all* alone."

"That's not fair."

"We came as soon as you called," James said.

"I know you did. Besides, it's not me I'm worried about." She wrapped an arm around RJ's neck. "It's Ralphy."

Michael blinked. "Ralphy?"

"RJ," she said.

"What about him?"

"I need you to take him."

"Take him where?"

"Don't be a smart ass. You know what I mean."

"Absolutely not." He shoveled two consecutive forkfuls of food into his mouth, briefly burning his tongue.

"Mikey, I'm all he has. Without me—"

"It's Michael."

"I know your name. I'm the one that gave it—"

"What else?"

"What do you mean what else?" She looked at James as if to say, what's wrong with him?

"On the phone you said you have things to discuss." A grain of rice flew from his lips. "What other things?"

"That's it. Just Ralphy Boy."

"Hear that?" he said to James. "Just Ralphy."

Deep breaths, James pantomimed. But it was too late. He was beyond breathing. "I haven't seen you in seven goddamn years and all you want to talk about is him?" He poked the dog in the neck. Ralph Junior smacked his jowls open and let out a low rumbling growl. Marilyn whacked the back of his head then shook a finger at Michael.

"Don't start that."

"Start what?"

"Playing the victim. You shut me out. I've begged you to come home."

"Home for what? So you could set me up with one of your friend's divorced daughters?"

"Excuse me?" James said.

"Don't worry." She swatted the air. "That was one time, way before you. Right, Mikey?" Then after an exaggerated breath, "I mean Michael."

"Yes, it was before him, but that's beside the point. It was only the most humiliating experience of my life."

"It wasn't that bad. She took the whole thing rather well. You know she's remarried now. Two kids and another on the way."

"*She* took it well? What about me?"

"You don't know how to let anything go." She turned to James, "Does he do this with you?"

The answer was yes, but Michael scowled at him. Don't take the bait! "And you can't admit when you're wrong," he shouted at his mother.

"Wrong how? By trying to protect you? Trying to teach you how to protect yourself? Sometimes it's better to keep certain things private, but you didn't want to listen. I was a single mother—"

"Here we go."

"I did the best— "

"If that was your best then—"

"Then what? What do you want? An apology? Would that make you feel better?"

"It would be a start."

"Ok, then," she yelled. "I'm sorry. Sorry for setting my life aside to raise you. Alone. I could've started over. Gotten remarried, had another family, but I chose you." It was a lie and they both knew it. She'd never met anyone bigger than Ralph's shadow. "I chose you," she repeated. "And what did I get in return? Nothing. You left. Never looked back. OK, so I made some mistakes. I didn't know what to do with this." She flapped a hand at each of them. "But I wiped your ass till you were seven and I never asked for a thank-you."

"Oh, I'm sorry. Thank you for raising *your* son."

"You're welcome," she shouted back, then laid her head against the high-back chair, turban askew.

"Maybe we should take a break," James said.

"I've got nothing else to say." Her body visibly trembled, but her see-through skin had a new, almost healthy flush.

"Neither do I."

The silence that followed started out hot and tight—punctured by the sound of forks on plates, ice in drinks—but slowly it loosened and cooled.

"He looks old," Michael said finally, referring to the white hairs on RJ's chin and around his eyes.

She took a piece of steak from his plate and held it in the air like a worm RJ swallowed whole.

"They usually don't live past nine. He's almost eight. He's too big to go cargo. Isabel's called all the airlines. You'll have to drive him. Not in that tin can. You'll have to rent a real car. You can use money from his trust."

"His trust?"

"Relax," she said. "He's a dog. You're the executor. Once he's gone it's all yours."

"You've got to be kidding me."

The corners of her lips shook and shuddered.

"I'm dying, Mikey. Taking him is the least you could do."

*

"SHE DOESN'T WANT FORGIVENESS," Michael shout-whispered at James, his own breath wafting back in his face, onions and garlic. "She wants a goddamn dog sitter."

They were alone in the backyard *getting some air.*

"I hate him," Michael paced. "I feel like an idiot saying it, but I hate that fucking dog." He stopped short. "What the hell are you looking at?"

"Stop." James grabbed his shoulders. "We're being watched."

Slowly Michael turned his head toward the back of the house. There, in one window stood the girl, the dog in another. "There's something about her," he said.

"She seems to be handling your mother well."

"I'm telling you. I'm getting a bad vibe. I think she's up to something."

"Forget about her for a second. What about the dog?"

"What about him?"

"We need to make arrangements."

"Don't tell me you want to drive that thing across the country."

"No, I don't. But we both know it's the right thing to do."

"The right thing," Michael shook his head.

He sat on the wrought-iron bench where his mother used to watch him practice gymnastics. Cartwheels and leaps he turned into arabesques. Loud claps. Bravo, Mikey. Bravo. How he loved her then. She was beautiful, with her perfect platinum bob and flower-scented hugs. Now, to keep from crying, he looked at the sky streaked orange and purple by smog and setting sun. "This isn't what I expected."

James sat beside him. "What did you expect?"

"I guess I didn't think she was *really* dying."

James put an arm around his shoulders. And when the ache in his temples became too great Michael laughed, "I always thought she was too mean to die."

*

IN THE DINING ROOM Marilyn said to the girl without opening her eyes, "That perfume. I can smell you coming from a mile away. What are they doing out there?"

"Giggling like a couple of schoolgirls."

She clicked her tongue. "Take me to my room."

There the girl helped her into a cotton nightgown. Marilyn looked at her turban in a silky puddle on the floor. Isabel looked at the ceiling. Both pretended not to see the sharp points of her bones.

Once in bed, Isabel propped pillows behind her back. "You know, I used to hate the way you smell," Marilyn said. "Now, it's not so bad. It's like the fertilizer my parents used on the farm. In March it was pure manure, but come summer it smelled kind of good. Like chocolate and coffee grinds."

"You saying I smell like shit?"

"Coconut-scented shit."

"It was my aunt's." She laughed. "I started wearing it after she died."

Marilyn surprised them both when she placed a cold hand on her knee. "Will you wear mine?" she asked. "After I'm gone I mean." It was an odd request, she knew, but suddenly she liked the idea of the girl moving through the world wearing too much of her favorite scent.

"I don't know. Smelling like a funeral home isn't my thing."

She slapped her knee. "It's gardenias, girl."

"Is it expensive?"

"You couldn't afford a drop."

"Okay then," She pulled the white coverlet up and tucked it around her shoulders. "But only cause it's free."

"Do you think they'll take him?"

"*El Caballo?*"

"He's not a horse. And don't make me laugh. I'm too tired to laugh."

"They'll take him."

"How do you know?"

"You're his mother."

"Apparently I wasn't a very good one."

"What's he got to complain about? Has himself a good-looking husband. Nice clothes. He sure as hell ain't missing any meals. As far as I can see, he's got himself a good life. He should be thanking you."

"You know if they don't, you'll have to look after RJ."

"Psst, then I'll make damn sure they take him. Strap him to the roof of that dumbass car."

Marilyn snorted. "I know you will."

Once she was alone she realized she never thanked Isabel for anything she'd done. She thought about calling after her, but as she fell into a fitful sleep she reasoned it would be awkward. The girl, like Marilyn, was tough. She wasn't hungry for sentiments. She didn't need a formal good-bye.

*

MICHAEL TIPTOED PAST RJ who was asleep in the living room. He ran into Isabel in the hallway. He looked at her with narrowed eyes, "Where's my mother?"

"*Que?*"

"*Donde-esta*-my-mother?"

"Ah, *aquí.*" She pointed to the door at the end of the hall. A few seconds after he brushed past her she said, under her breath, "*Gordo maricón.*"

"Excuse me?" He swung around but the hall was empty.

Surely she was locked in his father's office — the closest door not ajar — but he didn't knock. He was a patient man. If she had an angle, a fishing line in the water for his father's money, he'd find out soon enough.

The master bedroom was just as he remembered it. On a large Persian rug—gold, black and red—stood a four-poster bed. There, asleep, was his mother. He went to her side.

"Mom," he whispered twice, watching her chest hiccup full with air.

It had been an exhausting visit. He wanted nothing more than to go back to their hotel, curl up in bed with a bag of cookies and a bottle of cheap wine from the minibar.

He leaned down and pressed his lips against her forehead.

The rest of their time together was going to be different, he vowed. No more of the same old fight.

James waited for him in the kitchen. Together they found Ralph Junior sitting on his hind legs in the center of the living room.

"You can't leave without saying good-bye," said James.

"Yes, I can. He's a dog, remember?"

"Yeah. He's about to be our dog." He pushed Michael forward between the shoulder blades.

He approached Ralph Junior slowly, expecting a growl. But the dog simply looked up at him with human-like eyes. He touched his head—more of a tap than a stroke—surprised by the silkiness of his fur. "We'll be back tomorrow," he promised.

When they closed the front door behind them RJ barked. Three loud snaps that echoed through the house.

*

IN HER ROOM, ISABEL poured gin from a bottle she found in the desk, spilling several drops at the sound of RJ's bark. "Damn dog," she said. Then pinched her nose closed and threw the liquor to the back of her throat.

Outside an engine started. Through the lace curtain she watched the little blue car drive away.

Isabel's great-uncle was gay. The last time she saw him he wore velvet bell-bottoms and a studded choker. With their matching haircuts and tan slacks—different shades of brown—the old lady's son and his man looked like a couple of well-dressed Jehovah's Witnesses.

She smiled at this over another drink. And as she headed to the master bedroom she thought about waking the old lady for one last laugh. But she'd been given strict instructions, Do it while I sleep.

The old lady had stared Isabel up and down during her interview. "You sure a girl your size can do this job? You're sweating all over my furniture."

"It's a hundred degrees in here. Don't you got A/C?"

"No. I don't have an A/C."

"Then how 'bout opening a window?"

"Be my guest."

Despite her cousin's lecture on keeping her big mouth shut, when the closest window, an old push-up, got stuck partway Isabel cursed. *"Puneta, coño!"* she said, slamming the wood frame with the heel of her wrist until it flew open. By the time she returned to her seat, she knew she'd made a mistake. No way did the prissy old woman understand what she'd said. Still there was no mistaking the tone.

She and her ugly dog stared at her in silence.

"You're crude. But crude is good," she said as if she were trying to convince herself of something. "Makes me think you'd be of use, in the case that I need something more than assistance to the bathroom."

"Sure," she said, relieved. "Whatever you need. I'm your girl."

Now she hurried into the room before RJ — nails clacking against the wood floor — had a chance to follow her in. Whining in protest when she closed the door, he alternated between scratching and breathing at the space between the floor and the door.

Isabel, body humming from the alcohol, picked up an embroidered pillow off a side chair and took a seat on the bed.

The day they met, the old lady hadn't weighed much more. It was her probing eyes that had given her bulk. Asleep she looked tiny.

Don't do it. The words repeated in Isabel's head. A nasty command she fought by remembering her aunt's final days. That Medicaid bed, the smell of bleach and urine mixed with cigarette smoke from the skinny nurse who ignored their pleas for pain relief. Soiled sheets and catheters, breathing gone erratic, a scary sound the doctor called the Death Rattle.

Hands shaking, her blood loud in her ears, she placed the firm pillow over the old lady's face.

At first she was still. Then came the scratching: violent swipes and gouges at her arms, white lines across dark skin. If I fight, the old lady had coached her, push harder.

She'd offered her five thousand dollars. Isabel asked for ten. Somehow they settled on eight. Money she planned to put toward nursing school but first she'd take a vacation. Someplace tropical.

She squeezed her eyes shut and leaned her body weight forward.

Slowly the thrashing turned to jerks. The jerks turned to twitches.

When it was over RJ grew silent as if he knew. She opened the door, hiding behind it as he shuffled in, head bowed. In the hall she watched him through a two-inch crack climb onto the bed, legs turned coltish by the mattress springs. He stepped over the old lady, curled his enormous body into a circle beside her. Rested his head on her chest. Closed his eyes and sighed.

No Lie

Erica Bryant

I want to write a song
for girls who know the stank of no-lye relaxers

for what happened in our momma's kitchen or auntie's salon,
a raspy smoky bluesy note for internalized initiations:

you are black and your hair is nappy, so we learned how to speak pressing
   comb,
how to please others. We called it beauty, and vaselined our edges

didn't scratch our scalps, tended chemical burns, and we counted — four or
   six weeks and did it
again and again and again until we were convinced, and attached to our

new slaves, now clean and acceptable before the Lord.
The women in our families had meetings about our hair,

was it good or bad? They seconded and thirded strangely fruited notions,
satisfied white palettes, refined, straightened, managed, and never spoke of
   concerns

or mourned, not once. We did it and it was
beauty, and we slept, wrapped so our hair would lay flat

and we grew up and hardly mentioned how mad it really was
girls like us, grown in insecure soil

borrowed from massa. I want to write a hymn,
sharp and moody

for sharecropped self-esteem, for colonized girls who considered suicide but
   decided,
fuck you, and made ourselves stop.

WIND

Ross Bryant

wind at the tree line
pounding past needles and branches
low leaves fluttering over dark earth
old snow untouched by gale forces
a rock with ancient lichen
is unmoved
below the line
trees bow to unseen gods
some are sacrificed
roots splintering, trunks horizontal
rich soil lifted to the tumultuous air
thirsty wood
releasing odors
the final gasp
of a long life

LOVE ME TWO TIMES

Sarah Carriger

His name was James, never Jim or Jimmy, but James—to distinguish him from his father, Big Jim. Aunt Lou said it was just another example of his mother putting on airs; "Junior" was too common for *her* son. I thought it suited him. To me he was Jesse James, the affable outlaw, with his low-slung jeans and hip-shot smile. He was my first cousin once removed, but I'd never had much to do with him until the summer he was shipped down south to serve out his parole on my grandparents' farm. That summer I was told to have *nothing* to do with him *what-so-ever*, as if he could infect me with convict cooties or something. At least that was my mother's attitude; my grandparents were more forgiving or perhaps just more realistic. They were kind, unexcitable people, and it was difficult to imagine them as the source of my own mother, who got excited about pretty much everything.

The farm had become kind of a dumping ground for problem kids that summer. My parents had parked me there while they jetted around the country consulting specialists about my twin brother. It was the summer he got his first operation and the summer I got my first bra and my first bike and, to my mother's relief, finally resigned myself to the idea that I wasn't a boy (the bike she'd picked for me was embarrassingly pink with pearly streamers and flowers on the saddle—my mother was about as subtle as a kick in the teeth).

I had her old room, where I was surrounded by her creepy dolls with real human hair and eyes like stroke victims. James had been exiled to the shack down by the creek—as per my mother's instructions—but he came up to the house for breakfast and supper. Every morning I would stare at his reflection in the antiquated percolator that had pride of place at the head of the table. It was stainless steel with a hollow glass knob where you could see the coffee spurt up every few seconds like Old Faithful. I would watch as our reflected faces joined and broke apart like the blobs in a lava lamp until my grandmother would say, "June, what is your fascination with that thing?" I would look away, cheeks burning, while James dispatched his bacon and eggs with the efficiency of an engineer, oblivious.

*

WE WERE A GOOD WAYS north of Tipton, which was a two-bit town anyway, and hemmed in by the Mississippi River and the western shore of Reelfoot Lake. It must have felt like the back of beyond to a city kid like James, but he'd quickly taken on the coloring of a native—gotten himself some shit-kicker boots and a John Deere cap and a tin of Skoal chewing tobacco, which over the course of the summer would wear a faded white circle into the back pocket of his Levi's.

As soon as my grandmother released me from the household chores, I'd go find him, bare-chested and whistling, lean muscles popping with sweat while he worked at whatever task my grandfather had set him to—replacing rotted fence posts or mucking out the cow shed. "What's the forecast today, Junebug?" he'd yell as soon as he saw me. And I'd yell back, "Hotter than the devil's asshole" or "Hotter than a porn star's panties" or any mildly risqué nonsense I could think of to make him laugh.

I'd make camp nearby—laying out an old quilt and a pile of curled and yellowing National Geographics that I'd rescued from the basement. They were infested with silverfish and smelled like old cheese, but I didn't mind. I'd lie on my stomach and flip through the pages, kicking my feet languorously in the air like a 1950s pinup, while I listened to James whistle his way with gentle irony through "The Farmer in the Dell," "Old McDonald," "Turkey in the Straw." He was a gifted whistler. "Why don't you read to me, Junebug?" he'd say, when his lips got tired. And so I'd read to him about tribes in the jungles of Borneo where the men wore hollowed-out gourds on their thingies and the women pounded roots bare-breasted.

*

JAMES DIDN'T MIND HAVING ME around because I was his get-out-of-jail-free card. With me in tow he had the freedom of the open road. In my grandparents' thinking the responsibility for my care and safety would counter any impulse toward youthful hijinks—at least of the sort that had landed him in his current predicament. I lived for those moments when he would grab the keys to the truck and yell, "Saddle up, pardner! Let's get this show on the road." Often we'd just drive, in the late afternoon, with the sun turning everything golden, when the long shadows of trees bordering a field could touch something ancient in the pit of your stomach.

Saturdays were town days. We'd stop by the hardware store, with its smell of varnish and freshly cut lumber, then on to the Winn-Dixie to pick up this or that for my grandmother. I liked pushing the buggy while James collected items from the shelves—shortening, cornmeal, some chips that we'd share later sitting on the dock, waiting for the fish to bite.

Afterward, as a special treat, sometimes we'd go to Boyette's for catfish and cobbler. Boyette's was the only real restaurant in Tipton and stepping through its doors was like stepping into a time warp. Cypress paneling on the walls, black and white linoleum tiles on the floor, fans spinning overhead like dervishes. We'd sit knee to knee in one of the small booths next to the window, and when James stole french fries off my plate or laughed at my stories, I could feel my insides light up like the belly of a firefly.

When the competition arrived, I didn't see her coming. But she was like a black hole; I knew she was there by observing her gravitational pull. James had been sprawled cockeyed across the seat and although he didn't actually move, I could feel the shift in him. His muscles tensed and his gaze, which had been lazily wandering from my face to the fat greenbottle buzzing against the window to the man haw-hawing with the girl at the counter, suddenly zeroed in on something and held.

The name on the little tag above her left breast said Bernice, but she said her name was Tracy. Bernice was the last girl who'd worked there and they hadn't bothered to make new tags and she was just there for a little while—she was going back to college over in Union City in the fall, she explained, looking at James. I saw how he was looking back and started kicking the table with the toe of my sandal. James narrowed his eyes at me. The look said "Quit it," but I just kept right on.

I guess she was pretty. I could tell James thought she was pretty or pretty enough anyway. She had worlds of curly blonde hair spilling out of a clip at the back of her head and big boobs spilling over the top of her uniform. I looked down at my own chest, nipples poking out uncertainly into the world like the snouts of wild animals. I looked back at Tracy. I'd seen girls like her at the pool back home—slathering flat stomachs with baby oil and iodine, making eyes at the lifeguard, while I skulked next to the snack bar, wearing my towel like a burka.

"Ya'll aren't from around here, are you?" Tracy was saying with stunning originality. Her cheeks were flushed bright pink and the little gold cross around her neck trembled as she leaned over to swipe a rag across our table—giving James an eyeful. He took in the view and then leaned back in the booth with the cool of a professional gambler, but before he could say anything, I piped up, "I'm here because my brother is sick and James is here because he got arrested and kicked out of school and his parents didn't know what else to do with him." The words came out in a breathless rush, my voice high and squeaky. The look James turned on me said a good deal more than "Quit it." Tracy's eyebrows went up, but when they came down again I saw I'd made a mistake. She was intrigued.

"Maybe you can tell me what there is to do that's fun around here," James said, ignoring my outburst. I kicked the table again. He caught my ankle and gave it an unfriendly shake.

Tracy rolled her eyes at the lack of fun to be had in Tipton. "Maybe I could show you around a little, if you want. I get off work at six," she said.

"I'm stuck looking after my little cousin here, but maybe I'll get some time off later for good behavior," he said, and winked at her like they shared some joke.

My face felt hot and then cold. "Quit being such a penis," I said, the word exploding out of my mouth before I could call it back.

James looked at me for a minute, surprised. And then he laughed. "Quit being such a baby," he said, but there was warmth in his voice and he was looking at me, not Tracy.

On the way home James turned up the radio and we sang along to Elvis. *Love me tender, Love me true.* We passed miles and miles of fields dotted with the rusty skeletons of irrigation systems and then the state prison with its razor wire and guard towers and the notices not to pick up hitchhikers. I thought about James inside, smiling like Cool Hand Luke at the men who wanted to break him, and felt a dark, unexpected thrill.

"What was it like?" I asked. "Prison?"

James shrugged his shoulders. "I wasn't in for long and I was still seventeen so it was juvie, not a place like that," he gestured out the window. "Once you get the lay of the land, it isn't so terrible. Boring. It was boring."

"Did you like that girl?" I asked.

"What girl?"

"At Boyette's. Tracy."

His smile was more than a little wolfish, but he said, "She was OK, I guess. If you like the cheerleader type."

I chewed on that for a bit and then asked, "What type do you like?"

"The type that doesn't ask so many questions," he said, and winked at me.

*

WHEN MY MOTHER CALLED, it was always on Sunday evenings. After dinner, while Tom Brokaw droned on about Iran and the space shuttle, I would listen for the telephone. It took me no more than two rings to get from the den to the old olive green rotary in the back hall. I could imagine my mother sitting in some beige hotel room, her leg joggling a mile a minute, the ashtray on the nightstand overflowing with cigarette butts encircled with the bloom of her lipstick. She would start with: "Hi, sweetie. It's Mom," as if I were in danger of forgetting. And end with: "I hope you're being good for your grandparents." And in between: "Your brother's such a trooper."

"Is he getting better?" I'd ask, holding on tight to the handset.

I'd hear the long indrawn breath of my mother taking a hit off her cigarette and then the exhale and finally she'd answer. "We hope so, sweetie. We hope so. The doctors are working really hard."

I'd hang up fast, before the bright cheery shell of her voice cracked into a million pieces.

*

I STARTED SNEAKING DOWN to James's shack at night. The first time I did it the moon was nearly full and I remember the way the wisteria flowers glowed, hanging pendent over the back porch, raining white petals down on me as I passed. I remember the different smells — the chemical tang of the tomato vines as I passed my grandmother's vegetable garden and the rich loamy perfume of wet earth, the smell of manure from the pasture fields, and as I got closer to James, a whiff of rotting fish from the creek.

The first couple of nights I kept to the cover of the trees, although had he cared to look, my nightgown stood out like a white flag in the moonlight. Then when nothing happened, no yelling or alarm bells or barking dogs, I got braver and worked my way up to the window. Most of the time there wasn't much to see—James lying on his bed smoking or reading, his bare foot wagging along with the Grateful Dead or the Rolling Stones or Led Zeppelin. I wanted to go lie next to him, to be inside that circle of ease, but I stayed where I was, kneeling in the grass under his window.

The night I found that he wasn't alone, it took my brain a minute to sort out what it was seeing. Tracy's curly gold hair spread across the pillow and James's broad back moving on top of her while Jerry Garcia sang "Sugar Magnolia." I'd read my parents' book *How to Talk to Your Child about Sex*, but this was my first look at the real thing and it was clear the book had left a lot out. I could hardly breathe. The mosquito screen gave the shapes inside a gauzy, unreal look as they undulated like snakes. A moth was hurling itself against the bedside lamp—its drunken swoops casting crazed shadows on the sheets and across their bodies. They didn't notice. Not that. Not the bedsprings squeaking like angry bats. Not me, standing there in the wet grass outside the window, my mind zinging with panicked energy, taking it all in like it was a fatal car crash with body parts strewn across the road.

I don't know how long I'd been watching when Tracy arched her back and made a sound like a hurt animal as James sank his teeth into her tan shoulder. Then they both stopped moving, as if someone had thrown a switch. I backed away from the window and then turned and ran.

That night I lay in my mother's bed and listened to the whisper of the air conditioner and thought about what I'd seen. I erased Tracy from the picture and drew myself in. I put my hand under my nightgown and ran it over the nubs of my breasts and down between my legs where I knew the pleasure came from. I rubbed myself there and felt a liquid tingle. As I rubbed harder and the tingle grew bigger, my mother's dolls watched me disapprovingly from the top of the cedar chest. "You're a bad one," their eyes said. I imagined my mother looking heavenward and asking Jesus what she did to deserve this. I went to the bathroom and splashed water on my hot face. Then I took one of my grandmother's wash-cloths—scratchy and stiff from the line—and washed between my legs. But my mind kept turning to James and what it would be like if he touched me there.

*

THE NEXT MORNING when I came down to breakfast, James was already at the table, leaning back in his chair with a sleepy smile on his face. I stretched out my bare foot until it was poised between his legs. Not touching but close enough to feel the heat from his skin. He didn't look up but continued to smile into his coffee cup. My grandparents kept on eating, my grandfather pausing every now and then to turn the page in the *Lake County Courier*. Outside, the cicadas were already grinding away.

During the days that followed, while I did my chores — collecting eggs, vacuuming, peeling apples (so many apples) — my brain was busy constructing elaborate fantasies, pulling liberally from Cinderella and *Riviera Rendezvous*, my then favorite of the cache of dog-eared romance novels left over from my mother's girlhood. In the afternoons, I'd still go find James, but now everything felt different. He only had to look at me sideways for my face to catch fire. Everything I said sounded stupid and childish — nothing like the sexy dialogue I'd written in my head. And I messed with my hair so much, in my effort to look constantly alluring, that he asked if it was possible I had lice.

The activities that had comforted me earlier in the summer — swimming in the milky jade water of the creek, combing the woods for mushrooms, bird's nests, the translucent husks of molted jarflies — ceased to give me any pleasure. I spent hours in my mother's room reading romance novels and trying on her dresses, lovingly preserved with their colored petticoats in cellophane bags in the closet. I twirled in front of the mirror to feel the skirts swish against my legs while I imagined myself on a terrace in the Riviera — which I pictured as something like Florida — with James in a tuxedo kissing me under a silver moon. The dolls looked on, unimpressed.

*

"I THINK THERE'S SOMETHING WRONG with June," I heard my grandmother telling my grandfather, after the *News Hour* and Lawrence Welk, when they thought I was in bed. I froze at the sound of my name — the cookie tin, which I'd been attempting to stealthily pry open, forgotten in my hands. "Barely says two words together," my grandmother said. "Hardly touches her supper."

"Just worried about her brother, I expect," my grandfather said.

I slunk, cookieless, back to my mother's room. The dolls smirked from the corner where I'd exiled them. The truth is, I *hadn't* been worrying about my brother. He'd been sick for so long, he occupied a different world. I could still remember when we used to play together in the woods behind our house. We climbed trees and made forts and played Star Wars with sticks for light sabers.

The last time we'd played, my light saber had slipped and hit Ben in the eye—a danger my mother had frequently warned us about. I tried to convince Ben not to tell, but he started to cry and ran for the kitchen. When my mother heard what had happened she turned white and I was afraid she was going to hit me. But she sat down and carefully pried Ben's eye open—the lid was already swollen to the size of a golf ball—and breathed a sigh of relief. "His eye's still in there, just where it should be," she told us. "It's going to be OK. We'll go get it checked out, just to be safe." She sent me to the neighbor's and told me she'd be back soon. But she hadn't been. The scan my mother had insisted on revealed the first tumor.

Ben stayed in the hospital for a month that first time. When he came home, if I even got near him, my mother was on me in a second. "That's the last thing he needs. You sharing your germs," she'd say, shooing me away. And if I whined or sulked or otherwise made a nuisance of myself, my mother would say, "Think about what your brother's going through and he never complains." And he didn't. He barely said anything.

I had this vision of him being well again. I imagined us riding Big Wheels down the slope of our driveway, like we used to, while a dog—although my mother had said over her dead body were we getting a dog—ran along beside us barking joyfully. I could see my brother laughing as the dog tried to nip his ankles and my mother smiling at me with approval from the kitchen window as I called the dog away. "Come, Roscoe," I'd say. In my fantasy, Ben named the dog Roscoe but it would only listen to me. Our dad would come home from work early and grill hamburgers for us on the deck while Ben and I played fetch with the dog until it got dark.

They'd said that this trip would be the last one. That this time the treatment would work and we'd be together soon. And I was young enough to believe them or at least try to believe them, although I'd heard it all before. When my mother called on a Thursday night, I thought it must be good news. But when I picked up the phone, my mother's voice was tight, like she'd been crying. "Is Ben OK?" I said, alarmed.

"He's hanging in there like a trooper," my mom said. "Now put your grandmother on."

"But—"

"Just get your grandmother," my mother said, and when I opened my mouth to protest: "I don't have the energy right now, June."

It was my grandmother who broke the news that my mother and Ben would be staying in California for at least another month and I'd have to start school in Tipton. I thought about James leaving for boarding school in a few weeks, leaving me behind with the slack-jawed, mulleted teens we'd seen milling about in the Dairy Queen parking lot in town.

"It'll be alright," my grandmother said, seeing my expression. "I know you'll be brave like your brother. Now run on up to bed."

I climbed the stairs like I was on the way to the gallows. When I opened the door, there were my mother's dolls leering at me. "Fuck you," I said to the dolls. I drop-kicked one across the room, but found it didn't make me feel much better. I started to put on my nightgown, but then I remembered my mother's old slips — silky, filmy things with lace at the bottom. I pulled one over my head and it slid down my body like water. I snuck down the stairs and then I was out.

I ran through the high grass, the fireflies blinking like runway lights. The shack glowed in the distance, and I could hear the thump of a bassline over the crickets. I didn't take my usual spot under the window, but went right up to the door and stepped through.

He was asleep on the bed — naked. I don't know exactly what I'd been expecting but the sight of that mottled roll of flesh made me hesitate. It looked like one of the grub worms we sometimes dug for bait, like it belonged underground, blindly pushing its way through the dirt. "Motherfucker," I whispered. It was, after C U Next Tuesday, the worst word I knew, and saying it out loud made me feel briefly in control.

I took a deep breath and slid into bed next to him — keeping my eyes on his face and freezing like a thief when the springs squeaked (the words "caught in the act" emblazoned in neon over my head) — but James slept on. I lay for some minutes — it seemed like hours — with my head on the pillow next to his, watching the rise and fall of his smooth, tanned chest. The fan swept back and forth across our bodies, giving me goosebumps and rattling the pages of a magazine lying on the nightstand. Jim Morrison sang, "*Love me two times baby, Love me twice today.*"

I let my eyes drift down to the nest of gold wire between his legs and that strange animal, his penis, slumbering in the midst of it. As I stared, it began to grow and stretch like it knew I was looking and welcomed the attention. I held my breath and touched it with a shaking finger — gasping when it surged toward my hand. James stirred, and rolled toward me. He pulled me to him and mumbled sleepily, "Hey, I was just dreaming about you."

I felt his hot breath on my face, flavored with the cabbage we'd had for dinner, and tried not to wince as he squeezed my breast. I braced myself, but then, just before his lips would have touched mine, he must have realized that instead of Tracy's luscious D cup, he had hold of my not-quite B. He reared back like I'd stung him and, in his haste to get away, fell off the other side of the bed. If he'd slapped me it couldn't have hurt worse.

James scrambled up and stared at me. "June? What the fuck?" He stomped around the room looking for his underwear and cursing me. "What the fuck were you doing?"

My lip was wobbling but there was no way I was going to cry like a little kid.

"You need to get out of here right now! Go on, scoot!"

"No," I said, kneeling in the middle of his bed, suddenly conscious of the bust of my mother's slip hanging like two empty sacks.

"What the hell has gotten into you?"

"Why not me?" I demanded, crossing my arms over my chest.

"June, what are you talking about? You're like my little sister."

"But I'm not! I'm not your sister! And you're nothing like my brother. He wouldn't smoke pot or have sex with some random girl he picked up at a diner. He'll probably never get to have sex at all." I dug my knuckles into my eyeballs to keep the tears back and when I took them way, James had stopped glaring at me. He'd pulled on his pants and was moving cautiously toward the bed, holding up a hand like a lion tamer in case I decided to lunge at him.

"Hey now, kiddo. What's going on?" he said. "Is this about your brother? Has something happened?"

"I wish he would just go ahead and die already," I said. And the tears really started flowing then and there was nothing I could do to hold them back.

"Hey, hey," he said. "I know you don't mean that." He gathered me to him then and stroked my hair as I sobbed.

"He's not getting any better," I mumbled into his shoulder.

"I bet you'll be dancing at his wedding," James said. Then he stiffened. "They're calling for you," he said, pushing me away.

And then I could hear my grandfather bellowing my name—the sound still far off but coming closer.

"You need to get moving or we'll both be in a shitload of trouble. Go on—back to your *own* bed." I somehow got my legs under me and staggered out into the night. I trudged back in the direction of my grandfather's voice, then I thought about my mother's room with the dolls and the dresses and in the drawer her old hairpieces, from when beehives were in fashion, lying on their backs like dead pets. I turned toward the creek. The path was a bit overgrown and I tripped and fell a few times before the way opened up and I could make out the dark shape of the dock. I half jumped and half fell into the water. It was warm like a bath. I swallowed some water and broke the surface coughing. I panicked for a minute. *Never swim alone.* But I was a good swimmer. My mother had signed my brother and me up for lessons before we could walk. I lay back like we'd been taught and let the water hold me up. Floating like that, I could see the stars and all I could hear was my own breathing. I thought about what it must have been like before we were born — my brother and I. I wondered if we held hands, floating safe together inside my mother. I felt my heart rate slow as I drifted along in the mild current. I imagined myself drifting down the Mississippi all the way to the Gulf of Mexico.

HELLION

Doris Cheng

(from *Calyx*)

The summer I turned eight, I didn't know I was going to Hell. I was a sun-burnt savage, unbothered by existential dilemmas, and I obeyed only the commandments of finders keepers and "I didn't do it!" What did I know about Hell? I thought "Hell" was a part of speech, an adjective of sorts, like when white kids on the playground said "Hell, yeah!" or "Go the Hell back to your country, you yellow-faced monkey." Until a rainbow-colored Jesus Loves Me bus came through our apartment complex trawling for converts, and my mother, who worshiped at the church of all Taiwanese immigrants—aka the Church of Getting Something for Nothing—put me and my brother Ted on that bus so she could get a few hours of free babysitting. She didn't know these people, but she'd come across enough missionaries in her life to know that they practiced decent hygiene and were good for at least a free meal.

Even though it was an hour-long ride to the New Life Baptist Church of South Nashville—only ten miles away but we stopped at every broken-down housing complex to pick up bewildered-looking children—I barely noticed the time passing. Unlike my mirthless, frugal parents, whose idea of a good time was seeing who could extract one more drop of toothpaste from a seemingly empty tube of Crest, these people knew how to have fun. We clapped hands, we sang "Michael Rowed the Boat Ashore" and "He's Got the Whole World in His Hands," we ate Little Debbie snack cakes and played Count the Crosses and the Picnic Game ("I went to a picnic and I brought Adam, I went to a picnic and I brought Barnabas ... "). I didn't care that we were the only immigrant kids on the bus. Back then, our part of town was white and black, native Southerners who worked at jobs like driving buses and cleaning offices, and there was not much color in between—not like now, where you'll find a *mercado* on every corner. Since the black kids went to their own churches, it was just me and Ted on a bus full of white kids until, a few weeks later, some Mexican kids started riding it too.

One giddy Sunday, the bus brought us to a roller rink, where I experienced the greatest triumph of my young life: after tossing back a pitcher of purple Kool-Aid, I rode my sugar high around the rink without once touching the wall. "Well hey now, lookee you, Miss Wendy! You're a regular Dorothy Hamill on wheels!" gushed the bus counselor, Sister Dee, her eyes as big as moon pies. Looking at her face, contorted in what I took to be an expression of genuine awe, I felt myself straighten, my neck grow warm, like a seedling reaching for the sun. Had my mother ever had that kind of look on her face? A look of pride and disbelief—a look that said, "Well hey now, lookee you!" Hell, no.

How I rejoiced on that ride home! "Oh, you can't get to heaven on roller skates," I sang at the top of my lungs, my voice joining a raucous chorus, " 'cause you'd roll right by those pearly gates!" The bus shook from the firecracker clapping of thirty pairs of hands—everyone's hands except those of Juanita, sitting next to me, whose hands were clamped over her ears. I'd never spoken to her, though she was my assigned seatmate. She was two years older than I, a thickset girl with dark hair on her upper lip and twin nubbins pushing through the front of her tube top, but somehow, she seemed altogether babyish. I couldn't stand her. Maybe it was her lisping English (which made her sound, I imagined, like the love child of Cindy Brady and Speedy Gonzalez), or her dimpled fingers. Maybe it was the way her mother waited with her at the bus stop every Sunday, still dressed in coveralls from working the night shift at some factory, blowing kisses and waving frantically as the bus pulled away, as if her daughter was setting sail on the QE2 instead of just going to church. Imagine, I thought contemptuously, a big hairy girl like her still needing her mommy! And even harder to figure out was how this hairy, lumpy, clearly undeserving girl managed to inspire such love from her mother. It made no sense. But the fact of the matter was, I envied her. Juanita looked at me, her face as guileless as a cow at pasture. "*Es muy ruidoso*," she said. I turned my back on her and sang as loudly as I could: "Oh, I ain't gonna grieve my Lord no more, I ain't gonna grieve my Lord no more!"

Poor Juanita! She'd never done anything to me, other than being born to a mother who doted on her. And yet every time I looked at her, I wanted to slap her.

The Baptists had the conversion thing down. They pulled out every trick in the missionary playbook—the camaraderie, the happiness, the cookies, the happiness, the fun, the jokes, the sing-alongs, the happiness—how I devoured these things, all of it so scarce in my day-to-day life! But—along with the carrot came the stick. Heaven wouldn't exist if there wasn't a Hell, and the Baptists were never so happy as when describing the torments of Hell to little children.

"Hell is the inside of a volcano that's puking fire," our teacher Brother Shoney told us in Sunday School one day, spit shooting from his mouth as he said the word "fire." They called him "Shoney" because he was a big boy and he liked his burgers. "There you are, falling—falling faster than a bullet, so fast the wind is howling in your ears, and you're burning—it's hotter than Africa where you are, hotter than a pig roast on the Fourth of July, so hot your skin's melting like lard on your Meemaw's griddle. Satan's minions are gnashing their teeth, oh, they're ravenous, they can't wait to tear into you! And all around you the sinners are screaming—'Help me, Lord, I repent, I repent!'—but it's too late for repenting. Yep. Too late for all the filthy masturbators, murderers, thieves, homosexuals, Communists, feminists, practitioners of the dark arts. Satan's got them now." Shoney smiled brightly and dabbed the sweat from his forehead. "And if you don't accept the Lord Jesus Christ as your savior, he's got you too. Forever."

Recent transgressions flooded my mind, each seemingly more heinous than the other—lying about washing my hands, that time I threw away the frank and beans my mother served for dinner when she wasn't looking. Peeking at *National Geographic* while pretending to read *Ranger Rick* at the dentist's office. Would these be enough to send me to Hell? And what was a feminist, anyway? Or a masturbator? Masturbator sounded like some sort of kitchen appliance, one of those handheld ones used for mixing cake batter. Could I possibly—unknowingly—be such a terrible thing? I suddenly had to pee. I may not have understood what Shoney was talking about, but I did understand I was terrified. Up until then, the thing that scared me most was the spirit of Bloody Mary, who roused herself only if you were dumb enough to say you didn't believe in her and whose shapeless face Ted claimed to have seen in our toilet bowl. Satan, however, was in a whole different league. Satan was for all of eternity.

The little Mexican kid sitting next to me crawled under his desk, clasped his hands over his head, the way they taught us to do during air raid drills at school, and began to cry. Without waiting for permission, Juanita got up from her desk and crouched down next to him, speaking softly in Spanish. When he looked up, she untied the pink bandanna she wore wrapped around her leg and wiped his nose with it. Then she smiled at him in a way I'd never seen before—with such kindness, such tenderness, she looked as new as a freshly peeled scab. Disgusting, I thought. I was by no means a Goody-Two-shoes, but in my opinion, she deserved to be punished—for getting out of her seat obviously, but really, in my mind, for something I considered a more serious crime—coddling the kid, a crybaby, when everyone knew you didn't coddle crybabies. You taunted or ignored them. Otherwise, how would they ever learn the cardinal rule of survival? Which was that, no matter how scared or lonely or left out you felt, you never, ever, let anyone see you cry. A hard lesson, yes, but one that any kid in any schoolyard could teach you. In my case, it was a lesson driven home by my mother, famous for taking no prisoners when she saw a flagrant display of emotion. After Ted lost his pet rock and burst into tears, my mother led the charge, laughing, "Look, Wendy! Your big brother is crying like a baby over a rock! A rock! Can you believe it?" It was crystal clear to me then, as I pretended to chuckle along, that it was always better to be on the giving—not the receiving—end of mockery. As my mother liked to say, America was not a land for the weak.

Shoney paused, then he bent down to look at Juanita and the boy. His brow was furrowed and I imagined his displeasure at this interruption to his lesson, the anger that must be rising from his gut and preparing to pour from his mouth. Eagerly, I pushed the hair away from my face so I'd have a clear view of the punishment he would surely be serving upon Juanita. But all he said was, "Jesus loves the little children," then he picked up his Bible and kept preaching: "God's Word does not lie! Revelations chapter twenty-one, verse eight, sinners will die a second death in 'the fiery lake of burning sulfur'—" and I missed the rest of what he said because I had expected him to call Juanita to the carpet and couldn't believe it when the public shaming did not take place.

I glared at Juanita. Was there no justice in the world? No fairness? "*Tu no estas solo,*" she said to the kid under the desk, over and over again. "*No te dejare.*" Her nasal *n*'s and rolling *r*'s sloshed in my ears like dishwater. After her brazen flouting of the rules, this incomprehensible murmuring was more than distracting—it was infuriating. "Shhh!" I hissed. I needed to hear what Shoney had to say. He seemed to be some kind of tour guide to the Hereafter, and I needed his knowledge, his insider tips and shortcuts. I certainly wouldn't be able get this kind of information at home. For my parents, the afterlife was not a topic of conversation. They talked only about money. To be precise, my mother did all the talking, berating my father for sending money back to Taiwan, for not being man enough to ask his boss for more money, for throwing money away on toys, flowers, lottery tickets, et cetera. Metaphysically speaking, my parents were useless. Shoney was my only hope. If I didn't get the lay of the land from him, I'd end up taking a wrong turn and find myself in Hell, I just knew it.

"Can't you be quiet? Please?" My words were more of a demand than an entreaty. Juanita looked curiously at me but kept talking. It was strange to hear her talk in Spanish. Her babyish lisp was gone and her voice had become rich and fluid, like a glass of warm milk. I hated warm milk. "Ugh, don't you understand English? What's wrong with you?" But it was a rhetorical question. I already knew what was wrong with her—everything. Her thick accent, her tacky clothes, the complacent look on her face. The mother who blew kisses as the bus pulled away.

I have a hard time explaining what happened next. I—the Chinese girl who sat stone-faced when other kids made fun of my slanted eyes or my hand-me-down boy clothes—I was overcome by an anger so fierce it made my ears ring. I couldn't breathe. When Shoney stepped out of the room to fetch our Bible workbooks, an unseen hand—it must have been the hand of Satan—pushed me close to Juanita's ear and put these words in my mouth: "Shut up, you greasy bean eater! If you spics aren't going to speak English, you should get the hell out of America!" These terrible words came out in a whisper. I had Juanita's full attention now. Her cheeks reddened, her mouth opened and closed, and then her face changed in a way I'll never forget: it crumpled, then it recomposed itself into something unfamiliar and flat, like a patch of earth after a flood whose features, as the waters recede, are permanently altered.

The ringing in my ears had stopped by now, and I heard every sound in the room with bionic clarity—the squeak of Rudy's sneakers, the titters as Terry put a "Kick Me" sign on Hector's back. No one seemed to have noticed my exchange with Juanita. I could hear her breathing, uneven and heavy. She'd never tell on me, I told myself. She was too soft, and besides, she could barely put two words together in English. And what was there to tell, anyway? *She* had been the one disrupting the lesson. I'd only been trying to restore order to the class. I became aware of a prickly heaviness in my stomach, a feeling that I'd swallowed an oddly shaped foreign object. It was my conscience, of course—but to me, it felt like indigestion. I swallowed hard. I sat stiffly in my seat until Shoney huffed back into the classroom with our workbooks and crayons.

"We're sinners, all of us," he said. "The Bible tells us, 'Jesus, so that He might sanctify the people with his own blood, suffered . . .' He sanctified us!" With this he shook a fist in the air, and as he raised his arm, I noticed his armpits were drenched with sweat. "And what did he ask from us, in return for sanctifying us with the blood from his body? Not a whole heck of a lot—just for us to love one another. To be kind to one another. Imagine the pain He endured on that cross, to save our souls! Our wretched, uncaring, ungrateful souls! Think about this as you color page twelve." It was a picture of the crucifixion, a cartoon-like drawing of Jesus hanging from the cross, an armored, weeping Roman soldier at his feet. Jesus's head was cocked to one side and his eyes were raised upward in what was supposed to be an expression of suffering and forgiveness, but to me, it looked as though he was rolling his eyes incredulously. "No way," he seemed to be saying to the soldier. "Sorry is not going to fix this." My bladder felt as if it was going to burst. I raised my hand for permission to go to the bathroom.

Sitting on the toilet, I wondered if God had seen what I'd done to Juanita—if He was, in fact, watching me at that very moment, His celestial X-ray vision piercing the sheetrock like a toothpick through a cake. I launched into a silent argument with the ceiling: I didn't *do* anything! I told the ceiling. Juanita was the one who had sinned, not me. She shouldn't have been speaking Spanish in the first place. Because wasn't it true that if God had wanted us to speak Spanish in church, He would have written the Bible in Spanish? I was as tough as a mob boss on the stand, and I wasn't about to let anyone—not even God—pin anything on me. But as I stood at the sink and splashed cold water on my face, I remembered Juanita's cheeks. I remembered how red they turned after I spoke my terrible words to her. It surprised me, that rush of blood under her skin. I never knew that people with brown skin could blush.

When I got back to the classroom Shoney was walking up and down the aisles, patting a shoulder here, giving a word of encouragement there. "Wonderful job, Lorraine! Jesus would be proud of how nicely you colored inside the lines. Billy, what a wonderful shade of blue you've chosen for Our Lord's eyes." He was an earnest guy who welcomed every effort to praise Jesus, no matter how childish. I opened my workbook to begin coloring and almost fell out of my seat. Some-one had scribbled on—no, someone had *defiled*—my picture of Jesus. His two front teeth had been blacked out, he'd been given a Hitler moustache, and worst of all, in addition to the crown of thorns atop his head, he now sported a pair of horns. It was an act so obscene, so nakedly profane, that I threw my hands over the page, as shocked as if Jesus's private parts were showing. What lunatic could have committed so grave a sin? I looked around the room but saw no obvious wrongdoer. Some kids were coloring, others throwing paper, or whispering and giggling; no one was looking in my direction and no one, I was surprised to see, had been turned into a pillar of salt by God's wrath.

Could it have been Juanita? She was working intently, her dark head bent over her desk. I found it hard to believe that she, of the lisp and dimpled baby fingers, was capable of such cold-blooded sacrilege. I poked the kid in front of me, a sleepy-lidded boy named Darryl. "Hey! Did anyone take my workbook when I was in the bathroom?" He turned around slowly, but when he saw my picture, he slapped his forehead and opened his eyes so wide he looked like a cartoon character. "Oooh," he said, "somebody's gonna get it."

It occurred to me that the picture might be salvageable. Maybe—like the fashion magazines that turned a plain Jane into a foxy lady with nothing more than mascara, say, or a patterned scarf—I could touch it up, transform it with a few well-placed strokes. Eagerly, I picked up a crayon. But the vandal had marked Jesus deeply, pressing so hard the paper had become corrugated and dark waxy bits scattered about the page like soot. Sherman's march through Atlanta had not wreaked as much destruction as this. How was I supposed to fix it? All of a sudden Shoney was standing beside me. He looked at the crayon in my hand, then at the open workbook in front of me. He was quiet as he studied the picture, but he breathed heavily, his head cocked like a bird dog whose quarry has suddenly broken out in song and dance. After a moment he said, "Wendy, it looks like you've changed Jesus's face some. Is this how you give glory to Jesus Christ, Our Lord and Savior? Maybe this is funny to you, but I can tell you that God and all His angels in Heaven aren't laughing. Not at all."

I opened my mouth to say something—to explain—but, inexplicably, nothing came out. A strange paralysis clamped shut my mouth, leaving my tongue as stiff and dry as a piece of jerky. I noticed how Jesus's upturned eyes seemed to take in his new horns, two outlandish corkscrews that sprung abruptly from his head, and the suffering on his face took on new meaning. Shoney shifted from one foot to the other, unsure how to proceed. Finally, he squatted so his face was directly in front of mine and said, very slowly and clearly, "Maybe in your country, it's all right to draw on the face of Buddha or Hare Krishna or what have you. But they are false idols, and we call the people who worship them *heathen idolaters.*" He pronounced "idolaters" in the true Southern fashion, each vowel rolled and stretched like taffy at a pulling party. "Here in America, we honor each and every image of Jesus Christ, and *anyone* who makes a mockery of the suffering he went through on our account" — and here he looked at me sharply, his eyes glinting like chips of ice — "is a Pharisee and will burn in Hell." I nodded. I heard the sound of a gate close, far away. In that moment I understood that my soul had been judged and found wanting. It didn't matter that I wasn't the culprit. Shoney was God's appointed helper, and it was in his power to point me to the Promised Land — or consign me to Perdition. I wanted to tell Shoney that I didn't do it, that I would never, in a million years, draw on the face of Jesus — that I was *good* — but I couldn't. Under his unrelenting gaze, I felt myself slipping slowly, slowly, as if the film of my life had suddenly jammed in the projector, toward the place I feared most, the bottomless abyss I'd heard so much about. I could find no words to save myself.

Looking back, it's a mystery to me why I wasn't able to speak in my defense. *Maybe in your country … heathen idolaters … here in America.* Shoney's words left a ghostly echo in my brain. I'd held myself up as a real American to shame Juanita, and in the end, I'd been exposed as a sham. I wondered if it was divine justice for my cruelty to Juanita — the hand of God holding me back and serving up my just deserts. Then, too, there was the voice in the darkest corner of my mind: Maybe, it whispered, maybe I'd gotten exactly what I deserved.

Shoney continued down the aisle, and I looked at Juanita to see if she understood anything Shoney had said to me — if she could see the stain that now marked me, like an illness or a curse. Her head was bent over her desk, but when Shoney reached the end of the aisle, she looked up and met my eyes. Her face was expressionless. Then she smiled at me. It was a luminous smile, and like the one she had given the boy under the table, it was full of kindness. But there was something else there, something strong and alive, like the grip of a steady hand in deep water. It was the kind of smile a sister might give to a sister, or a mother to a child.

THEN ONE DAY YOU GIVE
A GUY YOUR LEGS

Jennafer D'Alvia

(from *34*th *Parallel*)

I t happens like this. You hang out in a place. Let's say Central Park, at the dance skaters' circle, and over some time, maybe a few months, you get really into the scene: You roller-skate around the rink, play chess on the benches, and shoot the shit with people who wander into the area—everyone from investment bankers, to Columbia professors, to guys who sell bags of weed on the edge of the pavement. The atmosphere's like a party, only better. Everyone's happy all the time. You don't know if it's the endorphins, the fresh air, or what—and you don't even care. You've finally found a place to go.

Eventually, you meet this guy in the park. He's part of the scene, just like you are. He's black and poor and a double-amputee in a wheelchair. You're middle class, white and able-bodied. In short, you're two guys who dig the scene, and you hit it off.

This guy in the wheelchair, Louie—he's always there in the park, watching you and giving pointers, because before he lost his legs he was a damn good skater. You've never seen him skate. That was prior to your time, but absolutely everybody says how good he was, so you believe it.

Little by little his advice becomes something more. Full-blown lessons. Louie explains everything to you: figure eights, edge work, loops, jumps; and when you're not getting it, he uses his hands to mimic feet, so he can *show* you what to do. The first time he does that, you kind of laugh, because you think he's making a joke. But Louie ignores you and keeps on patiently making the skate pattern with his hands, until you lock in, and his hands seem almost like feet, and you start to feel the motion he wants you to copy. The way he does that, somehow, reminds you of *The Karate Kid*, the scene where the old guy makes the kid paint all his fences and wax his cars, but the whole time he's teaching him the basic karate moves. You've always wanted to be a student of a real-life master, and that's what's going on now with Louie. That's how it feels.

You have a job, sure you do. You're an IT guy who spends his days going to companies and fixing their problems. You've always liked your work, but now your job feels like your hobby while the park stuff is your real life. Everything's gotten flipped around, everything you care about; and the lessons with Louie continue pretty much every day.

You never call each other. You and Louie just meet in the park whenever the weather's decent, and your skating gets better and better, until you feel like you're in the training montage of a movie, and for once, you're doing something that's good for your soul and good for you at the same time. You've had fun before, but never like this.

Then one day, you roll into the park, and Louie's right there sitting in his chair by the bench. He says he needs a favor, and you tell him you'll do it, without even knowing what it is.

"I've got cancer," Louie says, and the word sticks in his throat, like he didn't realize what it meant until he said it.

"Damn," you say, because you never would have thought that, though maybe you should have. Maybe you should have considered that Louie might not be the healthiest of guys.

He nods, then lights a cigarette. You try not to look at him until he's ready to go on. After a few puffs, he starts up again. It turns out he lost his Medicaid coverage, due to "an asinine thing" he did—as he puts it. He won a small lottery a few years back—five grand, and he never told the government. "I don't mean to make a long story long," Louie says. "But I think you should know the whole truth." He needs an operation— soon—or he'll die.

Louie pauses there, and by this time you're pretty sure he's asking for money. To tell the truth, you're not thrilled about this. In the back of your mind you've always kind of wondered if Louie might not hit you up for money one day. Of course, you were hoping he wouldn't. Him asking, you giving—the whole thing makes you uncomfortable. Like maybe that's all you're good for with Louie, and everything else you've been doing together doesn't mean one damn thing.

But then Louie starts on another tack. "I don't know if you know this about me," he says. "But I can dance the hustle pretty good." He smirks boyishly.

"I mean, at least I could when I was up walking. I used to win prizes all the time." His speech starts to pick up speed, and you can tell he's getting excited. "It just so happens," he says, "that there's a hustle contest in a few weeks' time with enough prize money to pay for my operation."

You don't know how to hustle. You don't even really know what the steps are. But, of course, Louie could teach you.

"You could train me," you blurt, and you expect him to perk up at that, but instead he looks confused.

He takes another puff on his cigarette, leans forward, and he says in a serious tone — like this is finally it, what he really wanted to say all along,

"Rich, I know it's a lot, but I need your legs."

"Louie," you say. "It's the least I could do." And you mean it. You're just relieved he's not asking for money. And, of course you want to help him. The only problem is you don't know if you can win the contest. And you say that too. You want to be honest with him.

"The thing is," Louie says — and now he sounds apologetic — "I don't need you, Richie. I just need your legs. I need to borrow them." He's talking so softly it's almost a whisper, and finally you get it.

He *literally* wants your legs. You don't know how it could possibly work, but you're sure that's what he means. You hear yourself say, "That's too much." But this is the least of what you feel. You want to run away from Louie, on the very legs he's asking for. They're your legs, yours.

Louie says that he knows, *he knows*, it's a lot to ask, but the thing is that the legs need to be the exact right size. If they don't fit perfectly (again he's talking fast), he might be able to walk on them, but he'll never be able to dance.

"And you and I have almost the exact same build," he says, and he looks at you, like he knows you'll be surprised. And you are surprised, which kind of puts your fear on hold for a second. You've always thought about Louie as being short. But now in your mind, you unfold him up out of the chair, and you realize that he's not short, or wouldn't be if he wasn't always sitting. He'd be exactly your height: five feet eleven.

"I always wanted that extra inch," Louie tells you, and winks. Then he flicks his cigarette to the pavement. You step on it and stub out the butt, before you realize what you're doing.

You look at Louie who's looking at you.

"It doesn't matter that you're white and I'm black," he says. "That's not gonna affect things — in case you're wondering."

"It's not that," you say quickly to cover his remark. "It's just that I *need* my *legs*." You can't even believe you have to explain it.

"Oh, don't worry," Louie says, "I'm not gonna leave you high and dry. While I've got your legs, you can have mine." He taps the right wheel of his chair.

You imagine it. You imagine sitting in Louie's wheelchair with legs that are amputated mid-thigh. And you look at Louie, really take him in for the first time. You force yourself to take note of exactly where his two legs end. Louie's looking at the pavement and biting his lower lip. This is the first time you're seeing him frown. Up until now it's been all about what Louie's been able to do for you: your skating, your learning, your fun. And you never actually thought about Louie, about his life outside the park. How does he carry his groceries? you wonder. How long does it take him to get home on the bus?

Every night when you skate Louie out of the park, you leave him loading onto the bus ramp for his ride back to Brooklyn. "See ya, Louie!" you call out, and then you're on your way. You skate up Broadway alongside the traffic. You love the feeling you get when the traffic lights stop the cars and let you go gliding through. Now you realize, once upon a time, Louie used to have that feeling too. You just can't leave him high and dry like that.

"Okay, Louie," you say. "I'll do it."

He doesn't move, but there's a flicker in his eyes, and you see that he never for a second thought you actually would. Then comes his grin—pure joy—and he's not gonna question your offer. He's not gonna ask you if you're sure. It's a done deal.

Friday night, Louie comes as planned. Just before he gets there, you start to have misgivings. You don't want to do it. You never *wanted* to. Of course, you want to help Louie, but again you're back to the fact—the irrefutable fact—that it's just too much.

You feel your legs stretching out below you and you notice that they're a greater portion of yourself than you ever realized. They're heavy, especially your quads, which have developed from skating, but it's not only that. Before, the legs always seemed to be just limbs—like arms. Just two out of four appendages, but now you realize, in terms of body mass, they're like half of you.

The bell rings, and Louie labors to make an entrance. His wheels push at the door, then roll back, then push again. He can't get through. Normally, you'd jump up and help, but your emotions are all jumbled up. How can you say no to Louie? How can you refuse a guy who labors like that, just to get through the door. It's only a couple of hours, you tell yourself.

Finally Louie rams the door hard, shoving himself inside. He seems larger in your apartment than in the park, and the chair is ungainly, like a bicycle dumped into your personal space.

You both say, "Hey," and after that neither of you knows what to say. It doesn't matter though, because Louie loses no time. He rolls up next to the bed and parallel-parks the chair, then uses his arms to lift himself up onto the mattress next to you. "You ready?" he asks.

"How does it work?" You didn't actually consider that before.

"Oh, this part is easy," he tells you. "It's all on the basis of pressure points." Louie leans over and presses his thumbs around on the middle of your left thigh, as if he's searching for something. Then he looks at you and says, "This may feel kind of strange, but it shouldn't hurt." You hold your breath. He pushes his thumbs, firmly now, into two points on either side of the thigh. When the leg separates you fall backward from the loss of weight. "Sorry," he says, but he keeps moving. As your leg joins to his stump, there's a whisper of a sucking sound. When he goes for the right, you use your arms to brace yourself. A couple seconds later the procedure is done. Surprisingly, there's no blood, not a drop.

Louie leans forward and touches his (your) toes. Then he shakes the legs a little bit, warming them up. Your pale knees bob up and down.

"They feel good," he says. "Just right."

He swings the legs over and stands up on them. Louie's surprisingly tall, as he walks around the bedroom, slowly at first, but then with more confidence. The legs really do suit him. His gait is graceful and unhurried, so different from yours. And you feel an odd jealousy at the way he's able to make your legs glide with ease across the floor. Aside from the color, it's as if they belong to him.

He takes a pair of black leather dance shoes from his bag and puts them on. They fit no problem. You ask if they're his.

He nods. "Yeah. I kept 'em."

When he finishes tying his shoes, he gets up and walks around, as if he only just put on shoes and not legs too. At the door, he turns to you. "You wanna practice getting on and off the chair?"

"No. I'm alright." He catches you by surprise with that.

Louie nods and purses his lips, as if he knows exactly how you're feeling. But you don't think he does. Louie never lent his legs out; they were just gone. He probably woke up in a hospital without them. You, on the other hand, are about to watch your legs walk away. It's strange even now to see them across the length of the room. It's like a photo, like they're already not really here.

Louie hesitates, looking at you. Then, he slips out the door.

A *Voyager* rerun starts, and the crew fills the bridge in their red and black costumes. You feel all the weightlessness of space around their ship, and your body is so light that you put your arm on the bed to steady yourself.

The scenes from the episode slide one into another. Alien hucksters smile and bargain with the captain, and always the vastness of space stalks them. By the time the danger is gone, and all the characters are back on the bridge, charting the next adventure, you know for sure that Louie's never coming back. It was all a ruse from the beginning: a leg scam. He must have picked you out because your legs were the right size, and then buttered you up with the teaching.

Why would Louie teach you for free, for hours and hours, days and days? Just for the fun of it? You're not exactly a skating phenom that any teacher would be thrilled to work with. You're just a guy — a guy with the right-sized legs.

You imagine your legs atop a hoard of limbs that Louie's got stashed in some grubby apartment in Brooklyn. Brownsville, the neighborhood name comes to you. You think that's where Louie lives. Is that where Louie lives? None of these details had mattered before. That was something you always liked about the relationship, how casual it was. It reminded you of childhood — the way you'd see a kid on the playground, and for no particular reason, the two of you would start hanging out. Louie was just cool, right from the get-go. He was different from the other New Yorkers who race around like they're stuck in fast forward. He suckered you in with that patient demeanor. You picture him strolling up Fifth Avenue in a new suit, your legs filling out the pants. Louie's got all the time in the world.

You're too depressed to look down at the bed where your legs once were, so you just keep your eyes on the TV screen: another *Voyager*, *Dead Eye*, commercials.

Finally, some time later, there's a noise in the hallway and then Louie steps through the door into the bedroom. You almost puke from relief. In fact, some of your lunch actually comes up into the back of your mouth, but you swallow it down- — he's back. Everything's okay. Louie's eyes are shining. He looks better than you've ever seen him, healthier, happier. He's wearing a grin from ear to ear, and in about two seconds you are too.

"How was it?" you ask him, even though you know the answer.

"Oh, man," Louie says, in his peculiar unhurried way, "I had a ball. I forgot what that even felt like, it's been so long." He looks up and shakes his head in a religious kind of way.

It's as if the air Louie's breathing is super-oxidized, he's got so much energy. You know that feeling from those special skate times when everything clicks and you're inside the rhythm, just bouncing and floating across the paving tiles.

Louie steps back into a hustling sequence with his eyes closed, as if he can still hear the music. You watch and see this incredible side of Louie that you've never seen before. Then Louie cuts the move short and stops to look at you. "Sorry, man," he says. "I should get these back to you."

"It's okay," you hear yourself say. "Take an extra minute." Now that he's back you can wait.

But Louie hops up onto the bed next to you. This time, he hands you a leg and tells you to, "Go ahead," so you fit it back onto your thigh and then the other. There's nothing to it really. You move your legs around, bobbing the knees up and down the way Louie did a few hours earlier. They're back and they work!

Then, as Louie swings over onto his chair, an amputee once more, it feels wrong, like he should have a pair of legs too. Everyone should.

That's when you wonder how he lost them. It's not the first time you've thought about it, but it's the first time you feel you have the right to ask.

"How did it happen, Louie?"

"Huh?"

"Your legs."

"Oh." The creases in his face deepen into waves of pain. "Car accident," he says with an effort. "The Bronx. Front of the car was crushed. Lucky—to be alive."

It's a speech he's probably made a thousand times, but it takes so much out of him just to get through it. You're sorry you asked. Without letting him see, you tighten the muscles in your thighs, calves, toes.

"Hey Louie," you say to change the subject. "How did you know how to do this—this leg transfer thing?"

He shrugs.

"No, really. I mean, I had no idea it was even possible."

He snorts softly, and shrugs again, this time with his palms up. Then he says slowly and clearly, "*Why* would you know it? Why would you *need* to?"

He snaps the brakes off and easily maneuvers the chair to the center of the room.

"You wanna take the legs on Sunday?" you ask. That's just two days away. You're a little surprised with yourself, but Louie grins at you.

"Yes, I do," he says.

You hang out with Louie while he practices for the contest, then cheer when he wins. After the operation and a couple rounds of chemo, Louie's back in his chair, back in the park and teaching you just like before. Only now when he wants to show you a move, he doesn't use his hands to imitate feet anymore. Instead, you just pass him the legs and watch from the bench.

Some days when you're tired, you let Louie skate the legs for a while. Other times, he just yells from his chair, "Hey, Richie, this is my jam," and you pass him the limbs and let him have a go.

Eventually, it occurs to you that it'd be easier to share the legs if you lived together, so you do that too. Louie moves in. Now, when you sit around watching the game at night, whichever of you needs to make a beer run takes the legs, and the other one just chills out on the couch.

You know this can't go on forever. For one thing, the cancer may come back. Or one of you may get a girlfriend. Or something else may come along to throw a monkey wrench into things, but for now it's just you and Louie sharing a pair of legs and a long, amazing summer.

ROAD TRIP WITH A
DEAD THERAPIST

Isabelle Deconinck

(From *Five Points*)

ugust 8, 1 PM

Taos, New Mexico. We're lounging at the edge of a pool, soaking up the dry heat, when my phone rings. I really wish people wouldn't bother me now. This is our last hour of vacation, the last stop before we embark on the long drive back to New York City, where D. and I will resume our separate lives in rent-stabilized, closet-sized studios. The phone rings again, slicing through the quiet of the afternoon with irritating insistence. I roll up the straps of my bathing suit, whisper, "I'll be right back," and hop onto the hot cement, away from the pool, to take the call.

"It's Norma," I hear. "D.'s therapist."

I'm confused. "Hi," is all I can think of saying.

"Susan died this morning. The cancer exploded in her body—that's what the doctor said."

Susan is *my* therapist. The cement is burning my feet, and I step back to a patch of soil with yellow grass withering over jagged cracks.

"She was surrounded by the people who loved her," Norma continues. "Then she sent everybody home and was alone with the nurse when she died at 2 AM"

I haven't asked for any of these details, but I take in every word.

"Do you have any questions?"

I anxiously search for one I should have thought of.

"Was it ... violent?"

"I'm not sure about violent, but it went very fast." She pauses before adding, "You were very special to her."

I want to ask what "special" means, or if every client is called "special" today, but my throat is as parched as the red earth my toes are gripping.

"I'm very sorry," she says finally.

Then the conversation is over.

I walk back to the towels where D. is still sprawled, face offered to the sun. She doesn't open her eyes when I crouch next to her.

"Do you have to answer every phone call you get?"

"It was Norma."

"What?" She flips off her sunglasses, frowning.

"Susan died." My voice is curiously flat, as if the sun had sucked out its last bit of energy.

"Oh shit!"

She sits down and wraps an arm around me. I wish I could lean into it, but instead I clasp my knees as if I were inside a fish bowl, the ripples of the pool warping its wall and the screams of a child bouncing loudly against it.

"You're right," I say choking. "I shouldn't have answered." Suddenly everything seems unbearably confining, even D.'s embrace, and I get up. I walk to the water where I dip my body, slowly, so as not to upset my precarious balance. Something is wriggling the air out of my solar plexus, forcing the ribs in, an odd, almost painful sensation. I must speak to Susan about this, I think, before remembering that Susan is dead.

*

NORMA HAD REFERRED ME TO Susan three years ago. D. and I had already been lovers for a while when I realized it was time to confront my inability to commit to anything permanent. Ever since, I'd been talking to Susan twice a week, tunneling into my life with the stubbornness of a mouse and entrusting her with feelings I didn't know were there.

"I promise I'll tell you if the cancer gets worse," Susan had said.

Then when did it get worse? Since our phone session on Saturday? And what about her call three days ago? I was washing a pear in the sink and tucked the receiver under my chin.

"I'm under the weather. I have to cancel tomorrow's phone session."

She had the breathy voice of someone in a hurry.

"It doesn't matter." But of course it did. I was looking forward to our time, her undivided attention as I cautiously exposed the hidden parts of my self.

The water was bouncing off the fruit, and I did nothing to prevent the droplets from wetting my sleeves.

"I hope you're better soon," I added after a silence lasting longer than it should. She didn't say she'd e-mail later, but I assumed she would. She always did.

August 8, 3 PM

"Maybe she couldn't face the fact that she was dying," D. says, studying the winding highway leading us to Santa Fe.

We've begun our trip back to New York City. The pressure in my chest is now a rope around my rib cage, tightening. I'm driving because I'm better at steering down a steep slope, although I'm not sure anymore. When the road doesn't curve around purple cliffs, it edges along abrupt precipices at whose bottom the Rio Grande glistens, oblivious to what else is happening. After the canyon, the view becomes spectacular. A stretch of red mesas dotted with sagebrush bumps into a barrier of mountains cut black against the bright sky. Such a view doesn't matter to Susan anymore, and it doesn't matter to me either, as I speed up through a series of hairpin turns. It's only because D. is there next to me that I slow down, ignoring the five cars tailgating me and waiting for the first opportunity to pass.

August 9, 9 AM

I'm having breakfast in a garden on the outskirts of Santa Fe. The branch of an apple tree is touching the rim of my plate. D. is inside the house, chatting with friends we've spent the night with. I don't want to chat with friends, so I'm sitting alone, slouched in a metallic chair that digs into my spine. All of a sudden, a presence fills up the air, enfolds me and lifts me up. It's in the dry, sun-washed foliage crackling like gravel with each gust of wind, in the faint gurgle of a hose already turned on, and in the offering of this branch, bowing under the weight of small green apples clustered under silvery leaves. I do not move for fear that Susan will go away.

2 PM

I-40. Crossing into north Texas — endless flatlands of straw-like grass with not even the shadow of a shrub to protect oneself. Trucks are everywhere, giant trucks growing into the rearview mirror, then roaring past our small, used Volkswagen at ninety miles an hour. They're like slaps. You know they're coming, you just don't know when. And it doesn't matter how much you prepare yourself, gripping the steering wheel. When one passes by, the car veers to the right, and it is with damp palms and a pounding heart that I realign the wheels inside the corridor of two straight, broken lines.

After Amarillo, one of Norma's sentences pops into my head: "She was surrounded by the people who loved her." I lean toward D., who's gazing through the window.

"And who are we, the patients? Professional acquaintances?"

An suv with tinted glass enters the right lane, cutting me off. I honk the horn and start chasing the car.

"Did you see that? Acting like no one else matters but his fat car!"

"Why don't you slow down." D. squeezes my thigh. "Of course Susan cared about you."

I release the pedal, but not before flashing my brights at the suv racing away.

6 PM

Western Oklahoma. Fields of upturned orange soil are scattered over the green farmland. How did such beautiful soil end up in this otherwise barren place? The trucks are nowhere to be seen at this hour, and the sky is picking up the color of the earth. I drive effortlessly on the empty three-lane highway, when words Susan said last week, last month, years ago, resurface: "Intimacy begins in your own heart," or "Don't run away from pain: Stay with it." Truths I refused to hear because I still had time to ignore them. I'm amazed they haven't fled with her death. On the contrary, they're louder than ever, shouting from the side of the road for me to finally let them in.

*

"WE SHOULD LOOK FOR A MOTEL," D. says, fidgeting in the passenger's seat. I continue driving. I drive until my elbows are stiff as cardboard, then park next to a Hampton Inn in Clinton, Oklahoma. The room has a smell of wet hair, and a suspicious, brown carpet upon which D. and I warily proceed. Suddenly I long to hear Susan's voice. As soon as D. steps into the shower, I dial her service, except for the last digit. My index finger trembles uncontrollably. What if the number has been forwarded, and someone answers? I blush like I've been caught red-handed. Water is pounding against the tiles of the bathroom, almost as loud as my heartbeat. I quickly hit the last "2." Susan's voice is still there, bodiless, composed, asking to leave a message. But it's not the caring one I remember, rising and falling peacefully, inviting mine to do the same after a long, hectic day. I hang up and start unpacking.

*

LATER THAT EVENING, I'm reading e-mails, kneeling on the bed that occupies our entire motel room. I learn from Norma that there'll be a memorial for Susan in New York City. I type:

"Can I help?"

I don't expect her to say yes. She doesn't. "It doesn't feel right for you to be involved in this way."

The only reason I don't slam down the lid of my laptop is that it's mine, and I'll be the one to pay if it breaks.

"She is trying to protect you," says D., pulling me onto the comforter.

"Protect me from what? Susan is dead."

"And what would you like her to do? You're lucky she's the one who told you and not a complete stranger. And didn't she say you could get in touch if you have any questions?"

"You're right, you're right."

I bury my face in a pillow. D. rubs my shoulders, sore from driving. After a while, her touch becomes lighter; she lingers in the small of my back and eases down the elastic of my underwear. I grow uncomfortable, as if Susan had stuck around and was hovering now in a corner of the ceiling.

"What's the matter?"

"Maybe later," I mutter.

Her fingers return to my shoulders, where they gently knead a knot. "I'm going to create a support group for Susan's patients," I decide between two grunts. "This way, we can reminisce about her together." I begin drafting a letter in my mind, which no one could refuse to answer, but at the thought of meeting other people Susan cared for, my neck muscles tense all over again.

"Forget it." I roll over. "I don't want to meet anybody."

"You can always talk to me," D. suggests, fluffing the pillow back to life before leaning into it.

August 10, 6:30 AM

"Can we talk?" I text Norma from a saggy chair, jammed between the bed and the wall. Dawn is peeking from around heavily starched curtains.

"Sure. Call me now. Just walking the dog."

"I don't understand," I tell her over the phone. "I don't understand how I can have my regular session with Susan, and the following week she is dead. Didn't she know she was dying?"

Norma gives me the facts, how Susan began losing her cognitive faculties on the evening of Saturday and was brought to the hospital, how they discovered that the cancer had spread to her liver, the lining of her stomach, her brain.

"Wasn't she undergoing chemotherapy?" I interrupt.

"It didn't work, and she was considering alternative options."

D. enters the room with a large towel knotted above her breasts and the imprint of goggles making wide circles around her eyes. I silently mouth "Norma" while pointing at the receiver.

"To answer your question," Norma continues, "no, I don't think she realized she was dying. She thought she was going to the hospital for a few days and could resume her work once she was out. She was a close friend, and it's a terrible loss for all of us."

D. is motioning to me to get up so she can retrieve her clothes. I can't think of anything to add on the phone but fear losing the connection.

"Is D. with you?" Norma asks abruptly. "Can you put her on the phone?"

I surrender the receiver to D., who pulls on her pants before leaning back on the chair.

"Hi, Norma .... Yes, I'm fine."

I could retreat to the bathroom, but having no use for it, I leave our room and squat in the crudely lit blue-carpeted corridor. Early risers greet me — a man who tips his cap without asking questions, and two overweight women who cut short their conversation, the fabric of their pants making an annoying swishing noise between their thighs. After ten interminable minutes, I get up and loudly knock: "Are you done?"

D. glances through the half-opened door before releasing it. "Where were you?"

"Waiting."

"Nobody asked you to leave."

I come in, my sullen face leading.

"And I'm certainly not the one closing you out," she says, and marches to the mirror to apply her dark lipstick.

10 AM

Back on the road, I replay the conversation with Norma over and over, the steering wheel getting stickier by the hour.

"Listen," I say to D., who's scanning the dial for a jazz station.

"You still want to talk about Susan?"

"Do you mind?"

She turns off the radio.

I repeat to her what I pieced together from Norma's scraps of information. The story gets fleshed out as we journey, just as the vegetation spreads denser and greener. Along a highway in Arkansas, silvery vines cover the trees of a forest. You can't see the branches or the trunks, only the luscious blanket of leaves smoothing out every angle. By the time we reach Little Rock, I realize that Susan was hospitalized the evening of our last phone session, that she canceled our next appointment from her hospital bed, that she didn't have time to say goodbye.

5 PM

"IF YOU WERE TO DIE TODAY, DO YOU KNOW WHERE YOU'RE GOING?" It's hard to miss the black and white billboard rising from the low bushes like some ghostly apparition. I glance at the side of the road, half-expecting an answer. Nothing happens.

"Maybe they want us to think about it a little bit longer," D. chuckles.

But the following miles offer nothing other than the same rows of bushes, more anemic and gray as we approach the next town, and bearing no hint of an afterlife.

10 PM

Another Hampton Inn. I want to know more about Susan, and I don't. "I don't really know you," I once told her during a session. "Of course you do," she replied matter-of-factly. I carried her answer back home like a gift, convinced that the Susan I knew was the one who really mattered. But tonight, kept awake by the tremor of a struggling air conditioner and shadows I do not recognize, I realize I know nothing. I lift D's leg, flung across me, and in the bluish glow of my computer screen, I Google Susan's full name. Death notices show up. I learn she liked dogs and cats and become uneasy at everything else I wasn't aware of. I learn she was a professional belly dancer—a talented one—and I panic, unable to fit this information into the Susan I knew. I jump back to the previous screen to erase what I've read, but it's all I can see now: Susan's arms gracefully curving in the air, her hips swaying with an unabashed ease I've only dreamed of experiencing.

*

A YEAR AGO SUSAN GOT PNEUMONIA, so we conducted our sessions over the phone. I got used to her voice softly speaking into my ear and occasionally interrupted by coughing. Three months later, I was back at her office, nervously pushing the button of an elevator that wouldn't go any faster than the speed it was programmed to follow. Susan emerged at the end of the hallway, beckoned me as usual, and spun on one heel, her brown, curly hair swinging behind her. I hastily followed and noticed that her pants were too big. Her jacket was draped in sharp angles. She'd lost a third of her weight.

"What happened to you?" I asked as soon as the door shut.

"Oh," she shrugged. "I needed to lose weight."

There'd been many elephants in the room since I began seeing Susan, but this one wasn't mine. A rash had broken out on her forehead, and I averted my eyes, because clearly I'd been staring. For the rest of the session, I was fixed on a knot carved into the wooden floor and did not leave it until Susan said, suppressing a coughing fit, "It's still me. I'm the same person."

"Of course," I compliantly replied.

*

IT WASN'T UNTIL THE FOLLOWING week that I asked the question. D. and I were spending a few days in Vermont, so I scheduled a phone session. I sat on the patio of our cabin, facing the tall silhouette of a mountain darkened by a forest of spruces.

"Susan—" I slipped into a silent spell, then heard myself saying, "Was there something other than pneumonia?"

"Yes."

"Do you have cancer?"

My words surprised me.

"Yes," she said again. "Although it's not an aggressive one, and I'm much better."

Her voice was calm as usual, but I sank deeper into the plastic lounge chair as if the mountain itself had fallen on top of me.

"Can I ask which organ?"

"Does it matter?"

"I guess not." But it did. Organs aren't the same. "It's the lung," I finally said. "Isn't it?"

"Listen, I have a lot of support and I'm really much better."

She had an edge I hadn't heard before. I said nothing. The evening was settling down. A cool humidity was crawling out of the woods, and I shivered.

"Will you tell me if it gets worse?"

She took a long, barely audible breath. "Yes, I promise."

*

AND SHE DID. She told me about the second round of chemotherapy eight months later. She'd just taken a week off. I entered her office, which wasn't really an office but a rented room with nothing in it other than two black chairs facing each other and a school table with a box of Kleenex. The windows were rumbling from the Park Avenue traffic while I unfastened my messenger bag.

"I hope you had a restful vacation."

I'd phrased the sentence so that she could answer "Yes," as I knew she wouldn't want to say more. Susan looked perplexed. Her hand was resting on the table, and I was struck by how exposed her veins were, long, purple lines traveling right at the surface of her pale skin, ready to escape. "I never said I was going on vacation."

"You didn't?" I slowly lowered myself in the chair, struggling to fit my over-sized bag between its legs.

"I had to start chemotherapy again. Although it's a small spot, smaller than the first one."

A fist was jammed inside my throat.

"What are you feeling?" Susan inquired.

I hesitated before mouthing, "Anger."

"Well, that makes two of us."

I glanced at her, startled. She was smiling that broad smile of hers, which used to dispel any shadows.

"Now, let's speak about you."

I stumbled, wondering how what I had to say could ever measure up against a lung spot, no matter how small, and I told her.

"But these sessions are about *your* life."

"Susan, are you going to stop working?"

"Of course not! I much prefer doing this than thinking about cancer."

So I spoke again, slowly, then more urgently, as if the act of sharing my private thoughts with her had the power to build a wall that could keep the cancer behind it.

August 11, 9:30 AM

"Why don't you let me drive?" D. asks, loading our bags into the trunk.

"I thought you weren't comfortable driving on highways."

"I can do it if I have to."

I hesitate at the front door, the parking lot already sun-struck at this early hour.

"Really, I don't mind," I say, and slip into the driver's seat. "Otherwise I'll just sit there and obsess about Susan."

"You're already obsessing."

D. settles in next to me and snaps the seat belt shut. I turn on the ignition. Our Volkswagen lurches forward. I swallow an apology and start again. The car inches ahead, obediently responding, and I sigh, relieved to be in control of at least this one thing.

*

ONE HOUR FROM MEMPHIS sheets of rain begin falling. The wipers don't work fast enough. Soon, the car ahead of us is reduced to two smudged red lights.

"We need to stop," D. says, wiping the fog that's formed on the inside of the windshield with crumpled tissues.

"And where would you like me to stop?" I ask, squinting. "We're on a highway. You see an exit? I don't."

The rain is hitting the roof with such force that I expect it to break through at any minute and pour over us. Then red lights are flashing in our faces. I press the brake pedal to the floor and slam my arm across D.

"Did I hit it?" I scream. "Did I hit the car?"

"No, you did not."

D. is rubbing her ribs. My hands are shaking. I want this rain to stop. I want this flow of cars to disappear. I want D. and me to not argue over things we won't remember tomorrow. I want Susan to be alive so I can tell her how much I already miss her. I want this cancer to show its ugly face so I can squash it between our car and the next one.

"Just breathe," D. whispers. "There's got to be an exit somewhere."

*

SOON AFTER, THE TRAFFIC JAMS. Fat raindrops are splattering onto the glossy highway. For the next forty-five minutes, I open and close windows, check the map for an exit, before finally dumping it in D.'s lap. Then we see it—a gigantic truck lying on its side, the cab hanging like a chicken whose neck has been snapped. A U-Haul has rammed into the guardrail, its back door ripped open, disclosing large sheets of yellow insulation dangling in the void.

"Keep moving!" A man with dripping hair and forceful gestures redirects the cars.

D. is sitting at the edge of her seat and clutching the dashboard with the tips of her fingers.

"Careful! Watch the glass."

But these are not pieces of glass. They're onions, hundreds of them scattered over the wet asphalt. I must be driving over some, even though I can't feel them, because the air is filling with their pungent smell. And it doesn't matter how quickly I close the windows; my eyes sting and I begin to cry. "Put on your signal and get to the right," D. urges. She points at a sign I can't read, then swivels her torso toward the back window. "Now!"

The tires squish on the slippery ramp. Soon we're driving through a town, separated from it by a curtain of rain that blurs the brick facades and encloses us in a deafening noise. .

"Now what?" I ask.

Just then, a towering sign appears like a smile lit up with missing teeth: "N NA'S DIN R EAT IN AND TAKE O T " I maneuver the car through the puddles of a bumpy parking lot, shut off the engine and headlights. D. retrieves an old, black umbrella from under the seat, and we hurry into a steamy room, where the smell of coffee and fried food commingles with a Southern drawl.

"I knew there was a place we could stop," D. says, grabbing the first available table. "You need to have a little bit of faith."

"I'm beginning to." My body collapses into a vinyl seat, and I toss her the car keys.

"Would you mind driving?"

August 12, 11 AM

We rest for a day in downtown Memphis. The blues are blasting through the open doors of shops and the sanitized aisles of Walgreens. We haven't encountered a city for days. People are everywhere, scurrying to work, hauling shopping bags, shouting on their cells, and miraculously getting out of my way as I wander down the avenue, shielded in a cocoon of silence. Since Susan's death, I tread more carefully, as if through wet cotton, like someone had let go of my hand and I'm learning to stand by myself.

"What planet are these people on?" I ask D.

"Come on!" She grabs my wrist and drags me through the sliding doors of a grand hotel, where a blast of cold air revives us. "Time to play." Then she dashes into a store displaying replicas of Elvis's clothes and eagerly rummages through the shelves. I trail behind, then find refuge on a stool against a wall.

D. is tugging at my elbow.

"Hmmm?"

"Do you like them?" She is fanning her toes in a brand-new pair of flip-flops. I wonder how much time we need to forget we're heading toward death and start thinking about shopping.

"Never mind. I guess this whole trip is going to be about Susan." She walks away, sandals slapping against her heels.

"Wait a minute!"

I jump off the stool. When I catch up with her, she shoves a shirt at me.

"Try this on."

Reluctantly, I make my way into a dressing room no bigger than a closet and put on the turquoise shirt—a color Susan used to wear, I can't help but notice.

"Let's see!" D. calls from the other side of the curtain.

So I come out. A faraway mirror catches my reflection—drooped silhouette with a punch of turquoise screaming for attention. I throw my shoulders back and start parading on the red carpet, getting taller and lighter with each step, as D. leans against the stool and gives me the thumbs up.

August 13, 4 PM

We're traveling along the Blue Ridge Mountains, a crest of forests delicately etched against a low, cloudy sky. On the other side of the road, a white fence follows the ups and downs of green hills, not wanting to be left behind. We could increase our pace and make it to New York late in the night, but I don't want to arrive. As long as we're driving, Susan is in the car. Already, she's journeyed with us through six states and 1,800 miles. When we return from lunch breaks at shady rest areas, I'm surprised not to actually find her in the back, her small frame wedged between the folding bike and cooler, watching over both of us.

*

WE STOP AT THE BORDER of West Virginia. I get out of the car, straighten my back, and rub one eyelid that's been twitching for days. Velvety woods are stretching to the horizon, the last hill barely distinguishable in the bluish mist. In the middle of the grass, a rabbit is staring at me, frozen. "Hi," I say, "Are you Susan?" It darts off into the dark underbrush. At the same moment, a flock of wild geese takes off right behind the car, and I duck my head. They're huge, silent birds, wavering under the pull of gravity, and I wonder if inside their puffed, creamy bellies, they're hiding the souls of dead people. They rise in the mauve sky, vigorously flapping their wings and extending their long, slim necks. Soon, all that's left is a black arrow, running across the horizon so smoothly you'd never know flying was ever a struggle.

"They've got a room!" D. hollers, bursting out of one more motel. The glass doors behind her mirror the sunset in orange. She cups her brows, waves as if we haven't seen each other for days, and rushes back to the parking lot, glowing in her tight jean shorts and tie-dye tank top. A scent of smoky pine floats by and I inhale it like it could vanish at any minute, like I've never inhaled pine before, letting it seep through folds of muscles and open new passages. D. reaches the car, panting.

"Let's stay here forever," I announce, grabbing her by the waist and sketching a few dance moves.

She hesitates, glancing around. "We'd better wait until we're in our room."

But I catch her moving lips, letting no air come between us.

THE OLD ECONOMY HUSBAND

Lesley Dormen

(From *The Best Place to Be* / Originally published in *The Atlantic*)

It was that summer, the summer we were fifty and the little Cuban boy went home to no mother, not the first West Nile virus summer but the second, the Hillary and *Survivor* summer, you know that summer, the summer the women were manhandled in the park and the kids lined up for Harry Potter, the summer we were fifty, all of us, fifty and holding, the ones a little older and the ones a little younger, fifty and holding, like thirty and holding only fifty, and it was summer and the ones who were rich were and the ones who weren't weren't but we were all fifty, every one of us, and holding.

We were in the city that summer because we couldn't afford a vacation and we couldn't afford a beach house, because our oven died and it was vintage 1929 or something and connected to the dishwasher in some complicated way having to do with converted residential hotels — in other words irreplaceable — and one thing led to another and now we had twenty thousand dollars' worth of European-made appliances on order. It was the summer we renovated the kitchen.

"Will you call the Miele place in the morning?" I asked Richard. "Will you remember to because I can't face it. Will you?" Our contractor was useless. Also he was in Brazil.

"I'll do it," Richard said. "I said I would."

"Because you have to, sweetie, OK?" What was I, deaf? He said he would.

One minute I was disgusted with myself for owning a fancy dishwasher I couldn't even pronounce — Meal? Mee-lay? May-lay? — the next I was in a rage over the incompetence of the people responsible for getting it to me. Those were the two ways I was. Everything that used to be in the kitchen was spread out all over the living room—one thing about a renovation was you saw all the stuff you never used with sickening clarity, the useless stupid juice glasses and the dust-encrusted early-eighties cappuccino maker and the rusted flour sifter and the grimy oven mitts from the Caribbean vacations, cartons of junk you dragged guiltily down the hall to the recycling room for the building staff to pick over. The bathroom was now the acting kitchen and a lot of stuff that used to be in the living room, specifically the dining room, was in my office.

We ate dinner there, in front of the TV. It was summer so there was nothing on. We were watching a biography of the actress Jane Seymour, Dr. Quinn, with the hair. How her first husband left her and her life was terrible, then she had a baby, then her life was terrible again, then she had another baby. Like that. Terrible, baby, terrible, baby, commercial, baby, baby, with some husbands thrown in and a castle and the hair.

*

RICHARD CARRIED OUR DIRTY dinner dishes to the bathroom—it was his week to cook and like a champ he'd brought in takeout burritos—and reappeared with dessert, from somewhere, on plates: pie. He kissed the top of my head. "Do you know that you're my fave?" he said. He said it a lot lately, probably picking up those voodoo vibes of double-dose Zoloft, of Tylenol PM addiction, of night-sweaty breakdown. Those crazy fifty-year-old women! He said "You're my fave" instead of "I love you" instead of "Take whatever hormone you want just don't get cancer" instead of "I'm sorry I already had children in my first marriage and didn't want any in my second and you didn't get to be a mother." Fine. He wasn't exactly sorry, but it was fine anyway. He was my fave, too. That was me, married to the one man who made me feel like my fiercest, most clear-hearted twelve-year-old self and not any of the men who made me feel that other way, that euphorically grandiose, desperately insecure, wildly libidinous twenty-five-year-old way.

We ate the pie.

Dr. Quinn was looking back, saying it was all worth it. I picked up the pie plates, headed for the bathroom, and considered walking straight out the door and shoving everything down the compacter. Throwing out was definitely doing it for me lately. I made a few mistakes: our income tax files from 1990 to 1995, a set of Berlitz tapes (French), the zip-in lining to Richard's raincoat. But why tell him now, when it was only July and he wouldn't need the coat until November. If I were a mother, my kids could be grown and gone by now. Or they could be triplets about to turn three. Or murdered or run over or autistic or kidnapped or cancer-riddled and bald or schizophrenic or in prison or nanny-shaken or searching for their real mother or late getting home from school. At least I'd been spared that, that's what I told myself, because I knew I'd never survive that, any of that, not a chance.

It was my first summer on earth as an orphan. Wasn't that every kid's fantasy? Well, it had been mine. I loved the Hayley Mills "Biography." *The Parent Trap* was a great movie. My mother died last spring. I was used to my father being dead—he died three years ago and I barely knew him. Now I was fifty, not a mother, not a daughter, and the kitchen was in the living room and I didn't know how I was supposed to behave.

We went to bed, Richard instantly asleep and making those putt-putt noises. I bounced around violently a few times, blew softly into his ear, huffed off to the living room sofa for a read, came back to bed and by then he'd quieted down. I fell asleep with my book open. At some point Richard woke, bookmarked my page, turned out my light, nuzzled my lips with my bite guard until I put it in.

*

HE WAS LONG AND LANKY, my husband, as straight-arrow decent as Jimmy Stewart. Not neurotic or tricky, not the least bit mean. He'd never taken a drug, not even pot. "Are you sure you're even an American?" I asked him. He never got pissed off at me, just came home with that open look on his face, now and then passing on stories about his temper—losing it with the pokey old people in the supermarket checkout line, with the virago in the laundry room who took his still-wet clothes out of the dryer, with the punk who threatened him on a street corner. When he cupped my head with his hand while we made love, I was startled all over again at the largeness of it, at what a man's hand can be, and I liked it, those big fingers twining my hair, I really liked it a lot, that largeness. I just kept forgetting how much I liked it, sexual memory malaise, like one of those eccentrically damaged Oliver Sacks people who couldn't remember a conversation beyond five minutes ago. The Woman Who Couldn't Retain the Memory of Pleasure. Doesn't every marriage contain its own evil twin? Maybe I was ours. Maylay, Mai Lai, malaise.

In the morning, Richard made the coffee in the bathroom and we asked each other how we slept and read the *Times*.

I was happy to get out of the apartment. Besides the money, it was why I took the job ghostwriting Winston Winter's book on etiquette. Three days a week I took the bus from lower Fifth Avenue to Winston Winter Lifestyles on upper Madison Avenue. Winston was Manhattan's most famous party and wedding planner. Today we were working on "Chapter Seven: How to Raise a Gracious Child."

*

I'D ALWAYS MADE A DECENT LIVING as a magazine writer. My specialty was sex and dating, the five-friend, two-shrink service piece dissecting the romantic lives of single women in their twenties and thirties and, occasionally, in their early forties, though not in any of the unmentionable decades after that, for *Marvelous Woman* magazine. I even wrote a column for single women called "On Your Own." Then one day I realized that I couldn't write another word on that subject. What else was there to say? How could I ask one more woman or one more representative for women what was going right or wrong in her life, what she wanted that she didn't have, what she wound up getting even though she had never claimed to want it and never asked for it. I couldn't even bear to read any more articles about women's lives, especially the serious ones written by the very smartest women that showed irrefutably all that remained wrong with women and the culture that served women despite everyone's best intentions and efforts. I couldn't bear thinking, Yes! Exactly! My brain hurt from nodding my head in so much agreement.

"Just do what you want for a while. We'll dip into the nest egg if we have to," Richard said when I told him how adrift I felt. He was an Old Economy husband. He never wanted to dip into the nest egg, ever. His willingness to dip into it now alarmed me. Was now the time for the dipping to begin? And if now wasn't the time, when was the time? I asked him again to explain the financial strategy of investing for the long haul.

"Isn't the haul getting shorter by the minute?" I said. "Well, that's one way to look at it," he said.

*

I SAID NO THE FIRST TIME Winston Winter Lifestyles asked me to write the etiquette book. Ghostwriter? Way too beside-the-point—whatever the point was. They said, "You don't understand! It's not just a guide to etiquette! It's a guide to the new spiritual etiquette!" Then they offered me a little bit more money, enough to make their original offer feel that much more insulting. I've noticed that people tend to offer you things when you say no to them, one more important lesson I've learned too late in life for it to do me any good. Didn't I have to earn *some* money? I mean, I'd never *not* earned money. Richard's salary had already taken a dive. After years of Wall Street money-managing, he was handling finances for a small foundation. He had an office near the Empire State Building. What about haircuts? Was the nest egg expected to pay for those? What about long-term care insurance? Not to mention the looming facelift expense. I was beginning to suspect that the whole thing was careering toward some horrifying endgame in whichpeople behaved either well or badly, in which strategies either panned out or didn't pan out, in which being a person with good bone structure meant one thing and truly understanding what it means to forgive and forget meant something else. I didn't know what I wanted to do. I wanted to train a golden retriever puppy to be a working companion for the handicapped, then weep when the time came to turn the dog over to its grateful new owner.

Maybe it would be good for me to take on an egoless project, I told myself. That way I'd make some money and empty myself at the same time, create room for something new, something meaningful. Not that etiquette was meaningless. Even the rudest people expressed outrage at the revolting treatment they received from others. No, etiquette was meaningful.

There might be travel involved, Winston's people added, and they pointed out that Winston Winter Lifestyles had an arrangement with the Four Seasons Hotel. Some exquisitely brought-up underling must have recalled me mentioning in a meeting that I had found the beds in that hotel chain to be the only beds I could sleep on without taking a ten-milligram Ambien first. I said OK, I would do it.

*

RICHARD LEFT FOR WORK. I watched for him from the window, and when he reached the corner I waved, adding a manic shimmy to make him laugh. An hour later, I collected my stuff and walked to the bus stop at University Place and Ninth Street, directly in front of the sexy lingerie boutique. I loved my neighborhood. I'd lived in it for over twenty years, half of those years the tail end of my long single-woman life, a drama played out just a few blocks adjacent to where I lived now. Every time I left the house I saw overlapping pieces of my present and my past: the dead-in-the-water blind dates, the still married ex-lover, former colleagues and current shopkeepers, the assortment of nodding-acquaintance neighbors. Once I saw the Pope pass by in his Popemobile. I'd lived here long enough to see my UPS man go completely gray.

A dozen tiny day campers on a leash drifted past Bagel Bob's. When I first moved to Greenwich Village, I never saw a single infant or toddler on the street. Where were all the families? Maybe on the Upper West Side. I was a suburban girl, transplanted to the city on the morning after the sexual revolution. Those were the days when you slept with every man who so much as caught your eye across a party. I tumbled desperately in and out of love, exempt from worrying about my future when love appeared, thrown back into teeth-grinding uncertainty when it vanished. One day, without warning, the new mothers appeared. They blanketed the sidewalks like startling spring snow, pale, dazed and puffy-eyed, bravely lipsticked, their babies in a pouch. But it was the mothers who looked newborn.

When the bus swung over to the curb, I climbed on along with three bus-specific women, capable widows with decorative brooches and sensible shoes. The bus was so civilized. I settled into a window seat, and we bullied our way toward Union Square. At Park Avenue South it turned north and began making stops again. By the time we began the crawl up Madison Avenue, there was standing room only.

*

I SAW WINSTON WINTER on *Oprah* once. He was explaining how to plan a wedding that included white doves, Byzantine place settings, robed choirs, and chandeliers made from the petals of orchids bred for that purpose. Apparently even ordinary Americans now wanted weddings that resembled papal investiture ceremonies from the fourteenth century or replicas of the exact wedding that Celine Dion had. On television Winston Winter appeared suntanned and buoyant, with very white teeth and an accent I couldn't place but that I recognized from Merchant-Ivory films.

I'd never imagined that sort of wedding for myself. I'd never imagined any sort of wedding, really, never pictured myself a bride at all. My single life was staged in a tiny studio apartment that often felt like a waiting room for marriage, but the Big White Day never seized my imagination as the denouement I was waiting *for*. The story I was in seemed more closely based on the disease model. I had turned out to be one of those women for whom the virus of infatuation—fever and delirium followed by a wasting, nineteenth-century-like decline, then protracted convalescence—was potentially lethal. At best the virus became latent, resurfacing as New Year's Eve Disease and other nuisance ailments. I noticed that some women had theories about men that, if not a cure, seemed to shorten the illness: Men were childish, men were selfish, men were insecure. Others relied on talismans and folklore, the equivalent of hanging garlic around your neck: Never prepare a cheese tray for a first date; always answer the door without your shoes on; when he calls, announce that you just got out of the shower. "Men like women who are full of life!" my mother offered—somewhat disingenuously, I thought, since we both knew it was the virus's cunning to mimic that feeling.

*

I DIDN'T HAVE ANY THEORIES. To me men were the great mystery, the source of all pleasure and pain. I admired them as poets—the way they described a woman as having a "thin waist," the dress she wore as "sort of greenish." Lacking language for unnamed experience, men were forced to invent it. "If no one else is president, why can't I be president until the new one gets elected?" a lover I wanted to break up with once said. Another, on his way out the door, reached for a song lyric to explain that he always found himself "slip slidin' away."

I realized I'd better get some theories. I was still working on it when Richard wandered into the middle of my love affair with a not-quite-divorced alcoholic Egyptian diplomat. I still didn't know how I managed to choose happiness—I barely recognized it. Richard and I married, eventually, in our own home and with the smallest amount of hoopla. That became my theory, but only retrospectively: You can choose.

At Thirty-Third Street, the bus passed the hotel where my father and his wife stayed the one time he came to New York, long before I met Richard. I was in my mid-thirties then and hadn't seen my father since I was a teenager. My mother had divorced him when I was six, remarrying twice more after that, never happily. My father seemed gentle and kind. I asked him two questions. "Do you think I'm pretty?" and "If you had one question to ask me, what would it be?" He said he did think I was pretty, that I looked like my mother. His question was: Why aren't you married?

*

Three years ago his wife phoned to say he'd had a stroke. Did I want to come? I flew to Cleveland. My father was in Intensive Care, in a coma. I stood by his bed and held his hand. I repeated his name. "Irv? Irv?" And "Can you hear me? If you can hear me, squeeze my hand." Those were the only words I knew to say at the bedside of a comatose person. His wife stood on the other side of the hospital bed and held his other hand. She looked over at me benignly. "Grace," his wife said, "why don't you try calling him Dad?" It turned out not to be like a scene from a golden age of MGM movie at all, more like a scene from a Lifetime Original Movie. I didn't want to be rude. But even when I tried substituting the word "Dad" for "Irv," my father still didn't answer and he still didn't squeeze my hand. I flew back to New York the same day.

All the parents were dying, the decent ones and the nightmares, the incest parents and the saints, the parents who doted and the ones who drank, the parents who lied and the parents who beat you up, the parents who always preferred your younger sister older brother dog, the silent fathers and the shopping mothers, the adulterous parents and the religious nuts, the ones who came to every game forgot to pick you up at the movies bought you the wrong birthday present didn't give you piano lessons made you try out for band, the ones that didn't notice you were gifted depressed gay fat thin suicidal talented bulimic and the ones who did. Who would be left to remember World War II and the cha-cha and the thank-you note? Yes, the end of Communism was huge. But the end of parents! I went to a funeral just a few weeks ago, the father of a friend. They had an open casket. A woman standing in front of it took out her cell phone and made a call.

At Forty-Second and Madison, roughly halfway to Winston's, I gave up my seat to an elderly man, then was jostled—a surprising rudeness—as I grabbed for the pole. The tricky blocks were ahead, the blocks that bordered my mother's neighborhood, the restaurants where we met for lunch, the office buildings where we went for her doctors' appointments. Although my mother had held on to her glamour almost to the end, glaucoma had demanded certain compromises: rubber-soled shoes and minimal makeup. Every six weeks we went to the ophthalmologist. I sat with her in the darkened examining room while the ancient, elegant Dr. Berg checked her eye pressure. My mother's feet, once snappy in sling-backs, sat meekly on the footrest like those of an obedient kindergartner, in Reeboks and slipping-down socks. A few months before she died, we went for an MRI. By then my mother thought she was being kept against her will at a spa, one where the guests had scarily whitened faces. "Do you have a locker here, too?" she asked me in a polite voice. I didn't know what to say. Who would know what to say? What was the right thing to say? A cell phone at a casket was clear. Everything else was up for grabs. The MRI room was as noisy as any Manhattan construction site. I removed my watch and my wedding band, as instructed, and sat on a folding chair at one end of the tunnel, holding my mother's foot as she disappeared inside. I wondered who would hold my foot.

*

ABBY WAS THE PERSON WITH WHOM I regularly shared Winston's etiquette advice. Abby had been my editor at *Marvelous Woman*. "The man is irony-proof," Abby often said in a reverent voice. She owned all of Winston's books. She was right. Everything about Winston was unironic. Abby was particularly taken with Winston's dictum about the proper moment to pick up your fork and begin eating your meal at a dinner party. "Once three or four plates are served, you may begin," Winston said. "A gracious host or hostess doesn't want any of her guests to eat food that has grown cold." "Really? He said that?" Abby seemed as surprised to hear this as Richard had been when I told him that Warren Beatty and Shirley MacLaine were brother and sister.

I wrote my first article for Abby, on contraception etiquette. It was while doing research for it that I came across "Emily Post's Rules for Debutantes." My mother had given me a copy of Emily Post's *Etiquette* when I graduated from high school. I had dutifully moved that book from shelf to shelf over the decades since without ever once opening it. How was I to know that hidden away in that seemingly useless volume were three rules containing all the guidance any young woman would ever need? Abby and I quoted them to each other regularly: "Do not lean on anyone for support unless necessary. Do not allow anyone to paw you. On no account force yourself to laugh." Emily Post didn't cover contraception etiquette.

I got off the bus at Seventy-Ninth Street and walked the few blocks to Winston's apartment. They were the same elegantly proportioned blocks I used to travel to when I was seeing my former psychotherapist, Dr. Isabella Gold. Week after week, year after year, I carried individual dreams from my apartment to Dr. Gold's office, dream by dream, one dream at a time, as if my job were to transfer an entire universe of matter from one place to another by teaspoonful. Then one day the work was done. All of the matter that had been in one place was now in another place entirely and I couldn't picture or imagine what used to be in either place.

That was New York in a nutshell, I realized. Things changed all the time. As soon as the change was complete, it was impossible to reconstruct the past. It couldn't be done. The former landscape would always feel like a dream or a lie.

Winston's building was small and elegant, with a long green canopy and an elevator man. The first time I came here, the elevator man repeated, "Winston Winter!" and took me to the eleventh floor. When the doors opened I found myself in a small red-lacquered jewel box of an entryway, with an umbrella holder, a gilt mirror, and two doors. One door led to the living quarters of the apartment, the other door to the office quarters. "Have a good day!" the elevator man said and left me there. I couldn't remember which door I had been told to knock on. I began to break into a bit of a sweat. It reminded me of a brainteaser my husband liked: Twins confined in a tower room with two doors. One door leads to freedom, the other to the executioner. One twin tells the truth, the other twin lies. Ask one twin one question to determine the door to freedom. What question? Which twin? That to me seemed to sum up everything.

*

AS IT TURNED OUT, it didn't matter which door I knocked on because no one heard me. Eventually the housekeeper, Margaret, wandered out with the recyclables and let me in. "Oh, he's so late, my boss!" she said. "Juice?" Then she pointed toward a room with walls the color of eggplant and I went in and sat down on a burnt-orange velvet sofa. Winston shouted from another room, "Give her some of that mango pango juice!" Occasionally he sang out an order to an assistant whose name was either Patricia or Felicia or Delicious. "Navy taffeta for the tables! And four dozen candelabra!" While I waited for Winston, I tried identifying the wonderful scent of the candle burning on the wenge wood table and attempted to add up how much everything in that one room cost and began to feel downhearted about my own apartment with its deficiency of silver cigarette boxes and 1930s cocktail accessories. Why hadn't I thought of eggplant as a color?

Today the door was open and I walked right in. Felicia Delicious was doing something with bubble wrap. "Good, morning, Grace. How are you this morning?" She was twenty-three tops. I wanted to throw my arms around her.

"Gracie, my love! Just finishing up the morning's e-mail. Get comfy, darling."
Winston was seated at his Art Deco desk, laptop open. He wore narrow pants
and the thinnest summer cashmere pullover, both the color of slate, and on
his feet were exquisite objects that seemed to be the marriage of an athletic
shoe and a Ferrari. His face looked as if it had just returned from Sardinia.

I put my recorder on the table and opened my notebook. I wrote down everything Winston said in case of tape malfunction.

He came around to the sofa, kissed me on both cheeks, and settled into one
corner. "So where are we today, my sweet?"

"We're beginning Chapter Seven," I said. "'How to Raise a Gracious Child.'"
Oh boy. Winston Winter on child-rearing.

"Very important! A topic dear to my heart. Because you know, Grace, good
manners begin with children. Margaret! Mango pango on a tray, please, thank
you! With instilling respect and integrity and compassion. With setting limits."

I smiled. That was my interviewing technique. I wrote down the words
"respect, integrity, compassion."

Winston lifted his exfoliated chin and sniffed the unironic air. "Let's see …
a section on those vile people who let their children run up and down the aisle
of airplanes …. Should we talk about physical punishment now or at the end?"

"I think it's probably best to stick to etiquette," I said. "Like, should you bring
your kid to a dinner party. Only because, well, that's more your area, right?"

"Never strike your child in anger."

I wrote it down.

He hit pause while Margaret set down a tray with juice. "What about you,
Grace? Do you and your husband plan on having children? Thank you, Margaret, lovely." How old did this man think I was? Did I register on him at all?

At lunchtime, we sat on tall stools in the handsome stainless steel and wood
kitchen eating Margaret's vegetable soup while Winston oversaw the cutting and
arranging in various sized vases of that day's delivery of orange roses. During
"Chapter Four: An Organized Home Is a Spiritual Home," Winston had opened
his kitchen cabinets and bedroom closets—spices alphabetic, Prada white
to black—and discussed his philosophy of creating a peaceful environment.
"Edit! Edit! Edit!" During "Chapter Six: Positive Energy in Difficult Situations,"
Winston addressed the etiquette of blame. "Let it go!" Every chapter seemed to
have an etiquette situation capable of being resolved by "Send a fragrant candle!"

It was close to five when Winston and I finished up. I walked to the subway,
feeling perfectly empty. Walking down the stairs, plucking my MetroCard from

where I'd stuck it inside a book, I sensed the absence of something. I took the local to Union Square and when I got off and had walked up the stairs and onto the corner of Broadway, I stopped. I rummaged through my bag. It was my wallet that was gone. Uncomprehending grief swam through my bloodstream. Then it swam out. I remembered: There was an 800 number at home, I had all my account numbers stored on my computer, I could replace my driver's license by mail. My legs moved again, and I walked toward home.

In the window of the coffee shop on University Place and Twelfth Street, I saw the two ancient sisters seated in their customary window booth having the early bird dinner. Both women had snowy hair and the tactful, pensive face of Miss Marple. I was always struck by how complex and subtle a variation each sister was on the other—the piled white hair, the parchment skin, the casually worn quirky piece of jewelry, the comfortably inward expressions—and by how deeply at home each sister appeared to be in the other's company. That's me and Abby, I always thought, when the husbands are dead. I wished that I knew everything about those sisters and their lives. Who had they loved and what had their little piece of New York looked like back at the beginning and which small luxuries had fallen away and which did they still cling to? Were they still moving forward or content to hang on? That was the mystery.

When I got home, I tried not to look at the boxes, at the gaping empty kitchen, at the living room mess. I went straight to my office and called American Express, and the bank, and then Abby, because you had to say out loud, "My wallet was stolen." I remembered the lengthy recovery time these routine losses exacted when I was twenty-five and thirty, the doomed sense that keys and credit cards and salad-bar coupons were not only irreplaceable but ominous metaphors for everything bad to come. But by the time my apartment was burglarized at thirty-five, I'd come to know the losses bluntly for what they were: stuff you missed and, eventually, replaced, even though you never got back exactly what you'd lost. Then I spoke out loud to the quiet apartment. "Mom," I said. I said it again. Then I flung open the hall closet and threw out every cheap umbrella I could get my hands on.

*

BEING FIFTY GIVE OR TAKE was like being an original Supreme. Some later groups could call themselves The Supremes, they could sing "Baby Love," but we were the one-and-onlys. And that was also our curse. Because no experience we had in our lives could be unique. There would be a brief window during which we naïvely thought we were having a unique experience — laughing at Steve Martin, eating sushi, forgetting the word for fear-of-leaving-the-house — and then that window would close. Five minutes later everyone would be claiming that experience. That experience would be on the cover of *Newsweek* and people we had the deepest contempt for would be selling miniseries based on it. Everyone's parents were going to die, even the parents of those middle-aged celebrities with twenty-five-year-old skin who paid Winston Winter to plan birthday parties for their toddler triplets.

*

IT WAS CLOSE TO SEVEN when someone phoned from Billy's Topless, a bar on Sixth Avenue.

My wallet was there, emptied of cash, but with credit cards in it. I said thank you, and that I'd come and pick it up, and thank you again.

Richard called just after that. How was I? I said I was fine and told him all about Winston and the wallet. I stood at the window talking to him like that, about my day, watching the midsummer sky turn to dusk. I could see Richard's office building from the window where I stood. The sky turned a deep navy as we talked, and then it was night, and the building's upper stories blazed with light. When I concentrated and counted carefully, I was able to find exactly where Richard was, up on the sixtieth floor. We knew we had a spectacular view when we moved into our apartment, but we'd always seen it in daylight. Not until our first night there did we really know how lucky we were.

We talked a little more that way, me at home staring out the window, Richard gathering up his things before heading home. We made dinner plans.

"Ready?" Richard said then.

"Yep."

He switched to speaker phone. Then he flickered the lights in his office, on and off, on and off. One, two, three blinks.

"Can you see them?" he called out. "Can you see them now?"

I could, I could see them, an improbable mile away, at not quite the top, a narrow band of flickering lights.

"Yes!" I said. "I can see them!" What were the odds of such a thing in such a city?

What were the odds? I remembered how happy I was. I was just happy.

CHEKHOV SAID

Therese Eiben

Three days passed before a report of the accident appeared in the newspapers: Gabriel Day, 18, killed on December 9 by a hit-and-run driver on Montauk Highway near Amagansett, New York. His mother, Nuala Day, 41, died December 10, an apparent suicide. A week later, the *Times* published an obituary of Matthew Quarles, an artist famous in the 1970s who had been preparing for a MOMA retrospective. Cause of death was listed as "natural causes." "Natural" in that a bullet to the cranium would naturally cause death, but specifics such as that went unreported.

There was also no mention the accident that killed Gabriel Day happened in front of philanthropist Henry Reade's Long Island estate. No mention that Nuala Day was Cherie and Henry Reade's live-in housekeeper and that the boy, Gabriel, had grown up there. No reference to the connection of the Reades, who were notable collectors of contemporary art, to Matthew Quarles. All of it, the delay in reporting, the scant detail, the timing and placement of the news article, buried in the Metro section, was the work of Henry Reade's able body man, James Waring. And so, officially, there was nothing to investigate. Unofficially, people talked. You might be surprised to learn who talked, given the public profession of grateful friendship with the Reades coming out of that elite South Fork enclave known as Dorsett Cove; how, as its oldest resident, Frank Holliday, said, "In our community, one man's tragedy hits his neighbors just as hard." Or maybe you wouldn't be surprised, because in the end everyone did. Talk, that is.

*

REESE WHITFIELD, WHO WITNESSED the accident, stood guard until the police and EMT had come and gone. Frank Holliday, Emerson Beale, and Trev Eeling salted, shoveled, set up flares, anything they could do to help the officials. Paul Partridge, a physician as his own father and grandfather had been, sedated Nuala once she learned her son was dead. She slept, temporarily protected from her grief, in her room off the kitchen, which the wives subsequently commandeered, firing up the Reades' eight-burner Viking range, doing as their mothers and grandmothers had done whenever a vessel capsized or a drunken houseguest went out for a midnight swim. If Nuala had been conscious she would have chased those Dorsett Cove matrons out. No one so much as got himself a glass of water from the tap in Nuala Day's kitchen.

Close to two AM, Sergeant Joe McGowan told Officer George Murphy, who had been directing traffic since nine that night, to go inside and warm up. Cass Eeling took Officer Murphy's oilskin coat. Louisa Partridge insisted he stow his holster, frozen stiff and rimed with ice, on the top pantry shelf. Eleanor Whitfield sat him at the kitchen table with pea soup and a hot ham sandwich. One by one their husbands joined Officer Murphy indoors. Sergeant McGowan cleared the scene and left with the forensics team and its evidence: photographs, tire tread casts, broken glass from a headlight.

Other than the sound of soup spoons tolling against porcelain, silence fell over the kitchen, its windows steamed, its floor slicked with ice melt, the deeply asleep Nuala Day nearby. Across the front hall in the dining room, where the planes of a Henry Moore sculpture gleamed under museum lighting, the table comfortably sat twenty, but the Reades' neighbors and Officer Murphy stayed where they were, several of them with plates on their laps seated in side chairs pulled from other rooms, the rest at the kitchen table.

"They should be able to identify the car easily enough," Emerson Beale said.

"Nothing's going to be easy about this," Cass Eeling said.

"It was an accident. Let's not make it out to be more than that," Louisa Partridge said. Cass and Louisa had been sparring for forty years, since they were seniors at Smith, where they graduated, preposterously, co-valedictorians.

"But was it a *random* accident?" asked Susan Holliday.

"An accident by its very nature is random." Louisa said.

"An accident by definition is *unintentional*," Susan said, "but what pulled Gabriel out in front of that particular car at that particular moment?"

"*Shhhhhh.* Don't wake Nuala!" whispered Betz Beale.

Susan continued in a lowered voice: "If it had been a different car, would he have run out into the road? If not, that would make it an accident, but not a *random* accident."

"Did you see the car?" Eleanor Whitfield asked her husband.

"I told Joe, it was all so fast—" Reese Whitfield dropped his spoon into the bowl and lowered his shaking hands. "I must have, but I can't remember."

Frank Holliday, still the tallest and strongest among them despite his age, shifted in his chair and averred that it was understandable given the circumstances.

"I heard it, though," Reese said.

He told them he was stringing Christmas lights through the pickets at his property line when he heard a big engine. First he thought it was a plane coming out of Montauk, but five minutes later—he was stringing lights along Indian Wells by then—he could still hear it: a heavy growl steadily increasing in intensity. He walked out to Route 27, right across from the Reade estate, and from there he could see a wash of light moving in a long arc against the night sky, the accelerating engine coming on like a jet ready for takeoff. The headlights swept off the horizon and bore down full beams straight on the road. Just then Gabriel appeared from behind the Reades' yew hedge, he was—crazy! Sick as that boy has been—he was wearing no shoes, no coat. He just ran toward the sound, ran straight down the middle of the road, arms out in front of him, palms up like stop signs. The car came into view sideways, braking hard as Jesus, gears crashing, everything dyed red in brake lights. Gabriel flew up and back, traveling for a moment with the car, which righted and then passed his trajectory, finally stopping when the boy fell. And then it was gone.

"So that particular car drew him out," Susan Holliday said.

"How many cars have an engine that big you can hear it ten miles away?" Trev Eeling asked Emerson Beale, who collected cars.

"Sounds to me like an E-Type." Everyone in the room knew that Henry Reade had a '61 E-Type. It was famous on the South Fork, nicknamed the Flying Penis. Beale had tried to buy it from him on several occasions. Thirty-four years old, mint condition. Some said the most beautiful car ever made.

"What are you saying? That Henry Reade wouldn't stop if he hit a man?" Frank Holliday was out of his chair, a plate falling from his lap and breaking into pieces. "What horse manure. We're sitting in the man's house and you're accusing him of killing that boy? That poor, sick boy?" Frank shoved a path between two chairs to stand against the vast silver doors of the commercial-sized refrigerator, a Traulsen. The Reades hosted many fundraisers in their Dorsett

Cove home. "Maybe the boy was just waiting for a ride, any ride. You don't know what kind of car it was. Henry Reade *loved* that boy."

"Besides," Beale said. "Henry arrived after the accident, on his way back to the City from Montauk, in the Rolls. He was with his man, James Something, or Something James, and a younger woman. They followed the ambulance to the morgue."

"James Waring is his body man, PR, branding, that sort of thing. I talked to him while Joe was interviewing Henry," Paul Partridge said. "The woman was Cherie's cousin."

"Cherie told me she doesn't have any family," Betz Beale said, her voice quavering, as though she expected to be contradicted. Out of earshot she was known as Timorous Beasty.

"She says that, but I never believed it," Louisa Partridge said. "Everyone has family, somewhere. Everyone has a past."

"Her name is Dorothy. She's a virologist at Columbia Presbyterian conducting trials on an experimental drug. She was here last month for that fundraiser for—" Paul Partridge broke off, not wanting to say AIDS in front of Frank.

"I saw her!" said Susan Holliday. "Tonight at the benefit, the cerebral palsy thing at the Montauk Lighthouse. Cherie Reade walked in with that James person and a young woman, must be Cousin Dorothy." Frank was shaking his big head like a wet dog working water of out its ears. Susan ignored him. "We go every year. Frank's sister's daughter— Anyway, about forty-five minutes later, Henry came in with a man. A handsome man. He I did not know, but they must have had two cars. Cherie left first, with the handsome man. Henry and the others after that."

"So who was the handsome man?" Louisa Partridge asked.

"More to the point," said Susan Holliday, "who was the handsome man *with?* Cherie? Or Henry?"

"Shut up, woman," The Traulsen rocked as Frank pushed off it to lunge at his wife, but Officer Murphy reached him first and, with Trev Eeling's help, dragged him across the hall into Henry's study. Sounds of a fight drew the other men in. Susan Holliday was herded upstairs by the women, where she fought their commiseration, which they were determined to administer.

Somewhere near dawn, Cass Eeling slipped downstairs to make a pot of coffee. While it brewed she rested her head on her arms at the kitchen table. Something niggled at her. She tried to identify it, but in an instant was asleep. If she had just opened one eye—even with her head still resting on her arms—she might have noticed a glint of the late-rising moon reflected in the sheen of the kitchen tabletop. Or had she managed to sit up, she might have registered the overturned furniture righted, the chairs from other rooms gone, the broken plate cleared away, the floor mopped, the soup tureen gleaming, Nuala Day's bedroom door ajar. Which might have led her to the top pantry shelf to look for Officer Murphy's holster, pushed in and among the ranks of *rouille*, quince jam, bourbon cherries, and other fancy condiments guests to the Reade estate brought as bread-and-butter gifts. The holster she would have found, its leather thawed by then and pliable, but not his gun.

First Girl

Elizabeth England

(From *The Journal*)

That spring when my mother left him, my father would choose a path off the Appalachian Trail and, every Friday, after a few drinks, he would call me in Maine where I was in college. He would leave on my answering machine the start time, the length of the hike, trail conditions. Our goal was simple: to climb mountains and point out things below that were familiar. Despite the slurring of his voice, I always understood my father perfectly. This time, I was to take Barkers Road to the fork and make a right; he'd be waiting at the trail head. It was expected that I would meet him.

My roommate that particular year was Victor from Cuba, Victor with the sleek black hair hanging like a dog's tail down his spine. He was a friend of a friend; we had nothing else in common. Besides studying, I spent most of my time doing what my mother often did: quietly putting down the toilet seat, slipping old-fashioned coasters under glasses, finding pennies between cushions and pocketing them. Victor rarely studied. He slept and baked fruit pies with lattice tops. When he heard the message from my father, he asked if he could come.

"Would you mind?" Victor was physical and, often, he would pick me up and flirtatiously throw me on the La-Z-Boy. If he hadn't been gay, we would've been sleeping together.

When I told my father about Victor, he said, "Is it serious?"

On Saturday, the morning sky was dark purple. Victor and I drove over the Maine border into New Hampshire and then across the White Mountains. Victor said once or twice, "Would you look at that?" The mountains still had snow on them, ringing their tops like halos. We passed covered bridges with small signs telling us their ages. "That, I cannot believe," Victor said about a distinctly old one.

When we stopped for something to eat, the waitress said, "What can I get you two lovebirds?" I turned red and Victor said, "She's just my kid sister." The waitress rolled her eyes and walked away. "You are the most beautiful thing, sis," Victor said, putting his hand on my thigh. He left it there until the check came. We could've been statues; we were that still.

Victor said that there was no way of seeing the opossum before I hit it. I felt the thump and pulled over quickly, without signaling, without looking behind me. "Breathe," he said. "It wasn't your fault." I imagined something large, a buck, a moose even. "We would be dead if it was one of those," Victor said. I got out first and looked. "Tell me, tell me," Victor said. When I didn't say anything, he too got out of the car and looked at the opossum with me. The soft belly pulsing, the skinny bald tail limp on the road, one eye blinking. Victor said, "Thank God, it is only that."

I had only one orange emergency cone and a large flashlight in the trunk to put near the opossum until we came back with help.

"No one will see that," Victor said, taking off his orange ski sweater. He put it on the pavement. It looked like a shrine, the cone, the flashlight, the sweater.

"Perfect," Victor said. He put his arm around me and squeezed. I was close enough to smell his patchouli oil. "Let's go find someone."

At the first gas station we came to, I stopped and told the man behind the counter what I had done. He said, "What do you want me to do about it?" He wore a checkered shirt with squares only slightly larger than the opossum's eye. I paid for gas and some gum and said thank you. "For what?" the man said.

At a payphone, I called my father. I left a message telling him we were still in New Hampshire and that I had hit an opossum. I said I was uncertain whether we would meet him at the designated time. Victor was sitting on the hood of the car when I came out of the phone booth. We smelled the yeast and flour of a commercial bakery, which, Victor found out, wasn't open on Saturdays. "This makes you feel as though you're eating," Victor said and put a piece of gum in my mouth. "Don't worry, I can't leave the little guy lying there either." From his front jeans pocket, he took out a cloth handkerchief and wiped my eyes, first one and then the other.

We got back in the car and drove slowly down the Main Street until I saw a store that had signs for missing kittens, unwanted puppies, pony lessons, fresh goat's milk, posted on its bulletin board. The woman filling a red cooler with

Dr. Pepper and chocolate milk told me to take an empty cardboard box from outside and slide the opossum in it. She gave me the name and number of her vet, Dr. Lesley. If I brought the animal to him, he would call the game warden who would take over from there.

"Use these," she said, handing me rubber gloves. "Save you a lot of trouble."

Victor was still in the car. His knees were wedged against the glove box. He was the longest man I had ever known. When he smiled at me this time, he looked different.

I drove slowly. I searched the road for animals. Victor turned on the radio. "There is no disco music around here," he said. I was holding the steering wheel tightly. Victor put his hand on my neck, his fingers resting lightly like a necklace on my collarbone. I pushed my shoulders down, I rolled my head in a circle, I inhaled. "You must exhale," he said. "Breathing is the only thing that works."

As soon as we found the opossum, I parked on the side of the road and put on my hazards. They made a ticking sound that reminded me of the metronome my mother used whenever she wanted to get our attention. The even, persistent click would make my brother and me stop fighting. It also made my father look up from the papers he graded nightly. We would all stare at my mother until she turned it off, said what she needed to say and left the room. I told Victor to get out of the car and stand watch. If a car came, I instructed him to motion it wide around the opossum and me. He practiced a few times, exaggerating the movements, until I laughed. "That's better," he said.

I searched the side of the road until I found a stick that was impressive, thick, smooth and easy to maneuver. I touched its blunt tip against the opossum's side and all the muscles in the animal's torso contracted. He tried to curl up like a caterpillar. I imagined his wounds were internal, a kidney that no longer worked, intestines that refused to function. Apart from the smashed right eye, he looked peaceful on the outside.

"Your mother," Victor said. "Is that who you look like, or your father?" He had his hands tucked in the pockets of his wool jacket. It was April but that day, it felt like February. I watched the smoke come out of his mouth.

"Depends on my mood," I said. The opossum was drooling. White foam curdled on the road. His one good eye stayed closed now more than open though when I came near him, he strained to watch me. I wanted to see his tongue.

"I think he's a child," Victor said. He was squatting next to me, his knee resting on mine, his eyes fixed on the opossum. He handed me the rubber gloves and kept the cardboard box.

I slid the opossum and Victor held the box. Whenever the opossum twitched, Victor said, "Watch it." He told me about his uncle who got bit by a rabid dog, the fever he got, how his wife couldn't take it so she left him. He lived, but then died young of a stroke. As Victor talked, I used the stick like a spatula, half-lifting the opossum, half-dropping him. Finally, Victor said, "Let me try." He put on the gloves. His face was serious, no smiling, no softness to his cheeks. His eyes looked first at the opossum and then at the box. Then, he picked up the opossum with both hands, one in front of the other as in tug-of-war. The opossum twisted his head around to bite Victor, showing his teeth, hissing and finally pressing down on Victor's hand, but not piercing the rubber. "Have you ever had a pet?" He asked me. The opossum was in the box, twitching.

"Dogs," I said. "Crazy ones."

"Why crazy?" Victor said.

"My father hit them in the head with the car," I said. "They would get in the way whenever he backed out of the driveway."

"At least it wasn't you he hit," Victor said.

This time, Victor drove. I rode in the backseat with the opossum who made a purring sound. He began to scratch the side of the box, his nails sliding back and forth against the cardboard. "He's nervous," Victor said. "Sing to him. Everyone likes a song." I hummed "Michael Row the Boat Ashore." "That must be American," Victor said. It was repetitive and I could keep it going for a long time. "That's nice," Victor said. The box bumped into me when Victor turned into the vet's office. The opossum's eyes opened, even the hurt one, and we stared at each other until Victor parked and opened my door.

Dr. Lesley wasn't in, but his assistant took the box and said, "What is it this time?" She had long nails, which she protected, using only the pads of her fingers to write our names and addresses, the time and place of impact. I told her it felt like something larger. "That's when they hit both tires, not just one," she said. She then gave the opossum a shot and both eyes closed. "Sign here," she said. "He'll be fine."

I drove the speed limit. Victor said he had never seen a place as big and lonely as New Hampshire. "Where is everyone?" He said.

We crossed the state line into Vermont, and when I got to Barkers Road, I took the right and saw my father's Buick empty and locked under a tree. Victor tied his sweater around his waist and I took off my sweatshirt. Both of us changed into our hiking boots and looked for the trailhead.

At the beginning, the ground was as muddy and slow-moving as my father had described. There was a small stream to cross, a few logs to climb over, but otherwise the walk was easy. Fiddlehead ferns were beginning to unfurl, bluebells were sprouting up through the mulch. "So this is spring," Victor said.

We made it to the clearing at the top of the mountain with few stops.

"The payoff," Victor said. "This view of everything." He was breathing hard, but there were no sweat rings under his arms, no large effort expended. He pivoted, looked out and down. There was a breeze, which we hadn't felt in the woods. Victor's hair had come out of its leather tie and now blew around his face, sticking to his skin. "So where is this father?"

I circled the top, looking near a cluster of rocks on the east side and then checking a path on the west side. I called his name. My father wasn't there.

On the way down, I called out a few more times until Victor said, "He should've known better."

"But we were late," I said.

"About the dogs, I mean," Victor said.

When we got to the trailhead parking lot, my father's car was gone. "Waited four hours, guess it's serious" was written on an old A&P receipt tucked under the left windshield wiper of my car. Victor didn't ask to read the note. Instead, he picked a violet, smoothed my hair back and stuck the flower behind my ear. I closed my eyes as his fingers touched me. He said, "You are the first girl I ever wanted to kiss."

SHE-MONSTER GETS FIRED

Kim Farrar
(From *New Ohio Review*)

Here you are again, running from the villagers
with their torches and pitchforks. You thought
you finally fit in. You filed down
your neck-bolts, got rid of your high-waters.
You watched Oprah, kept a dream diary,
a gratitude journal, pictures of your thinner self
on the fridge. You tried to keep your need
for electricity minimized: licking the outlets,
rubbing your hair with a balloon for just a crackle.

You knew it would happen. Every morning—
the affirmations, the meditation, the positive thinking.

You longed for lightning and rain.
You did everything right to escape
the old ways of staring into the well.
It took years of practicing the right laugh.
You did your best. Married up.
Got a job teaching ESL. Now and then,
a grunt would slip and
crickets   crickets   crickets.

People liked you. You were funny.

But one day you found refuge
eating flies in the faculty lounge;
soon you stopped hiding
your green undertones with foundation.
You missed being the girl

who loved her square head,
touched her thick-stitched scars like Braille.

The villagers yell, Kill her! Kill the monster!

You're barreling through the woods,
nettle whips your ankles as you soar
over logs in your clodhoppers.
You're filled with the old familiar joy
of being free and incredible.

THANK YOU FOR MAKING TODAY BEAUTIFUL

Patricia Follert

(from *Epiphany*)

THIS IS MY DEMENTIA. It sleeps next to me at night and wakes testy the next day. It doesn't like to shave or shower or wear clean clothes. What is this, asks dementia, as I pull back your bedclothes, what is this? This is only morning, I say, like all the other mornings, only you don't remember.

*

THERE IS AN INSTANT when understanding breaks like an egg in your hands. Oh, you can look back, over your shoulder, at what was, but it's gone now, lost in the rush of diagnosis. "Darling, you have dementia." Sounds like cocktail talk.

*

THEY HAVE SHOWN US the scan. Small areas of white deformity scattered in your superb brain like road detours. You never know where you will end up. Have we told each other everything? Do we want to? Early onset, they say. It sounds like a weather report.

7:30 am. The ordinary days. The reassuring weekdays. The marital tidiness, the orderliness of it—rising and breakfast and the kiss at the front door. He is already in the office in his head and you bar the door to keep out the pain of his absence. Already you anticipate his return and this shapes your restlessness into a whole day of grocery shopping, a yoga class, dry cleaners, the Chinese laundry, a manicure perhaps. 6 pm. The scent of cold air on his cheek and a paper cone of subway lilacs.

This is what you carried in your pockets—a gold Cross ballpoint pen in sincere blue ink, a solid gold die from an old girlfriend that was stolen from the bedside table in a hotel that I replaced as a wedding gift because I saw your fingers mining for it and missing it in your suit pants pocket, a Swiss Army knife, a gold Tiffany key chain bestowed by another ex-lover that sang with keys, a dark-brown, leather billfold with a discreet gilt monogram with credit cards and large-denomination bills medical cards a fold of fives and tens and ones in your side pocket for tips an initialed Brooks Brothers diary annual Christmas gift from a besotted mother-in-law an address book small change which never lasted long a small plastic comb in your breast pocket and a white, starched handkerchief in the left back pocket of your pants.

The people you expect to hear from never write. Those you wish would never write do. The people who learn from people at second and third removes offer unsolicited hugs, a presumptuous intimacy, and speak in whispers as if raised voices could raise the dead. Then the handyman follows you down Main Street asking again and again do you know what you are going to do, do you know what you are going to do, he starts to call you Funny Face and you know he has been having a secret life with you so you fire him. The owner of the Italian deli offers to move furniture or just "get you out of the house." The pool man who tells you to call any hour for any need until you protest the cost of his snowplowing moonlighting and he snubs you in town. The owner of the hardware store who drove you home when you lost it in his store because you lost your keys and you and the dogs are locked out and the Village Hall people say they do not do that and the Village Police say they do not do that when all you need is a ride home.

Painter Hung Liu
Introduced Herself Saying

Gail Ford

"The Chinese language only has present tense.
I eat rice (now)
I eat rice (tomorrow)
I eat rice (yesterday)."

I eat rice, the leaves are red outside the window
I eat rice, the leaves, bright green and budding
I eat rice, the branches are bare of leaves.

Painter Hung Liu climbs the scaffolding.
She paints a running brook across gray rock.
The rocks are wet (now)
The rocks are dry (yesterday)
The rocks are sand (tomorrow).

I eat rice, my hands are small, skin smooth
I eat rice, my hands are calloused and sunbrowned
I eat rice, my knuckles protrude, the second joint of each finger twisted.

Hung Liu is dressed in traveler's cotton
Is dressed in paint-flecked overalls
Is dressed in Chinese silk.

A bird is in her mind
The bird is on the wall
The bird's feather is blue and at the very tip of her brush.

I eat rice, a torn ligament aches
I eat rice, my body young and supple
I eat rice, my granddaughter feeds me, one morsel at a time.

Hung Liu paints an antelope on a cave wall.
There is silence. A hand strikes a gong.
The struck note goes on and on.

Painter Hung Liu's hand is on the knob.
The door is open (now)
The door is closed (now)
She climbs the scaffold (now)
She walks out into the world (now)
The brook burbles on the wall.

First Kill

Janet Franklin

When he shows you the picture he took in Baghdad
after his father baked his famous crab cakes,
after the Seahawks started killing the Rams,
after you went out back to make a phone call
and found him just standing there holding a cigarette,
after his mother had told you how she'd taken him
down to Tahoe since he'd been big enough to fly,
her son, who needs two beers to fall asleep
and leaves the TV on static all night,
when he shows you the photo
he's had in his phone since before he had Junior
he doesn't blink, he looks at you and you look at him
and the two of you are a couple of people
standing together in the wet grass on a starless night
off a dirt road in Skagit County, Washington,
twentysomething miles southwest of Mount Baker
and fourteen miles east of the bay and past that
the ocean, but the whole family's still inside
so you hand him his phone and go back to the house,
except you don't, neither of you do, not really.

JUDY GARLAND GETS DRESSED

Christina Frei

(From *Third Wednesday*)

With the help of my wardrobe assistants
I am fitted out in a white cotton blouse,
sleeves long enough to cover my wrinkled upper arms,
loose enough to hide my hunched back,
make me look taller, younger.
The blue gingham dress goes over the top.
It's not my taste (it never was),
which runs more to the racy red satin or black silk.
I like to look sensual. That's what got me
where I am. But I swallow my vanity
along with another martini while someone braids
my hair. That and the gingham does the business.
Someone asks me to sing, so I put down
my cigarette, open my one adequate feature
smeared with Estée Lauder Poppy Red
and croak a ditty about a cow jumping
over a moon, *hey diddle diddle*, and wink,
which makes everyone laugh because they know
I've had one vodka and a few blue tablets
too many and that's how we get the job done.
I close my eyes and Bert comes in
to get his face painted brown and whiskered,
and Jack is there too in his metal can outfit
which makes me smile when it clanks.
He pretends his private parts
are also made of tin, and sticks them out at me
and when I mockingly raise an eyebrow,
that sends everyone in wardrobe into gales
of unapologetically fake laughter

until it suddenly and inexplicably stops
and I sneak another blue tablet plus a couple pinks.
Then everyone starts to resemble clown-pigs
so I grab my green-tinted glasses in the hope
of being magically transported to something
approximating a city made of emeralds but all they do
is transform everyone into green clown-pigs
and even though I try to laugh, I can't
because my face is frozen with fear. I put on makeup
with shaking hands—lots of mascara, lots and lots,
and still I need more because I'm ugly like a pig too,
my small eyes, my turned-up nose, jowly cheeks.
I need a balding wizard with his trick mirrors
to make me believe in myself. I need a kind witch
to brew me some kind of miracle potion,
or donate magic shoes that will take me home to Liza.
Hey, big boy, I slur, turning to Ray, *can you do my zipper up?*
I'd rather do it down, he says, and I startle
when I see it's not Ray. Not Jack or Bert either,
and everyone laughs again like there's a button you push
except mine broke a long time ago.
Someone hands me a towel on my way out
because my mascara is running down my face
and it's going to stain my blouse, and then I'm on,
clasp the microphone on a spot-lit stage, sing
with all my might: *somewhere over the rainbow skies are blue*
except it is almost midnight and there is only black.

IN THE CONCESSION

Annette Frost

The storms were wind and sand and shadows.

    They came at night. They came ahead of sleep

and rattled the hibiscus bush. The storms were

    red and bleak. And brown and gray and made of breath.

The storms bent the young millet stalks and made them

    women, hunched and not alive, not dead. The storms unslept

the sleeping things. Loosed scorpions from the grass

    thatched roof, dropped them like rain. The storms

were snakes. And roaches. They surged and brawled.

    They made the treetops moan and shake. The storms gave

legs to silent walls. They carried dust and rubbed it

    inside mouths. They came, a rushing wall of brittle sand,

but moved so slowly from far away, a red wall coming. They broke

    instead of knocked. The storms were men.

THE GOOD WIFE

Rebecca Gee

Father tells me he's teaching me to be a good wife
As he demonstrates the way he wants me to kiss him.

I look over his shoulder at the porcelain kissing-angels that mock us.
If my arms were long enough to reach those sleek golden heads

I would set them in motion to see their frantic bobbling up
and down, slowing bit by bit into a weak nod, dying into

stillness. Mother does not allow me to touch the angels because
I might break them and I know what they do when at play.

It's hard to be still; my skin feels stiff and hot like Grandma's horsehair
loveseat on a summer day. Will he cover me in plastic slipcovers

so I stay as good as chaste for my husband-to-be? "Don't be afraid to please,"
he tells me, his hands heavy as pewter.

I stare at the plastic fruit in a bowl on the table at his elbow.
At a distance, the fruit looks like perfection, but it's

bitter and unyielding.

PRODUCT RECALL

Judy Gerbin

I screwed up, again,
counting the colored rubber bands.
I lost track and ended up
with too many of the red, which match
the color my face turns
as my coworkers watch me start over
for the third time. On top of that
I've been assigned an extra double bin
to finish by end of day.
Even the spider plant
on the corner of my desk
seems unfriendly.
I want to quit.
Yet I'm terrified
I'll be fired.
I cannot lose this job
after all the years spent
on this particular ladder
which consists of one rung. Being
on the top and bottom simultaneously
has given me an elasticity
of soul and an ability to let things
roll off me.
Besides, where would I go?
Due to budget-slashing, the bands
have gotten thinner, their colors duller.
The red looks like creamy tomato soup,
the blue is closer to gray. They feel dry
and they break easily. One just
dropped to the floor but I leave it.
I can't seem to focus

on these rubber bands like I did
when I was just starting out,
my life ahead of me, full
of promise, full of unknowns, moist
like something planted and ready
to shoot up through the ground.
Maybe there is something
better to pursue. I wonder
about the opportunities in paper clips
and Post-it notes. Or something larger.
Is it too late, something, perhaps, out of doors.
In the grasses and trees, something
with breath and warm blood. Something
with guts and sharp teeth. Or something
of the sea; odorous, leviathan,
with a perverse, a singular
mind of its own.

DOOR OPEN!

James Gibbs

There wasn't really a trial, it was more of a hearing. No jury, nothing like that. And it was so long ago; Redmund was twenty—not that much older than the boy, then. And kids can be bad too. People forget that. Reddie was just finding his way at community college. And then Robert's heart attack—suddenly no father for him. A hard time for me too. But Reddie's a good boy. He's just ... affectionate, and funny. Quick, easy to laugh; boys look up to him. It's like he's still one of them. Like he always will be.

I do the math, count it out, and I can't quite believe it. I can't believe it's already 1983. I can't believe I brought him into this old world back in 1952. Little Reddie, with his little hands and little thumbs, and all that black hair, all over like a monkey! Scared me half to death and back. People in hospitals—people like that—they didn't warn us *anything* about life back then: none of the crazy possible things. Like that hair. The first thing is you're scared it's your fault—some what-for you deserve somehow. The second thing is you just decide: this is my life now. I held on and I knew I'd love him even if he *was* a monkey. I held on and told them not to let Robert in. Not to let him see. The nurse laughed at me. Saying don't worry, he'd be normal, soon enough. He would shed. The doctor would explain it all to Robert—"Mr. Pritchett"—before they let him in. Save him the shock. Men: back then we left them out, where life was concerned. Thirty-one years ago, sweet little Redmund. Not a monkey at all, now. *Now* he has that caterpillar mustache and the muttonchops, like the pictures on all the awful heavy rock records he listens to. I banned those records from downstairs, at least when I'm at home. Even a guilty mother has limits. And anyway, he's free to play them up in his own room just about whenever he wants. His room, his rules. That's how we keep the peace.

Reddie takes the trays off the folding tables with a funny act of playing the waiter, dish towel over his arm. Backs ass-wise through the swinging door to the kitchen. Starts the water for the dishes. I switch off the TV clicker, and sit here in my big old chair that we brought from the other house. I feel the throb in my knees — always there now — and with my hands all clawed-up like lobsters, I *can* believe how old I am. And let me tell you, still a surprise: one minute you're a little red-dirt girl in West Virginia with chores, brothers and sisters, noise and life, and the next minute: this. The quiet TV, dimming down. The sound of water from the tap in the other room, running out one pipe and down another.

It is what it is. Every weeknight, Reddie comes home from work. I cook. We watch his shows because mine are all daytime. He does the washing up. After that he reads his science fiction, I read mysteries, and we both smoke the Pall Malls I buy out of Robert's social security. After which I pull myself up the narrow blue-carpeted stairs and hie me to bed. Every weeknight.

Every weeknight except Thursday. Thursdays, Reddie's got Scouts.

In bed, I look up at the ceiling and think of the ways that other people make do. Like: Is it too late to start drinking? Would that help me to sleep?

Reddie has a lot of names. He seems to like it like that. Robert gave him three: Redmund Earl Pritchett, real Virginia names. He's Reddie to me, but only me. At work he's Red, or Earl. Good job, at the hospital, with computers; record-keeping, and he brings home most of the paycheck. The Boy Scouts call him Red too, even though they're apparently supposed to call him Pritchett, sir, like in the army. As if. Yes, sir. Red, dude, cool car. Sometimes he revs the engine for them. Boys always love that.

*

WHEN HE'S AT WORK, like now, I pick up the house. Strip the sheets from his bed, gather the clothes from the floor. At the hearing the judge said I was responsible for him. Real slow, he said it. I told him, a mother's always responsible. Someone makes a mess? A mother is the one to clean it up. Reddie was sent home.

Then there was the scene at the church, and church was done. All that "love" those people had? They folded it right up. Put it away, so easily. After that the rest wasn't a shock: the scenes at Kroger's. (Then driving to Easton to pick up dinner.) The post office. The notes in the mailbox. Trying to get them before Reddie saw, which he did anyway, sometimes.

We had just enough of Robert's insurance money to make the move here. Start clean. Wash off that red dirt one last time. Stay clean, no matter what.

There's a poster just above Reddie's bed, for a band called Iron Maiden. Now the name sounds pretty promising, at least compared to the others—The Black Sabbath, Judas Priest—you can almost imagine this maiden: a robot woman, something out of Reddie's sci-fis, beautiful and strong. But oh no. Instead, on this poster, is a ghoul: a monster with a peeling-off face. I chuckle a little on my careful way down the basement steps, arms full of dirty laundry. He's a real horror, to match the music (electric oompah-loompah, if you want my opinion). Am I supposed to be impressed when I see that face on the wall of Reddie's room? Scared? As if Halloween should last all year now. It's funny because Reddie's not like that; he's sweet.

I fold on the kitchen table, mate the socks. I iron Reddie's blue work shirts. I leave his Scout uniform to the side. He irons that himself, just so, going around each patch.

I have my Salada tea, and a man on the *Donahue Show* is claiming he met Jesus in Rio de Janeiro. Jesus spoke perfect English even though he looked like a local and had nothing—not even any shoes on his feet. I don't believe in that stuff anymore, but I believe there's forces in nature that make us good and bad, and our job is to protect the good. Make the bad as small as possible. We're all here on this earth together and we can't get off, so we've just got to take care of each other as best we can. No matter what mistakes we make.

When we first moved, Reddie used to cry. I wanted to hold him and rock him like a little boy but I didn't dare.

*

TWO MEMORIES:

One: Reddie coming home from school. He must have been just seven or eight, carrying a dead bird. A fat Virginia robin. I screamed and screamed. Like a wild bird myself. It could be diseased! Get it out! Reddie wasn't crying, he was calm. Hadn't killed it. He had just found it, and he wanted to fix it.

Two: Reddie home from work, here, in *this* room, the day he told me about teaching Scouts. He still had his hospital ID hanging from his neck. He had the Scoutmaster's guidebook, holding it in just the same way, with both his careful hands, like the body of that bird. He was ready for no. Ready for this will not work. Ready for whatever screams I might have left in me.

But in the end, I helped him study.

*

ON SUMMER WEEKENDS Reddie's out with the troop, camping, river rafting, even climbing, can you imagine? He's got some color and he's filled out, stands up straighter. Like Robert used to do, years ago, putting on his hat, walking out the door like a man with somewhere to go. He's started making the coffee in the morning, and I come down and find him at the table, with a mug set out for me.

When he first brought home the Scoutmaster's guide he would quote from it all the time, reading with an unlit Pall Mall in his mouth. Almost on page one, it says, "It is easier to build a boy than it is to repair a man." And I don't know about the boys but Reddie *is* getting better; he's mending. He's with the Scouts, working outside. So much better than hidden away upstairs listening to his awful music. That ridiculous poster of the monster might still be pinned to the wall, but Reddie's out in the world, in the sunshine with the boys, smiling and getting tan.

I make sure things are safe too. On every overnight there's always an assistant Scoutmaster. Or at least one of the boys' fathers comes along, to chaperone and keep an eye.

*

THIS WEEKEND THERE WAS NO TRIP; everyone wanted to be around for the big Gallery10 opening: the new mall. Today was the very first day, balloons and everything. Even the parking lot is six stories. It's dark and gray, full of cars going the wrong way — but when you cross through the big white doors it's like the whole world is made of quartz and brass. Alabaster tile. Everything sparkling and perfect, skylights above. Like being inside Champagne. I wore earrings and an old church dress, and I was glad. I was glad I rose up, to match the place. Even if Red was dressed more like the parking lot: big arms sticking out of a sleeveless T and that thick caterpillar mustache sitting right in the middle of his face, waiting to cross.

We stopped in the pet store, and it was full of people, like a party. Reddie held a puppy in his arms, kissing the fur on its head. Beautiful. I said I wondered should we bring it home and he said, Ha! Too much work. You can get one if you want. Then he went to look for his Halloween ghoul records at Sam Goody, so I went to A&S, the big big store at the end. I got lost in Towels and Sheets.

But then, right in the middle was a huge bed, layered in whites, like a centerpiece: a cake. Sinking into those soft down pillows, I had the idea that I could leave Reddie. Leave him and the dark little house, and the big sprung chair, his old trophies and everything else, leave it all, leave the vigilance, the checking up, all the worry the judge laid on me, and just move in here, to the Gallery10. Move in and stay. Sleep on a different bed every night in this great bright place all alone. Never use the same towel twice.

Back at the food court, I stake out a seat while Reddie brings a food-of-the-world tray: kebabs, spring rolls, schnitzel, and tacos, and it's like you really can have any delirious thing you want, here. Reddie says it's a spaceship—from one of his stories—where you can live for a hundred years while you travel to a new solar system.

"You'd have kids, Ma. And they'd have grandkids. And then their kids would finally arrive, and have a brand-new planet."

So I feel guilty for leaving him out of my fantasy, of living in Towels, forever.

Sitting here in the food court with Redmund, I can see that he really is a man. I'm round and indistinct, even in my nice dress, and he's like everyone else here: body on display in sweatpants and gymnastic clothes—no suits, not a single tie to be seen. What Robert would think I have no idea. But Reddie does have the body of a man. He looks around the food court, amused, alert for a joke, as usual, but he's all straight lines, strong. Powerful arms. Curly black hair, thick on his head, tumbling down a little, across his forehead. A few curls of hair from below the collar of his shirt too. It wouldn't surprise me if half these spandex-clad girls were dreaming of him under their piles of cotton-candy hair.Who can even imagine what they're thinking? They're probably wondering why he took his mother out to Gallery10.

*

ONE OF THE DEALS I MADE with Red is that I come along to troop meetings once a month, just to see how things are. We make an excuse for me to come: sewing badges, things like that. And I get a chance to see the assistant leaders, Steve and Perry—Eagle Scouts—and look into their baby blue eyes and I have never, once, seen anything amiss. Nothing to hide. Nothing that they need to say to me. The younger boys run drills for Reddie and stand at attention for inspection, tucking their little tan shirts in. Reddie straightens their little web belts, makes sure the buckle is centered just so.

Sometimes I think that maybe we moved for nothing. Isn't it proof that Reddie's accomplished all this, without another "event"? It says in the guidebook that to teach people you find the right balance of guiding them and giving them freedom.

Now.

September is the busiest month. The little Cub Scouts are leaving the den and joining our troop. They're called tenderfoots, which just makes you picture it.

Reddie has to get them up to speed and plan all the overnights before the chill sets in, and for me there's the fund-raising and the big bake sale. The tenderfoots are in and out of the house, learning new things for their very first badges. There's one upstairs now, Tyler. After the doorbell I found him standing on the step, shy, looking out from his bangs. He said hello, like his mother had told him to. She was waiting in the car in her professional clothes, squinting up through the long fall light to make sure someone had let him in safely. She gave me a little official wave. Put her sunglasses on, pulled away.

Tyler is beautiful, but with a great big birthmark on his neck like a bruise on an apple. I saw it just as he was stepping in, while I held the door. My heart just goes out to anyone even a little bit different. It's like I said, we all have to take care of each other.

He's upstairs with Reddie, practicing knots, and I'm here in the kitchen baking. Running the mixer for the frosting. Thinking about leaving the bowl for Tyler to lick, if he wants to. Like I get to be a grandma after all, for all these boys.

I went upstairs ten minutes ago to get a dish towel—I put them all up in the closet there so I have an excuse—and the door to Reddie's room was closed, like I thought it would be. This is a no-no. We made a bargain. I knocked on Reddie's door, just like I've done a hundred times, and opened it quick!—no waiting around. This is what I do: I sing out, "Door Open! Door Op-en!" I do it with a little waggle of disapproval in my voice, which I just can't help, even if it does drive Reddie nuts.

Under the awful poster, the boy was on Reddie's bed, in his summer shorts, with thick blue rope in his little hands. Reddie was folded up in the chair opposite, hugging his knees. He was watching the boy's fingers and the rope intently, checking the knot, I guess. He wasn't close. He wasn't even on the bed.

But still, *Door Open*, that's the rule.

Door Open.

As soon as I get this batch in the oven I'll find some other little reason to go up there. In case it's closed again.

Maybe the frosting.

Eat, Eat, Eat

Sherine Gilmour

Hung ducks silent and red as a sunset,
rolls stuffed with bean curd (only 60 cents),
rolls stuffed with coconut custard (only 65 cents),
dumplings puffed with pork fat (5 for a dollar),

back-alley lo mein,
homemade tofu in bright orange jugs
served on wax paper squares with a mysterious syrup.

At the market, I fill red plastic bags, my backpack, my mouth
because my great-grandmother grew up on a farm
that only had one cow.

Because my grandmother watched her father eat his fill
(he worked at the factory so he ate first),
and then she married my grandfather
(who stabbed someone with a fork
for saying hello while he ate his steak),
and later she taught my mother how to get by
(coffee and water).

Because at least one basement, one attic, and several closets
brim with sugar packets, ketchup packets, and coffee creamers
(you never know).

Because to this day, the women in my family
vie for the role of who eats last.

But here, I can wander Canal Street,
Centre Street, walk all around Confucius Plaza

and rarely feel plagued
that I could ever have too much,

that anyone would resent me taking
a little more on my plate, ordering a few extra items.

Here, everyone acts like lovers
feeding each other on a first date,
throwing bread to pigeons,
eating on a stoop together from steaming Styrofoam boxes.

When my great-grandmother took care of me,
I had something to eat every morning.
Her husband had died with factory lung,
and her house teetered and steamed,
boiled and brimmed.
The stove was covered in kettles,
oven filled with pies.
"Eat, eat, eat," she scolded and sang, sang and danced,
tried to shove dollar bills into my hands,
which my mother always returned
despite our empty cupboards and sour milk.

When my mother slept late (vodka),
I had to wait
to eat, but not now,
now, I can taste a thousand things
(a thousand-year egg whose ashen skin
splits to golden yolk safe within).

The girl behind the counter wears an apron
over her small plump belly.
I love you, paper sack stained with butter.
I love everything stained with butter.
I nearly cry with relief and joy
as we work through the language barrier,
point and nod

(I'll take one of those, one of those,
and three of those, thanks).

Who else can I buy for?
Myself, my husband
(our dog?),
friends, strangers, old teachers
(can I mail food to poets?).

Dear lychee nuts,
dear pork fried rice,
drink boxes of strawberry juice, plum juice,
salted lemonade,
follow me home
over the bridge, the river, like the pied piper.

I don't want this to end.
Say we'll always be together.
I don't want to wait to inherit ketchup packets.
Promise me I'll never be alone and hungry again.

PATRIMONY

Nancy Green

(From *Bellevue Literary Review*)

After I received my inheritance, a small, unexpected gift from my father, I decided to go back to school to get my PhD in psychology. I became a doctoral candidate at Rutgers, doing my dissertation on cognitive therapy, with a focus on client motivation in the treatment of mood disorders.

One day I was at the office of my advisor, Dr. Dominic Zampano, waiting to discuss my statement of purpose, the part of the dissertation where I define my keywords and concepts. Judging from the notes he had written on my latest draft, Dr. Zampano was unhappy with how I had defined motivation. My definition "lacked precision." I had to admit, among all my keywords, motivation had been the hardest for me to define. I'd spent weeks on it, reviewing mountains of literature. Aaron Beck, Albert Bandura, not to mention Pavlov, Freud, Watson, Skinner, and a slew of others. Each had his own definition of motivation—but what about me, what was Deirdre Cantwell's definition? Frankly though, I thought I'd nailed it in my introduction. So I was feeling frustrated that Dr. Zampano had waited to raise his concerns, after I had gone ahead and written four chapters. Still, I recognized that greater precision is always desirable. So I felt open to his criticism and told myself that's what advisors are for.

I sat in the waiting room, eager to talk to him. The room had no personality. It was a compact, windowless space with cinder block walls painted a neutral hue. No pictures. The bookcase was empty except for three copies of the *Diagnostic and Statistical Manual of Mental Disorders* and a souvenir mug from the 1996 American Psychological Association Conference, Orlando, Florida. A scuffed Naugahyde chair stood opposite mine, and in the corner, in a gray plastic tub, a ragged plant thrust its dry, tongue-like leaves into the filtered air. So there I was, waiting to meet with Dr. Zampano, when I became aware that he was late; an awareness—not an obsession—a simple awareness within the broader continuum of my thoughts, thoughts that ranged flexibly, but that included at various intervals: *he's late, he's late*. And I could hear him talking on his phone behind his closed door, so I knew he was there, and I knew that he knew I was there (he'd buzzed me in). I doubled-checked my calendar. Our meeting was definitely scheduled for three o'clock, and the clock on the wall said three-eleven.

Waiting, I found myself glancing again at the notes Dr. Zampano had written on my draft (in his tiny, feathery pencil script, so I had to squint even with my glasses on). I glanced at one note in particular that floated in the margin of page twenty-nine: *You call this a definition of motivation, Deirdre?* I tried distracting myself because I did not want to think badly of Dr. Zampano. I did not need the stress. I'm not a child, I told myself; and he's not my father.

Everyone knows that people write things they would never say face-to-face. Best not to read into his note until I had the opportunity to speak with Dr. Zampano in person, I thought, to find out what he really meant.

By now it was three-thirteen, but I tried maintaining a neutral, mindful mood. I told myself to think objectively about time: how we tend to anthropomorphize it (e.g., *"I'm killing time," "time stood still," "Father Time"*). And I thought about how I would have to define "time" as a keyword in my dissertation if I were a doctoral candidate in astrophysics instead of psychology. And just then I heard Dr. Zampano chuckling in a low, vaguely intimate way behind the door, which suggested to me that perhaps his phone call wasn't business, but personal. This made me personalize his lateness—as if Dr. Zampano was deliberately ignoring me out of some petty or even sadistic need of his.

Automatically, I created a narrative about him and his motive for acting in such a rude, dismissive way toward me. The story (in my mind) was about a vain old man stuck in Rutgers instead of the aimed-for Stanford. He was talented, yes, but not enough to make it into the big leagues, and early in his career had been surpassed by a brighter, more ambitious colleague who rose to prominence—a psychology superstar like an Aaron Beck or an Albert Bandura—eclipsing Dr. Zampano, leaving him behind in bitter disappointment. Dr. Zampano languished in his faded, Naugahyde-furnished office in academe now. My story included me as well, as the thirty-year-old, up-and-coming psychologist with new ideas about what motivates clients, ideas that he found threatening, and so he retaliated by making me wait.

I did realize that this was a construct, a fiction created by me to explain Dr. Zampano's behavior, and rationalize my annoyance, and that I was personalizing his delay way too much. Aaron Beck defines *personalization* as a common type of cognitive distortion or error in thinking. Its most extreme forms—persecutory delusions—are seen in paranoid patients. Less dramatic forms of personalization are found in neurotic patients who tend to exaggerate the extent to which external events are related to them. So I was aware that I was thinking (erroneously, vis-à-vis Aaron Beck) that Dr. Zampano's delay had something to do with me (although there was nobody else but me in the waiting room).

I told myself (self-talk) that I was being overly sensitive, merely projecting my own needs and expectations onto Dr. Zampano. (I had learned to be precisely punctual from my late father. My sisters and I would never even *think* of keeping him waiting.)

I coughed now, and cleared my throat a couple of times, hinting of my presence. But by three-fifteen I found myself trying to remember my past interactions with Dr. Zampano. Had there been any friction between us? Anything to warrant his rejection of me (if indeed it was a rejection, and not a projection on my part, i.e., of my own erroneous drama). And I remembered once when we were in the elevator together and Dr. Zampano said "Hello, Deirdre" to me, and then "Have a nice day," as I was getting off at my floor. Very human. I recalled other similar, vivid scenes in the elevator. No friction. But then Dr. Zampano always seemed slightly aloof, and he'd held his graying, bearded jaw stiffly, in a way that suggested to me, once I thought about it, that he felt out of place crammed into the elevator with doctoral students and junior faculty, and that he wanted something more—his own elevator maybe, at Stanford or Harvard—to lift him straight to the top floor without his waiting at anyone else's stops. But his failures aren't my fault, I thought, and I shouldn't be blamed.

I waited. The only sound was the low, electric whir of the clock; that, and the sound of Dr. Zampano's voice on his phone call, which, judging from his intimate and vaguely patronizing tone, I assumed—again, perhaps erroneously—was with another woman. And I had the recurring thought—recurring, not intrusive—that I did not want to think badly of Dr. Zampano. There could be hundreds of explanations why he was keeping me waiting, I told myself. The issue was: what could I do about it? Knock, I knew that. Self-efficacy is a key concept for Albert Bandura, the father of cognitive theory. So of course I thought of knocking, but how? I didn't want my knocking to give the wrong impression, by conveying impatience, or any other sort of fussy, intolerant attitude. I didn't want it to sound like a condemning knock, as if I were angry about the wait and blaming him. My knocking had to be candid, but not confrontational. It had to be a neutral knock. I decided to give Dr. Zampano a few more minutes.

I could use this time, I thought. Between my dissertation and my internship at the clinic, I barely had time to breathe, so why not see Dr. Zampano's delay as a gift? Finding what's positive in a challenging situation, or even a tragic one, is the hallmark of emotional health. Isn't that a main thesis of my dissertation? I flipped the pages open to the case presentation of my patient "Angela V."

I was using her case to illustrate certain key dynamics in the motivational process. She's in an abusive relationship with a man and can't seem to leave. She keeps hoping that the man will change and start treating her with respect, like a human being. Hope is a central aspect of many motivational theories. I have written seven pages on hope alone, where I take pains to distinguish it from wishful thinking and/or blind optimism. Let me use this extra time to polish the "Angela" section, I thought. My chair's battered Naugahyde twin stood across from me. I put my laptop on it, spread out my session progress notes, and grabbing my red pen, began to read:

Therapist: You mentioned that you were at the end of your rope. Have you thought of leaving him? [Open question]

Angela: What?

Therapist: Leaving him. [Reiteration]

Angela: Hell no! That's just what he wants me to do, so he can get with that bitch Melanie.

Reading, I was aware of the temptation—a temptation, not an actual impulse—to change Angela's answer into something a little more ambivalent, like "Yes, I want to leave, but I'm afraid to"; something to show that she was at least conflicted, and making progress, which would better illustrate my point about motivation. Everyone knows that researchers sometimes skew their data to fit the hypotheses they want to prove. But I could never imagine myself fabricating Angela's answers. Either you're ambivalent or you're not. I scrolled down:

Therapist: I understand. Hell no, you're not leaving. [Reflection, including affect]

Angela: He's the only man that's ever loved me.

And of course it was frustrating to see Angela's continued attachment to the man after all the sessions we had done. *You call that love, Angela?* I'd wanted to say. Still, a therapist is there to listen, not argue. (I had learned how to listen from my late father. My sisters and I wouldn't *dream* of contradicting him.)

Besides, I did not want to view Angela's attachment to the man personally, as if she was deliberately staying in an abusive relationship in order to undermine my dissertation. I just hoped I could help her find the motivation someday to unearth the authentic Angela buried deep inside.

Now it was three-twenty, and I thought I heard Dr. Zampano saying good-bye, a faint, plaintive farewell before hanging up. And I started to feel stressed again, realizing that I'd be inside his office any second, having to defend my definition. I tried imagining what he was unhappy with, so I could be ready with my answers. (My sisters and I learned to be ready from our late father. We never knew what mood to expect from him.)

I glanced anxiously around the room, at the trinity of *Diagnostic and Statistical Manuals of Mental Disorders* on the bookshelf, static and silent as Stonehenge, at that plant in the corner, gasping. The clock whirred undeterred. You're not a child, it seemed to be saying. But I was wrong: Dr. Zampano's call wasn't over. There was a long silence, punctuated by that muffled, salacious chuckle. I imagined the woman on the other end of the phone: young, attractive—another doctoral candidate? At any rate a woman who was flattered to be receiving the undivided attention of an eminent, though ultimately disappointed professor.

Listening, I couldn't help wondering what it would be like to be in a relationship with Dr. Zampano. Obviously, it must be lonely. Nonetheless I started imagining how Dr. Zampano kissed, and I wondered whether he was a gentleman in bed—attentive, caring—or self-centered? It had never entered my mind before— sex with Dr. Zampano—and I resisted it entering my mind at that moment, against my will (conscious self). Still, the image—a stock image, not an elaborate fantasy—of us embracing, undressing, moving as one, made me think: did I unconsciously want to sleep with Dr. Zampano? Any clinical psychologist worth her salt would have to consider that possibility. Freud, the father of psychoanalysis, defined *Eros* as the primary instinct, the basic motivating force for human beings.

And so I tried to remember my past interactions with Dr. Zampano. Had there been any frisson between us? Anything that could be interpreted as erotic? Perhaps that would explain my hesitation to knock innocently on his door. Was I harboring some latent need to be pursued by him? Seduced? Some desire to have Dr. Zampano find me in the waiting room with my laptop open, my session notes spread out across the Naugahyde chair, anticipating?

And I remembered one night last week when I was working late in the library. The light was low, and I lay on the carpet between the stacks, alone, jotting notes. And Dr. Zampano found me there. He held a monograph tightly in his arms—his own research? I've since wondered. He stooped down gently, all the while eyeing my notes with an appraising stare, and in a soft voice he whispered, "Hello Deirdre, how's it coming?"

"Good," I'd said.

We chatted intently in hushed tones as I recall, about Aaron Beck if I'm not mistaken. Nothing personal. Very professional. And I'd said, "See you next week at three o'clock," as he stood up to leave.

I recalled other collegial interactions with him in the library, and several in the elevator. No frisson. If I had any unconscious desire to sleep with Dr. Zampano, I wasn't aware of it. So there could be hundreds of other explanations, I told myself, why I was still sitting alone in the waiting room, not knocking on Dr. Zampano's door. The issue was, what should I do about it? Again, not what I personally, as in me, Deirdre Cantwell, should do about it. Not "I" in the narrow, erroneous sense of that word. Rather what should I, as in *anyone*, objectively, do?

That's the challenge, I reminded myself. Finding the right motivation in a stressful situation, or even an infuriating one, is what makes us human, and different from wild animals acting on blind instinct. Isn't that a main thesis of my dissertation? So I'll knock when I'm good and ready. Let them laugh, I thought, staring at his closed door.

And at that point I felt an unavoidable sadness for the woman on the other end of the call, or girl really, if I was correct in assuming her existence, and her subsequent preoccupation with Dr. Zampano. Because, rightly or wrongly, I got the feeling she was probably young enough to be his daughter. And I guessed that, ostensibly, she was someone who looked up to him, and who wanted security, stability, and that undeniable validation one experiences from winning the affection and approval of an older, more worldly, authoritative man: a father figure. And I knew she'd learn inevitably (i.e., the hard way) that a relationship with Dr. Zampano—evidently a laugh a minute—would wind up, over time, to be one-sided. I just hoped that she, whether real or imagined, was the sort of girl who wouldn't become cynical and embittered by her disillusionment with Dr. Zampano, but would maintain a healthy skepticism the next time, knowing that she's not a child, and feeling confidant that she can stand on her own two feet.

At that point I returned to my dissertation, and, scrolling down, combed through my transcript looking for even just one ounce of motivation on Angela's part to leave the man:

Therapist: You believe he's the only man who has ever loved you? [Reflection]

Angela: Yeah. Besides he's a good father. He has a job, and gets my kid things. He's like Santa Claus with him.

Therapist: He's like Santa Claus. [Complex reflection]

Angela: Yeah.

Seeing Angela's words—the *real* Angela, not the motivated one I wished she were—I wondered what it must be like to be her. And I realized it must be lonely. Telling herself that a man is a good father to rationalize staying with him, staying in an abusive relationship.

I checked my watch. By now it was three-thirty, hopelessly late, but I found myself thinking about Angela's child. And I remembered meeting him once at the clinic—a tiny, sallow-skinned five-year-old. He sat in the waiting room, playing on the floor with a pair of plastic, multijointed action figures—perhaps Christmas presents. He hopped the toys across the carpet—in his mind a gigantic speedway—puppeteering them in loud, frenzied pursuit; crashing them in an incredible, pretend explosion, only to pop them up again, revived.

It starts so young, I thought, the imagining, the pretending, the illusions. And without warning, I found myself missing my father, but no more, I had to admit, than when he was alive.

Keep Moving

Patrick Hansel

(From *Perfume River Poetry Review*)

We belong to the dust, the dust
belongs to no one. Ask the bones
of Domingo, who crossed into Arizona
with his six-year-old son, walking
through the mountains, avoiding
the desert snakes and the eyes
burning a hole through the sky.
On the third day, they ran
out of water, and on the fourth
Domingo began to run out, his skin
tightening, his eyes wandering
through heaven and earth, the heaven
you make in your mind when flesh
begins to die, skin for skin,
bone to its bone, the heart's fierce
surrender. There comes a moment
in time where the mind can accept
what the body knows. We belong
to the sun, the sun belongs to no one.
Domingo placed his right hand
on his son's head, drew a crooked cross,
commanded him on. The son
obeyed with his feet. The last order
of the living is the first wish of the dead:
Keep moving.

A ROOM THAT HAS LIZZY IN IT

Michele Herman

(From *Outside In Literary & Travel Magazine*)

In September even the birthday parties stopped. Now they're starting back up again, but quietly. They're mostly at home after school instead of the usual Saturday extravaganzas at the Chelsea Piers bowling alley. No one's even hiring magicians to do the old disappearing-underpants trick; we have no stomach for vanishings.

Today—a warm, particularly acrid-smelling Thursday in October, 2001—happens to be Benny Spiegel's ninth birthday, and I'm on my way to the middle-income West Village Houses to pick up my two sons at his party. Call me perverse, but I can't think of anyplace I would rather be than Benny the Terrible's birthday party. Somehow I have landed in a generation of strivers, but I don't ask much as I stroll down workaday Washington Street breathing through my mouth. I walk this street every day: to the Grove Street School to pick up my boys, to the post office to kiss my slides good luck as I send them off to galleries, to the library to hunt for a Friday night video. How at home I feel with cobblestones under my shoes, the Hudson River by my side. Even the dog pee that leaves a sticky sheen on the lampposts belongs to pets who know my scent.

The West Village Houses couldn't be stingier on the outside, clad in small maroon-washed concrete blocks trying their hardest to look like brick. But inside they are a little society of helping professionals—social workers, guidance counselors, even a bona fide nurse or two. I open the metal door and, like the neighborhood dogs, take a whiff. I detect vanilla and butter and cane sugar, and though I am four floors away I know instantly this is the smell of Benny Spiegel's birthday cake made by Janeen, the baking babysitter from

Jamaica. I rush up the institutional stairs toward my children and our friends and the solace of buttercream. When I push the button marked Spiegel a harsh buzzer sounds, welcoming me in its unceremonious way into the last bastion of Manhattan nurturers.

Mara, Benny's mom, lets me in.

"My landsmen," I say, stretching my arms wide to include all the moms and kids and Janeen in the galley kitchen. Mara herself, I should point out, is not a nurturer, but a nurturer's spouse. Her husband, Barry, is a clinical psychologist, but she works for the Board of Ed, which gives her insider knowledge, which is one reason we sometimes call her Queen.

"Spider-Man," she says with some regret by way of greeting, showing me her living room, where the kids are gathered on her impractical off-white carpet around Benny's impressive Lego collection and the moms are madly chatting the way moms will. The room is strung halfheartedly with plastic spiders and fake spider webs.

"He had to have Spider-Man, Brooke," says Mara. "Thank heaven it's almost Halloween." We're all feeling funny about Spider-Man these days. The movie is due out soon, and it stars Toby Maguire, who's adorable, but on the down side, the posters have all been pulled because they showed Spider-Man scaling the Twin Towers. In the middle of all the spiders, a yellow cartoon-character piñata hangs from the ceiling fan.

"Pikachu," I say with a fondness I didn't know I felt for the squeaky pansexual Pokémon. Mara apologizes for mixing her birthday-party metaphors. But I don't mind this relic from a benign ancient civilization.

Eventually we hug, and stare into each other's eyes. We all do this these days, with new license. I notice that Mara has not plucked her eyebrows. They are growing in dark and choppy, as if they've fallen out of their V formation, and I fear this is brash old Mara's only way to cry for help. I scan her up and down for signs of additional neglect, and sure enough her toenails have just the tiniest circle of red polish left, and her toes look as if they've been squashed together too long, like old garlic cloves. "You okay?" I ask, and she waves me away with the kind of half-answer we all trade in lately: "Yeah, yeah, peachy."

I keep an eye on all the moms, on Shlomit our kibbutznik and Desi our dance therapist and Arlene the mother of twins and Lizzy, especially Lizzy. When I go to sleep I don't see the towers fall and rise and fall again a mile away from my bed; what I see in the dark is a tiny collage of crosshatches, formed of the worry lines around my friends' eyes.

I scan the room for Glen and Danny, my boys, and find them with Jinsong, a new Chinese boy in Glen's class who shares Glen's belief that life is one great physics experiment. They are attempting to saw their slippery Spider-Man plates in half with plastic knives while little brother Danny cheers them on. I kiss the sweaty tops of their heads and get the day's news. I ask Jinsong whether his mom is coming to pick him up because, speaking of peachy, Jinsong has a new baby brother I'm in love with; I want to have my party pleasures all lined up.

Finally, I scan for Lizzy. I always feel better in a room that has Lizzy in it. I find her leaning over the kitchen counter, deep in conversation.

Hungrily I make my way toward her.

Mara puts a hand on my forearm, and I jump. "I wouldn't go over there if I were you," she says. "Mara," I say. "I've been sitting at home alone all day, listening to public radio. They just did a segment on the plague, and they weren't talking about the Middle Ages. I think I can handle the conversation over there."

Lizzy and I met nine years ago on a bench at Bleecker Street playground. It was November, and our babies were packed into their strollers, and it started to drizzle. The other mothers briskly packed up those little yellow Cheerios dispensers they had and slid them into their diaper bags with the Provençal patterns. They left in pairs or trios, as they always did, with their shirts tucked in. I was new to the neighborhood then, and new at this job, with an asthmatic baby, a career as an illustrator slipping from my fingers, and a husband working long lawyer hours but not making partner. It was not clear any of us was going to be okay.

At exactly the same moment, this woman and I turned toward each other. I went first. "Do you ever feel like you're going to lose your mind?"

"I was going to say 'fucking mind,'" she answered, smiling.

She pointed to a building across the street. "See that pile of laundry about to fall off the windowsill? That's my apartment," she said. "Race you."

We got to her dim hall laughing and out of breath. We shook the rain out of our hair and left shoes and strollers and puddles all over the tiled floor.

She had the same dining chairs from Workbench as ours. Glen was crying in that starved, enervated way that could crank up to an attack. Or maybe it was another ear infection. I sat down at my chair, pulled up my shirt and nursed him.

When her baby was successfully transferred to his crib, she held out a hand for shaking and introduced herself. Then she told me I looked like a hot meal would do me good.

She fed me leftover spaghetti with pesto warmed in the microwave, on a Winnie-the-Pooh plate.

"This is the best meal I've ever had in my entire life," I told this stranger named Lizzy, "and I don't even like pesto." I asked for seconds, and thirds, and somewhere in the middle of the helpings I began to cry. Lizzy looked around for a Kleenex and when she couldn't find one she shrugged and handed me a Pamper. With my mouth full and a strand of spaghetti not quite sucked in, I added "never touch the stuff," and my crying resolved itself into laughter. We laughed like lab partners at the delight of trying to fill me up faster than Glen could empty me. I blew my nose into the diaper, and we laughed some more.

At home later that night, as I lowered Glen to his crib trying not to set off a screaming fit, I noticed something foreign in his fine brown hair. I fished out a fragrant green spaghetti strand and clutched it like Scarlett O'Hara with her radish and thought that maybe I wouldn't lose my mind after all.

Now I look among the gang, my gang, to see if everyone is here, but my eye lands instead on a familiar red-and-white paper on the kitchen counter. It's a Metro-North schedule, opened like an altarpiece triptych to the page headed "Leave New York." Oh, no, I think. Please no. She's loud and annoying and has garlic toes, but please don't let Mara leave.

But I have walked straight into what I've begun to think of as "the conversation." Here in Manhattan it drones on in the background all the time. It starts furtively, like preteens discussing sex. It used to be easy to ignore. The first snatch I hear is this: "I say, if you're going to move, really move. Go to Camden, Maine."

And now they begin the list. They are talking about benign things, wonderful things like backyards and the rolling hills of the Taconic Parkway. I like these things as much as anyone.

"So what do you guys think about Nyack?" asks Arlene. She's never quite gotten over having twins, and needs our blessing on every decision she makes.

The group decides Nyack is a viable option. They move on to highways. I listen patiently while they approve of the Palisades and the Merritt. Mara is measuring out miles in the air between her thumb and forefinger.

I look over at Lizzy but I can't get her eye. She and I always say, when our time comes, reserve us a room at the Village Nursing Home, and then scatter our ashes from Pier 40. We've picked out the bench in Abingdon Square where the late-morning sun shines and where we'll feed the pigeons just to annoy the yuppies.

When Arlene says Nyack for a second time, rolling it around on her tongue like this year's Beaujolais nouveau, I take a swat.

"Cute," I say, "but wrong side of the river. No trains. You'll need two cars."

Moms begin firing out towns, and as quick as they say the names I shoot them down. I hardly ever leave the city limits, but somehow I have stores of intelligence on every burgh they mention.

"Cold Spring," says Shlomit, who was in the Israeli Army and can be very commanding. As if on cue, we hear the military sound of a low-flying helicopter, a sound as common these days as Mister Softee's jingle. We know the drill: we freeze, look toward the ceiling, and then, when it stops, release all our hot breath into Mara's living room and try to pick up where we left off.

Cold Spring is easy: "Way too many antique stores and three incredibly overpriced restaurants, the kind where the menu actually says 'fine dining.'"

Desi says Katonah. "Great art museum, but racist." I tell them about friend of a friend who was racial-profiled there. "Not once, but twice," I say.

I dismiss Larchmont's highly reputed school system, tell them Irvington is the boonies, Montclair not half as integrated as they make it look. Meanwhile I look around the room to see who's serious, to see whom I stand to lose. But it's no use—I can't stand to lose any of them.

Finally I can't take it. "The West Village!" I scream and they all look up at me as if I've started voguing across the off-white rug. "Why not consider that? Especially seeing as how you've all already made lives here and your children attend school here and you have jobs here and own apartments here and have made very good friends here."

Lizzy has been uncharacteristically quiet, so I walk over and sling an arm around her. "Looks like it's you and me, my dear." I note, with alarm, a faint smell of cigarettes on her. She quit smoking before Sam was born. I know it's the fall trend, falling back into conquered bad habits. But Lizzy isn't trendy. Lizzy can't start smoking again. Her mother died of lung cancer.

"Brooke," she says. "Nip it."

I protest; I am just warming up. I tell them, with the satisfaction of a really well-placed cliché, that you can run but you can't hide, even though I suspect it's entirely possible to spend a lifetime hiding in Irvington, Westport, East Hampton. Janeen calls from the kitchen with a two-minute warning on the birthday cake. I try a different tack.

"I'll tell you about life outside the city," I say, and from my arsenal I recount for them the scariest, most spiteful suburban story I can think of. They're all in a tight circle around me now.

"It's Wednesday," I say, "and you take your kids out to eat at Chuck E. Cheese because" — I look around the room and name husbands — "Avi … Roger … Barry … James just called to say he'll be late again. At first you don't want to take them to Chuck E. Cheese and you're sure you'll never be *that* kind of suburban mother."

Lizzy is tightening her jaw and neck tendons in a way that says shush up now if you know what's good for you. I know she's trying to save me. But they made me listen to them and now I'm going to give it right back to them.

"In fact you hold out for a long time, but all of your kids' friends go there and talk about it at school until it starts to seem as normal as wearing running shoes all day. And you pass it in the suv on the way home from soccer or Hebrew school or guitar or ikeido or the orthodontist, and your kids beg, and you know that they're at the developmental stage where it's important not to be too different, so you put on the blinker and you turn into the parking lot."

"What a lovely parable, Brooke," Arlene interrupts. "A novel way to tell us you have a little problem with the suburbs."

"And Chuck E. Cheese surprises you," I continue, "because they serve a bowl of strawberry applesauce, beautiful pink applesauce." Like a geisha, I cup my hands toward the circle of moms in a beautiful-bowl-of-applesauce gesture. "It's right there on the table without you even having to order it. The kids love it and you love Chuck E. Cheese for being so attuned to your desire to get some good healthy food into them and not pander to their worst tastes. And because everyone's so happy and having their needs met, you make Chuck E. Cheese a regular stop on Wednesday nights, when the afterschool schedule is especially nuts."

The kids are getting restless. A fight is breaking out over the Bionicles, but I am not ceding the floor.

"And then one Wednesday night you go — " I pause dramatically, " — but there's no bowl of beautiful pink applesauce. There's a new menu and you hunt and hunt but there's no applesauce anywhere on it, only a lot of gooey greasy foods with …." And here I waggle my fingers while sliding my hands back and forth, a gesture that in another story might be raindrops or piano playing, but here can mean only one thing: "a big slab of jack cheese on top, sweating from the microwave."

"You ask the waiter about the applesauce and he doesn't know so he calls over the manager and he says, oh, the kids weren't eating the applesauce so it didn't pay. And there you are at Chuck E. Cheese in your running shoes, in your fat jeans, on the molded plastic seat." I have no idea what kind of seats Chuck E. Cheese has; I've never been to one.

"But all this is okay," I conclude, "because suddenly you remember the time back in college when you thought you might make a good political speechwriter someday, and you decide to send an e-mail to the executives of Chuck E. Cheese or whatever corporation owns it, getting them to reinstate the applesauce policy, and maybe you'll start an e-mail campaign among your friends. And you feel like a real activist—"

Just as I'm finishing up my speech, the door pushes slowly open. We all stop and stare as Jinsong's mom's small dark head pokes in. She is holding the peachy baby, the first baby born in the neighborhood since September 11. She never lets this baby out of her sight. He is tightly wrapped, as always, in his white blanket, and she clutches him to her chest like a poultice. Somehow she has managed to take off her shoes. She nods hello, several times, with more downward motion than up, as if apologizing for her presence, and then stands in the doorway next to the Razor scooters, looking terribly far from home. Even the littlest of the neighborhood kids know that if you dig deep enough in the Bleecker Street sandbox you eventually reach China, the far side of the world. It hits me suddenly that I am asking far too much. I am asking more than my friends or my city or my world has to offer.

Lizzy walks toward me and grips the fleshiest part of my upper arm. She says my name and leads me forcibly into Mara and Barry's bedroom, where I realize I've never been. The off-white carpet continues in here. Everything else is pastel and frilly. The dresser is covered with photos. "Look," I say, pointing to a wedding picture. "Barry has hair."

"Brooke," says Lizzy again.

"Stop saying my name, would you?" I say. I know what she's going to tell me. I realize now I've known for days, but I averted my eyes and my ears each time she got too close.

"I wasn't ready to go public yet, but after that ...." She points to the living room and hunts for a word to describe my little performance. I fixate on a photo of the kids in their Fours class play, *Caps for Sale*. How I remember that day. There's Noam, Shlomit's son, still blond, with a stack of caps on his head. There's one of the twins with her chicken pox newly crusted over. And, as always, two monkeys side by side: my Glen and Lizzy's Sam. In the back you can just make out an exhausted-looking Lizzy and me on little nursery-school chairs, each with a nursing baby in our lap.

"Where?" I ask, but I realize I already know that too. Her favorite brother lives there. They always vacation there.

She squinches up her face like a student knowing that whatever answer she gives will be wrong. We say it in unison: "Brattleboro." Somehow my "Brattleboro" is spoken with conviction, hers with a question mark, as if we're rehearsing each other's parts.

We're silent for a minute.

"That's off Perry Street, right?" I finally say. "Right in the Grove Street School catchment zone."

We laugh. But then she gets down to business, rattling off practical reasons, the thin outer layer of reasons, for the move. Most of them revolve around her brainy husband, James, and the Internet and his portable business.

I look her in the eye. "Don't go. Tell him you changed your mind. Tell him you lost your fucking mind."

She lets out a sigh. "It's not just James. I'm not as brave as you are, Brooke. You make it hard."

I feel tired suddenly and sit down on Mara's bed. Lizzy leans on the blond dresser. I wonder why married people's bedrooms are so weirdly virginal. I wonder how we all misread so many signs.

I am not brave. I'm afraid that without Lizzy I'm just a woman on a Manhattan bench who doesn't have the sense to come in out of the storm.

"What about all our plans?" I say, panic rising as I think of how many of my days are predicated on Lizzy, and Glen's on Sam. "What about baseball camp?" I skip to the last page: "What about scattering our ashes from Pier 40?"

"I'm so sorry, Brooke. I had to make other plans." Her voice is shaking but the message is firm.

"Listen." She puts her hands on my upper arms to steady me and delivers a pep talk about a house they just saw online. "There's a whole guest cottage. You'll come and stay. There's a horse farm right down the road where they give lessons practically free." She bounces up and down, mimicking Danny as a horse-besotted toddler: "Hawssie! Hawssie!"

"I don't want horses. I want you, here." I point to the firmament of Mara's silly pale carpet. We hug, something we rarely do, and I feel the fleshy sensation of her breasts up against mine. I remember us after Danny and Sylvie, our second babies, were born three weeks apart, in our big nursing bras with the clever snaps, always riding up in the back from what felt then like an enormous motherly weight we were carrying. I look into Lizzy's familiar face, her limp hair, her crooked nose, the crease where her dimple hides. On the news there has been talk of sacrifices to come, lots of talk. What a fool

I have been to think I could gather my loved ones around me and pull the drawstring tight.

In the living room, I hear Janeen and Mara shushing the kids. The room goes dark as someone pulls the blinds. I've been away from my boys for too long.

"I guess it's time," I say, and Lizzy and I go back to the living room. We find a spot on the side near Benny. Mara, looking like a proper queen, carries the cake with its nine candles and one to grow on.

"By the way," Lizzy whispers. "There are no Chuck E. Cheeses in Vermont. There's a clause in the state constitution."

"They send them all over the border," I whisper back. "New Hampshire takes them in like orphans."

"You know the New Hampshire state motto, right?" she adds. "Chuck E. Cheese or die."

"Don't go," I say one more time, as if I have a say.

The kids tell Benny the Terrible he belongs in the zoo, and, true to form, he bops the two nearest ones on the head. His round baby cheeks are lit by the birthday candles, and he's beautiful. They're all beautiful. All I want is to stand here with the moms and watch the kids grow. I want to watch Jinsong's baby brother grow big and goofy like Jinsong, and break the big kids' Legos and beg for treats from Mister Softee. I haven't made other plans. I haven't even stocked up on bottled water. I don't see the point. All I want is to grow old with these people.

I look at Lizzy, but there's no light on her. She looks drawn and pasty. She's in a car that James is driving up the New York Thruway to the New England Thruway. She's growing staticky like WNYC, and I'm losing her.

*

WALKING BACK HOME WITH the boys down the narrow sidewalk on a block shrouded with eternal scaffolding, I let the tears come. In each of my sweaty, shaking hands I am gripping a Spider-Man goody bag. Under my arm I carry two pairs of blue jeans that Benny Spiegel, raised on Janeen's pork stew and coconut patties, has outgrown. Mara thrust them at me on my way out and though we didn't particularly need them I took them without a word. The little buildings along Washington Street mock me now that Lizzy won't be here to cast her crooked silhouette on their bricks. The blues bar on the corner, Roy Lichtenstein's studio, the just-renovated townhouses all filled with pregnant supermodels—right now I hate them all. A woman in heels on her way home from work comes toward us and I have to push my oblivious boys aside to make room for her to pass. I feel like taking the whole maroon hulk of the West Village Houses and its do-gooders and shoving it out of my way. Now look what you've done, I want to say to the world at large; you've driven Lizzy away. Tears and snot are dripping onto my shirt. Glen is eyeing me fearfully, not having a clue what's wrong. I don't have a Kleenex. I wasn't prepared for this. So I grab the wad of Benny Spiegel's freshly laundered hand-me-downs and blow my nose.

PERSONS IN NEED OF SUPERVISION

Joel Hinman

A rching up out of Forward Facing Dog, Sarah Nielsen had an inverted stroke. "Inverted" because rather than lose capabilities, she gained them. She was down in the basement of the Marriott Hotel and in one convulsive second vast dead zones of Sarah's psyche zapped online. Suddenly she was a woman unstuck. Why such misery and for so long? It had been, she realized, an inside job, her own insidious self-sabotage. No longer shoddy or pathetic (*her words*), Sarah became maniacally determined, starving herself to her ideal weight, quitting her job and reigniting her husband's sexual appetite—some mild bondage and a few blow jobs in the shower brought him around—and then deciding she would become pregnant. When six months of procreational sex produced no result, she started IVF, and then, after three unsuccessful treatments, she turned, without thought or hesitation, to adoption. Even if her marriage to Neil might never amount to much, she would have a baby.

So, she told Pam as they carried margaritas to the deck, wasn't it just a kick in the head that her happiness should now depend upon a shambling chemo-wigged disaster mouse like Lynette Greibel?

"Oh my God!" Pam gasped. "Lynette has cancer?"

"I'm talking about the hair being a disaster. She doesn't have cancer, not that I know of. You've heard how women in primitive tribes put dung in their hair? It's that filthy. Every time I think of smacking her in the head, I stop myself. You know why?" Pam, who had been along from the beginning, didn't. "Because all I can picture is a second head made of particle dust appearing alongside the real one .... Like a squid's defense mechanism."

"What about Morrie at Hair & Beyond?"

"Lives in Dixonville. Here is the problem." Sarah numbered them off on her fingers. "The woman lacks any sense of personal boundaries, can't self-edit, tears the house apart looking for her cell phone when it's dangling from her belt. I'm in too deep. Ooh, that's strong, we better get some chips. What I keep asking myself is, how I could have let this happen?"

Pam looked at the college clock tower rising above the sycamores and waited.

Sarah's voice dropped to a gravelly whisper. "We have our last visit with Amber Saturday. The weekend after, the other couple gets their turn. Then Amber chooses."

The only reason Sarah and Neil were finalists was because Sarah made it so. After Neil received the prestigious Davenport Chair in Astronomy and Astrophysics and Sarah learned the college was fundraising and recruiting off her husband's accomplishments, Sarah went after Dean Liu, arm-twisting support for a group dedicated to crafting an appeal that would be "specifically tailored to a subliterate sixteen-year-old dropout expecting a child born out of wedlock." Sarah chased the college's best talent: developmental psychologists, neuroscientists, rhetoricians, graphic designers, obstetricians and behavioral scientists. "It isn't a birth mother letter," Sarah proclaimed on GoToMeeting, "more like a private webinar." The voice of Cassandra rang from a French professor in Adolescent Psychiatry. She sat at the end of a conference table staring out from beneath hair that appeared to have been shaped by beating wings. Flinging her hands above her head, she warned Sarah that they must assume "the girl to be extremely isolated, as if she were living in her own biosphere, communicating perhaps with a few peers or maybe a boyfriend."

*

Now Saturday morning had arrived and Sarah and Neil were traveling south in the darkened fuselage of the Expedition. Thirty miles outside Dixonville Sarah's phone rang. It was Lynette Greibel.

The hours Sarah spent talking to Lynette—more than she could count—shuttled between tedium and exasperation. Long rambling digressions, stories studded with redundancies, needing to be reminded what she had just said: it was like listening to an alcoholic.

This time Sarah could hear Lynette talking even before the phone reached her ear. Lynette was at St. Joseph's. Her oldest had fallen off the roof of the car. No, the car had not been moving. It was Sarah's view that Lynette's entire life consisted of an unbroken chain of chaotic events. Upheaval followed calamity followed crisis. Still Sarah wasn't without sympathy. For all her rollicking dysfunction, Lynette was practically a single mom, raising three kids while her husband orbited the country in a Freightliner. And Open Heart Adoptions operated out of a P.O. box and the sun porch of a two-bedroom rancher. Although she didn't think Lynette should be allowed to run a quilting bee, let alone an adoption agency, Sarah was in hurry and by geographical accident Lynette worked in an area where the blighted economy had people selling babies.

Expecting the long haul, Sarah wedged her foot against the dash and popped open a can of self-heating coffee, waiting for the exothermic reaction.

After telling Sarah that she and her son were waiting on the neurologist, Lynette began reminiscing about the amazing job Sarah had done on the birth mother presentation. This being old news, Sarah became suspicious. She was wondering why Lynette had started in with the flattery.

"Wait a minute, Lynette!" Sarah interrupted. "I'm not blowing this off. We've been driving all morning and Neil skipped a conference in Hawaii." Neither was true but, as she told Pam later, the dice were rolling.

While Lynette explained that adopting parents weren't allowed to spend unsupervised time with birth mothers, Sarah glanced at her husband for support, but from the spellbound smile on his face, Neil Neilsen was out drifting past spiraling nebulae in some lost corner of the cosmos.

"Look," Sarah said to Lynette, "Amber's gonna pop any second. This was supposed to be *our* quality time. I'm genuinely sorry about what happened to your son, but no way I'm postponing."

"*Hold on!*" Sarah faked. "I'm losing service ... " Cutting the call, she reached for the NASA coffee. They got the temperature right, though the taste still left a lot to be desired. When she looked out she could trace the line of flood-blasted trees along the Seneca River. To the east the road followed the blue shale hills of the Alleghenies. The first time they had driven down to meet Amber it had been winter. Sarah remembered how the mountains, stripped of leaf cover, possessed an aching fragility. Beneath the bare branches the fire roads stood out like sutured wounds against the snow. Later she would explain to Pam she wasn't aware she had begun scheming. All she saw was the opportunity: Amber without Lynette.

They passed the "Entering Dixonville" sign. Truth be told, the only time during the whole process she'd been demoralized was when she learned that Open Heart Adoptions was based in Dixonville. The town was an urban legend, renowned as a capitol of hillbilly racism after a boisterous Klan rally in the nineties. Neighborhoods were still ethnically segregated: the Poles here, the Mexicans there, blacks across the river. When your car wasn't recognized, people stared at you with suspicious hostility.

In Amber's part of town, the houses were American mutt: single family homes mixed with boarding houses built originally for coal workers. Amber's was a boxy firetrap clad in chocolate-brown shingle. But it was a cinch to find the house. Who else bolted a dog pen to the side of their home? Raised on house jacks, the cage was the stepfather's inspiration, proof of his cleverness. On their first visit when giving them a tour he had suddenly flung open a door off the living room to reveal a weary German shepherd sprawled on an old bath mat. "Other people walk their dogs," he said. "Pooch still gets fresh air."

Today as they pulled up, the stepfather reclined in his Barcalounger on the front porch, waiting.

Sarah told Neil to stay in the car. She was so busy trying to remember the stepfather's name she didn't notice the kid on the banana bike. He swerved to avoid her, but then glanced back, before pedaling away. He was a black kid with a pick comb protruding from his Afro like a tail fin.

The stepfather watched Sarah approach. The porch looked like a drawer that had been yanked open, the contents exploding everywhere. Coming up the steps, Sarah sidestepped a milk crate filled with auto parts, on the rail a broken Atari nested alongside an Easy-Bake oven.

"Lynette called," the stepfather squinted. "You ain't supposed to see Amber." Hand trembling, the man lit a cigarette with a Zippo lighter. Sarah saw there was some kind of fireball on his wife-beater. Not for the first time she wondered why he hadn't been killed in a bar fight.

His name came to her, "Why's that, Juney?" She stared him down.

"I don't give a fuck," he said. Sarah could tell this was a favorite line. He was proud of the way he could vary the delivery. She watched him lean forward to park the Zippo next to a battered Maxwell House coffee can. When his shirt fell open she glimpsed a little crop of red-tipped warts grouped by his armpit. They looked like pencil erasers.

Although this was her fifth visit to the house, she had only once laid eyes Amber's mother, a woman who looked like she was living with an ambiguous diagnosis.

Ignoring the stepfather, Sarah stepped toward the screen door and shouted, "AMBER!"

You could see clear down the hall, even out the back door to the railroad tracks. A warm unpleasant smell drifted out of the house, sink traps and spoiled food, the smell that rose when you lifted the trash can lid and remembered raw chicken. Sarah was fighting a gag reflex when Amber stepped into view.

Their eyes met. Sarah nodded to indicate she knew Amber had been hiding. The girl loathed her stepfather, but somehow he always seemed to be hovering when they visited. His possessiveness made Sarah wonder if something had happened between them, something she didn't want to contemplate.

When Amber came out, Sarah almost gasped. Her belly, obscenely distended, had begun to drop. Her skin was translucent, her eyes glassy, her hair a watery, almost colorless blonde. Sarah thought of that science show where chickens didn't have the nutrients to yellow the yolk. Amber's knees and elbows stuck out painfully. For once she wasn't dressed like a biker chick. She wore a summer dress, the most feminine thing Sarah had seen her in and her hair was held up by—of all things—pink barrettes. Suddenly Sarah felt a scalding sense of shame. There had been times, she discovered, when her reactions, more like reflexes, made her disgusted with herself. Like the time she'd caught herself snooping in a cupboard trying to figure out if Amber was getting the protein the baby needed. Now the same shiver crawled across her skin; if Amber was carrying twins wouldn't that solve a lot of problems?

Sarah slid her arm around the girl's shoulder and said cheerfully, "How 'bout the girls go shopping!" For a moment she saw the girl's guard drop. Even when Amber's face was slack, there was a wariness around her eyes. She wasn't cagey or blatantly dishonest but sometimes Sarah had a sense of animal cunning.

Amber lumbered—*lumbered*—down the stairs. Hesitating, a hand outstretched toward the railing, she peered over her belly searching for the bottom step.

"Hey, Juney," Sarah called back, "tell Lynette we're at the mall." While this wasn't an out-and-out lie, it was a bit of willful misdirection. Like anyone else Lynette would assume this meant Amber was headed for the Marquis Galleria, a shopaholic destination featuring national chains. Instead Sarah was going to lead them to a smaller shopping center where Neugenbauer's Department Store wore the tiara. Without Lynette around to meddle and with adequate time for some girl-on-girl shopping, Sarah planned to clinch the deal.

When they got closer to the s u v, Sarah shouted for Neil's help. Watching her husband rise from the driver seat, all six feet two inches of him, Sarah found herself seeing her husband as Amber might. His movements seemed stuttered and awkward; the motion of each limb began with a jerky thrust as if he was punching through bags of cellophane. His head no more than a balloon loosely tethered to his neck.

Neil unfolded part of the back seat so Amber could squeeze in. Most of the cargo hold was filled by a wooden packing crate—an optical tube for a refractor telescope—with "Astro Master" stenciled on the side panel. Climbing back behind the wheel, Neil twisted around.

"It's part of a Celestron telescope," he said. For a second they both stared at the wooden crate. Then they looked at each other. Amber even smiled. Sarah couldn't believe what was happening. Wasn't there a kind of tenderness to the way they were gazing at each other? Her mouth hung open. Here was something she had never considered: Neil charming a teenage girl, and being charmed by her? It made her wonder. Had she become so insistently self-reliant she'd ignored Neil's possible contribution? And why hadn't this occurred to her before?

"Make sure you fasten your seat belt," Sarah said to Amber, but the girl was already texting.

At the shopping center Neil dropped them at the curb. Once inside Neugenbauer's, they stood in the cavernous entrance. The aisle in front of the entrance featured nothing but glazed statuary of shepherds tending sheep. Bric-a-brac and keepsakes made of birch bark or brass, displays of perfumed candles and crystalline bath salts: Sarah realized how grotesque it must look. Glockenspiel music—the demented sound of tinny hammers—seeped out of the ceiling. Walking ahead, Amber hunched her shoulders as if the merchandise might reach out and touch her. Sarah had considered running Amber by the teen department but instead caught the girl's arm and pulled her through the store out onto the mall's concourse.

"Jesus," Sarah muttered, and the girl whipped her eggshell face around as if to say, see, see what I live with! Glancing around, Sarah thought the shopping center's promenade looked like a replica of the dreariest part of the 1960s. Better they keep moving. On the left, they passed a vacant storefront where it looked as if savages had torn the guts out of what had been a U Save. Pegboard shelving lay toppled on its side, with heaps of fissure tile spread across the linoleum. Pompeii-like, it was like a shopping cave furred with ashy brown insulation.

They had only gone a hundred feet when Amber began to complain. She was tired; she needed to sit. Sarah brought the girl to a busted fountain, at the junction of two concourses, where Neil found them.

They sat beneath a flyblown skylight. The mall was dead except for a couple of teenage girls in greeter vests scurrying past Yarn to Be Free. All of the depressing qualities of Dixonville seemed to have gathered in the mall's bleak emptiness.

When Amber heaved herself to her feet, Sarah thought the girl had decided to pack it in. Tell her and Neil to forget about the baby. But Amber just needed to pee. She waddled off, returning a moment later to retrieve her cell phone.

"Remember what *that* was like?" Neil said.

"I never got pregnant," Sarah said.

"No," Neil said. "That age."

"Neil, are you visiting us from outer space?"

Neil gazed up at the skylight. "When I was a teenager," he said, his voice unexpectedly soft, "I couldn't figure out other kids. I wanted to impress them. It was trial but mostly error. I tried everything to get along but the more I felt, the more it hurt." He paused. "We've got to be patient with her."

"When are we supposed to be *patient?* This is our last visit."

"Our attitude. Let her become whoever she is going to be, which, granted, isn't that clear right now. We've got to keep the options open."

Sarah studied her husband. "Where do you get this stuff?" she asked.

"I have students. Plus, I was pretty much a late bloomer."

Sarah thought there was more to say, but here was Amber trudging back toward them. Because she didn't lift her feet, her flip-flops sledded across the floor.

Sarah turned to Neil, whispering, "I need her alone for a few minutes." Neil looked as if he hadn't heard.

But when the girl settled, Neil asked, "How about some ice cream?"

"Sure," Amber said.

"What flavor?" She wanted vanilla. When he asked if she wanted sprinkles, dimples appeared.

Watching Neil depart Sarah felt increasingly desperate. She remembered what the French psychiatrist had said. How do you bond with a girl who won't engage with anyone?

"Amber?" Sarah said, her voice pitched to seem so relaxed as to sound dis-interested. "After the baby, are you going to go back to school?"

"I hate school," Amber said.

Sarah risked a glance. What a mistake. The girl raised her eyes to give Sarah a dose of her soul-scarring apathy. It was like getting blasted by a ray.

"School's not for everybody," Sarah said. "What about working?"

"Oh, yeah! Right!" Sarah recognized her tone. It wasn't far from the stepfather's not giving a fuck.

She studied Amber. In truth Neil has struck a chord. Sarah could see herself in the girl's withholding. She had spent decades chained to an image of herself as one of the walking dead. Chronically chubby she had lived without hope until she had lost the capacity to imagine herself as anything but a crummy victim.

"You know, Amber," Sarah said, "if you had your own money coming in, you'd control more of your life. You could learn to type. Get a job as a secretary. Imagine having your own apartment, own car. A big TV, a fridge stocked with the foods you like. Ice cream and a soft nightgown. Taking a bath when you felt like it."

Sarah heard footsteps. Neil held out a vanilla cone to Amber. He gave Sarah a frozen yogurt.

For a moment they ate in silence. Then something made Sarah look up. Over near the bathroom, a black kid was staring at her. She thought nothing of it, but then, a minute later when she glanced back, he hadn't moved. There was, Sarah realized, significance to his immobility. She twisted around to Amber.

"Who is that?" she asked because not only was he staring, but he looked vaguely familiar.

"Darryl," Amber said.

'What's he want?" she asked.

"Talk to you."

Sarah threw her yogurt in the trash. Darryl's briefs rode three inches above the waist of his jeans. The lines of his hipbones disappeared beneath his jeans, about where the flatlands of his stomach vanished. Up close his eyes were hooded. She wondered how old he was, fourteen? fifteen? When she saw the pick comb she realized he was sleeping with Amber.

"What's up, Darryl?"

"Stepfather gonna keep the money," Darryl said, his voice matching his posture. Enunciation wasn't something he cared to be good at.

She thought about this. In a way she was relieved. This, not something darker, was the reason for the stepfather's proprietary behavior. "He's her guardian," Sarah offered.

Darryl's eyes widened. "I the baby daddy," he said.

"I thought that other kid"—she struggled to remember the name—"Billy was the baby daddy?"

Darryl was reaching for his cell phone. "Nuyh," he said, "Billy only think that cuze she got him drunk and took pitchers." Sarah batted the phone away, but not before catching sight of a pink torso.

"If you're the father, why didn't you tell anybody?"

"Issa niggah," he said.

Darryl's language was the trigger for a kind of neurological overload, a surge of feeling and repulsion so overwhelming, Sarah thought she might slip to the floor. She stood there, swaying a bit. Darryl must have understood because he leaned in with the closer. "You gimme the money. I get you the baby."

She handled it badly she would say later. In the clear light of day she should have hashed it out with Darryl. In the months to come Sarah wondered why she fled. Was it the undiluted despair and helplessness, or the cynicism and accusation? Or did she need to flee because she had just been outsmarted by two sixteen-year-olds?

She may have said something to Darryl before she wheeled around. If so, she doesn't know what it might have been. All she can remember was her need to get away.

"What happened?" Neil asked, alarmed.

"Let's go!" she rasped. When she glanced at Amber the girl looked satisfied, or was that a look of pride?

Sarah didn't have a plan anymore. Despite Lynette's absence, she'd lost control. She was stumbling along the concourse, while puzzling details from the last couple of months came together. Now she understood why Amber had at first refused a sonogram. And why Billy's mother had waived paternity rights. They were down at the end of the concourse running out of mall when Sarah looked up at the providential sign: "Fashion Depot."

Inside the over-lit window was a tableau of female mannequins, all posing as professionals. Some wore skirts or shirtdresses. A few wore blazers with polka dot blouses. One of the mannequins didn't have fingers, a fin jutted out of its sleeve.

Hauling Amber into the store, Sarah was on autopilot.

"Where's the manager?" she demanded.

A glance at Sarah and the salesgirl was hollering, "CHERYL!"

From the rear offices came a woman in her late twenties. She frowned when she saw Sarah holding Amber's arm.

Later Sarah told Pam it wasn't a hunch, or intuition, but deep imprinting. Some engrained habit called forth by the "Sale" signs. Only minutes before she'd been stripped of all of her personal power. The socioeconomic superiority that had guided her and given her confidence had turned to dandelion fluff. She'd been played by a couple of kids, desperate kids, perhaps, but kids nonetheless. Then, as she stood under the fierce glare of the florescent lights, a thought dimly flickered and restoration came. "You don't always recognize the form of inspiration," she told Pam. "This time it was the pent-up power of credit."

"*This* girl," Sarah said, pointing at the mystified Amber, "this girl needs everything you got!" Sarah made as if to lasso the store.

Cheryl pointed. "Like that?" she asked.

"NO! no, no! *After* the baby."

Sarah turned to Amber. "You know what you need?" Amber clearly didn't. "You need skirts, blouses, pantsuits, sweater sets. We're gonna remake you right now!"

But Cheryl saw and Cheryl understood. "All righty!" she beamed.

It was a shopping orgy. All hesitancy and uncertainty were banished, overruled by purchasing power. Cantaloupe and Pink Champagne. Periwinkle and Eggnog. Short sleeve, long sleeve, shirtwaist and pleated skirt, sateen and cotton. They tore things off the racks and ripped them off the carousels; running back and forth between the displays and the counter until a bale of clothing sat by the register. At one point, catching a breather, Sarah gave Amber a look that said, this is what happens when you mess with me. As the bill was being tallied Cheryl told Sarah that when she first saw her she thought Sarah had caught a shoplifter. Neil started to question the bill of $2,900 but Sarah dropped him with a look.

That wasn't all. Sarah had more. They would store the loot at Billy's house, the patsy Amber had fooled into thinking he was the baby daddy. Billy's mother was a willing accomplice, once Sarah explained.

Silent, exhausted by expenditure, they drove to Amber's house. Sarah had that caramelized glow that comes with spending a lot of money. When Sarah asked Amber if she liked any of it, the girl blushed.

Neil reached back and patted Amber on the knee before she got out.

Sarah and Amber stood on the porch. For once the stepfather wasn't around. Sarah looked at Amber. "Whatever happens, Amber, we're not going to see you for a while."

"I know," the girl said.

"But the whole time, we're going to be sending you good thoughts."

Amber nodded. She still looked too young for any of this. Sarah could see the girl was trying to think of something to say. "Don't," Sarah said.

Finally, Amber leaned over and kissed her on the cheek. A touch so light Sarah could barely feel it.

*

"YEAH," PAM SAID, "Dr. Fauque was just as you described her: the hurricane hair, smoker's cough, heavy French accent. I was gobsmacked but Bradley loved her. *'Eet ees his nest! Eet ees his stink! He makes like a protection with zee smell'!'* She and Sarah were standing in the kitchen. It was the first week in October.

"The woman knew more about Amber than anyone else."

"She worked it out," Pam said. "He leaves the stuff that needs to be washed in a basket outside the door and I don't have to go in. And believe me that's a relief." Pam pulled a bottle of rum and some lime juice from her bag. "Wanna do daiquiris?"

"I think I'll stick with wine."

"She described it as an olfactory barrier. You'll love having a teenager."

"Did I show you the postcard?" Sarah asked.

"No!" Pam said.

Sarah opened a drawer and withdrew the card. While Pam read it, Sarah opened a bottle of red and poured herself a glass.

Pam turned the postcard over. "West Virginia?"

"Could be, or they could have gotten someone to mail it. Who knows. They took the clothes, of course."

Pam reads, "'I was going to give you the baby.' Wow!" Pam squinted at Sarah, shaking her head. "You know she's encouraging you?"

"That hurt at first, but weirdly she and Darryl have become a kind of model for Neil and I. Bonnie and Clyde. Did I tell you we are seeing someone?"

"That's big, "Pam said, following Sarah out onto the deck.

"Neil drove down there and met with Darryl's parents. They don't know where they are either, but Neil wanted them to know he would have taken the baby." Sarah paused. "He wants to send them money."

"Go, Neil. All this changed him," Pam said.

"It did. In some ways he was more upset than I was. Now he's much more present but also calling me on my shit, talking about how I kept him out, treated him like a cosmonaut on shore leave. 'The tyranny of low expectations' he told the therapist."

Studying the postcard, Pam said, "The baby's large."

"I know. Already thirteen pounds."

After Pam left, Sarah stayed on the deck. The slanting light backlit the maples and sycamores, the leaves glowing. Above the trees, the spire on the clock tower was a brilliant white. Her wineglass was empty. Sarah said something to herself and picked up her cell phone. She dialed.

"So, Lynette," she said. "Where are we at?"

CALL AND RESPONSE

Lucinda Holt

When I really wanted something I couldn't have, my grandmother would say, "Whores in hell want ice water, but that don't mean they're getting any." This line shut down tantrums and whining, rich people's luxuries. It wasn't until I was ten or eleven that I had a sense of what a whore was. But I had always understood that my grandmother's words meant my expectations, my very heart's desire, would not be met—at least not in this world. And arguing about it wouldn't make any difference. I used to wish for hamburgers and French fries when my grandmother made beans and corn bread. And I never mentioned to her that Tracy, my friend down the road, had roller skates and a remote-controlled Barbie Corvette. And I never said to her that Tracy's mother hardly ever made beans and corn bread or that her father always had change for the gumball machine at the Hitching Post—the convenience store on the main road. But when my grandmother died all I had a taste for was beans and corn bread.

I was thirteen years old when she died. I don't recall how I learned she died. I just remember someone saying, "Your grandmother—she had a stroke." The impersonal "she" as if it had happened to someone else—someone I didn't love more than anyone else in the world. When people died, my grandmother would always say they had "gone to Glory." I didn't know where Glory was. It was heaven I assumed, and I wasn't sure if I believed in heaven. My grandmother must have thought it was a decent place to go because though she said "gone to Glory" with some resignation, there was always a slight smile on her face. But I couldn't smile about my grandmother leaving me on the earth so far from her Glory.

*

MY MOTHER HAD DIED not long after I was born, and my father had left me in East Texas with my grandmother when he set off to California looking for work. When my grandmother died, my father was called and had to drive all the way from Los Angeles to get me. He worked emptying trash cans, vacuuming floors and cleaning toilets at some defense company. He made more money there than he would have stocking shelves at the Piggly Wiggly or working at the Dairy Queen. During that time between my grandmother's death and my father's arrival, I was left with distant relatives.

I found myself sitting at a little wooden kitchen table with Sister Stewart and her son T—given name Thomas but known to most as T, TBird or Thunderbird. I actually wasn't all that hungry, but if someone had put beans and corn bread in front of me, I would have eaten it. That's all I really I wanted, but T had bought hot link sandwiches. Spicy Texas sausages from Lockhart, cut in halves, covered in barbecue sauce on big slabs of white bread. T sat next to me. I can still remember looking over at him and having him look back at me with a smile. Was that smile supposed to comfort me? It didn't. I can still see the bits of sausage and bread tossed together in his open maw. I hated him for enjoying a sandwich while my grandmother was dead. I wasn't really clear about how T and I were related. I just knew my grandmother had said his mother, Sister Stewart, was her third cousin, though I would be hard pressed to explain what a third cousin was. In their kitchen, there was a lone bulb dangling from the ceiling. In the places along the walls over the countertops and stove where cabinets used to be, there were black scorch marks that licked out over the walls. There were always fires, floods and domestic disasters in this little house. You see, Sister Stewart was crazy. This was my first time sitting at a table with her, being this close to crazy. Usually I would see her at distance—matted hair, large pendulous breasts swaying under her patchwork dress as she walked barefoot. Once when my grandmother was still alive, I saw Sister Stewart on the side of the road, yelling "This is a dry and thirsty land!" I asked my grandmother, "What's wrong with her, Granny?" My grandmother looked at me incredulously and said, "Why she's crazy. Ain't nothing for it." But there was nothing crazy about the old woman sitting across from me with a smile on her face.

"How you, sweet Regina?" That's what she said to me.

I hesitated. There were no words that could answer that question. "I...," and that's all I could muster. My hand was on the table, and Sister Stewart enveloped it with hers. Her hand was soft, and my face was wet with tears. Sister Stewart got up out of her chair and held me close. She smelled like cedar, and I noticed that some of the patches on her dress were the same upholstery fabric as one of the old chairs in the living room—a dark green velvety fabric. But there were also patches of candy-striped fabric worn thin, cotton squares of pink polka dots on a white background, a brown polyester that reminded me of a man's suit and a striped brown and blue that could be from a man's tie. For some reason this random patchwork made me cry even more. And Sister Stewart just held me close, saying, "Yes, yes, yes." And when she sat back down, her patchwork dress had a big wet circular mark from my tears.

"Your grandmother was a good woman. She will be mourned and missed by many, but none as much as you, sweet girl." And then Sister Stewart picked up her knife and fork and began to cut and eat her sandwich with such care. She had small hands with fingers that came to delicate points. "It's a blessing to have a long life, but you live long enough you'll know loss. Both of my parents were dead by the time I was five years old. I've known so many people to come and go, I can't count them anymore. The worse I'd say is to lose a child. My second husband threw my third child out of a fourth-story window." I wondered if I had misheard her, and my face must have shown it. "It's true," she insisted. "That's what brought on my first episode. I was in a hospital for weeks, just sick with the grief of it." She put her knife and fork down and just sat, staring past me. I looked at T, not knowing what to make of what was happening. He shrugged and said, "Don't worry, she be alright." T would know. He was the person who used to get her off their roof when she got up there, preaching while just about everybody gathered around to watch.

After we ate, Sister Stewart sat in a chair on the little cement square of her back porch, reading her Bible. I sat with my legs crossed on that warm slab of porch looking out in the distance. T poked his head out of the back screen door. "Miss Gina, come here, let me tell you something." I went into the kitchen, and there T was, smiling.

"Listen here, pretty girl, I'm about to step out. If she gets to acting up, you run down to Dr. Brady's and tell him."

"You're leaving?" I asked, suddenly afraid to be alone with Sister Stewart.

"Yeah, but she'll be fine. Dr. Brady has her on this stuff that's been working pretty good. You don't have to worry. Call the fire department if she sets something on fire. But don't call the police. They don't come round here no way unless they trying to mess with you. Just run down to Dr. Brady's." He gave my arm a little squeeze. He took a cigarette out of a pack tucked into his shirt pocket, lit it, took a drag and stepped out the back door. I heard him say, "I'm headed to the store, Momma. I'll be back. Gina be here with you."

The thing about crazy is that it's unpredictable. It seems fine one minute and then it's not.

I wanted to hide in the house away from Sister Stewart, make myself invisible until my daddy arrived, but for all intents and purposes, I was her sitter until T came back. If something happened to her, it would be on me. Through the screen door, I could see her going out into the yard. I braced myself in case I had to chase her down. But she just turned in a circle, looking up at the sky. It had started to rain lightly. The rain dappled her face and hair. She looked happy. I went out on the porch, and I could see the sun was still visible even though it was raining. When dark clouds twisted like dirty dishrags in the sky, dropping rain while the sun shined through a break in the clouds, my grandmother would announce, "Devil must be beating his wife." I never knew what the devil had to do with the weather or why he had a wife for that matter. Sister Stewart, who was barefoot, tramped back up to the porch and shook herself dry.

"Sure feels nice out there. Let's get inside." In the living room, Sister Stewart read her Bible. And I sat quietly the way I used to with my grandmother when there was a storm. There was no storm yet, but something was coming, bearing down and stomping its way across the Texas plains.

When it was time to sleep, Sister Stewart brought me sheets to put on the love seat. I felt relief that we had made it to bedtime without incident. I lay in the dark on the love seat, thinking of my grandmother. At night she would recite the poetry of Paul Laurence Dunbar and James Weldon Johnson because she wanted me to know that there were "Negroes," as she called us, who wrote poems. Occasionally she recited nursery rhymes, like none I'd ever heard. They were frayed threads pulled from the past—a time when "This Little Piggy" wasn't a piggy at all.

Once at bedtime, when I was probably only seven or eight years old, she took my big toe between her fingers and started, *This little nigga said I want some corn.* She didn't smile or laugh. She just moved on to the next toe. *This little nigga said where you gone get it.* She continued on to the next toe: *Out of Massa's barn.* She tugged gently on the next toe: *This little nigga said I'm gone tell it.* And at the last toe, she said, *This little nigga cried wee, wee, wee all the way home.* I remember she pulled the sheet up over me and said, "Go to sleep now." I can still recall the pressure of her kiss on my forehead, as I lay there with the singsongy rhythm of the verse colliding with words like "nigga" and "Massa." I couldn't imagine Tracy's mother reciting verses like this to her at night. Had Tracy ever lain in bed hearing about little niggas thwarted in their longing for corn? I knew she hadn't. But I also knew this was all part of the past, passed down to my grandmother and now to me, like some tattered doll. And I held on to it—who we were and where we came from. This was our nursery rhyme—my nursery rhyme.

This was all a part of my grandmother's love, which wasn't a vague feeling, cloying and heavy as pound cake. Her love was strident. It yelled at me to stay in the front yard where she could see me from the porch. It was meticulously washed and ironed clothes, leftover pot roast and vegetables cooked into hash that would last and last when we were hungry. Her love was a firm hand combing and plaiting my hair at night. Her love swore. "Careful getting in and out of that tub, you'll fall and bust your damn head open." Her love was vigilant in its pursuit of anyone or thing—accident or natural disaster—that might come between us.

I dozed off at some point and then woke to the sound of thunder like someone ripping the sky open. I smelled cigarette smoke, and then jumped when I saw the red eye of a cigarette floating in the dark.

"Didn't mean to scare you." It was T, sitting in the chair across the coffee table from me. I saw the end of the cigarette move up to what must have been his mouth and then down again as he rested his arm on the chair. My eyes started to adjust to the dark. And now I could also see the glint of gold from the gold tooth in his mouth and moisture in his eyes. A flash of lightning lit everything up like the lights had all been turned on for a split second. I could see T's face and shirt were wet from the rain. And before the thunder responded, I could hear a drip, drip, dripping on the carpet. Was it something leaking or just T's clothes dripping on the carpet?

"Thank you for watching Momma today. I sometimes just need a little time to myself." Though it was dark, I pulled the sheet up around me and drew myself over to one side of the love seat. I didn't know what to say to T. We sat for a while with the sound of heavy rain pelting the little house and the occasional call and response of lightning and thunder.

"Miss Gina, you're getting prettier by the day." I still didn't say anything. But what was there to say in response to this comment? Thank you? Was I getting prettier by the day? If those words had come out of someone else's mouth—someone who wasn't focusing on me so intently, I might have liked the idea. It would have felt good and sweet. But there was nothing good or sweet when T walked over to the love seat. When he sat down, there was no avoiding the wet heat of his body next to mine.

"If you were a little bit older, I'd marry you." Though I couldn't see T's face, I could hear the smile in his voice. What was a little bit older? Fourteen? Sixteen? Did he know I was thirteen years old? I knew I wouldn't want to marry T — the man who it seemed had spent his whole life caring for his momma. And if I didn't want to marry him, why did he think he could marry me?

I hated T for scaring me, for sitting next to me in wet clothes, for eating with his mouth open, for leaving me with a crazy woman and for saying such a nice thing about me being pretty and then messing it up by trying to force me to marry him. It was all — all kinds of wrong. And then T rubbed my back, making big circles. It felt nice. And I hated that the touch of someone so awful felt so good. And I thought of Natasha and Angela who said Pastor Littlejohn tickled girls who came to his daughter's sleepovers as an excuse to touch them where he wasn't supposed to. Angela bragged about it, as if having some old man grab you meant somebody wanted you. Natasha laughed and called him a nasty old man, but I couldn't imagine bragging or laughing about this. I wondered if I was about to be one of those girls, groped or used by some relative or family friend in the dark. It happened all the time. And while I'm not sure how I feel about God, I silently called on my grandmother, the one person who had always been there but wasn't now. But, of course, nothing happened.

The storm carried on. Lightning struck again, bringing a moment of light. Then I heard Sister Stewart stirring in her room, her bare feet slapping the floor and then the screen door slammed. I knew she must have walked out the front door. T's cigarette was still burning in an ashtray on the coffee table, and I felt his weight shift on the love seat. I could just make out his silhouette in the dark. He had his head in his hands, and he let out a deep sigh. There was a boom of thunder that seemed to shake the little house. I could hear Sister Stewart yelling, "When you walk, your steps will not be hampered; when you run, you will not stumble." I did what seemed to make the most sense then. I ran — out of the house and after Sister Stewart.

She was walking pretty fast for an old woman, and I had to run to catch up to her, slipping occasionally in the mud in my bare feet. T was behind us. I glanced back and he was standing in front of their house, yelling for her to come back. "Momma! Gina, get her back in this house!" Sister Stewart was intent on going somewhere, and I was going with her. In a matter of moments, we were both soaking wet. By the time she turned right onto the road where the cemetery is—what some old people still call the "colored cemetery"—T was driving alongside us in his truck. He had the window down. "Momma, just stop and get in this truck." Sister Stewart didn't even seem to register that he was there. "Gina, I'm gone stop this truck. You help me get her in." I had no interest in helping T, so I ignored him like his momma. At this point there was little time between the call and response of lightning and thunder. T stopped his truck on the side of the road just across from the gates leading into the cemetery. A low metal fence had recently been installed around it. I guess it was more of a protective gesture than anything else because it did nothing to keep racist vandals from defacing the headstones. Sister Stewart hoisted a leg up and over it with ease. I followed.

Sister Stewart headed straight for a little marker on the far left. She was saying something, but I couldn't hear her over the rain and thunder. I just stood there with her. I touched the wet stone that read, Caroline Stewart, 1937–1939. And then Sister Stewart pulled me down onto the ground, and we sat together. She had her arms around my shoulders. And I don't really know if what happened next really happened or if it's just how I remember it. A spark of lightning danced for a moment along the gate we had just climbed over. I felt a crackling sensation ripple through my body where it contacted the ground. Not even a second later I heard a loud crack. I saw T across the road shaking his legs. He swears today that it was ground voltage, and it gave him some kind of nerve damage in his left leg. I still don't know if that's what really happened. Maybe the lightning messed with my memory. Maybe I was crying, but it's hard to say. I just remember being heavy with the rain soaked into my clothes and all that had happened and letting it seep right there into the ground in the cemetery where my grandmother would be buried.

A DRIP

Carey Ann Hunt

Florescent light. White walls and a sink. Dripping. Slowly.
Surrounding sounds were louder.

Occasional beeps. But they too were lower in volume than the singing. A
   gray-haired, frail elder lay in repose on a bed. Ashen.
Wrinkled. Beads of sweat laced her brow.

Dripping. Without sound. The long hand just past the two and the short
   hand on the six. Ticking. A figure sat sidesaddle to the elder's left. A red
   silk scarf draped around her shoulders.
One hand upon the elder's heart.

The other hand moving through gray combed hair. Slowly. Singing.

On the elder's other side in similar fashion sat another figure. Matching
   earrings and necklace. Holding the elder's hand in her two. Still. Singing.
At the foot of the bed another figure was positioned. Leaning in. One hand
   placed on the shoulder of the figure to her right.
The other on the elder's thigh. Singing.

Away from the bed, towards the window, stood a figure holding a baby.
   Rocking. Shiny eyes and wet cheeks. Singing.
"Ferryman ferry me over the river. Ferryman ferry me over the river. Over.
   Over. Over." Singing. Heavy labored breathing was heard during pauses.
   Coughing. Sputtering.
Long beep. Singing fades. Sniffles crescendo into sobs. Breathing deep.
The clock still ticking. Sink dripping. Beeping silenced.

Outside the window green leaves were soaked. Dripping. Swaying.

A brown bird perched. Turned in the direction of an eastern-facing
   mountain. Singing.

WILDING

Scott Hunter

I got "wilded" once.

I thought of this again on my way home the other night, when I stopped for milk at that bodega on Ninth Avenue that I almost never go to. It was years ago. When "wilding" was a thing. You never hear about it anymore, but it was real. Marauding bands of young men, maybe eight or ten, teenagers mostly, terrorized people in the streets of New York City. Just, like, on their way home from school, or after hanging out in the park at night. Back then, half the streetlights were burned out. The crack epidemic was almost over — everyone had died — and AIDS was finally being taken seriously because a straight white boy from Indiana got it and died before his prom. Wilding was in that era.

With wilding there was often nothing worth calling a crime. It wasn't exactly "mugging" — maybe no one was robbed. It wasn't exactly "assault" — maybe no one was even touched. Wilding might mean nonverbally threatening to beat the shit out of someone just to laugh as he trembled backward over a garbage can. Grabbing and hurling a briefcase just to see the papers fly into mud puddles. Or tearing at a woman's blouse and watching her cower in her bra. Victims were left gaping at the ruins, while the boys galloped around the corner, like mustangs over the sierras.

I got wilded after my friend Dan and I had just seen an off-Broadway show, something his girlfriend had no interest in. It was late, and we were hungry. We stopped to read the menu at La Luncheonette, by those housing projects with the broken windows and the outside hallways with chain link that curls up at the top to prevent people from jumping or babies from falling. It was cold and we were coatless. But the menu looked heavy, with complicated food that might take all night to get served, and Dan had to go to the office the next morning. Probably he just didn't want me to have to pay so much for a meal. He knew I'd insist on paying my way even though I made no money working entry-level on Seventh Avenue while he had a job on Wall Street.

Dan and I were college friends, but more like acquaintances. I never wanted to get too close to him because then I'd fall in love with him. He was handsome—tall, dark, with high red cheekbones—and fit. I told myself we were not quite friends because he played basketball four days a week and I thought of myself as fat. Of course, in part we were not quite friends because he was waiting for me to come out to him. He'd leave openings in our conversations which I filled with awkward silences, or bad jokes. Or an abrupt change of subject, to put the focus back on him. Still, I liked that he knew things. And he liked experimental theater, and his girlfriend preferred *Cats*, so sometimes I got the call.

That night, we skipped La Luncheonette. It's still desolate, that block, despite new luxury high-rises. Back then, with the projects and cars without tires in the parking lots, it seemed more vacant. As we walked, we began to feel the presence of these overgrown kids: peripheral glimpses of a dirty blond boy, black and brown kids of varying heights and weights. The diversity of those projects is still confusing—Chinese boys in Tupac T-shirts speaking Spanglish. One of the boys coming up on us looked white at first glance, I can still see his freckled face, had a red-headed afro, close-cropped, and black features—wide round nose, broad lips. Freckles like Howdy Doody. So freckly. He was probably seventeen. I've seen freckly black people since then. But this kid was riveting. Wide green eyes, bright with confidence, with initiative.

They followed us, and they walked faster than we did. Started loping. You could feel it. Dan and I stopped talking about where we might get food. You could hear them cursing, laughing, talking shit about girls, the projects, complaining about the cold. A lone streetlight flickered through fog. When we reached an area near a chained back entrance to the projects, the sidewalk widened, and that's when we could really feel them all around us. Dan and I mistimed stolen glances at each other. I was seeking his signal, sensing we should make a break for it, too tentative to act on my own. The boys stopped joking with each other. They got quiet. The silence was sudden. Teenage monsters, breathing.

First, with only the sound of big fast footfalls, one of them grabbed my briefcase. You never know how you'll react in a situation like that. You say, "I'd let them take it, *life* is more important than *stuff*." But there was no "your money or your life" moment. No "gimme the case." Just a big freckled hand, invading, snatching at the soft, satchel-like case, and me instinctively clutching it, pulling it in. I can't think now what I might have had in it — I owned nothing more valuable that the case itself, which I'd felt forced to purchase by a boss who wanted me to look more professional, but it was Coach, and I liked that it said I was serious but relaxed enough to work in the Garment District.

Well, the kid lost his grip, but pounced forward, shoved me, and I fell on the briefcase. As I rolled and looked up, the kid reared up to stomp on me with a big white high-top sneaker, the $150 kind. Somehow, I stopped his foot with my free hand, caught it before it started to come down with any force, and in that moment our eyes met, Freckleface and me. That's when his face — every detail of it — imprinted on my memory. He jerked his foot away, the sharp edge of the outsole stitching on those high-tops tearing my fingernails, and hopped back. The smile, I guess, is what registered as confidence.

While all that happened, one of the others, a tall heavy-set kid, punched Dan from behind, the long-armed right hook reaching around, tagging his eye. But Dan turned, and squared up, as if to fight. Put up his dukes. And that was it. A fast, shadowy blur of action. They all bounded off. Long, leggy bouncing strides. A fading whoop or holler. As if Dan being ready to fight, and me fallen atop the easy-snatch bag, made everything more trouble than it was worth. Their point was made, they owned that cold dark street.

Dan said, "Let's go!" and took off running — he dashed across the avenue to that bodega I stopped at the other night, only I didn't realize it at the time. Instead, I got up, disoriented, dizzy, and didn't see where he went. I heard hoots and howls from those kids trailing off in another direction. My knuckles and nails were bleeding. My trousers were ripped at the knee. I still had the briefcase. My ears were ringing. My pulse surged in my head, and I ran. Stopped at the corner, looked this way, that way, and didn't see Dan. I don't recall feeling, in that moment, any sense of abandonment. Only a need to feel safe. Only that Dan was smart, knew to take care of himself, and I should do the same. So I ran home. I lived a few blocks away, on a brownstoney street where faded Neighborhood Watch stickers dotted a few doors and windows. The dead-bolt sounded snug, secure. I sat at the kitchen table and examined my wounds. The briefcase leather was scuffed, an outer pocket torn. I cracked ice in a towel for my raw, scraped hands.

Sitting there, out of breath, pulse pounding, I thought of Dan. What if he hadn't got away? Had he gone the other direction — might the wilders have doubled back? I pictured him getting ambushed by wilders. By Freckleface, confident, smiling. I looked at the phone, and in the very moment I was deciding whether to call 9-1-1 or the local precinct, it rang. It was Dan.

"Thank god!—*Where'd you go?*—I lost you!—*Are you ok?*" We both uttered variations on these questions, talking over each other, loud, fast. He was calling from inside the bodega, using the shopkeeper's phone, not the pay phones outside. He'd already called 9-1-1, a squad car might come, he doubted it would be any time soon, wasn't sure he could stand to wait. Then he was interrupted. I could hear the shop owner complaining about his making a second phone call, Dan arguing that the pay phones outside were all broken, that the shop owner should complain to the city about the burned-out streetlights. His fear was morphing to anger. I broke through, told Dan to hang up and come over, reminded him of my address.

He arrived in seconds, out of breath, his eye swelling. I got more ice. We cursed the bodega owner. We retold our versions of the incident, each of us recounted waiting for a signal from the other, wondering if we'd be able to outrun them, wondering how the tall guy's arms could be so long. We cursed the teenagers. Relived the whole thing, saying over and over, "That's never happened to me—has that ever happened to you?" and "We just got wilded—did they get anything?" and "We're so lucky—are we lucky?" As our heart rates returned to normal, we got quiet. We rearranged the ice cubes in our towels and dabbed at our own wounds.

"Dude," he said, looking not at me, but at the ice cubes he was adjusting. "I didn't mean to leave you hanging—I thought you were right behind me." He retraced his logic—crossing the avenue, to the store, to the brightest light, it seemed the natural place to go. "I should have made sure you were with me."

I apologized, too, for running off. The apologies were a reflex of our formality, I realized later, testament to a distance between us. Friends would have been tighter, inseparable in a moment of crisis, brothers able to see through the fog of war together. But back then, it was only an awkward, confused silence needing to be broken. So I told the old joke about how, if you're chased by a bear in the forest, you don't need to be faster than the bear, only faster than the people you're with. He'd already heard it, but we laughed anyway, too loud, too long. As the tension subsided, and rational thoughts replaced fear and relief, Dan realized he hadn't waited to see if 9-1-1 sent a squad car, so we decided to call the precinct directly.

The police came over right away. Two beat cops, blue uniforms. Hats, big boots, belts. Weapons. Whenever I remember that old apartment, I think of the feeling of that night, that sense of too many too-large people in that too-tiny space. The cops asked if we could describe our attackers. Dan had almost no visual memory of them. But I described Freckleface perfectly, his tall and lanky frame, his oversized white shoe, and that face. That confident green-eyed smile. Every detail.

"Wow," Dan said, grinning. "You really took a good long look at that guy." He said it with a look in his eye that I read as suggestive.

The cops laughed. Dan laughed.

"I was being attacked!" I said, stammering. I looked down at my scraped-up hands, adjusted the ice in the towel. Another awkward moment hung in the air. "You really didn't see anything?"

He shrugged. He hadn't seen anything, it happened so fast, or couldn't remember, at least not in comparable detail. The cops said that often happens, memories go blank, but later things come back to us sometimes, and that's why they would put a detective in touch with us. They wrapped things up, even offered to drive Dan home—he lived down by Ear Bar—and he accepted. There were hurried, formal good-byes. No back slaps. No handshakes. No "see you tomorrows." They were gone, and I suddenly felt left out. Like they had picked Dan for the team and not me, like three guys ditching me and going out for beers. That's what came over me in the quiet of the apartment, alone behind the dead-bolted door. I knew it was silly. The cops had been good to both of us. They were calming. I should have felt grateful. We were unhurt. His eye was bruised and my hands were scraped up, but we were fine. I used all remaining energy to get down on my knees and sponge away footprints tracked in by the police on the old wood floor boards. I went to sleep thinking about Dan's black-and-blue eye, a manly wound in comparison to my fingers scraped pink and white, and now dressed with tiny Band-Aids.

The next morning, a detective did call. Early. He asked me to come to the precinct, said Dan would be there in an hour, and he hoped I could be there too. The surprising efficiency made me eager to participate in this act of civic duty. I'd walked past that precinct office many times. Double-height ceilings made the room feel huge. Paint was peeling from the upper corners, hanging in big dirty-white curls revealing dark green underneath. Light around prewar glass fixtures was smoky, and the smooth black and white marble floors seemed almost soft from so much traffic. The half-walls were high, the benches were low, and the cops all seemed oversized and elevated. I felt like a third-grader at the principal's office. Gruff chatter and ringing phones created a stark contrast with the quiet of the Saturday morning street outside.

I greeted the desk captain and he looked me over without expression, pointing to a conference room. I saw Dan through a big windowpane, standing in a sweat suit, already done with a run. He was laughing with the detective, who wore a white shirt, loosened tie, frazzled hair that matched an oversized mustache. For a second I wondered how long Dan had been there. He seemed already to have found an easy camaraderie with the rumpled detective, just as he had the night before with the beat cops. His eye didn't look too swollen, just some black above the red of his cheek. As I walked toward the room, I ripped the baby Band-Aids off my fingers and threw them in a dented metal trash bin.

I walked in and Dan hugged me. Taken off guard, I didn't hug back, I stiffened. We never hugged. Dan was already talking about the night, the incident, the aftermath. He was animated, said he was glad to see me looking so normal, that his eye didn't hurt, but on his run that morning he could feel blood pounding in his cheek, and temple. I showed him my scraped-up hand and fingers. Told him he looked worse off, and that I was grateful he'd turned to face the wilders. His willingness to fight back saved us, I said.

"Can you start at the beginning?" the detective interrupted. He introduced himself to me, we shook hands, and he offered us chairs at an old metal table. The cops from the previous night weren't around. The detective had their report. He asked me to retell the tale, and I did. The detective nodded along, interjecting questions, clarifications. In different ways, he wondered open-endedly about motive. I looked to Dan now and then, trying to remember which of the details were from my memory, and which were things I'd picked up from him the previous night at the kitchen table. Mostly Dan nodded in agreement or shrugged. The detective asked, "Did they say anything?" and "How about then—did they say anything then?" I didn't understand why he was asking, and answered no, they hadn't said a thing as far as I could recall. He looked over his notes and said, "Yeah, that's what your, uh, friend Dan here said." He was pensive, skeptical.

"Some of, um, your people," the detective said, looking at me as if maybe he and I shared—or should share—some essential knowledge, "they don't always like to report all the details of an incident. Like, maybe things were said. Name-calling." He paused. I replayed his outer-borough accent in my head—*name-calling, name-cawling, kwalling.* He went on, "It's a new thing we do, investigating for any of these so-called hate-crimes."

He parceled out the information slowly. Let it sink in.

"Some of your people ... they don't like to be identified as the victim of something that might be ... maybe considered ... you know, an incident of, um, a … gay-bashing." Like wilding, gay-bashing was a relatively new crime, a new name, new penalties. Then he added, "Or some such." For years after that, when I wanted to leave someone an out, I would add an "or some such" and recall that morning at the precinct.

"Dan's not gay," I said too quickly, insistently. The detective looked up from his notes. Dan laughed. The detective smiled. I hadn't come out to anyone at that point. There was a colleague at work with whom I'd furtively discussed *Paris Is Burning* in the break room, a couple of people from previous part-time jobs I saw at a club once. People with whom I was open in certain situations, but hadn't had that conversation. There hadn't been a need. And there was a dorm-mate who'd moved away for law school with whom I'd later acknowledge in a letter how we both knew the other was gay, and how sad it was that we hadn't talked about it. I knew I was blushing as I looked back and forth between Dan and the detective.

"That's true," Dan said, smiling. "I'm not. But *they* didn't know that."

I wasn't exactly *not* out. Always thought my haircut and colorful sock collection spoke for me. It didn't take a police detective to identify me as gay. But I still wasn't fully identifying myself as gay. I hadn't walked in the Pride Parade. Hadn't marched at an ACT UP rally. Had never been to The Center. Didn't like hanging out in smelly bars with porn on silent TVs and drag queens hosting lip-sync contests. That's what I thought it meant to be gay. So I had no dating life. I steered clear of sex the way I steered clear of crack—something that killed you. I didn't know how to be friends with the few gay guys I knew. And that, I realized there at the table in the precinct conference room, was also why I wasn't even quite friends with the straight guys I knew, like Dan.

"After all," Dan continued, "I was walking with *you!*" With this, he laughed harder. As if my outing myself, albeit inadvertently, was cathartic for *him*.

And this is when it began to dawn on me. In that old conference room, with paint peeling off the walls, and a rumpled detective seeking to understand what crime had been committed the previous night on that Chelsea street. How foolish I'd been not to see in Dan's teasing the night before at my place with the beat cops the very recognition—the acceptance—that I yearned for. A laugh was all it would have taken to step toward the light, dim and flickering as it was. And now, there in the conference room, he looked at me with the same expression he'd had the night before. A joke at my expense, but with a warmth in his eyes that I was now able to see. So there it was. He knows I'm gay, and was still happy to wander the streets with me. Go to the theater. Get a bite to eat. Like friends do. I was finally sorting it out.

So many ways I had held myself back, thinking that telling him would come between us, when in fact, it was the not telling that kept us from connecting.

I unclenched my grip from the arms of the metal chair. Overcome by a strange sensation of lightness, I sat back. I pictured us walking on that dark street, talking about the play we'd seen, about the food we might eat. I saw us a foot apart, not in step. I played out the wilding, and saw him run one way, me the other. I thought about Freckleface and the band of kids whooping as they bounded off. Off to another crime, or to a corner for a smoke. Talking shit about girls. They hadn't said anything about fags. I hadn't felt hated. Only that they were a wild band, and we were two people wandering for food in their territory.

"If that was a gay-bashing," I said, turning to the detective, opening and closing my fists, feeling the little scabs crack, the scraped-up fingers looking stronger, "it didn't go down like most gay-bashings. The ones *my people* tell me about."

Dan laughed at this. Understood my train of thought. *"Your people,"* Dan said. "Do they tell you that punks like last night call you names while they bash your head in?"

"Yes," I said. "Things like 'fuckin' homo.'"

"Faggot?" Dan offered.

"Maricón." I nodded, feeling myself falling in sync with Dan.

"Queer," Dan said. Having fun.

"Cocksucker!" I continued. We were on a roll.

"Whoa—easy," the detective interrupted. "I get it, I get it."

"That's how *my people* say it normally goes," I said. "A proper gay-bashing has, like you said, some name-calling." The part of me that was using his language, making sure I was understood, also wanted to pronounce *name-calling* the way the detective did. I didn't imitate him. But I did add an "Or some such."

There was a moment while the detective made notes, nodding. He seemed to be moving from skepticism to acceptance. He was disappointed, but he didn't entirely appreciate how we seemed to be making light of the situation. "Don't get me wrong," he said. I replayed his accent in my head again—*wrong, ru-wong*—and he went on. "It's not like I wish you'da been gay-bashed. We don't wish that on anyone."

And then he began telling Dan and me all about Freckleface. The detective knew him. He didn't say so, exactly, said he couldn't be certain, but based on the description I'd given, he was pretty sure. A kid he'd known for years. In and out of trouble. More a bad-luck kid than a bad kid. A projects kid. A hate-crime accusation might change something, the detective said. Might give the police a new threat. Something to hold over the kid's head to bring him back in line, keep him on the straight and narrow.

"You'd be surprised what might jolt someone into accepting their reality," the detective said. "Help them find their better self, see their own potential."

I wasn't convinced that could work for a perpetrator. But I could see how it might do that for a victim. I started to feel lucky that my jolt was so gentle.

Afterward, we stood on the street in front of the precinct, Dan heading the opposite way. Out of habit I searched for something new to talk about, anything that would let us linger there together a bit longer. For a moment I thought maybe I should thank him, but I knew that didn't seem right. Nothing more needed to be said. Still, some old habits ...

"Do you think it's messed up that the cops would drum up evidence to nail that kid?" I asked. It was the kind of speculation we might have discussed at length, playing out scenarios, me guiding the conversation, hoping for a way to bring up the Thing that was always in the back of my mind, but never daring to do it. Everything was simpler now.

"Maybe," he said, and thought for a second. "No. I don't think so. I think that cop not only wants to help that kid, he also wants to serve and protect *your people*."

We smiled in agreement. In sync.

"I gotta get to the office," Dan said. "So much stuff to do before Monday."

"Yeah," I said. "I gotta go, too. So much gay stuff to do." We laughed, and we parted.

As time went on, I saw Dan again a couple of times before his company transferred him to California. Went to his wedding. Now it's mostly just Facebook updates. And then the other night, all these years after the wilding, still living in the same neighborhood, I found myself buying milk at that bodega where Dan had called the cops, had called me. It's cleaner now, and brighter. In front, the hollowed-out pay phone shells have been gussied up with an Internet connection. As I was paying, I looked through the door and I saw that boy. Freckleface. There was no mistaking it. He was older, of course. And taller. A man. Had a scar on his face now, and a tattoo on his neck that was unfinished, a little messed-up-looking because of the freckles. Looked like someone who'd done time. And now, there he was leaning against scaffolding, resting a big dirty high-top sneaker on a fire hydrant. He seemed to be trying to joke around with some of the other project guys, maybe pretend his troubles weren't troubling. There were nicks in the red afro, and the wide green eyes were tired. But it was him. Still talking shit, you'd could tell by how the others reacted. With a chipped tooth, the smile didn't have the same confidence. I got my change, took the milk, and as I left I nodded at them because we all live around there. They nodded back. It's everyone's street, everyone's bodega.

I e-mailed Dan about it. His reply came fast: "Did you get his phone number this time?"

Probably Last Meeting
of Bluebell Ridge II
Homeowners Association

Philip Ivory

(From *The Airgonaut*)

Meeting called to order at 6:00 PM by Brenda Greenwood at the clubhouse. Members present: Brenda Greenwood (President), John Kornacki (Vice President), Sally Durwitz (Treasurer), Verna Siliphant (Secretary), George Krebbs, Phyllis Mantle. Members not present: Stu Halloway.

Minutes of May 9 meeting approved. Treasurer's Report approved. At end of May: $1,452.26 in checking account and $27,438.55 in reserve account for total of $28,890.81.

Old Business: Regarding letter we sent April 16 to Bill Slate, President of sister community, Bluebell Ridge I, in which we proposed melding of communities to combine resources, reduce expenses, streamline services to residents: Brenda read reply dated May 22 from Bill averring that merging of communities cannot be considered until seismic fault (with occasional lava spillage, as on Memorial Day two years ago) under Bluebell Ridge II be corrected. Repair to be verified by town council and UCLA Department of Seismology. Sally said budget for present year will not allow for repair to earth's crust. Motion made to revisit next year. Passed.

On another issue: John reported that Stu Halloway (absent) acted without Board authority, threatening to send homeowner Hannah Horsley (lot 41) to "a stinking gulag" for unauthorized removal of creosote plants growing in common area.

Sally added to complaints about Stu, saying occasional motions he has made at meetings to exonerate Stalin for historical crimes are "real time waster."

Sally added Stu is "probably a communist" and also "Norman Bates crazy." Phyllis pointed out alarming situation: USPS person now only delivers mail to residents on Moonbeam Drive (Stu's street). This is because Stu made him his "best friend" and "milk shake buddy at Hardee's" and told him other streets in community are bad.

Brenda banged on table and asked for motion to be made about Stu. George made motion Stu "is terrible." Passed.

Phyllis raised issue of her request that HOA pay for removal of dead acacia tree in her front yard because it will fall and crush her, and maybe her grandson if he is sleeping on living room couch. Brenda said tree is homeowner responsibility. Phyllis said tree was there when she moved in, does that mean her grandson should have to die from it when he hasn't even been to the Harry Potter theme park yet?

Unplanned 20-minute recess resulting from Brenda banging on table with fist to change subject from Phyllis's tree, reverberations of which caused circuit breaker in back of clubhouse to flip so AC stopped working. George volunteered to fix.

Meeting resumed. AC fixed. Phyllis complained about excessive banging on table by Brenda scaring people and causing recesses. Brenda said that should be in New Business. Also said banging is part of her function as President.

George suggested instead of banging, just using words or mime. John said excessive size of Brenda's fist could be part of problem, saying fist is not human, more "circus sized." Phyllis suggested Brenda's fist is growing larger every meeting in supernatural way, so banging is a hazard to health/safety of other Board members.

Brenda asked for other opinions. Sally agreed with George's no more banging idea. Brenda said that is not another opinion, but same one. Sally wondered if table in clubhouse is in danger of breakage due to fist banging. Potential replacement of table is not listed as line item in yearly budget. Should it be? Motion made, not passed.

George offered to fetch yellow wraparound ruler (*Secretary's note: research proper term*) to measure Brenda's fist size. George to follow up with measurements at subsequent meetings, so we will know for sure if some "demonic shit" is going on with Brenda's "humongous troll hand."

Brenda banged on table to say time for New Business.

New Business: Brenda asked for volunteers for July cookout. John to bring hot dogs, burgers, George to bring drinks. Agreed not to tell Stu although he is Board member. Phyllis and Verna on dessert detail. Time: Saturday, July 21, at 10 AM.

George said residents have complained about sulfur fumes in clubhouse and pool area. Homeowner Jane Foley (lot 22) said they made her nephew puke at Easter. Sally said probably related to volcanic venting due to earth crust problem.

Brenda asked for other New Business, and Phyllis said John appears to be dead. Not breathing or humming "Bolero" in usual annoying way. Sally said perhaps pacemaker was shattered by Brenda banging on table to announce New Business. Brenda asked that remark be struck from record as assertion unfounded without autopsy.

George suggested recess due to John probably being dead, but Sally said we need to keep going so we can finish so she and Herschel can watch *Shark Tank* at 8.

Brenda banged on table, said we're not leaving until we discuss repair to irrigation lines near south perimeter. George told Brenda in addition to giant hand, her tongue is now swelling like giant toad's tongue and dripping slime that sizzles.

Brenda, unable to speak in human way, emitted rumbling wail like wart hog while banging on table for order.

Windows spontaneously shattered. Bedrock beneath clubhouse and pool area gave way. Board members fell into crevice, some screaming from lava burns (very painful and frightening).

Brenda, clutching John's limp body with giant clawed hands, sprouted reptilian wings that could not bear her weight. She and John fell into chasm below, consumed by smoke and fire. Others tumbled after them, clutching at roots, trying to climb on top of each other, but falling, falling to certain death. George, falling, shouted resignation from Board as fiery boils erupted in his flesh.

Only Verna and Phyllis left alive, on ledge, singed and choking from fumes. Can hear sirens. Mutual motion made that Stu Halloway be formally asked to serve as interim President. That motion entered here in hopes that FEMA or other professionals will find these notes and take appropriate action.

Respectfully submitted,
Verna Siliphant (Secretary)
Bluebell Ridge II Homeowners Association
June 9, 2016

CLEAVED

Kathie Jacobson

(From *Twisted Vine*)

cleave¹ (vb) to cling, to adhere
cleave² (vb) to split or cause to split, esp along a natural weakness

*J*ust above the equator, as the earth swelters in a shriveling drought, impoverished men lose reason. Homes are burned. Humanity evaporates in the sun as bodies chase and flee. Death litters the so-called road to safety. The news reports this is a land on the verge of genocide. (The verge? you ask.)

A baby cries alone in a field. A mercenary, hearing, carries her home. Peacekeeper, they call him. (Peace? you ask.)

One day he will tell her unspeakable stories, answer her questions with tales of a bludgeoned mother. One day she will whisper like a breeze beside his bed.

CLEAVED

Conscripted boys approached—machetes high, pumped biceps as they cleansed the village, erased names, fileted the pious, cleaved hands from arms, legs from hips. Heads oozed in tortured piles. Rage littered the sky; sheets of ash that once had been walls burned on the breeze. Terror nestled in eyes of onetime friends.

They would have carved you from your mother's arms, emptied you onto the growing mound: no earth for cover. She slipped her pinky into the palate of your new-made mouth, shallowed her breath, slid beneath the pit where feces stewed.

When boys whooped victory and ran from there, she wrapped you in her skirt, bared her legs to thorn and insect bite, clutched you, a bundle in her arm's curl, and fled.

You slept and she hastened to the running road where dirt turned red. She stumbled on clumps of mud-red dirt marooned between the fallen. Bodies tangled on the path like gnarled roots above the ground.

Life trickled through her shredded skin, stained your blanket. Blisters cracked on her nose and lips; she had no eyes, no face; left you wrapped between the tufts of grass without a note; left you no name.

Singing your sleepy, your mother tucked you in a nest of matted weeds. She brushed her lips whispering against your forehead. Saying this is the place where your father stood, where your father stood in the time before.

You knew her smell. A whiff of overripe melon and still you turn, confused, expecting. You knit your brow to squeeze memory from scent. Who? you ask, and want to know.

GENOCIDE

In another era, you might gather flowers from that field. You might stand there, blades of grass slipping between your toes, your knees bowed as you bend to pull small red blossoms that scavenge moisture from the sand. On the road, gray-whiskered men would shuffle, cigarette smoke trailing them. You would know the yellow globs of chaw that linger where boys spit on the uneven stone path. You would carry a sack with a mango. An orange. You would feel no hunger.

That day the grass thirsted, reedy and long, half of it trampled flat. Weighted.

You could see the sky burnt colorless by the sun from where you lay on the ground. You could see grass scrape against that faded blue. You could see, if you looked that far, the haze of heat as it rose. You could hear the rattle of dry seeds as they complained about the wind. The creek bed, scratched like chalk on a slate board, lay soundless. The road thundered with passing feet. You could see them, if you had known to look, from this spot in the field, a mile from the dusty square where fires blazed. You would have seen their shoulders bouncing, their heads jostling above the tufted grass. The sound of them, their voices, shiver you awake. The baritone of panic. The alto of flight.

You lay wrapped in bright colors a mile from the dusty square where fire blazed, blanket corners knotted to keep snakes from your skin. Smoke filled your lungs. Sweat dried to salty film on your cheeks. Hunger wailed from your lips, lifted from the grass. And they turned.

Beside your nest, a girl stood, her nappy slipping. Boys cracked blades against her bones, their swings more savage because they towered over her small frame. A boy nicked your hand, raised his cleaver as if to open you like a casaba. Your mother's wail raced around the edges of the sky and he turned toward her. She waved her arm like a worried bird. She extended her arm like a broken wing and hobbled on the ground, lured rebels like foxes from your nest of matted weeds. She drew their knives and left you sleeping without allegiance on the sunbaked ground.

She hobbled on the road, dizzy, shrieking. The boy grinned and she saw teeth, not yet finished in his mouth. She saw his face, still soft and whiskerless.

Her torment shaped you, pierced you like prayer and changed the structure of your ear.

Beside you the girl. Beside her, hands.

In blood pools, flies paddled drunk. Because they bathed in blood-red pools, flies did not settle in your eyes.

PEACEKEEPER

He was a man drawn to fire. He was one of them. He belonged to no one. A map of battles scarred his dreams.

His first wife left him over silence at the table where they chewed corn and beef, their forks squeaking against porcelain plates with pink and blue flowers on the rims. His biceps grew with lifting body parts and corpses to clear the roads. He tore sleeves from his shirt. His palms chafed where blisters grew, then popped, then peeled, skin hanging thickly from a final border. His second wife recoiled at the gloveless leather of his skin.

Dry-eyed, distracted, with a belly that did not swell, his second wife shrugged one shoulder when he told her he was leaving. A soldier goes when he is called. A wife waits: in her bathrobe, in her dress, in her kitchen, in her garden. She knew he would go. When she married him, she knew he would go. She watched him in the mirror as she glossed her lips. He looked at the glassy version of her eyes, finished her shrug.

Both shoulders rose then fell to attention.

HIDDEN

You are Lucy McHenry Mack. You were never a baby. You did not cry or gurgle. You did not blow bubbles with the flow of air through saliva drooling from your lips. You did not smile. You did not babble. Your flat eyes held emptiness, stared at the air where your mother should have been if your mother did not let you go. Did not drop you. Did not leave you soft upon the ground. Did not wrap you in colors and tuck you between tufts of grass that lingered like hair on the head of a man with cancer. Did not forget you in a field where the grass crackled with the slither of snakes and the stomp of insect feet. Did not squirrel you away from the whistle of swinging blades.

UNDONE

Before, he kept time to the rumble of the march. In his mind, he heard Coltrane. Dolphy. He slept dreamless and woke with sour breath. He breathed into his hands, inhaled his air to know he was alive. His feet trod with precision on hard earth and soft flesh in equal measure.

After he tripped over an infant's cry, found life small and helpless in the field, his stomach churned. After, he saw people lying breathless, eyes wide with fear. He slept only when exhaustion sealed off dreams. After, he could not close his eyes against the corpse-filled acres. Death loomed, visible.

He carried the baby from town to town, in the crook of his elbow, his hand a gentle armor, his AK slant against his shoulder.

SHOULDERED

Inside a padlocked gate, an old house crowded orphans, head-to-toe, in beds; their bodies sore with underuse, their ribs wrapped in skin.

Light dribbled from chandeliers dangling from the wood-beamed ceiling. Grime layered like sedimentary rock on children's skin. Cholera lurked.

He carried you there as he knew he should. He could not let go.

The second wife beamed like headlights when he Skyped a picture.

His face scoured your cheek when he roughed you good night. Rough tendered you. Like him, soft voices caused your spine to curl, your head to shrink like water evaporating in the sun.

The soldier rode you on his shoulders, the ones that shrug and you held on. You clapped your hand and gripped. You held on across the desert and the sea. You held while the soldier dozed on the plane that carried you. His arms surrounded. Like a nest. You held while paper mounded in an office.

You held on and arrived at a house, its window boxes filled with pink. Petunias dangled like skirts of fancy girls; pink, like shirts on the machete men who severed your mother and pruned your hand.

Birds flitted through leaves of a tree that tapped your window in the wind.

They pinned a medal on his chest. A choir sang.

HOME

At breakfast his wife shrieked, smile faded, when your hand lay wooden on the table. She did not expect a broken child. He boiled water, poured tea and sighed into her wailing. You ate cheese still in its paper. You would eat grasshoppers or crickets without barbecue.

On the street children pointed at your arm when your body grew too big for the hand toned to someone else's skin. In school girls would ask. Some, shy and halting, turned their gaze to your shoes as they spoke. Some, bold, squinted at your eyes. Boys did not wonder about your hand once your breasts bulged forward.

You did not miss your hand.

Where is your mother? That bothered you.

You were certain. She was walking in the desert still, her feet badly burned against the barren sand.

TENDER

The second wife peered from across the room or through a kitchen window as you tendered dolls into nests on the ground and then, with great care, removed their limbs. You made a study of plastic links: slide-and-washer, pin-and-donut, ball-and-socket. You swiveled arms at shoulders, legs at hips in concentric circles, flat or angled. You cut elastic bands and heads poured off shoulders. Sometimes you filled a doll with petals from the garden, pressed a limb back into service. Inside, petals resolved to dirt.

When the soldier shivered in the night, woke, his forehead wet with sweat, his pupils grand against the dark, this second wife walked him to your doorway.

One day, she whispered, you would sew limbs onto broken children.

GROWN

At any hour, you saw the sky and every color interrupted you, drained motion from your limbs. A doctor told you that your teeth would fail. Poor nutrition. Eating sand.

You bit holes in your lips and lost your taste for melon. You stomped and begged to know your name, the one before he cradled you. Rage darkened your eyes, filled you like a messenger's sack. You held a knife against your skin. The second wife cried behind the door. The soldier watched. You pushed him away, staggered between surrender and blame.

In the news, they sent boys, now men, to prison. In your sleep, the men, still boys, amputated dreams.

You studied people in the street, attended to the curve of lips, the slope of nose. You followed every black-haired man with peppery whiskers, your gaze a question: perhaps the one with shiny shoes who hid his eyes with dark glasses, perhaps the one with slip-on clogs and sockless ankles. Words filtered across the tables, syllables stretched in accents: thick from the south, twang from the middle.

At the end of the war they slipped into the crowd like any other man, no tattoos scarred their foreheads, no feathers tarred against their skin.

The soldier held you when you cried. His shirt stained wet. He looked over your head and across the road. Taught you to see nothing.

CLEAVE

The soldier walks with a cane linked to his belt loop so that he does not lose it from his grip. His steps slow, his lean heavy as he swings his right foot forward, presses upright on his strong left. He carries a cross-body bag with a wallet, some papers, all he has seen. A folded buck knife waits inside a leather pocket on his belt.

You cleave to this man with red and gold bars pinned on his coat. His shoes shine like mirrors. In them, you see your face. His uniform drapes loose from his shoulders and lines web from his lips. You watch his wrist below his sleeve. Dark hairs curl on his arm.

One day two mothers will come to you. The first mother, his second wife, with her hair pulled from her face, her eyes drawn with care, the skin on her cheek grown thin, transparent, will offer you a hand. You will not take it. You will stand, your shoulder grazing against hers. The second mother, your mother, will stand apart. Her feet will sink below the floorboards. She will swat the air like she is pushing aside a tangle of vines. Her eyes will not blink. Her lips will part as if words have found their way into her mouth.

You cannot hear her. She has been gone so long from the field where she left you. She is wrapped like a chain around your neck. She is threaded through your braids. She is in the curve of your waist, the sap of your naval.

The soldier will lie down.

You will test his cheek, run your finger up the rough of his whiskers.

The second wife's shoulders will shudder and you will lift your arm to cradle her.

THE BOAT AND THE WATER

Elizabeth Kandall

Confession: I did not want this boat,

Not its sunny dock at Chelsea Pier or its down-home dock upstate, not its
   deluxe cabin down

below where the children could eat popcorn and watch videos on a double
   bed, not the glossy

wood polyurethane shine, not my job of throwing the rope or holding the
   wheel, not the way

you moved several tons of steel and fiberglass out into the choppy current
   and skillfully slipped

her back into the skinny spot between the other boats like you were dancing
   a move with the

swivel of your hips. Not even the tears that swell in my throat when I think
   of you swimming off

the back of the boat in sight of the lighthouse, where you work to string rope
   to buoy to

enclose our little place, to hold our family in this wide open water. I wish I
   could have

embraced this. I could not, but love, I'll concede: whatever boat you are, I'll
   be that boat's

water; deep and shallow, wide and narrow, under and all around, the white
wake behind, I'll be

the vast open sea and the currents that swirl and the ones that pull you
toward.

ECHO LAKE

Timur Karaca

(From *Narrative* magazine)

When I was eight years old, I watched a girl drown. I was at Echo Lake for the summer with my family—still intact and functional in those days. The girl's name was Alexis Swenson. She was five. I was playing with a group of kids in the woods behind our cabins, when Alexis, ignored because she was the youngest, darted in and snatched up the lacy white sun hat that was a marker in our game and made a break for the lake.

She was laughing. Something animal in me was sparked, and I chased her. It felt so naturally like a new part of the game. When she saw me behind her she ran faster—her sun-bleached ponytail bouncing against her nape, the sun hat whipping in her small hand. She'd had a head start, and I hardly made up ground as I chased her down to and across the beach, then out to the end of the dock.

I don't know how she went in—whether she jumped or lost her balance. When I reached the water she was almost submerged. Her hair unfurled along the surface, and her arms reached out over a blur that must have been her legs going like mad below. She was already much farther out than I ever could have reached.

I squatted, then kneeled, then lay down on the edge of the dock, to get as close to her as I could, as though that might make some difference. The truth, of course, was that I couldn't swim—a truth, unfortunately, that no one else knew. I had completed a year of lessons at the Y, and had, through my own skill and conniving, managed to be promoted, undeservedly, over to the deep end with my peers. I had become master at keeping within an arm's reach of the wall when we practiced treading water and at finding the shallowest lanes when we swam laps. I couldn't have stayed afloat in that lake for more than thirty seconds, let alone rescue a panicking five-year-old girl.

Eventually, I called for help. I ran halfway back up the dock, but I didn't want to leave her. At some point, someone's father appeared on the beach and came running. Then there was a commotion of men on the dock and all the kids and some other of the adults came down from the woods and the cabins and watched from the beach. My father was there. He didn't say anything at first. He put his arm around me and massaged my shoulder, and then he turned me away from the commotion.

I didn't see her after they pulled her out, but somehow I have a memory of her puffy face, vacant eyes, hypoxic-blue lips, and a strand of lake grass clinging to her hair. It's the memory my mind constructed after my parents told me that Alexis had been rushed to the hospital but had died. We were sitting in the family room of our cabin, the three of us, the lake and the woods uncharacteristically quiet. From the trees outside, pollen was falling and swirling like snow through late-afternoon shafts of sun. My parents delivered the news with care; they didn't dance around the facts or coddle, but they also weren't, in their way, without empathy and tenderness. In short, they did everything right, everything one might ask of parents in such a circumstance. They listened to my spare and jumbled version of things, but didn't press me or judge, didn't presume my feelings. There was surprise, of course, when I confessed the extent of my deceptions at swim practice, but any anger they were careful to direct only at my instructors. "We put him under too much pressure with those lessons," I heard my mother tell my father later that night as I lay awake in bed.

The truth is that no one ever overtly blamed me for what happened, including Alexis's parents. Before they left the lake early that summer, I ran into her father, repairing an upside-down boat in front of their cabin. He didn't ask me what had happened or reprimand me in any way, but he also didn't forgive me. He stiffened as I walked by, and he went on with his work, looking down, hiding his face below the bill of his cap. I think that just about anything else would have been better. The smallest, stiffest nod or an honest dose of rage or despair could have changed everything.

Later that summer, a boy a few years older than I was and already with a reputation as a bully, teased me about being scared of the water, which sent our playmates into nervous titters. His parents must have gotten wind of the incident because he was absent from the woods and the lake for the next two days, and when he reappeared, he wore a haggard look of shame. None of the kids ever said anything else to me about the drowning.

In the fall, my parents enrolled me in extra afterschool classes and took me on weekend trips to museums and the zoo. They didn't exactly pretend that the incident hadn't happened, but they never brought it up. If they sensed I was down or preoccupied, they smiled or mussed my hair, and then there was a new activity or an outing. I sometimes had nightmares (which, curiously, had more to do with falls from a height than with drowning), and for years afterward I continued to think about Alexis when reminded of her by some near or actual catastrophe; my older sister Margaret's diagnosis of leukemia (though she would survive and remains, to this day, in remission), my parents' separation and eventual divorce, my father's heart attack. But months and years would pass, and it seemed I wasn't thinking of her at all. And then something would happen, and there she was again: the laughter and the white hat, leading me down to the water.

Years later when my father was ill, we sold the Echo Lake cabin. I was thirty and recently married, and Laura was pregnant with our first daughter, Samantha. My father would never have the chance to meet her. I visited him frequently in the hospital, where, among other things, I helped him manage the sale. It was both the first time in many years, and the last time in the twenty years since, that anyone brought up the episode of the drowning to me. He was proud of me, he said. He wasn't sure he'd ever told me. "A lot of kids would have been crushed by a thing like that," he said, and then he proceeded to commend me in more general terms, for going to college, starting a family of my own, and so on. I thanked him and changed the subject—his heart was weak at that point, failing him, and I didn't want him getting upset. Days later he took a turn and needed a mechanical pump to keep him going, a palliative effort buying him a little more time. He was gaunt, his arms and chest bruised. Intermittently delirious, he rambled incoherently, and he brought up the drowning again. "Can't swim," he said, "said he didn't care, never wanted to." He said it just like that, in the third person, as though I weren't there in the room with him. At least that's how I remember it now. At the time, of course, I didn't ask him to repeat himself or clarify. He was already on to the next related item, according to his mind's broken logic. I just held his hand to keep him calm. At the time I gave little thought to his words, and soon my father died, and ten days later, Samantha was born.

Now, I'm sitting in a hospital again, at Samantha's bedside. She's twenty years old, in a coma, recovering from what appears to have been a drug overdose.

It's late, and the nurses have kindly allowed me to stay past visiting hours. It's quiet. There are only a few beeps and clicks from around the ward, the rhythmic pull and hiss of Samantha's ventilator. They've drawn a curtain around us, and it's dark, but I can see her by the light of the monitor that shows her vital signs. I can tell that they've cleaned her, that someone has washed dirt or something else from her cheeks and her chin and neck. Someone has combed and gathered her straight brown hair neatly into a ponytail and laid it on her shoulder. There's a plastic breathing tube that curls from her mouth and fogs with her breath. Her skin is pale, her lips puffy. But her face is calm, her eyes closed, and it occurs to me that I know this face, or that I've imagined it before, but it's not Samantha I've seen like this, it's Alexis, or my constructed memory of her, drowned and brought up from the lake.

Samantha had been found on the beach, unconscious and hardly breathing. There looked to have been a bonfire or a party of some sort, but there was no one left with her when the paramedics arrived. Someone had called 911 anonymously. They'd found bottles of pills in her purse—Vicodin, Percocet, oxycodone. She didn't move or respond when they tried to rouse her.

I got to the hospital first, and Laura arrived a short time later. We stood and watched her for a full twenty minutes without speaking. Lately, things have been bad between Laura and me, but with Samantha in the hospital our deepest differences suddenly felt insignificant. Laura leaned into me, and we watched Samantha's chest rise and fall.

Later, during the nurses' change of shift, we were asked to leave the room, and we walked downstairs to a waiting area near the lobby. There was no one else there, and we sat on either end of a sagging plastic couch. It was late afternoon. An arc of sun fell on Laura, lighting her cheek and her straight brown hair. "You should go," I said. One of us would have to leave soon to pick up our younger daughter, Jordan. I could see Laura's mind working as she thought about what to tell Jordan. Samantha'd gotten herself into trouble before but never anything this serious. Laura would be vague until we had a better sense, at least, of how Samantha's condition might evolve. "I'll stay," I said. I couldn't imagine leaving her. Laura nodded, gazing down at the tiles on the floor, and wouldn't look at me. It seemed there was something I should say, something hopeful, or a gesture I should make. But nothing felt quite right, and then it was too late—Laura stood and readied herself to leave, and I was reminded of a time when Samantha was twelve years old and got caught smoking in the girls' room at school. Laura and I met at the principal's office (I'd had to take the train and was late), where Samantha sat quietly letting her hair fall over her eyes and face as we heard the accusation. She said almost nothing and kept silent on the ride home. She folded herself over in the back seat, clutching her pale, bare knees, and I was taken, not for the last time, by how small and young she looked. "What's going on, Sam?" I asked, as though she were waiting for me to ask, as though it could ever be that simple. I thought that maybe she just hadn't wanted to talk in front of the principal. But she only shrugged. I looked over at Laura, to see if she might want to take a different tack, but she wasn't looking at me just then either, and she didn't turn or say anything, though I was sure she must have felt my stare. She faced away, chin in hand, staring or pretending to stare at the sun's red reflection passing across the buildings outside her window.

After Laura left I resumed my wait at Samantha's bedside, and watching her and wondering about the murky depth of consciousness she was navigating, I thought about Alexis and Echo Lake. One summer Laura and I had taken the girls to the beach—the ocean, not the lake—and the surf was a bit rougher than expected for that time of year. Samantha must have been about eight, and Jordan was still a toddler. The girls and I waded out to my knees—their waists—and I kept a tight grip on their hands. Samantha was already a strong swimmer, but the waves made me nervous. We told her not to go in without us, but later that afternoon I saw her, a hundred yards or so up the shore, in up to her chest. She was jumping the waves and laughing, but every other one seemed to knock her down, and I would lose sight of her for a moment. Then I would find her again, her pale body in the light, submerged in the green, and the tide would pull, and she would slide a few feet deeper and farther out. I sprinted to her and pulled her from the water. She coughed and sobbed, and tried to push free as I carried her back up the beach. I set her down, and Laura wrapped her in a towel and dried her. When Samantha calmed a bit, I kneeled and asked her why she went in without us. I pushed a damp twist of hair from her temple, and she recoiled and wrapped herself up tighter. "I was fine," she said. On the drive home, the sky went gray and humid, and the girls fell asleep in the back seat. Laura seemed unsettled. "What happened out there?" she asked. I thought her question was strange, and then I thought that maybe she hadn't seen Samantha out in the water before I got to her. I explained about the waves, how they knocked her down, about the undertow and how it can take even an experienced swimmer by surprise. But that didn't satisfy her. "The way you grabbed her," she said, "and pulled her out—I thought you were going to hurt her." I didn't know what to say. When it happened Laura had been a hundred yards or more up the beach, and I told myself that from that distance the scene might have looked very different. Replaying the events in my mind, I couldn't find anything I'd done that wasn't necessary. I glanced over and met Laura's eyes, and I felt that she was looking deeply into me. Her look was of concern, and tenderness, but I also saw that she was afraid. That look was new. We drove for a time in silence. It got dark. Then I told her about Echo Lake. I'd never told her. Somehow, it had just never come up. I was aware that I'd been nervous at other times, when the girls were near water — sometimes I was conscious of recalling Alexis and the drowning, sometimes not. I told Laura what happened, and she listened quietly. Afterward, she put her hand on my knee and said she was sorry, she hadn't known. The rest of the way home we didn't talk, and later I wondered if there was more we should have said. But we didn't, and that was the last we spoke of it. When we got home, we carried the girls inside — Jordan in Laura's arms, Samantha in mine — and tucked them in and kissed them, their skin still rough with salt.

I'm sitting here with Samantha now, looking from her face to the monitor, trying to make sense of the small alarms and lights that beep or flash from time to time. Laura texted earlier to say that she and Jordan were home safely, that Jordan had gone to sleep. I replied that there was nothing new here, I was still waiting, that I would stay as late as they would let me. It's almost midnight. The night nurse is friendly. She looks to be about seventy and reminds me of my grandmother when I was a boy. Her movements are deft and assured as she adjusts the monitors and pumps. She talks to me while she works. "You should go home," she says. "You need to take care of yourself too." I thank her but tell her that I'm not tired, that I'd like to stay. She stands beside me and watches Samantha over my shoulder. "She's a beautiful girl," she says in a near whisper and smiles. It's the look and smile of someone who has raised children. "Feels like they're put on this earth to drive us mad sometimes, doesn't it?" she says. "All we can do is love them," she says, and I can only nod. Her voice even softer, she says, "It's not your fault, you know," and after a moment it gets hard to breathe, and I feel the blood rushing to my skin like it wants to get out, and I know I shouldn't answer her, but I can't stop myself. "Why would it be my fault?" I say, and the skin around her eyes slackens, and I can see the fear pulling at her face, though half of the smile is still there, trying, maybe, to coax me back. "Why the fuck would it be my fault?" I repeat, my voice rising, and suddenly I'd like to undo her smile all the way, smear it clean off, and I'm standing and my hands are shaking, and the nurse sets her syringes and coils of IV tubing down and rushes out the door. After she's gone, I stand my ground, the breath whistling in my nose, and then her place at the door is taken by two large men with badges and black sweaters. Sizing me up, they look tired but no-nonsense, and somehow I'm glad they've finally come, as if they've been following me for a very long time.

EVE

Jennifer Kearns

(From *EDGE*)

People, there was no snake.
Let me set the record straight,
not half of that dumb book was true.
Nor was Paradise that great.

All I did was serve the man a peach.
No apple. You scholars got that wrong too.
Poring over papers and arguing
did tomatoes or peppers grow in those climes?

It was a peach, plain and sweet.
Plucked from a tree in our yard.
In between sweeping up droppings, pelting prowling jackals away,

in between cooking and cleaning and listening
while he jabbered to voices in his head.
Something about a coming storm, he said.
No time to help, too deep in conversation.

And when I meekly asked if he might ever
come sit, talk to me, play with our boys,
still so small and slippery in the tub,
he would sit up on the couch and sigh,

stroke the livid scar that laced his side,
moan how much his body ached,
the missing rib, his trunk all a-kilter,
yet still I asked for more?

We got evicted in the name of social progress;
he left me, one-two, for another woman.
A snake charmer, no less.
Wouldn't you know.

So I made my way here, alone.
None of that "crawling on her belly, eating dirt."
To life on this dreary isle washed in rain,
where the locals still eye me up in the only pub.

At night I dream of my garden,
the soughing trees, the animal chatter.
I curse the day I tried to teach him anything
but I would return now willingly

And stay naked.
Even toiling among the banks of nettles.
Even at night when the chill wind blows
and our fingers turn to ice.

APPLE PIE

Eleanor Kedney

(From *The Offering* / Originally published in *Connecticut River Review*)

I found my father sifting,
fine white flour falling into drifts
in the belly of a yellow bowl.
While he turned the crank
and metal moved like a scythe
scraping against mesh, he was quiet,
young in natural light,
his cheeks ruddy, his dark hair
slick with Brylcreem, combed high,
the tip of his tongue on his lower lip
as when he wrote Christmas cards,
marking extra dots above i's, adding
curlicues to the tails of g's and y's.
I wanted to know his thoughts.
The Cortland apples, peeled and cored
while I had slept, waited on the counter
dressed in cinnamon and sugar as if this
was a special occasion, though
he often made pie early in the morning
—his pie pleased and inspired praise.
He'd serve me a piece complete with swirls
of whipped cream and look into my face.
He was a kid that way. I didn't pretend
I could someday make pie and it would taste like his—
the crust flaking when it hits the tongue,
the apples spicy-sweet and buttery—but sleepily
I listened to what he wanted to tell me
about measuring Crisco and chilling dough.
He had no written recipe, only his ease

cutting in shortening, his wrist moving back
and forth as if rocking a cradle.
Big fingers handled dough like delicate fabric,
easing it into a pie plate, fluting the crust
with his thumb, his mark. He set the timer
and it loudly ticked away our minutes.
The morning of his wake, my mother threw away
the last piece of apple pie to make room
for cold cuts, salads, and sodas.
I lifted it out of the garbage and ate it.

El Camino

Robert Kendrick

(From *Concho River Review*)

Kim says Doug's Chevy's all mine if I want it,
the house next to go. She still sleeps with his clothes.

Forty-nine miles to Nebraska & back,
let the big block breathe. A run just our age.

December moon honeys the T-handle shifter
bright as the nickel plate .38

he pressed to his neck, action tuned to release
cam & spring from the least point of pressure,

his talent for turning desire into speed
& smoke, handwork that propels me

between frost-capped cornfields.
Dead stalks keep topsoil from drifting,

roots clutching dirt until rot. Pull one up early,
ground loosens under those closest.

I've dreamed of this music—finely milled piston
& ported exhaust, waves of horsepower & torque,

polished hood pins & the next mile of asphalt,
just as the first key gleam promised

when Kim pressed it to my palm
& insisted *just once, then decide.*

Uprising

Maggie Kennedy

(From *Meat For Tea*)

6 point at most,
unintelligible from a speck.
Each tri-apple ant
a farsighted blur,
in formation a running,
ceaseless ticker tape,
emerging from under
a floorboard to
   behind the couch
       around the table
            across the stove

  up
  down
      the fridge
  into the cat's bowl
and back again.

I vacuum and scour,
wipe out dozens on hundreds
but the parade returns,
silent but rattling.

You are big with reserves of fat.
You toss bags of untouched food.
You are armed with weapons of destruction.

We are tiny, just itty-bitty.
We are poor and unarmed.
We are many, many more.

##

A teardrop of a country
I never bothered to know,
a street vendor sets himself ablaze
because they took his vegetables
because they cast him aside
one too many times.
The smoldering shame of how
he let them define him:

speck

This is how revolutions begin.
Not with a bang,
but a dismissal.

As I battle the crowds at the mall,
a president is fleeing to Paris.

As I walk my 10,000 steps a day,
copycats douse themselves in gasoline.

As I surf for a distraction,
thousands on thousands gather in a square.

##

Being seven,
being intrigued with all things bug,
A. takes matters into his own hands,
sets traps of raisins under radiators
and waits.

Additional troops arrive.
They crawl under our cuffs,
faint tickles that erupt in
slaps and swearing.
They float in our soup, die in

our undergarments.
They invade the coffee maker,
their teeny bodies indistinguishable
from the black grounds
we spit in the sink.

A. captures them in Tupperware,
pokes holes in the lids with a fork.

We debate inside and outside:
Squirrels always outside — Can you imagine the mess?
Cats and dogs inside and outside.
Mice outside ... OK a caged pet at Johnny's house.
Ants outside, not inside
except OK an ant farm for your birthday.

But who says? A. asks.
I do, I say, and he slinks away.

##

How many specks before
I pause to name them?
    Terrorists?
            Freedom fighters?
To envision something I never considered,
the dots adding up like a Seurat painting,
all the points of color combining
to form a variegated version
of what's right in front of me.

##

The man at the hardware store explains:
The poison is sweet to the workers
who forage for food,
they won't be able to resist it,

wingless females having never had
children of their own
will hurry back to the nest
to share the candy with the queen
and her offspring, and
in their hopes of something more,
they wipe out the colony.

##

An army hazes a square.
It knows no other way.

##

Their absence feels strange at first.
I hesitate before leaving food uncovered.
But within hours, it's as if they were never here.

##

The next spring, a single ant on the counter.
One day later, a trail.

SATELLITES

Hani Omar Khalil

Between the second and third acts of *La Rondine*, after Magda seduced Ruggero in the bar at Bellier's, but before leaving him in a plaintive exchange of *Please don't go*'s and *I don't want to hurt you*'s, before you pitched me a scenario where the Sputnik chandeliers high above us crashed violently onto the audience below, before racing together from the Met in sub-zero weather to ring in the New Year at the Oak Room, before restraining me along the way from every unprotected crossing, no matter how empty, before saying, over venison and gnocchi, "if it's 11:00 PM, then my brother is doing lines already," to which I had no response, before kissing me at the stroke of midnight, no different than usual, before catching the fireworks in Central Park from across Fifty-Ninth Street, with Champagne (for me) and seltzer (for you), before spending what turned out to be our last night together, before declaring us over barely even to Epiphany, before the uninvited appearance of all that is no longer useful, you tried telling me something; you tried telling me something, in your way, and maybe I tried telling you something too, in my way, but because our ways were very different, yours casual, confident, and unsmiling, mine risk-averse, sensible, and ill-fitting like the suit I'd worn, it became lost, amid a cacophony of donors and dowagers amassed at intermission beneath the concrete and terrazzo double stairs, lost beyond the orbits where you gravitated, but where I — like an errant space probe or a fading solar flare — could never reach, lost before a parade of couplings more perfect to you than ourselves, lost in the succession of names dropped, always so effortlessly, lost in anticipation of a third act, which, unknown to me, was already well under way, all your way of saying *I want to be honest* ..., and because I remained dumbstruck by the impossibility of you, because I was raised to be good and not brave, I bent instead toward harmony, tried reconciling to the tonic, hoped out loud I wasn't complicating anything for you, my way of saying *Not yet, please not yet* ..., but you insisted there was nothing, offered me another fig from your pocket, which I always declined, pointed out again who in the room was a patron and who a spectator, who peerage and who parvenu, who satellite and who star, and with this disjointed ritual, with the glinting absence of any us in your eyes, we continued, headstrong into the future, toward our finale: Ruggero, all swept up and about to be destroyed, and Magda, longing like a swallow for migration to the sun, arms outstretched into darkness, to carry her home to a gilded turmoil.

I WATCH HIM, MY HUSBAND

Jay Kidd

(From *Atlanta Review*)

I watch him, my husband (that word, so strange)
as he rides his bike in front of me on our way to the beach,
notice how his knees splay out just a bit,
his ankles turn in just a hair,
how his shoulders are relaxed as he steadily pedals
along in a way that seems so effortless, so easy,
and I realize that I am getting to see him as a boy—
that he has always ridden a bike exactly like this
so I ask him about being a boy and riding bikes
and he tells me that he rode his bike to school every day with his friends,
a small fact I had never known
even after twenty-seven years of being together,
twenty-seven years after that first night
when the scent of his cologne
slid down the back of my throat
as we kissed on the street in the East Village
and I would say to my roommate that
I had just met the man I was going to marry
which was the word I used to mean forever
in that time when silence equaled death,
but who could have predicted, what crystal ball
could have foretold that we would be here,
in this new century, as husbands
with a house and a pile of junk mail, with a drawer
full of cuff links and collar stays and a vase stuffed full with poppies,
or that we would have bike locks and helmets and bottles of water
and be riding past sand dunes and tidal flats
and deep into a beech forest stopping to watch
as the sky turns impossibly pink

TRUST

Liz Kingsley

(From *New Ohio Review*)

First he slept with someone else and later while he was busy sleeping, she slept with someone else. No, before he slept with someone else, she slept with the lawyer across the street who gave good oral argument. She did not tell him about the lawyer. Their time together was privileged and she knew her rights. While she was with the lawyer, he slept with the decorator. When she found out about the decorator, she confronted him and said I trust that you know about the lawyer. He said he in fact did not know about the lawyer, but that now he no longer trusted her. She said that she had stopped trusting him after a flirty consultation they had with the decorator about their living room, which is why she slept with the lawyer in the first place. He said she had no reason not to trust him, but that he sensed she didn't, so he figured he might as well go ahead and sleep with the decorator. She said that's exactly why she can't trust him anymore. He slept with the decorator on the outgoing living room sofa. She said the lawyer has a trust account, into which she deposited the money they were planning to pay the decorator for the incoming living room sofa because she didn't trust him to go through with the renovation in light of their domestic destruction.

ALL DRESSED IN GREEN

Peter Krass

(From *Rattle*)

In the latest issue of *Quagmire* I find 7 new poems by Billy Collins.
In the new *Kiss My Quarterly*, 12 poems by Billy Collins.
Coming soon in *Broken Meter*, 18 poems by Billy Collins.
On NPR radio, Billy Collins reads "Wish I'd Written That."
In my sleep, Billy Collins stars in a major motion picture
directed by Billy Collins, produced by Billy Collins
and featuring a supporting cast of thousands of Billy Collinses.

Tonight, at my local Barnes & Starbucks,
Billy Collins is giving a reading.
So naturally I go, all dressed in green,
color of envy, money and snot.
Other striving poets fill nearly every seat,
each wearing something green,
each moving their lips as they quietly pray,
"O gods of poetry, whoever you are,
please let a magic morsel fly
from the mouth of Billy Collins
to infect me, like a virus,
with whatever he has: the virus
of being published,
the virus of selling books,
the virus of success."

I sneer at them. "Stupid poets," I say.
"That's not how life works."
But when Billy Collins appears at last,
smiling and nodding, clearing his throat,
I find my seat in the very front row,
open my mouth as wide as it goes
and breathe.

Domino

Cori Kresge

Because they would not let me have it,
I would have to get it for myself. The moment
they weren't watching, I was quick
to rig a teetering
scaffold of cane-backed chairs, an
upturned bowl,
a cereal box, a
tin
pot, two
minutes to slake
an addict's thirst,
climbing for
the
top shelf bag
of sugar to
plunge my
pudgy hand into
the sack.
Just one
little domino on the brink;
high on the thrill
of pure
forbidden
sweetness.

IMPLAUSIBLE

Iris Lee

(From *Urban Bird Life*)

I want to be the girl who brings the bucket of water
to the farmhands on hot August days when the sky
stretches thin its milky blueness.

I want the farmhands to push back their caps,
rub their dusty hands up and down on the legs of their overalls
before shyly passing that bucket around

and gratefully drinking the water
I'd hauled up with aching arms
from the well in the yard

while white and red chickens fluttered around,
beaks open, hoping for a trickle from the dripping bucket.
I want the farmer's wife to be plump but not fat,

with a soft tummy and comfortable large breasts,
and curly short hair going nicely gray. I want her
to toss the chickens their feed

with a balletic gesture of her arms,
so that the pale grains cloud the air
before raining down on the warm brown earth of the yard.

I want the tractor to be silent in its shed,
the barn cat to curl at my feet and my life to be summer.
I know it won't. I can live with that.

ANYONE CRAZIER THAN YOU

Andrée Lockwood

(From *Epiphany*)

"I have a great idea," says my psychiatrist, Dr. Essex, tipping his head back to finish his beer. It's 1985. I am twenty-three, eating a cheeseburger and drinking a glass of Chablis at one of the glassed-in, sticky-table restaurants on Seventh Avenue South. Dr. E's been a little down recently, and my company cheers him up, so we've taken to going out to eat on Mondays and Thursdays after my sessions.

Since he got remarried my father doesn't pay my shrink bills anymore, and my $238-a-week take-home doesn't cover $100 sessions, so Dr. Essex and I have worked out a barter system. We hang out at his office; I maybe help with some Xeroxing or whatever in return for my appointments. I'm being treated for depression, drinking and promiscuity. Dr. Essex always says, "Bottom line, Nadine? Don't fuck anyone crazier than you, cut down on the sauce and you'll feel better." That's what I appreciate about him. He's a behaviorist, so he skips the arcane shrinkology and gets right to heart of the matter.

Anyway, Dr. E's been having a hard time. His mother dropped dead at B. Altman's in October trying on raincoats, and his father has Alzheimer's. His father calls like a million times a day, wanting to know where his wife is. He had cancer and he speaks through a voice box. I answer the phone sometimes when I'm working there, and this spooky mechanical voice croaks, "Hilda? Hilda? Is that you?"

I've had a bad week myself. I had to miss two days of work to go home, board the dog and bring my mother a suitcase at Milford Hills, the fancy drying-out tank she ends up in every couple of years. Then, when I get back, I find out that Ellen Bird Girl Pillsbury got the associate editor promotion instead of me. Ellen still thinks she's Student Council president. She wears giant clip-on power earrings and each time she picks up the phone, say 150 times a day, I have to watch her do this little bird dip with her head as she slides off her earring to snuggle the receiver up close. I'm always bitching about Bird Girl to Dr. E, who says, "The ear is an underappreciated sexual organ, Nadine. You figure it out."

I'm an assistant at the New York office of BrightonBooks, the famous English publishing company. It's full of the kind of B.O. Brits who look good from a distance but all wear nylon shirts and no deodorant. Sometimes just standing in the doorway of my boss Simon's office is a trial. Simon told me that Alan, the senior editor, didn't think I presented quite the right image to work directly with authors.

I'm telling Dr. E that I guess Alan thought I was presentable enough when he was finger-fucking me in the taxi after the office Christmas party. Dr. Essex says, "The moral of this story? Don't shit where you eat." I'm still bummed out so he goes on. "But you're smarter than they are. Go to Bloomingdale's and get yourself a new outfit. Keep your head down, look the part, and in six months it's you with the promotion, okay?"

I can tell he's getting a little impatient. He doesn't like to talk about my problems at dinner — Dr. E.'s got strict boundaries that way. He tells me again how I'm very healthy in comparison with a lot of the people he sees, and that reminds him of some shithead at the hospital. Dr. E went to medical school in Mexico. He's obsessed about the way the Harvard- and N Y U- or even the Case Western Reserve-trained doctors look down on him despite the fact he has the same degree they do *plus* a psychiatric add-on. I tell him that in my experience, good schools are full of assholes who have no idea of real life, etc., until he calms down. "Enough of this morose shit," he says. "We need to rock and roll." That's when he thinks of the Pink Pussycat.

Me, I'm not crazy about sex shops, and it's the third time someone over the age of forty has dragged me here this winter. Too giddy, too many multicolored fumbly gadgets. Just give me your basic car or bed or elevator. Or once even the emergency stairway at *Newsweek* in return for Jamie Scadden fixing me up with an interview, although that was a disaster — security guard, *blowjob interruptus*, and I never even got a callback. There's a couple next to me checking out the dildos and handcuffs, super expensive because who's going to be comparison shopping, and I want to say save yourselves $79.95, go get a bottle of wine and maybe one of those cute little maid aprons and have at it.

"Can you believe all this shit, Darlene?" Dr. E gives me an alias, right there on the spot. He's always careful about using pseudonyms to protect people's privacy. His receptionist's name is Irene Mulhune, but he had a plaque made for her desk that says Mrs. Mahoney. He tells patients he and his wife live in Manhasset, when in fact I know it's Massapequa. "Always base a lie somewhere close to the truth," he says, "that way you can't go wrong."

We've been here ten minutes, and I'm getting tired of exclaiming, "Oh, wow!" every five seconds, but I put on my good sport face because I can see Dr. E is almost giggling with excitement. He's trying to act like Margaret Mead, seriously comparing the different Ben Wa balls. The thing about Dr. E is that he's got a very immature side, which I just try to ignore. The whole place is mirrored and as Dr. E leans over the counter his ponytail sticks straight up and for a minute his bald spot looks back at me like some little blanked-out kid with a topknot. Across the room the salesboy is playing with his nipple ring. I'm really not in the mood to go back to Dr. E's office tonight. Then his beeper goes off and I'm saved because it's a Bellevue call, which means long and messy. Dr. E hails me a cab and does his protector routine by writing down the medallion number in his little book so the driver knows someone's watching and not to pull anything.

I get some clothes at the Presidents' Day sale, and just for the hell of it I get my hair cut to my shoulders, very Ellen Pillsbury, all charged to my father's MasterCard, which I have for emergencies. It's Simon's birthday and the whole BrightonBooks editorial staff is in the conference room with cake and white wine. But the big news is that it's Howard Skoll's first day back in the office after three years. Howard Skoll is a legend. He won the America's Cup in the sixties and he invested the money that got BrightonBooks off the ground in the u.s.. Howard's sailing picture is in the lobby, along with all the fake, heraldic intertwined double B's and the framed book jackets. In his picture Howard is tan, blond and smiling. In person he looks like a faded Polaroid.

Alan has his hand on Howard's back, guiding him around the room and Ellen is next to Alan, and the three of them revolve like some precision skating team. Today Ellen's forgotten to put her earring back on so she's listing to one side. Roxanne Bertoli and I are knocking back the Soave when the team glides over to us. Alan says, "And this is Nadine." I swear he emphasizes the *this* in some smarmy shit-Brit way. I stroke my cheek with my middle finger but make it look absent-minded so he's not sure. Ellen tilts her head and smiles brightly as Howard Skoll pauses and takes my hand. He looks right into my eyes and says, very sincerely, "I look forward to working with you," and that confuses me so I just say "okay" in a kind of sulky way and then turn to Ellen and say, "Hey Bird Girl, you dropped an earmuff."

I'm in the doghouse because Ellen complains to Alan and Alan speaks to Simon who calls me in for A Talk. The offices have wooden doors, but the walls are glass, so everyone can see the whole pantomime. "Nadine, *really*," Simon says. Simon isn't too bad, actually, so I try to refrain from stupid Simon Says jokes. He lives in the Village with his boyfriend, Eric, so he's immune to me. At our first out-of-town book fair I leaned in close to give him a shoulder massage and he lifted my hands, looked me straight in the eye and said, "There's no need for any of that." Simon tries. He's a great one for pep talks and I can tell he's decided his mission is to help me live up to my potential.

Today he's reminding me about the two directions one's life can take when Roxanne knocks on the door because I have an emergency phone call. "Tell her I'll call back later," I say, but Simon insists and leaves the office so I can have some privacy. My mother is crying. "You forgot to pack my favorite green sweater," she sobs. "Did you tell Daddy where I am?" As I hang up the phone I can hear one of the Jamaican nurses in the background saying, "Come with me now, honey, come on, Lucille." One of Simon's obsessively sharpened no. 2 pencils rolls onto the floor. I step on it until it snaps and kick the pieces into a little nest of dust under the desk.

Howard Skoll asks for me. He's looking out the window of his new office blowing smoke rings. "I need to get myself set up and if I could borrow you from Simon for a few weeks I'd be very grateful." Alan and Simon are already in on it, of course. Simon beams—missionary scores conversion. Alan is giddy, as if in some way glory is being reflected back on him. "Nadine, this is an extraordinary opportunity. Do try and be your most responsible self." Bird Girl sniffs, "At the top you're going to find that things are very different, Nadine." Normally I would tell her I know all about being on top but for once I keep my mouth shut.

The first week it's all painting, boxes, drop cloths and new bookcases. The movers bring in a couch, a drinks cabinet—locked—and a fish tank. I'm in on time every day. Simon actually pretends to faint, lies right down on the carpet next to my desk one morning, ha ha—and I color-code the files and call IBM to order French and German Selectric balls.

Howard comes in around ten, cigarette, coffee light no sugar, and I give him his messages while he feeds the fish. He flicks his gold lighter with the enameled schooner on the cover, tells me where to make lunch reservations. Then I go back to my desk and he closes the door. Howard has the one office with plaster walls, so when the door is shut it's anybody's guess as to what's going on in there. I tell Dr. Essex that I can't figure out what Howard does all day. "He comes from money," he says. "He doesn't need to do anything." I look at the floor and cross my eyes when Dr. E gets proletariat since I know he grew up in Greenwich. "But don't worry about his job. *Your* job is to look busy."

So I retype hundreds of Howard's furry old Rolodex cards, then do another set for my desk. I'm not used to being so popular. Everyone in the company feels an urgent need to detour past my desk and stop and shoot the shit all buddy buddy as they shift from one foot to another hoping Howard will open his door. Howard gets quieter every day and it's spooking me out. He's stopped asking to see new manuscripts. Up close his skin is all pickled looking, as if he's been swimming in vodka. Sometimes I listen at his door and all I hear is the muffled clink of ice hitting the glass, and a terrible low sound that might be weeping.

Dr. Essex is on an office redecoration kick, so he shows me a million different shades of beige and swamp green because he thinks they're soothing. I tell him those colors just depress patients so much they don't feel like arguing. Macy's has a giant sofa sale so we're checking out the miniature room displays, which can make even the most stable person go multiple personality — optimistic Early American — no, wait — black leather swinger! A busybody saleslady gets us in her sights. "Something for your daughter's first apartment?" and naturally we're out of there one, two, three, which is just as well because I'm distracted by the Howard thing. I finally realize who he reminds me of — Ashley Wilkes, Ashley at the end of the war when everything is gone.

Alan takes me to lunch, gin and tonics, thanks for pitching in, but really he's pumping. "How is Howard settling in? Does he have everything he needs?" If Alan wasn't such a backstabber I might tell him but instead I'm Lucy Loyal. I talk to Simon, swear him to secrecy and tell him about the clinking ice and the crying. He's worried because apparently Howard has a history. I could have told him that.

At spring sales conference the salesmen fly in, the editors get creative with slides and lapel mikes, the mascaraed publicity girls have the vapors. Simon practices his pitch to me at least ten times. I ask Howard if he wants to rehearse and he smiles vaguely and says, "That's kind of you, Nadine, but not necessary." I tell him I'm happy to but he says, "No. Thank you. I'm just going to lie down a few minutes," and as he turns to go back to his office he pats my shoulder. His hand is papery, with dull blue veins bubbling under the skin. "I wish," he says, and stops. "Well. You're a good girl," as he shuts the door.

Roxanne and I are setting up, wrestling giant book covers onto the Hilton's spindly little easels when Alan grabs my elbow. Howard hasn't shown yet. I let it ring twenty times from the payphone, twice, and then decide just to run back and check. It's starting to rain so I awning-hop along Fifty-Third and up Madison to Fifty-Seventh. The twelfth floor is deserted, fluorescents buzzing grimly. Howard's door is locked; I knock, and then I smell smoke. When the firemen get there they grab me, hard, and shove me into the stairwell as they lift their axes to chop down the door. I sit shivering on the scratchy concrete stairs rubbing my aching arm, eyes tearing against the smoke. The alarms start screaming, the sprinklers let go — then there's the ambulance, police and fire inspector. Finally they come to take Howard's body away and Alan puts me in a cab and sends me home.

It's a monsoon out so when I get to Dr. E's office I am soaked through. My shoes are disintegrating and my dress is so wet that the little pink roses look like they're bleeding. Dr. Essex hands me a towel and an old robe, and I drape my clothes over the flaking bathroom radiator. He hasn't shaved and he tells me he's been sleeping here for a couple of days. "But fuck it," he says, "this is about you."

I tell him about Howard, that Howard's dead, but I'm spacing out, suffocating in funky brown velour from fumes of Old Spice, old skin and old pizza. Dr. E and I talk it through: bad choices, ruined lives, good choices, better lives. We both just sit there feeling sad. "Hey, we need some Dr. Billy," he says suddenly. Dr. E is a Billy Joel freak. We pop beers, and Dr. E is getting a little silly the way he does and when "I've Loved These Days" comes on he jumps up and dances around, singing along, *"we're going wrong, we're gaining weight, we're sleeping long and far too late,"* and then he says, "Wait a second, I know, stay there, don't move," and he runs into the bathroom. The next thing I know he's standing in front of me, all hairy legs and wrinkly brown socks, pretending to play the sax solo, wearing my pale green dress. I laugh so hard I spit beer all over the floor. I laugh so hard I puke.

STILL

Ann Lovett

Two days after the hurricane and it's
perfectly still. Silent in the house and nothing
moving outside but a tufted titmouse
that flits back and forth to the feeder by
the kitchen window. A walnut tree stands
blunt as a post at the edge of the woods,
its top snapped off twenty feet up
and dropped on the waterlogged lawn. Sun
pours in now; gold washes the floor
with light, shadows sharpened by edges
of window, tree, table leg.
I hear myself
breathing. I feel my tongue
against the round stones
of my teeth; the chair presses against
my back. Today stands open
like a paper bag. Just about
anything could
happen. It could still fill
with air or close
with the punch of a fist.

Playboy

Lela Scott MacNeil

(From *Gertrude Press*)

It came down to this: my nineteenth birthday, waking up on the floor of what must have been a holding cell, staring at what must have been my own vomit, realizing that the only goddamn person I could call was the girl who put me there.

The concrete floor burned my cheek like the aftermath of a slap. Past the texture of the vomit I could see white painted bars, and beyond that, a pair of menacingly shiny shoes.

"Wake up, sweetheart," said a voice, followed by an accusatory rapping. A headache was rushing in through my eyes. I tried closing my eyelids, but the damage was done.

*

"Pizza Purse," I said into a dirty phone at the end of a long, gray hallway that smelled of piss and disinfectant. Pizza Purse was something my nutjob ex-boyfriend started calling her, after the time we were all hungry and wasted, and she pulled three foil-wrapped slices of pizza out of her purse like she was some kind of magician. That was the exact moment I fell in love with her, although it took me another year or so to figure it out. She always said she hated the name, but I was pretty sure she meant she loved it.

"I told you not to call," she said.

"I'm in jail," I said

"I know," she said.

"You owe me," I said.

The dial tone growled in my ear.

I guess I did a couple of things to make her mad. There was the thing where I threw up on her shoes. It happened more than once. I have this idea I'm the girl who can drink whiskey all night but someday I'll have to admit to myself that I am not that girl.

There was the thing where I wouldn't tell my mother about her. The way I saw it was, I knew what she was going to say so what was the point. I knew the exact words because she had used them when she found the *Playboy* under my mattress when I was fourteen.

There was the thing when I let go of her hand, walking down Fifth Avenue, because why does everyone in the whole fucking world need to know our business. When I got home from school the next day she and everything she owned had disappeared. It looked like the apocalypse had come, but only for her. And for me too, if I'm being honest.

*

WHEN I SHOWED UP at her restaurant the morning before she got me locked me up, I hadn't slept in at least two days. Maybe more. I'd found some pills in the pocket of my coat. At some point you stop counting. They were serving brunch. There were yellow Christmas lights everywhere, so thick you could barely see, and everyone was wearing blue lipstick. Even the customers. That's how I remember it. I remember demanding a Bloody Mary. I remember her telling me to leave, her voice clawing at my ear like a wild thing. I remember not leaving. I remember finding myself outside, the February air plugged into my lungs as if into an electrical socket.

I remember sneaking back in through the back door. Jumping up on the bar. Singing "Celebration," by Kool & the Gang. Maybe it was "Holiday," by Madonna. One of the bartenders getting ahold of my ankle. Jumping off and grabbing the Bloody Mary pitcher and refilling everyone's glass. Even the half-full Mimosas. Especially the half-full Mimosas. Mimosas are bullshit.

*

THE FIRST TIME I TOOK her on a date was the week I got back from my father's funeral. It was also the week I started taking my drinking seriously.

I took her to Medieval Times. We had to take a bus from Port Authority. I'm afraid of busses the way other people are afraid of flying, but she wanted to go, and so I wanted to take her. On the way there my wallet was stolen. On the way there I managed to lose my wallet. It depends who you ask. Either way, she had to pay.

The truth was that it wasn't a date, but I wanted it to be. The truth was that I didn't know if it was a date or if it wasn't. Her hair was dyed so blond it was white. She wore fuchsia lipstick every day, no matter the weather. She had a tattoo of a peacock feather on her upper thigh that she would show you if she was drunk enough. Getting her drunk enough was one of my goals back then. It still is, but I've given up trying.

At Medieval Times they gave us paper crowns, and we sat in the front row like queens, and watched the horses dance. At Medieval Times we cheered for whichever knight they told us to, the red, or maybe the black. At Medieval Times she fed me whiskey from a flask, and when I pressed into her, she stayed.

*

WHEN MY COURT-APPOINTED LAWYER asked me about my grades, I asked him why it mattered. He told me to watch my tone and so I told him the truth. "Well, what the hell are you doing here, sweetheart," he said, and talked the judge into community service. People never understand how I can do so well and still be such a screw-up. I knew I was lucky but that wasn't how it felt.

*

IT WAS NIGHT AGAIN by the time they let me out. It was raining, and the street was a black river. I could feel the water sneaking into my socks and curling up between my toes. I could feel it washing the puke out of my hair. My mother had baptized me as a baby and I had never believed in any of that, but maybe it was time to start.

*

I WAS SMOKING A CIGARETTE on Avenue A when, "Hey, sweetheart," a voice rumbled, as if it came from somewhere deep below the asphalt. I looked and saw a homeless guy, standard issue, face all ripped up from so many nights out under the stars. I felt myself scrunch, ready to be disgusted, ready to start walking.

"Hey, look at the moon."

I looked up and he was right, the moon was ridiculous. Big and round as that swimming pool where my father tried to teach me to swim when I was five. I still don't know how. The moon wasn't swimming pool colored, but standing there next to the homeless guy, I would have been happy to jump right in.

I reached into my pocket to see if I had any cash. I had been expecting him to ask me for money, but when he hadn't, I wanted to give it to him. I remembered I had spent my last twelve dollars on cigarettes. I pulled out the pack and shoved them into his crumpled hand. I walked away so I didn't have to be there for whatever happened next.

*

ON THE DAY THAT I LEARNED my father was about to die, they were repaving the street outside my apartment window. The smell of tar filled me. Every movement stuck.

My mother told me to come home, that there wasn't much time. I asked her why the hell she hadn't told me sooner, but she started to cry so I dropped it and hung up.

I walked outside to see Avenue A stripped of its skin. I know how you feel, I said. I said it loud, because no one in New York ever looks at you like you are crazy, even when you are. Or maybe everyone in New York knows that sometimes things happen, and talking to the asphalt is the only rational response.

Back upstairs, I drank my Diet Sunkist and watched *Who Wants to Be a Millionaire*. I knew that the hoarseness in his voice when I called him on my birthday was more than bronchitis. Turned out, it was a tumor that had wrapped itself around his vocal cord and crushed it, the way the root of the eucalyptus tree wrapped itself around the water pipe in my front yard when I was a little girl. Eucalyptus trees do not belong in the desert, my mother said, and called the men who came to cut it down. I knew she was right, but it was my favorite tree. I did not care that it was home to hundreds of birds that shit on our car.

Eucalyptus trees are red inside, and when you chop one down, it looks like a giant severed limb.

I was right, it was not bronchitis. For the first time in my nineteen years, being right held no satisfaction.

I couldn't get a flight home until the next morning. I ordered steamed vegetable dumplings. I ordered them because they are the only thing I can always make myself eat. I ordered them because something had to stay: Me, slouched sideways on my roommate's overstuffed white leather armchair, legs strewn across one arm, back against the other. Eating vegetable dumplings and watching *Who Wants to Be a Millionaire*. A show my father hated. A show for people with common minds, he said. Maybe I want to be common, I said. I watched it every chance I got.

I still keep all my clothes on the floor because he kept his rooms so neat you would think nobody lived there at all.

I began to make phone calls. The nice thing about your father dying is that it is an excuse everyone understands. One call, and I was released from my classes for the rest of the semester. Another, and my boss said take as much time as you need. At eighteen, I was always looking for this kind of excuse. That was the month I learned that sometimes what you want stops being what you want, once you get it.

*

REMEMBERING THIS, I WANTED to tell her about it. I wanted another good excuse. Something that could get me back inside her warmth the way my father dying got me out of everything.

I walked toward her restaurant, pretending that this was a new idea, that I hadn't planned on going there all along. On the way I stole a deodorant from a deli run by this old man I knew never paid close enough attention. I stole Old Spice, because once she told me she liked the way it smelled on me. I made a promise to myself to come and pay the old man back as soon as I had money. I knew from experience about the promises you make to yourself, but maybe I'd keep this one.

"Where you going with that, sweetheart?" said the old man, pointing to the deodorant shaped lump in my pocket. His face seemed to be collapsing in on itself, but taking its time. The Old Spice was shaking at the end of my outstretched arm. He waved his hand.

"You need it more than I do."

I tried for *thank you* but it came out as a grunt. The air smelled like a slow death. I couldn't tell if it was his or mine.

"We have lady deodorant back there, you know."

This time I managed a *no thank you,* and pushed my way back out into the thickening night. Her restaurant was only a few doors down, and I stood with my face pressed into the window, like a child. I was sure everyone was watching, and I should have cared, but I could not remember how to care. She was beside me then. Her presence nearly knocked me over.

"You know you can't come in here anymore," she said.

"I wrote you a poem."

"I stopped reading poetry."

"Please."

Her sigh lasted until I thought it might not end. I can think of worse things than being stuck next to her sighing for all eternity.

"I'm off in fifteen. I'll meet you there." I knew she meant Odessa because that was where we always met. I decided to decide that was a good sign. She disappeared into the red velvet light behind the door. My blood was trying to bite through my cheeks. I wanted to press my face to the cold window again because maybe it would calm my blood. I wanted to press my face to the window like a child again because children are forgiven. I turned away from the window and set my feet toward Odessa.

The rain had stopped and the traffic lights were dancing their reflections down the shining streets. I opened up my lungs and pulled in as much air as possible. It smelled like cigarettes and the secrets of strangers. It was the sort of night where you could become someone else, if only you tried hard enough.

Odessa was empty because it was Tuesday, and everyone else had better things to do at two AM on a Tuesday than hang out in a crappy Ukrainian diner waiting to hear whether or not they got to keep on living. I felt a sudden kinship with the lone waitress behind the counter. I ordered potato and cheese perogies, with sour cream and applesauce. Her favorite. I couldn't stand them. She told me I was crazy for loving Chinese dumplings and hating Polish ones. I told her that was what she loved about me. "I keep you guessing." I think what I meant to say was that I kept her on her toes, but that was just another thing I never quite got right. After the perogies arrived I remembered how I had no money. In the fluorescent light my empty hands looked dead, although I admit I don't know what dead hands look like.

When she arrived she filled the place, leaving no room for anything else. The waitress, the cracking green booths, the plastic plants, all of it pushed to the side.

"They're cold," I said, pushing the perogies in her direction.

"You hate perogies," she said.

"Maybe I'll like them this time. They're just dumplings, right?"

"I'm sorry I called the cops."

I grabbed a perogi and shoved it into in my mouth. Fair was fair.

"I've made a decision," I said, mouth half full, "I'm calling my mother."

"I'm sure she'll be happy to hear from you."

"I'm going to tell her about this amazing girl I met, maybe you know her?"

"I'm gone, Katie. I'm already gone."

"You're right here. I see you." I picked up her hand and breathed it in. It smelled like that orange and vanilla Bath and Bodyworks bullshit that I had hated right up until that moment. She pulled it away and stood up. She put a twenty down on the table.

"Let me get this," she said.

"Thanks for not making me pay for my own execution."

Her lips pressed into my eyelid like a slowly exploding berry.

"You're going to be okay," she said, before letting herself be swallowed by the darkness outside. While I tried to work up the courage to walk back to my half-naked apartment, I leaned against the side of the restaurant and looked up at the moon I had traded my pack of cigarettes for earlier that night. It could have been the lack of sleep, but I swear I heard it whisper how maybe she was right.

GRAFFITI DREAMS

Marnie Maguire

E ven when I was a hyper dyslexic kid, I wanted to be a professional calligrapher. I dreamed of holding that thin, dainty pen between my fingers, and pressing ink to paper to spell out things that looked like long, lanky tongues licking their way to the end of the page. But fuck, I spelled calligraphy with a *k* and could barely comprehend the moves and grooves of a *p* and *h*.

I held tight to this dream like you do with the lottery: hopeful, but with practical disbelief. That is, until I discovered graffiti.

*

IT WAS MY MOM WHO bought the cans of paint. This was her idea of keeping my dream alive. She took me down to the Toronto lakeshore, where I stood, small and shivering. In front of me was a gigantic gray elephant of a building. Behind me was the polluted, stinking lake. The breeze coming off it just about chilled me senseless, which was not good. I may have been twelve, but I knew, even then, that I had to have sense for the two of us.

"Well, go ahead," she told me, and shoved a can of paint into my gut.

I froze. This was illegal, and my mom was probably high. It was midnight on a school night, and I was choking on fear while she apparently felt nothing.

There was a purple fleece pouch in my pocket, an empty whiskey bag that most kids used to carry marbles. I kept a collection of color-coded words in it instead. I took it everywhere. The feel of it gave me comfort. I had memorized each word, its shape, its sound, the way it felt in my mouth. My body practically danced with each word. I knew each and every one that well. Even as I shook my head, no, to defy my mother, I was thinking, "Which one would look really good up there on all that wall?"

*

MY MOM WAS REAL BIG on encouragement: "Stop being such a chickenshit and paint something before we get caught."

I wouldn't even look at her.

"If you don't hurry up, and we get caught, Children's Aid is likely to haul your ass away from me."

When my mom said stuff like that, I wanted to take the paint and spray it right into the whites of her coke-oh-so-sure-of-herself, hazey hazel eyes.

But then I heard sirens, and I guess I had as much sense as my mother because I grabbed the first word my fingers found in that whiskey pouch. I don't remember what word it was, but did it ever look glorious up there in a curly chemical cloud of silver and blue.

BACK

Andrea Marcusa

(From *In The Words of Womyn International 2016 Anthology*)

On a recent visit home, Dad was back—no longer vague, but alert and sitting on the living room couch next to the fire, eager for conversation. (It was just like Mom said, six months on Aricept and his addled mind was restored.) He gazed at me as though he'd never been any other way, never months, maybe years of a vague, gentle man looking around the kitchen every five minutes asking, "Where's your mother?"

His thoughts went places that I hadn't seen it go to for ages-—the Middle East, nuclear fusion, the speed of light. Even when he hit a blank patch, he'd hop ahead or back to a different topic, the way a stereo LP used to skip on his turntable in our living room. A few missed lyrics but the tune still intact. His confusion eased. Now, laughter, ideas, a sharp gleam in his eye.

I told him I was setting up Mom's computer, careful to leave out that this job was now mine because he could no longer manage it, and he joined me in the study, saying his ancient printer would work with her new laptop. I nodded, sure this was his dementia talking, not the clear reasoning of the man I once knew. That old printer used one of those thick, spiked plugs that hadn't been sold in years. No way it'd work with Mom's sleek laptop. But, when I checked, there was a thin slat for a USB cord, just like he'd said. That's when I knew he was really back. My daddy one of those medical wonders you read about, hear about. Keen, alert, observant and back in every way.

I unraveled the new power cord and set the empty packing box on the floor, a giddy child's joy spreading through me. In my excitement, I somehow knocked hard into the sharp corner of the desk with my hip. Pain shot up my spine. I grabbed for the spot and rubbed furiously, blind to the cup on the desk holding a fistful of pens. It rocked back and forth, then tipped. A dozen tiny plastic missiles clattered across the hard wood floor.

"What the hell do you think you're doing?" my father snarled. "What's wrong with you? Can't you do *anything* right?"

I jumped, then froze. He'd used an ancient, vicious voice from years ago, a voice I'd wiped from my mind. A voice I'd tricked myself into believing belonged to another man named Dad, from another world, and another family, another life. But it was him. His lip actually curled.

Thanks to modern medicine, Dad's war had started up again.

It was only later, the shock stinging like a fresh burn, that I remembered one of Dad's favorite sayings.

Be careful what you wish for.

ETCHINGS

Nancy Matsunaga

(From *Calyx*)

I t is not true that tattoos can withstand fire.

At least, not the tattoo on Jordan's wrist. It is melting as she watches, the purple dye dripping, sliding across her hand, a hot river. It takes an eternity to travel from the blue line of her vein to the mole just underneath the knuckle of her ring finger.

She wonders where it will stop. She wonders if the butterfly that it once was will sear up to the surface of her skin and evaporate into the thin June air. She wonders whether some part of it will remain, whether the skin will harden across it, etch it into her bone. She holds the Bic in her other hand, her right one, and stares at the flame on her left wrist as it starts to lick and spit toward the ceiling.

She is standing in the kitchen of her parents' summer house and it is midnight, midnight at least because her older sister, Lizbeth, is asleep and the loons down at the lake are trilling like a ward of insane asylum patients. The light at the Turners' place next door is out and she can hear their voices starting up, the hoarse rasping of Sheila Turner *Get out you motherfucker* and the lower, calmer register of Adam Turner *Sheila please the children* and now the sleeve of her bathrobe is a torch and her mother's voice is shrieking above everything *Dennis the extinguisher* and she feels nothing, only hears the sizzle as the cloud of chemicals sprays across her arm and body.

And then she is lying on the sofa, her mother kneeling beside her, *Drink this,* and she takes the huge white pills offered without asking what they are for. The room is shadows, nothing clear, but she knows that he is not here—her father; if she listens, she can hear his voice from the other room, speaking low on the telephone, but she doesn't want to listen so she closes her eyes and listens instead to the humming inside her head.

She had walked down to the shore alone that evening, went there to hear the quiet lapping of the water like milk, to get away from the wall of her mother's silence, her sister's chronic sarcasm, the rumbling of her father's discontent. She had failed at something, displeased them somehow—was it the new spider inked across her left shoulder or was it that they had somehow learned about Matt? She wasn't sure, and she wasn't sure it mattered; in the end it always came to this, and she'd managed to ruin another family vacation, only one day into it.

The voice in the other room stops and Jordan's chest tightens and suddenly she can feel everything. It is as though a gaping hole has opened up in her arm, as though some demon has gouged away at it with a curved, hot claw. She moves her eyes to look, but there is pain there too, the millimeter shift in her vision sending new waves of it rippling through her body, so she closes them again. Her father is coming into the room now, she can hear by the soft thuds on the floorboards, THUD *thump*, THUD *thump*, his right leg always landing harder than his left, some old tennis injury. *Mom* she whispers and what she means to say is *I don't want him here* but what comes out is a groan. Her mother shushes her, pats her shoulder, shifts the towel on her arm to a new side so the cool can again suck out the searing heat.

"They're on their way," she hears her father say.

"Did they say how long?" her mother murmurs.

"Rumford's an hour. You know that."

"This is not my fault," her mother spits. Jordan has never heard her mother speak like this to her father. She wonders what she knows. She wonders what she's seen or imagined. The burn sears again. She wants to grab her arm right where the pain is, and squeeze it until she wrings everything out.

*

IT HAD STARTED WITH THE ETCHING. It was an impulse she had, childish perhaps but she had followed it. The first one on Lizbeth's door jamb. She had taken her pen knife and carved a careful *Fuck* just below the latch, where her sister might see it and then again might not. She attempted a skull and cross-bones but the look was too Tic-tac-toe instead of Rat Poison. She thought she needed to do better. *Cunt* on the inside of the locker next to hers—she'd wedged it open, BANG metal on metal while Matt walked by without turning his head.

Better words, she thought, *I can do better.*

She borrowed Lizbeth's SAT prep book. *Ersatz,* she etched into the seat of the oak chair she sat on in Mr. Lacuna's office, while he closed his eyes and leaned way back in his desk chair as if to maximize the distance between them. Mr. Lacuna, Mr. Laconic. Her therapist. Her ersatz doctor.

"So, Matt was your third … partner," he was saying. Jordan finished the Z without watching her knife, looking instead at Lacuna's face for the moment the eyes opened. Snap, like Venetian blinds. The eyes transparent as glass.

"Do you think you know what love is?" he asked. It was a trick question, Jordan knew. There was no right answer. He looked for ways to assert his intelligence over hers. Only he wasn't more intelligent, they both know that, so he muscled his way around with his age and theoretical experience. *You will understand this when you're older* he would stare, or *Oh to be so young and naïve* he would smile condescendingly. When his eyes landed on her breasts he always looked away too fast.

"Excuse me, where is your wife?" Jordan demanded one session. When they'd started, there were two ersatz doctors. Now there was only one.

Lacuna, Laconic, cleared his throat, "We only work together for the full family sessions."

"Where is my family?" Jordan asked.

"Your … mother"—he pieced the words together carefully, as though they might break if strung all together too closely—"thought … individual … sessions … might be more … helpful."

"You don't agree." She sat up from her slump. Her black thrift store polyester dress slid across her bare legs, revealed the lace of tattoos up her inner thigh. His eyes brushed across them, snapped back up to her face, the clear glass clouding.

"I was interested," he admitted, clearing his throat again, "I was interested to see where things might … go … with everyone present. To explore those relationships right, on stage, as it were."

Ah, that was it. On stage. With Mrs. Lacuna, aka Dr. Eva Frank, as the stage director, fitting the part perfectly, all sharp angles to her husband's softness. The cat's-eye glasses with the tiny diamonds in the corners that flashed each time she turned her face. All angles and order. She had announced the case in the first five minutes, as though to make clear to herself what she was doing there. *Everyone is worried about you Jordan, your mother, your sister. They learned about your risky behavior.*

Perfidious. If she had been at home, she might have etched it on her sister's headboard. But for lack of a surface, she imagined etching it right into the skin of Dr. Frank's forehead as she sat there enumerating all of their shortcomings. And the four of them there, her parents and her sister and herself, all gape-mouthed, actors stripped of their scripts, nothing more to say. Had she really thought, this Dr. Frank, Mrs. Laconic, Mrs. Can't-Shut-Myself-Up, did she really think that theirs was the kind of family who actually spoke about these things? Out loud? To each other? That any one of them would dare to say the word *sex*, even in a completely noncontexualized way? They were all the accused, they were all prisoners bound at the hands and feet to their chairs, unable to move in their shock, the admittance of everyone's guilt.

Well, except her father. His part in the whole drama anonymous. He acted guiltless and embarrassed, looking away from all of them, ashamed of these women, these girls, his family. Maybe he found solace in Mr. Lacuna's presence, the two men, mute, distant and beyond all the static of the women rubbing up against each other. Or maybe he just thought Mr. Lacuna was a weak and silly man with a tyrannical wife.

*

BY THE TIME THE AMBULANCE ARRIVES, the horse pills her mother gave her are starting to work. Jordan sees everything as though from underwater, faces rippling and dissolving. She lies back and lets arms enfold her, laying her across blankets cooled from the outside night air.

"One of you can accompany her in the ambulance," she hears someone say. THUD thump, THUD thump on the creaking porch steps behind her. Her blood turns and turns inside her body. Someone, a woman, takes her right hand and turns it over, smooths it out as though preparing to read her future. She realizes she is still holding the Bic. The woman removes it gently, holds her wrist to take her pulse. She can feel her father's shadow across her face and can imagine the crease between his brows, the worry lines edging his eyes. She wants to roll away from him so he cannot see her face. She is too aware of her lips, too self-conscious of her tongue as it slips out to wet them.

When the door slams behind her she expects darkness to descend inside the ambulance, like the back of a Mafia van, but of course it is bright white, like the inside of a doctor's office, like the inside of the gynecologist's office her mother made her go to after their first appointment with the Lacunas, after it had been made clear to all that Jordan had been screwing every boy she was able to. ("Sexually active," the gynecologist had called it, and spoken like this, coming from this woman doctor's voice, it had sounded so important and, at the same time, so normal.) Under the bright lights Jordan cannot sleep, but she also cannot open her eyes, the lights piercing through her envelope of tranquillity, penetrating like needles through her eyelids. She feels her father take her good hand. He strokes it with soft, back-and-forth caresses. Fatherly caresses, she wishes she could think. And maybe it is, this time; but there have been too many that are not fatherly, and she cannot tell the difference anymore. She pulls her hand away, sensing her father's sorrowful helplessness at the gesture. If men cried, she thinks, he would cry. And she would be the reason.

*

WHEN HE HAD SEEN HER first tattoo, he had recoiled. The first one she had chosen carefully. It was just an experiment. A small dagger, on the skin of her neck just below her left earlobe. (That one had hurt like hell. Just as she had expected. Just out of her line of vision, it was strange not knowing when the needle was about to start, when it would stop. There was a timelessness to the pain, like it might just go on and on forever without stopping. A part of her relished this, and it was why she kept going back for more.)

She had thought she would keep it hidden for a while, but there was no hiding the enormous piece of gauze covering that side of her neck. She had come home, supposedly from an after-school book club, and tiptoed into the kitchen to microwave a fast dinner for herself. He was behind her before she realized it, his hand touching her neck.

"What happened?"

"It's nothing." She whirled around, trying to tilt her head to cover the gauze. "I just got a little cut."

"A cut?" He was standing too close, as always, and his hand still rested on the gauze, tenderly, one finger brushing her earlobe. The molecules boiled inside her, but she had nowhere to step back to, the corner of the counter sharp in the small of her back.

She gasped as with a sudden gesture her father ripped off the bandage, revealing the raw, red, shiny patch of skin, the dagger still wet, a drop of blood surfacing. He stepped back, his lips curled in disgust, and his expression made her feel proud, made her feel strong, and she stood up straight and the disgust she felt at herself disappeared.

"What did you do to yourself?" he asked. She smirked at him and sidestepped away, making her escape.

Now she knew what she needed to do. The etching had been just a kids' game. She went in for a second tattoo, and then for a third, a fourth, a fifth. Beneath the fritzing fluorescents of the tattoo parlor she closed her eyes, learned by feel how the needle would travel, skimming across her skin, under her skin, in and out, the room filled with its low buzzing, punctuated by clicks from the lights. The tattoo artist with his wire-rim glasses, his thin body, his steady hand. She didn't care that she was the only girl ever there, that the other customers were fat men with black Harley Davidson shirts and shaved heads. She liked it like that. No one expected her to talk to them, no one talked to her. Lying across the low table, as though she were getting a specialized spa treatment; or sometimes sitting in the folding metal chair, cold and hard against the backs of her legs. She opened her eyes to watch when she could, to see the drawing emerge dot by dot and then disappear again as her blood rose to the surface, thin and red. Her body gradually, surely, being covered with an intricate pattern, the tattoos approaching each other but never touching, interacting in a strange harmony, a tiger's mouth opening wide, smiling across the head of a phoenix, brilliant blue, rising out of the flames of a dragon's mouth.

When she was there, she could forget everything. She loved the feeling of her head spinning and spinning. She was light as helium and her head buzzed along with the needle. When she was there, nothing else mattered. She didn't have to think about her father loving her more than he should. When she was there, it was only her, and the needle, and the blood, and that soaring dizziness. When she was there, all time, and fear, all shame, stopped.

*

SHE MUST HAVE FALLEN ASLEEP, because she doesn't remember being taken into the hospital. It is dark now, and she can't see what's around her very well, but she can hear the soft beeping of a monitor next to her, and feels a pressure on her right index finger, where the monitor is connected, keeping track of her pulse. Bags of fluid are suspended over her, a tube leading from them into her veins. Another machine hums quietly and shows red blinking numbers. She doesn't know what they mean. 86. 99. 92. She watches them blink and change, blink and change. She is alone in the room. 90. 98. She keeps watching them blink and change, blink and change, and she breathes in time until she falls asleep again.

When she awakens next, it is morning. A nurse comes in and takes her temperature, makes some notes on her clipboard.

"Are you ready to see your family?" she asks.

Jordan is silent.

"Shall I tell them you're still asleep?" Her voice is kind and almost conspiratorial. She pats Jordan's good arm. Jordan blinks hard.

"They didn't do this to me," she tells the nurse. "I'm sure you think it's child abuse, but it's not."

The nurse nods once. "Okay, honey," she says. "Don't worry about that right now."

"When can I go home?"

The nurse sighs. "Don't worry about that, either. Let's just see how this goes."

*

HER LAST VISIT TO LACUNA'S OFFICE had been the day before their trip to the Maine woods and the day after her sister's graduation from high school. Lizbeth would be off to Princeton the following year. Jordan would be alone in the house. Well, of course, not *alone*. In his office she sat rubbing the knuckle of her middle finger, trying not to think about the itch on her shoulder from her latest tattoo. The office was overheated and dry. Jordan looked toward Lacuna but not at him, staring instead at a spot in the middle distance.

"I think I'm losing your attention here," Lacuna said, clearing his throat. "We were talking about your relationship with your father." His face was long and blank.

Jordan blinked and looked at him. *Spurious.* She no longer made the etchings but the words still rose to the surface of her mind like the droplets of blood in the tattoo parlor.

She had been thinking about a lunch she'd had the week before with her father. He'd asked her to visit him at work. *We haven't spent time together in so long*, he'd said, and she wanted it to be like when she was a little girl and he would bring her in, show her the photo of her that he kept on his desk, the engraved nameplate that made him seem like such an important person. She agreed to meet him. She should have known better. She shouldn't have let him shut the office door behind her. When he hugged her and whispered in her ear *I miss you honey* his hands had slid down the small of her back, over the curve of her hips. She had pushed him away, her eyes burning, and run out the door.

"Why are we talking about my father?" she asked Mr. Lacuna. "I have no relationship with him. None at all."

"None. At. All," Lacuna repeated, adding the usual pauses between the words. Jordan scowled.

"I hardly even see him," she said. "It's my mother I want to kill." She tried to say it as nonchalantly as possible. She was looking for a reaction, of course, but she understood as she said it that this, too, was true. She waited for Lacuna to react. Instead he leaned back slightly farther in his chair. Jordan wondered if he would ever topple right over. That, she thought, would be something. That would be worth the time she spent here.

In the end, nothing was enough. Not the words, not the tattoos. Not the solitary walks where she taught herself how to inhale cigarette smoke without breaking into a coughing fit. The feeling of the smoke filling her chest and making it constrict. Not even her late-night conversations with Lizbeth, those rare nights at the summer house when her sister was feeling generous, when they would go arm in arm down to the shore, sneaking a bottle of Kahlua with them, drinking it straight, giggling and staring up at the unstoppable stars, confiding their loves, their obsessions, pretending for a night that they were best friends. Not even that. There was something hard across the sky, something she couldn't scratch or break through, something closing in around her like the cell walls in *The Pit and the Pendulum*. She had to push back the walls so they wouldn't squeeze her, but she couldn't find the way. She could only imagine the world in fire, the flames sucking out all the moisture, burning everything away, devouring matter and leaving a vacuum, leaving nothing, leaving endless, timeless, blackness.

*

THE HOSPITAL LIGHTS TOO BRIGHT. The IV drip continuous, monotonous. Jordan slips in and out of sleep.

"What's this one supposed to be?" Matt asks her, his finger tracing the line of the infinity symbol just under her navel.

"Eternity," she says, her voice thick with the desire to not intrude upon the silence, to not say a wrong thing and ruin the moment. She keeps her eyes closed and smiles. What happens next? Do they drift off into sleep together, outside there in the park under the trees? Or are they in his basement bedroom? She can't remember. She squeezes her eyes closed tighter, fighting her mind as it returns to consciousness.

"Are you with me?" the tattoo artist asks. "I think we lost you for a minute. Skip breakfast this morning?"

The room is still spinning. Jordan laughs and laughs and laughs.

"Kiss me," she says to the tattoo artist. He leans in toward her face. He kisses her. His tongue is warm. His hand is on her cheek, as light as air.

She opens her eyes and he is not there. Everything is melting away—the sketches on the dark walls fade and all that is left is the cold matte white of the hospital walls. It is her father leaning over her, hand on her cheek, watching her eyes.

"She's back," he says.

"Oh, good," her mother says, and Jordan turns her head and sees her mother sitting on the other side of her. "Maybe we can finally go home." In her mind Jordan feels the heat of the Bic again, feels the hot metal of the starter under her thumb, remembers the *click, click* as she started it once, twice, three times before it finally caught, the suctioning sound as it grabbed hold of her arm, devouring the lighter fluid she had poured there. She tries to remember the pain, the pain she couldn't even feel in the beginning, but already the feeling is slipping away from her. ("No one can remember pain," the nurse had told her. "It's our best defense mechanism.") She tries to remember the sensation but it is like trying to remember a dream, and as she wakes it is vanishing, vanishing. She looks down at her arm and though it is still covered with white gauze, she knows it will be fine. Perhaps there will be a scar, the tiniest mark that, after years, only she will be able to see. With everything she tried, everything she went through, nothing ever stuck, and nothing ever changed.

She closes her eyes. "Where's Lizbeth?" she asks.

"Back at the cabin," her mother says. "Let's go."

Jordan opens her eyes again, stares at her mother.

"*You* go," she says. "I'm staying here a little longer."

"Don't be silly," her mother says. "The doctor said if you were up to it, you could come home today."

"Well," says Jordan, "I'm not 'up to it.' So you can go ahead. I'm pretty sure the doctor won't object."

And her words cut through the air and circle around them and etch a line in the hardness, a small line but a line nonetheless. It was a beginning.

Purple Head

Sarah McElwain

(From *FictionNow*)

This happened a long time ago, on a New Year's Eve. My boyfriend wanted to go to the Academy of Music in Northampton to see the new Polanski movie. I did not want to see this movie. I worked in what was then called a school for the retarded and had enough surrealism during the week. It was snowing hard and I'd have to drive. My boyfriend could no longer drive. He'd faked a seizure at his job at Main Street Records to collect unemployment, but that meant he'd had to surrender his driver's license.

I'd spent all fall reupholstering a couch, piecing together vintage patterns of rose chintz on my iron Singer. I wanted to stay home, sit on this couch, drink too much wine, and eat olives. We had a fireplace.

*

IN *THE TENANT*, ROMAN POLANSKI plays a shy, Polish immigrant who rents a Paris apartment in which the previous tenant killed herself. He believes that the landlord is driving him to commit suicide the same way that the beautiful Simone Choule (played by Catherine Deneuve) did, by jumping out of the third-story window. Soon we see Polanski preening in a blond wig and sexy dress, applying blue eyeshadow and lipstick, cooing into the mirror, "I think I might be pregnant." During the final scene, when the surrealism kicks in and we see Polanki's head (or is it Simone Choule's head or is it the wig?) fly out of the window over and over, my boyfriend squeezed my hand so hard I thought it would break.

*

WE WERE SITTING IN THE CAR when the church bells started chiming at midnight. We heard cheers and noisemakers. "Happy New Year!" I said, leaning over to kiss my boyfriend in the passenger seat. I expected him to say "Happy New Year!" back. Instead, he said, "I have something to tell you."

He said he didn't want to start the new year with a lie. Then he told me that for the past six months he'd been having sex with our neighbor.

*

THERE ARE LAWS AGAINST DRUNK DRIVING or while under the influence of drugs. There should be a law against driving while in shock. Part of me remained in the driver's seat, hands clutching the steering wheel, while another part flew into the backseat and observed from the corner. My hands shook as I tried to navigate the car out of the parking lot. The road home was now an alien landscape; all the familiar landmarks had become shadowy and abstract. When my boyfriend screamed, "watch out," as I skidded toward a snow bank, it sounded like we were underwater.

We made it home. After I closed the front door, my rage erupted. I could only think of hurting him. Using the hardest thing that I had—my head—I charged him like a bull. He stepped aside just in time and I bounced off the wall, leaving a skull-shaped indent in the plaster that would come out of our damage deposit three months later.

*

IN THE MORNING I SLAMMED the front door for the last time. Stuffing everything I could into my Karmann Ghia I drove across the river to my cousin Pauline's house in Pelham. Lying on a mattress in the attic, staring at the rafters, I felt blindsided. We'd been talking about children. How could I have been so stupid? While I'd been out working the 11 to 7 shift every day, he'd been home, supposedly working on the dystopian novel that he was writing. Instead, he'd been next door fucking the neighbor. "Did everybody know but me?" I asked Pauline. "No," she lied.

I raked through the last six months for clues. I thought about Christmas Eve. A week ago when I'd been so confident that I'd asked my boyfriend what he liked least about me. He said it was the way I shuffled cards. At the time this had seemed stupid. I shuffled cards like a pro. But now I searched these words for deeper meaning. I'd told my boyfriend that the thing I liked least about him was how when I got home from work every night all the kitchen cabinets were always open. Even the hard to reach one over the refrigerator. What he was he looking for? And why couldn't he just close the fucking cabinets?

When I finally went downstairs on Sunday night to eat spaghetti and drink wine at the kitchen table with Pauline and her new boyfriend, Glen, it turned out that I'd lost five pounds. Pauline said it was from all the tears.

*

RED-EYED AND HUNGOVER, I arrived for work at the State School on Monday morning. I told my coworker Violet nothing. The last time I'd seen her I'd been a different person. I'd wished her a happy new year, waved good-bye, then driven home to my future.

She was a solid, singsongy Jamaican transplanted to cold western Massachusetts, who'd worked at Children's North for ten years and lived on the grounds. She wore pink polyester uniforms under layers of sweaters and snow boots. I wore jeans—heavy Levi 540s—and sneakers. It was our job to take care of children who could not take care of themselves. There was no time for art therapy. By the time we got all of them ready for lunch, fed and toileted, it was time to start this process all over again.

*

ON FRIDAY NIGHT I was driving back to Pelham when I saw an apparition. Sitting on a mound of garbage on top of a snowbank among the last of the holiday garbage—a mountain of cardboard boxes and a tinsel-covered Christmas tree—was a purple Styrofoam wig head. I pulled over, ran back, and grabbed it.

Bald as a purple egg, it had blank black oval eyes with spidery lashes and a red Cupid bow's mouth. I put it in the seat next to me and drove around with it like that all week. Sometimes I talked to it, but mostly we just cruised around together, listening to the radio. Where was its wig? I wondered.

*

BY SATURDAY NIGHT, I knew what to do with it. I waited until 9:00 then drove across the river back to Northampton. Thelma Houston was singing on the radio ... "I can't survive." I was on the other side of this song now.

Our house was dark but there were lights on in the neighbor's bedroom. I parked up the street and walked in the shadows back to the house with the head under my arm. The front door was locked. I didn't have my key, but it wasn't hard to climb up to the second-floor porch using the drainpipe, even with the purple head under my arm. I pried open the bedroom window and slipped inside. The room smelled different. For a moment I panicked. I wanted to take the purple head downstairs to see if the kitchen cabinets were still open and tell it my side of the story. Show it the dent in the plaster and the couch that I'd reupholstered so beautifully.

Instead, I put it in the bed. Lying on a pillow in the dark, it had a startled look that reminded me of Liza Minnelli. I covered it with the quilt, then slipped out the window. I jumped down from the porch, walked to my car, then drove back to Pelham.

The phone rang around midnight.

"You crazy bitch," he said. "You almost gave me a heart attack."

"Surprise," I said.

And I felt a lot better after that.

*

THEN ONE MORNING my car wouldn't start. I sat in the freezing car turning the key in the ignition. Listening to the *er-er-er* sound.

Glen drove me to the bus stop in Amherst. I'd lived for twenty-four years without ever thinking about public transportation. The bus dropped me off at the front gate to the State School, then I had to walk up the long, icy driveway, past admissions all the way to Children's North at the back of the grounds. I was an hour late for work.

*

ON FRIDAY MORNING, Glen towed my car with his truck to the towny garage in Pelham Center. Louie, the owner, said he could fix the starter motor, but in his opinion it wasn't worth it. The engine was good, but the body was rotted. The best he could do was to transplant my car's engine into a better body, one with a blown motor.

He looked at me. "I'll see what I can do. I got something in the lot that could work. How about $150?"

My paycheck was $95 after taxes. "Thank you," I said, relieved. I could manage this.

I took my stuff out of the glove box. It was such a cute car! Driving it, sometimes I'd felt like Amelia Earhart flying in my tiny, two-seater in the dark with just a dim instrument panel and radio. But the canvas top no longer snapped on all the way and the heater had never really worked. My taste in cars, it turned out, was like my taste in men. I'd chosen looks over reliability.

*

I CAUGHT RIDES ALL THAT NEXT WEEK, waited for the bus in the desolate shelter, and walked the long, cold road to work. But I didn't care. My erotic flame had been ignited by Louie. I couldn't stop thinking about his black fingernails and callused hands. When he finally called on Friday morning my heart was pounding. "It's for you," Pauline yelled up to the attic. I hurried down in my nightgown.

"Your car's done. You can pick it up tonight."

"When do you close? I work until seven."

"That's okay," he said. "We'll stay open till you get here."

*

GLEN PICKED ME AT WORK. When we pulled into the driveway of the dark garage, he gave me a funny look. "Want me to help you with this guy?"

"No," I said, jumping out. "Thanks for the ride." I waved.

"Don't get burned," he warned.

After Glen disappeared down the road, I looked around. It was dark. There was only a dim light in the garage and the office seemed open. I went inside. It looked the same as I'd remembered it from a week ago — same girlie calendar from Pelham Auto Parts with the days X'ed out in blue ballpoint, same green leather car seat used as a couch.

"Hello," I called.

Louie appeared. I felt nervous but relieved. He was the car doctor and I was the patient.

"Hey, there." He smiled, ducking his head to fit in the doorway. He was taller than I had remembered. "Your car's almost ready." Turning, he yelled at someone in the garage. "Bring Renée Richards out front. Then you can go home."

I was very aware that it was after hours. In a few minutes we would be alone. But I didn't know if the attraction I felt to him was mutual. I'd recently been betrayed, deceived, and humiliated. I no longer trusted my perceptions about what went on between men and women.

The keys came flying through the air. Louie caught them effortlessly, lifting his right hand so they sailed into his palm.

"Looks like Renée's all set to go," he said, holding the door open for me.

We tramped out front in the cold dark. Instead of my green Karmann Ghia, there was a white vw bug.

"Meet Renée," he said, opening the door.

I understood that my Karmann Ghia's engine had been put into a different body but I didn't get the reference. "Renée?" I said.

"Renée Richards. The sex change?" He tried to say this in an offhand manner but I could tell that he was very pleased with this joke.

I still didn't get it.

"The tennis player who got switched into a woman."

"Oh," I said. It was 1976 and the news was full of Renée Richards, formerly Dr. Dick Raskind, the six-foot-two tennis player and ophthamologist who had recently transitioned into a new body.

Louie got in the car and started it.

It occurred to me that I'd made assumptions about Louie. He was much more sophisticated than I was, even with my college education.

"Watch this," he said, revving the engine. He'd attached a silver flex hose to the exhaust—in a way that wouldn't kill me—bifurcating it so that one end warmed my feet and the other end hooked onto the dashboard. "You can use it as a defroster," he said, sweeping it across the windshield. "Or a hair dryer." He aimed it at me.

"Cool," I said, surprised by the hot air in my face.

He smiled. His front tooth was crooked. Why did this imperfection suddenly seem so drop-dead sexy?

He sprayed me again with hot air and my hair flew around in a flurry of static electricity.

I laughed. The sound scared me. It had been a long time since I'd heard the sound of my laugh. It was higher and more girly than I remembered it.

"C'mon inside," he said. "I'll write you up a bill."

He took my arm and helped me through the snow.

In the office, he sat down at his messy desk and pulled out a pad. I sat on the leather car seat. I had never had sex in the backseat of a car. The front seat, yes. The back seat, no. I wasn't one of those girls who climbed into the back seat. Back seat sex was intentional; front seat sex was more just one thing leading to another.

When he handed me the invoice it was for $100. I looked up.

"It's a good, round number," he explained. "Makes things easier for the bookkeeper."

"Thanks?" I said, trying to make it sound like a question. I wasn't sure why I was getting this discount. I searched through my bag for the envelope then counted out four twenties, a ten and ten singles. I could have dropped the money on the desk, but our hands seemed magnetized. Somehow I levitated off the car seat onto the desk. Suddenly I was sitting on top of an old-fashioned blotter stuck full of cards. We were leaning in for the kiss, when the phone rang. Instantly we pulled apart. He picked it up.

"Soon," he said. "Yes. Yes. With tomatoes."

I knew it was his wife.

Pushing back in his chair, he drew his hand through his hair, which was long and dark with metallic gray strands. Holding the phone to his ear, he turned and smiled at me.

I saw his children waiting for him at the kitchen table. I saw the shaggy mutt rescued from the shelter with the faded bandana tied around its neck begging for scraps. And the wife, heavy but still beautiful, talking on the kitchen wall phone while she stirred a pot on the stove and kicked the refrigerator door closed with one foot.

I slid off his desk back onto the car seat. I'd been about to do what had recently been done to me. The circumstances were different, I wasn't married, but the geometry was the same. Last time I'd been the betrayed one. In this new configuration, I'd be assuming a different role.

I went out and got in my car. It wasn't as cute, but the engine sounded good. At the stop sign, I unhooked the hose and sprayed myself. My hair flew around and I laughed again. Not so girly this time.

*

MY NEW CAR, RENÉE RICHARDS, the Karmann Ghia in the white vw bug body, became a celebrity in Amherst that spring. Sometimes when I left it in the Faces of Earth parking lot, I'd return to find a crowd of people standing around it, pointing at the hose hooked to the dashboard and laughing.

One night Louie called me again. My heart pounded when I heard his voice.

"I got a guy here who wants to buy Renée for $600."

That was twice what I'd paid for the car (or was it cars?). And if I sold her I'd just have to buy another car. Either that or quit my job. I still had no real place to live. If I wanted to move, to start over again in a new place, this was my opportunity. Whenever anyone asks me why I moved to New York City, I say it was because of a car.

ON THE AMERICAN PLAN

Joanne Naiman

Before Arthur Rosen came along, I never thought too much about my parents' marriage. I did look forward to every Christmas vacation — when my mother and father and I along with thousands of other Jewish families went on an annual exodus to Miami Beach.

The only time my parents displayed any public affection was during those trips. At noon by the shuffleboard court, my parents would cha-cha or rumba, or pull me in to join them on a conga line or for an Alley Cat. They'd take me on cloudy days to Parrot Jungle or Alligator Farm. My mother and father would wrap their arms around each other while they watched a man put his whole head in an alligator's mouth, as if this sight were as romantic as a full moon.

In Miami too, my mother basked in the tropical sun and blossomed into the mother I wanted all year long. I'd feel the heat of the day still trapped in her tanned arms when she'd hug me and whisper wisecracks in my ear — wisecracks she usually reserved for her friends in New York. We'd gawk at the old ladies with diamond rings large enough to shade their knuckles. "Rich or poor," my mother would say, "it's good to have money."

My mother, father and I walked the Miami beaches together for hours, me in the middle holding each parent's hand. I loved the tangy scent of the ocean as it foamed around our toes, cooling and tickling them; the hard-packed wet sand that left our footprints — a fleeting but actual imprint of my family walking side by side side.

We lived on Long Island. Back home, my parents sectioned me off as if I were Berlin right after the Second World War. Education was solely my father's territory. Everyone knew he was a genius. And he was sure I took after him. He'd work late into the night on his legal briefs, then play chess against himself.

An ancient lemon-colored chess book with a broken spine sat on the other side of the chessboard where another player should have been. I would have done anything to please my father. Chess was the world my father loved most, and he badly wanted me to enter it; but its strategies were a language my father spoke that I could never decipher. It sounded like so much gibberish that for my entire childhood I thought my father played not *chess,* but *chest.*

My mother was the witty one. So she was in charge of overseeing my social skills. But I was a latchkey kid who always walked into an empty house. It's not that my mother worked. In our social circle, it was shameful for a wife to have a job. It meant you needed money—which secretly we did. My mother just wanted to be anywhere but home—all day long she'd run errands and come back just in time to make dinner.

*

IN 1968, MY FATHER DIDN'T come with us on vacation. My grandma, my mother and I stayed at the Mimosa: "Right next door to the fabulous Fontainebleau," my mother bragged to friends. She bragged too that her close friends, the Rosens, were staying at the Fontainebleau at the same time. The Rosens were really my father's clients, who seldom saw my parents socially. My mother also didn't mention the Mimosa was a skinny down-in-the-heels hotel scheduled for demolition. I was only twelve years old when I saw the Mimosa. It looked so sad surrounded by the big fancy hotels on Collins Avenue, Millionaire's Row.

I was sad myself because I missed my father, but he couldn't take off work. The year before when he came down, he lay poolside writing on long yellow sheets of paper, his black socks and shoes still on, his pants pushed up to just above the knees. At home, I never saw his knees. They looked sweet, mammalian, their bony structure reminded me of the faces of the sea lions I so loved at the Miami Aquarium.

"We're on the American Plan," my mother told my grandmother our first day of vacation. I knew the American Plan meant breakfast and dinner were in the dining room, and for lunch Grandma took everything surreptitiously from the breakfast table that would fit into her purse.

I watched as packets of Melba toast disappeared onto my grandma's lap. Then she inspected the lox and frowned. "I'm not taking this. I don't trust fish to travel."

"For God's sake, Mom, it's just going to the fifth floor. And Cara will be eating in two hours. If it makes you feel better, we'll lay the lox across the air-conditioning ducts while we're at the pool."

The second day my mother announced excitedly we were going to tour the Fontainebleau and maybe even run into the Rosens. She tried on several outfits: "They're daddy's richest clients. When I say richest, I mean filthiest."

We lived in a brand-new upper-middle-class neighborhood on Long Island. Jews flooded into these areas in the late '60s. In those days, really rich Jews lived side by side with the merely upper middle class, because many of the wealthiest areas on Long Island were still restricted. And many Jews still saw the outside world as threatening. In these suburban enclaves, the rich showed off their diamonds, furs, their yearly remodeled houses and Caddies in the driveway—safe from the prying eyes of goyim.

Doctors and lawyers were the lowly workers in my neighborhood. The really successful men were "in business." None of us kids understood the term—but if you were lucky enough to have no clue how your father made his money, chances were your family was really wealthy. These were the families that stayed at the Fontainebleau.

My father worked hard at his legal practice, but we were still poor by everyone else's standards. My mother didn't feel equal to anyone who had more money; and everywhere she looked she saw families richer.

Even if we couldn't afford the Fontainebleau, I believed my mother belonged there. She looked beautiful wearing a white silk shift, her gold sandals covered with so many seashells, as if the ocean had washed over her feet, and left behind pale pink shells clinging to the tops of her toes. Her sandals slapped smartly against the hotel's marble floor. The lobby seemed even sunnier than the sunny day, with its dozens of glittering chandeliers. My mother let her fingers trickle through water in the fountains—there were so many, it sounded as if it were raining in parts of the lobby.

But I held my breath. We were imposters walking into a world where we didn't belong. Maybe my mother could pass for Fontainebleau material, but I couldn't—a skinny girl with kinky hair and cat's-eye glasses, which were completely out of style. And a baggy bright orange shirt, which my mother insisted I wear in honor of Florida oranges. My grandmother had a European accent. I loved to hear her talk—her language was littered with little idiosyncrasies. But I was afraid she might slip up.

"This elevator is mind-bottling." she said when she saw the gold filigree of its door, and I cringed.

"It's really you!" my mother said, and ran up to a man and woman around my parents' age, lounging comfortably on a sofa in the lobby, as if the Fontainebleau were their living room. "Cara, Mom, you know Arthur and Sylvia Rosen. They're Daddy's oldest clients."

"Hello, Lila! Not oldest. You make us sound ancient. Longest. Will you look at Cara! I haven't seen you since you were a double for Shirley Temple," Arthur said.

I smiled. It was the era when every girl wanted stick-straight hair. It was nice to be reminded that once I'd been considered cute for having curls.

Arthur had a full white mane of hair. And he was dressed entirely in white, complete with white patent-leather loafers. Even at twelve, I could tell that, for a grown-up, he was handsome. He could have been one of the dozens of Fontainebleau's statues come to life. Suddenly he pulled me toward him in a large bear hug.

When he released me he said, "What do we have here?" He produced a Kennedy half-dollar from behind my ear. He pressed it into my palm. "Your ears are a silly place to keep pocket change. Put this somewhere safe."

"Mine?" I was thrilled when he nodded. My grandma and I were kindred spirits. Grateful and amazed when any small gift unexpectedly came our way.

The most memorable thing about Arthur's wife, Sylvia, was her diamond necklace, with its huge sapphire pendant lodged so deeply into her cleavage it looked as if it hadn't been fully mined from her mountainous breasts. Her skin was wrinkled, and she looked older than Arthur.

"And you, Lila." Arthur leaned in and kissed my mother's cheek. "You have to watch what falls out of your wallet." Just like that a twenty-dollar bill came falling from my mother's suddenly open pocketbook. Arthur picked it up and handed it to her.

"Don't be silly. I can't keep this," my mother giggled.

"Keep it, or it will just end up in some waiter's hand," Sylvia said. "Tomorrow, you're ours. We've got ourselves a big brand-new Cadillac and it's begging for company."

*

THE NEXT DAY, ARTHUR DROVE UP alone, dressed again all in white in a matching white Cadillac with red leather interior. It was a convertible. The top was down. "Sylvia sends apologies. They only had one appointment left at the hotel's beauty parlor. Of course she grabbed it."

"Of course." My mother nodded, looking bowled over at the news that the Fontainebleau had its own beauty parlor.

Arthur opened the front seat passenger door for my mother. I was sure she'd refuse to get in. She called convertibles death machines and let me know if I rode in one, I'd end up upside down with the roadway on my head.

"I can't believe we're driving in this!" she exclaimed. She sat down and wiggled her backside a little. "This leather is so soft, I might just melt right into it."

"Look at you! You look like sorbet. Like you could melt in someone's mouth yourself," Arthur said. My mother wore an outfit we'd cut the tags off this morning. Canary yellow.

Grandma and I got in the back. The seats smelled like the new leather of the briefcase my father had just bought because his finally fell apart. There was so much space between my grandmother and me, I could have stretched right out and not even reached her with my toes pointing. My mother caught me playing with the automatic windows. I thought she'd be mad, but she winked at me. *Sumptuous. Lavish. Luxurious.* I tested myself on the appropriate vocabulary words.

"We're heading her down Collins Avenue to show her off," Arthur said and peeled away from the curb. He pulled from his linen jacket the fattest cigar I'd ever seen. "Cuban. I make it my business to know a guy who knows a guy, whenever I want something." He blew perfectly round smoke rings. He called out the names of hotels we passed: "The Shangri-La, Carlton, Delano, Dorchester, Eden Roc, Gansevoort, Marseilles, Essex House, Ocean Spray." They were like sprawling modern castles. Lining the avenue were palm trees filled with coconuts, which hung like small brown moons waiting to drop to earth. The air held the scent of salt water, mimosas and cigar smoke.

"You're going to have to stop me from turning to the people on the sidewalks and waving. This car by itself is a whole parade!" My mother wasn't even looking at the sidewalk—just Arthur. My grandmother clutched her handbag on her lap and stared straight ahead. She coughed whenever a breeze blew cigar smoke directly in our faces.

"Ready for this," Arthur said to my mother. "A new feature called Cruise Control. It's set for fifty-five miles an hour. I don't even have to put my foot on the gas. I can dance." Arthur stomped his feet so hard against the car floor that I heard them even with the top down. The back seat vibrated.

Arthur continued stomping. He blew smoke rings as he sped along. He weaved in and out of traffic and ran through stop signs on Cruise Control. My grandmother uttered under her breath: *Slow down, you Schmendrick.*

"Lila, dance with me." My mother crossed her legs at her ankles and swiveled them back and forth. Arthur swiveled his legs toward her. For a brief moment their knees touched, just the way two people's glasses do when they toast each other.

We made a sharp turn at a corner. A sidewalk with a gigantic palm tree came rushing toward us. Arthur lurched away just in time. I felt the lox from lunch leap into my throat. Please, please, please, I thought, don't let me vomit in this beautiful new car. Nothing I'd ever do in my mother's eyes would be as horrible.

By the time Arthur slowed down and headed for our hotel, I was doubled up, holding my stomach. My grandmother hadn't spoken a word.

"Thank you for that lovely dance." My mother waited for Arthur to come around and open the car door for her. She had no patience with my father when he tried to open doors for her.

"Lila, Sylvia wants to make it up to you. Tomorrow night, our guest at the Fontainebleau for dinner. Eight o'clock."

My mother croaked out a "Fabulous!"

*

THE NEXT NIGHT, MY MOTHER shimmied into her shocking pink silk dress. "Zip me." She stood in front of me. I cautiously zipped her up, imitating the way my father did it, thinking about how serious but pleased he looked carrying out this task.

"Mom, you're going to be the prettiest!"

"It's not a contest," my mother said, "though it would be nice if I won." She smiled and kissed me on the cheek. "We can't forget the finishing touches." I nodded. My mother bobby-pinned to her hair a freshly teased fall, then sat on the bed and slipped on her pink rhinestone sandals. When she stood up, she wobbled.

"Why are you wearing such dangerous high heels?" my grandma asked.

"You know this dress calls for these shoes."

My grandmother didn't contradict her. I was frustrated. I had no idea why my mother's dress *called* for her rhinestone sandals. This was the kind of nuanced wisdom I would need to become a beautiful grown-up woman, and I feared I might never acquire it.

My mother dotted her wrists with perfume. "And now, the crowning touch. I'm going to lipstick." She seemed to be addressing our whole hotel room, and my grandmother and I were merely a couple of its audience members.

My mother stepped into the bathroom. I followed. She had a dozen or so lipsticks on the counter. "Bungle Jungle Red. What do you think?" She didn't expect me to answer. She had already spread her lips wide open and was slowly drawing shiny color across her top lip, which curved in the middle like a tiny waist. "Did I ever tell you a saleswoman at the Elizabeth Arden counter at Saks said I had perfect lips?" I shook my head. She had told me, but I liked being reminded. I secretly suspected my own lips looked a lot like hers, and possibly one day soon they also might be a lush puffy palette for brilliant reds and oranges. But I was too shy to ever ask my mother if she agreed. She kissed a tissue over and over again, until it looked as if it were covered with glistening cherry frosting.

We heard a loud knock at the door. My mother rushed toward it but my grandmother got there first.

"Hello, all you beautiful ladies." It was the first time Arthur wasn't wearing all white. He had on a blue dinner jacket that perfectly matched his eyes and echoed Miami Beach because it was the chlorine blue of swimming pools and the beach umbrellas at the Fontainebleau. In his breast pocket was a white handkerchief as crisp as a lady's starched linen shirt. His glance swept right over my grandmother and me, as if he were barreling down the road, and we were traffic lights that had just changed from red to green. He stared at my mother. "Apologies from Sylvia. She isn't feeling well, but she insisted we go without her. She doesn't want to ruin our evening."

My mother was already smiling, so I couldn't tell if the news made her happy. But my grandmother gave my mother a big frown. "Lila, I need to show you something," she said. My mother shook her head. My grandmother shook hers back, and they disappeared behind the closed bathroom door. Arthur was still standing in the hallway.

"How you doing, sport?" I didn't like being called *sport*. *Sport* was the nickname of a boy or a dog. I shrugged my shoulders. Arthur didn't seem to notice. He was eyeing the bathroom. He appeared so much larger than before, looming in the doorway. I didn't want him to come any closer. For one thing he stank, as if it he were saturated in cigar smoke, with a hint of what I knew was bourbon, because it was the popular drink of the men who played pinochle all day around the pool. He grabbed the sides of the doorframe with both hands and teetered back and forth on the balls and heels of his shoes. Every time he leaned forward, his potbelly crossed the threshold into our room. I didn't know if he was waiting for me to invite him in, but I didn't budge.

Arthur looked at his watch. Then he looked at the bathroom door again. He tapped his foot. "You have to treat a dinner reservation at the Fontainebleau like a doctor's appointment. Not a minute late. You capiche?"

I didn't capiche. I didn't understand what it meant, but I suspected I wasn't allowed to do it. But I realized he was criticizing my mother, and I didn't like it. "Mom's always early."

"Look, sport, do you think you could hurry her up?"

"I'm not allowed to interrupt." That wasn't true. But I decided right there that my father didn't like Arthur Rosen. His richest client. *Too big a shot.* That's what my father would have mumbled behind his back.

Arthur sighed. I knew that sigh. It was the bored, frustrated sound of a grown-up made left to wait around with a kid they didn't want to talk to. Any second he'd ask the required question: *How's school going?*

"Any good five-fingered discounts lately?"

"Excuse me?"

"You don't have to pretend. I'm with it. Girls your age. Shoplifting's your favorite hobby. Lipstick, gum. Are you one of the gutsy ones who stuffs clothes down her pants?"

"It's against the law." I blushed.

"Scared, huh?" Arthur laughed. He was still laughing at me when my mother came out of the bathroom, her mink stole wrapped around her naked shoulders.

My grandmother was behind her, holding a balled-up tissue. She never raised her voice when she was angry or upset but she'd tightly ball up tissues as if she were making little fists. She whispered to my mother, "For the last time, don't go. A married woman, this is how she acts?"

My mother came over to me and bent down, "Good night, sugar puss." Even if my eyes were closed, I'd recognize her: soft mink brushing against my arm, florid scent of Arpège, those warm lips pressed to my cheek. My stomach dropped as she walked over to Arthur, and they left.

*

WHEN GRANDMA AND I WENT into the hotel dining room for dinner that night, the maître d' said: "You're usual threesome, I presume."

"Two. My mother's out."

"Sick," my grandmother said, quickly embarrassed. "She's out sick with God knows what."

*

"POOPSIE, YOU DESERVE A TREAT," Grandma said after dinner. "How about bingo." I couldn't believe it. The card room was one of those inner sanctums I thought was reserved for adults. Like my mother's mah-jongg gatherings. When the game was at our house, I wasn't allowed in the den. But I'd sneak close enough to watch and listen. I loved the music of the game: *One bam. Two crack*; the secret songs of grown-up women, the mah-jongg cards the women read from like tiny librettos; their high-pitched laughter and bickering always with a happy ending.

We sat next to a woman Grandma had befriended at the pool.

"This is my granddaughter I told you all about."

"Such a pretty girl! A *shaineh maidel*. I'm Hilda Fishman but call me Hilly." She had a thick Yiddish accent and wore what my grandmother called a *cashmere wig*—expensive, platinum and gigantic.

She put a bingo card right front of me and round translucent red chips. "These are the fancy chips. At the Y you can't see through the chips, so you have to keep moving them to check your numbers."

Grandma nodded. "This is high-class bingo. They even have the numbers in a cage so you can watch them spin. At the Y they pull numbers out of a sack." I was sorry to hear my grandmother say that. She lived alone in her tiny apartment while we had such a big house. And now I knew her bingo games were second-class.

"It's Bingo!" Hilly stood up and shouted, then tapped me on the shoulder: "Number fourteen. Your card."

I'd never won anything before. I received applause when I claimed my winnings because I was the only kid in the room. My prize was a shiny patentleather pocketbook, the type grown women called a *clutch*. I clutched it. I couldn't wait to show it to my mother. This would be the first grown-up pocketbook my mother and I would share.

"Wonderful, isn't it," Hilly said. "Make sure, sweetheart, to enjoy this. Because one minute life's lovely. The next, it's more terrible than hell."

I turned to my grandmother: "Holocaust," she whispered to me.

*

IT WAS ALMOST 9:30 WHEn Grandma and I went back to our room. I rushed in. The room was empty.

"Where's Mommy? She can't still be eating."

"Such fancy restaurants, people chew slowly," my grandmother said. Though she was frowning. "Get ready for bed, and I'm sure Mom will be home by the time you've washed your teeth."

"Mommy always lets me stay up on vacation," I protested. I didn't want to risk falling asleep and miss giving the clutch to my mother that evening.

"A few more minutes." I watched my grandmother change into her night-gown. Without her bra, her breasts hung down like long thin animals without bones. She dropped her dentures in a glass of water. In the moonlight they took on the eeriness of an ancient sea creature.

Grandma sneaked a quick glance at the bedside clock. It was now after 10:00. I lay on the bedspread with my shoes and socks still on. I wanted to make it very clear I wasn't going to bed until my mother came home.

My grandmother crumpled up a tissue.

"Mom's really late, isn't she?" I panicked. My mother was *never* late. She prided herself on arriving places early.

"Not late. She's on Fontainebleau time," my grandma said. "Even walking through that lobby takes twenty minutes. Let's see what's on television."

"No! Who wants to watch in black and white."

"Don't be that way, poopsie. We'll find something even if we don't have a colored set."

"You can't say colored, Grandma. It's color."

"Why not? Isn't the picture colored?"

I felt worldlier than my grandmother, wiser. I didn't want to feel that way. I started to put my head in her lap, but she seemed so fragile; a tiny wrinkled woman engulfed in a field of polyester blue poppies.

The phone rang. My grandma scooped it up. "What? We've been back at least an hour. I can't hear a word. Call me from a place quieter. Are you at a bar?"

Grandmother hung up. "Mom's calling right back. She said she's been trying to get ahold of us."

Grandma and I sat on the edge of the bed together and waited for the phone to ring. For fifteen minutes we said nothing.

I stepped onto the balcony. Below me, the ocean swirled and frothed, dark and dangerous.

When the phone suddenly rang again, I ran inside. "What? What?" My grand-mother said. This time I put my ear next to hers. Live music and laughter came roaring at us over the line.

"Buddy Hackett. Late show" were all the words I could make out, then "Intermission." My mother's voice bubbly and happy, "Lucky to get tickets." Then she hung up.

"Get your sweater," my grandmother said. She put her raincoat over her nightgown, which stuck out of it, and threw her dentures into her mouth.

"Grandma?"

"No big worry," she said. "We're going to make sure Mom gets home safe after the show." Before she pulled me from the room, I grabbed the clutch.

MY GRANDMOTHER HELD MY HAND roughly and rushed us toward the Fontainebleau. The night was clear and the moon shiny. The Fontainebleau was as bright as daytime. Women were in long evening gowns and minks, the men in dinner jackets. I stared at the floor trying not to look at their expressions as we walked by. Even with her raincoat on, you could tell my grandmother had her nightgown underneath. And she'd forgotten to change out of her slippers. The show was all the way across the lobby. My grandmother charged ahead, while I stood far enough away so we didn't look like we were together.

"There!" My grandmother said angrily, and pointed to a placard with the picture of Buddy Hackett. "Let's sit on this sofa, out of sight." It was a blue velvet sofa, round and big as a playground merry-go-round except it had a high, high back. It was the perfect place to hide. We'd see anyone walking out of the show without them seeing us.

Grandma and I were silent. I opened and closed the clutch's clasp. Of course my mother *had* to love it—real patent leather, with the same leather smell as the Rosens' car.

*

GRANDMA SAW THEM BEFORE I DID. She jumped up and muttered: *No!* My mother was walking barefoot out the door, her feet naked on the floor. Arthur Rosen held her sandals in one hand; his other hand was wrapped around my mother's waist.

My grandmother was face-to-face with my mother before I realized it. I ran up too. "What the hell are you doing here?" my mother asked.

"I was going to ask you that! Cara and I want you to come home now."

"No!" My mother took Arthur's hand. She caught me staring. She said softly, "Pumpkin, go to sleep. It's way past your bedtime."

My mother had never called me *pumpkin* before. It frightened me. The mother I knew called me *sugar puss*. She didn't stand barefoot on a marble floor, a fat man's hand touching her best silk dress.

"I won this clutch for you!" I held it up. It was perfect. It gleamed as shiny as anything else in the Fontainebleau.

"You won something? Huh?" My mother didn't even look at the clutch. She didn't get the point at all.

"We can share it." I tried to give the clutch to my mother, but right at that moment Arthur whispered something in her ear.

She nodded. She held up a finger. "In just a sec. I promise," she said to him.

"Come on. The night is young but we're not getting any younger." Arthur laughed. My mother laughed too, in a way I'd never heard her laugh before. I realized then my father was not enough for her. My father and I together would never be enough.

I didn't notice my grandmother raise her hand. But I saw her slap my mother. I heard the loud crack too. My mother's head jerked to the side. She touched her cheek. She never uttered a sound. She pursed her lips, and her eyes went wild. My grandmother burst out crying.

My mother stood stock-still for just a moment. Then she bent down and looked straight into my eyes. "You understand, don't you, pumpkin? I just need some fun from time to time." Her cheek was so bright red where my grandmother had slapped her, as if it had been pounded raw.

My mother had never asked me to understand anything before. I wish I could have said then: "Yes, I understand that for just one evening you want to feel glamorous and slip away from the loneliness of your marriage."

But I was twelve, and all I understood was my mother had just thrust a terrible secret at me that we both knew I would keep forever because I couldn't break my father's heart.

I nodded. "Good," my mother said. She blew me a kiss, took Arthur's arm and walked away. My grandmother was still crying. But I was as deaf to her sobs as to the background music in the lobby. The fountain near the couch was filled with pennies that people had made wishes on. I threw in the clutch. It bobbed to the top. I held it under water until it sank itself.

THE WORLD OUTSIDE MY BELLY

Rachael Lynn Nevins

(From *The Mom Egg*)

My sweetheart, this is what life is: waiting for the B23
in the rain. The air is full of the scent of lilacs, and the bus
is late. There will be days in May
as cold and gray as October, and you will forget
to buy milk for your breakfast.
Sweetheart, I tell you, don't go looking for real life
anywhere else
but in the heaps of dirty clothing on the bedroom floor.
The dishes in the sink. The late nights at your desk,
your weary eyes, the moon in the window.

DANCERS

Mark Fenlon Peterson

(From *The Milo Review*)

"Smile and relax, rest a moment, you look stressed," Angel says softly. She shuffles to the reflector and adjusts it for a more sensual light. "Next, we'll try the same position but you'll give me a Julia Roberts." Lauren doesn't budge. She remains on the floor with her shoulders hunched, one knee is crossed over the other and pressed to her chest, her hands rest on the patella, her head is tilted toward the floor and straight black hair conceals her face and sparkles like studio snow drifting toward a stage. Then, suddenly, when Angel is behind the tripod again, Lauren lifts her head and turns her interlaced fingers, cracks the knuckles, rests one hand on the floor and the other back on her knee. Her mouth slips into a large and toothy smile.

Lauren is the first Asian soloist in the New York City Ballet and will be the Sugar Plum Fairy this year. The company needs promotional photos and this is a four-hour session; the dress and tiara shots are done and Lauren is covered by a simple leotard. She is excited to be the star.

"Perfect!" says Angel and snaps three shots. "Can we go brighter?"

Angel will strike her own forehead this evening when she looks back at these shots and realizes this pose is a replica of an Egon Schiele painting. She will delete them for their lack of originality. Yes, there will be hesitation and regret due to the quality of the photos and the drama that happens in the next few minutes, but originality is critical in her mind, and Angel won't allow her work to be considered derivative. The fact that ideas and art always echo the past is lost on her. But, here in this moment, the photographer seeks solely to capture what she imagines is the truth in this dancer, the aura and strength of the person inside the beautiful skin. She searches so she may discover the inherent qualities of charisma.

Lauren briefly touches her chin with her index finger, raises her head and her lips ever so slightly to be brighter. Angel taps her remote and the camera clicks three times.

"Great! How about solemn?"

The chin lowers slightly, and Lauren changes her expression to be a perfect replica of the Mona Lisa half smile.

"You're better than an actress!" There are more clicks and another "Perfect!"

The camera keeps snapping and Lauren holds the pose, and Angel says, "And now move your head from side to side."

Her face hides it, but Lauren's mind percolates while she poses. She thinks that the ballet is not likely to want these pictures for the Christmas Playbill. The Sugar Plum Fairy is renowned for a regal and graceful beauty. Or perhaps they'll want to show the athleticism of the ballet; they will choose the shots with plenty of leg like the ones that Angel shot at the start of the session.

Lauren thinks of her legs as her best feature and in these thoughts she loses focus on the pose and lowers the hand from her knee to caress her thigh. She knows her legs are the perfect mix of length, strength and size. She asks herself, What is this photographer doing? This turtle pose, this half fetal position, this covered-up body is not what she has worked so hard to have on the front of the *Times*!

With the strength of the foot that is planted on the floor she lifts herself in one swift movement, takes three steps and with her hands raised in front of her, fingers and palms pointed straight, she opens her mouth slowly and shouts, "This is not right!"

"Okay ..." Angel steps backward, sets the camera clicker down and lowers her hands like a criminal surrendering to the police.

"No, it is not okay, what do you think you are doing? Are you stupid? What do you think Julia Roberts has to do with the Sugar Plum Fairy? Where did you get this idea? Do you think I want to be seen this way?"

Lauren continues to advance, appearing to become taller and taller while Angel shrinks as she steps back. Lauren's body is taut, veins visible in her neck as she continues to shout. "I want to know, what made you think this would be a good idea? Are you an idiot?"

Lauren stops and stares at Angel. Angel does not know how to control her face like an actress, her eyes have welled up, she is not articulate and she is unable to speak under stress. Lauren leaps closer and shoves Angel with both hands against her shoulders. Angel offers no resistance and simply falls backward onto her heavy bottom.

"Well, what do you have to say for yourself? Can't you speak? Are you an idiot?"

"Well ..."

"Yes, speak, or are you an idiot?"

The fall released a surge of tears. Angel's hand lifts to cover her eyes as if attempting to erase herself from this moment. Angel is not pretty, but her bright blue eyes are the surprise on her urban face and these tears surfing down the creases and aged acne scars are a shock. Lauren pirouettes and stomps in her slipper-clad feet as she paces to the other side of the room and back.

"Well, what is it?" she says again.

"I ... I ... I ... I don't know, I find the pose sexy," says Angel.

"You think the Sugar Plum Fairy is meant to be sexy?"

"It's innocent and mysterious and exotic all at once."

"The Sugar Plum Fairy is innocent and mysterious and exotic? Are you warped?"

"Uhhhh ..."

"You are an idiot!"

There is silence in New York. Lauren's mask of righteous anger is a park monument of solidity in the room. Her nostrils flare and her eyes are aimed at Angel's forehead, which is now the one facing the floor. If this hits the media, this outburst will be portrayed as a tantrum, the subtext as proof that even those with dream lives have their difficulties and failures. And that is true, but isn't this unmediated state also a form of acting?

Quietly, Angel says, "No, not the fairy. You. You look innocent and mysterious. It is wonderful."

"Mysterious? Are you racist? Trying to conform me to some expectation because I'm Asian?"

"No, that's not at all ..."

"Do I sound exotic now?"

"Uhhh ..."

"What do you think you are doing?"

Angel leans forward with her arms out. She is plump and over fifty; she gets on all fours before she can start to raise herself from the ground. One knee lifts, one hand pushes off the knee, the other hand lifts from the ground, then out into the air for balance, the leg straightens, and the other foot drags up from the floor until a crouch is achieved.

"I'm getting up," she says. And then, both legs straighten until she's standing. She has found a face for herself. The blue eyes are calm and hard. Surviving and taking care of herself is one thing Angel knows how to do well. She photographs people because she does not understand them; she photographs them to find something she understands, and perhaps, to find someone that cares about her. The inner strength that has carried her through many lonely years is visible when she is fully straight and she looks at Lauren without dropping her eyes.

"The shoot is done."

"What? We have two more hours."

"No, we are done. I have what I need."

"Don't let me bother you, we need to get this right."

"It is right."

"You understand what I mean? I'm sorry I yelled but the pictures should glorify the ballet, they aren't about my being Asian, or young, or anything. It's about the dancing! That's why I'm upset."

"Look around you, they don't care." Angel unscrews the camera from the tripod, "You have two extra hours for yourself, go enjoy yourself."

Lauren stares at the polish of the wood floor; it shines as brightly as the space under the barre. "But where will I go?" she says.

*

ANGEL DIDN'T ANSWER and Lauren walks out of the building with her cell to her ear, mindlessly walking uptown on Eighth Avenue and trying to connect with anyone. The symphony of walkers parts as she strides up the street, a lifetime of dance imposing a long step in her gait even when walking without direction. Both men and women turn and gawk at her beauty. She calls the Cavalier, then the Spanish dancers, and the Chinese dancers, and Clara, and Drosselmeyer; she doesn't call the Arabian dancers because they are mad at her for getting the part, and when none of them answer, she calls her mother in California. It's still early and her mother doesn't respond either. She has no one left to call. Well, no one but her boyfriend, and she can't call him.

It's October fifteenth and she enters the park at Columbus; she sways seven feet in front of the coffee hut wishing for a large green tea, her bag and money remain at the practice studio. Lauren is in a world of her own thoughts, unconscious of her expressions and her posture and the image she portrays. It's an unmeditated expression, and there is nothing we can clearly see or say about her except that she looks lost in the world around her.

The bored woman inside the hut says, "Do ya need something?"

"My boyfriend is cheating on me."

"Men are fucked, my dude cheats all the time, I take him back and show him what he's missed and he stays good for a month or so and takes the kids out. What else are you gonna do with them? Did you want something?" The attendant is a short Cuban or Dominican with pink hair. She might be twenty-two or as old as thirty-five but she speaks with the tone of the wise, as if these are the undeniable facts of life.

"I'd like a tea but I don't have money."

"Ya look like a woman with money." She leans over the counter and takes a long and slow grilling look over Lauren's body, noticing the thin-soled shoes, the long legs covered in tights, the red skirt, expensive sweater and long hair. "If you don't have money, you must be autistic. I'd know how to get money with that body. You wouldn't find me working here."

"That's not what I mean, I left my money at home."

"You need money for a coffee."

Lauren has stepped forward and leans slightly forward on the balls of her feet. She doesn't acknowledge the compliment and slowly comprehends the words, then says, "You are right. I must be autistic, I do things I don't understand, makes me feel like half a human."

She leans a tiny bit more until her right hand fingers lightly touch the counter, the light contact holds in her tears.

"That's all people, girl, don't think you're special. And blame your man, he's the one that eff'ed up. Make him pay!"

The attendant turns and pours a small coffee, and places it on the counter. "I didn't do this," she says and turns away. She hides her face when she can't control the expression, and Lauren reminds her of her own disappointments.

Lauren says thank you and waits for something more, she wants to say she doesn't really know what her boyfriend did, she wants to keep talking to defend her boyfriend, but the attendant has walked into the back room without another word. She continues to wait, still leaning, but both hands are wrapped around the cup and resting on the counter. When she realizes the attendant is not going to return, a few tears do fall and diffuse on the counter.

Her body tightens, she wipes her face with a napkin, she stands straight and continues to cherish the gift of this coffee between both hands and then strolls confidently into the park.

*

AT THE TOP OF UMPIRE ROCK the expression on her face is a smile, as if she is enjoying the children playing below her, as if she is one of the mothers, or more likely, a college student earning a few bucks as a passive babysitter. It's clear she is not paying much attention to what's around her, although the blank smile would suggest to an observer that she is not unhappy.

After an hour, the coffee long gone, she stands and stretches, and takes a few steps before her legs tingle with pins and needles, she takes a few more steps and one foot slips into a crack in the rocks. She does not fall but she cannot move. The foot is trapped. She flails her arms, she pulls on the foot, but the legs remain numb and won't operate effectively. Awkwardly she lowers herself to the ground and finds herself in the same pose that she held for Angel.

"Why was I mad at Angel?" she says out loud to herself. No one is near and she doesn't answer her own question. She pulls on her leg, and from this new position it slides out. Her slipper is ripped in two places, and her ankle hurts. She touches it gingerly but there is no swelling and the touch does not bring any additional pain. She stands, the blood flow returns to her legs, and she walks slowly and cautiously the rest of the way down the schist and out of the park.

At home, she pulls out a bag of ice and ties it to her ankle. Her apartment is a tiny studio with room for a bed, a closet, a bathroom, a sink, two kitchen cabinets, two-burner stove, and a refrigerator that has never been used except to store ice packs.

She calls the general manager of the ballet. The apartment is a sublet, and the primary tenant left his furnishings and pictures, which are colorful and befitting his career as a Brazilian gay porn star named Tony. There is one picture in particular that never fails to capture Lauren's eye. It is Tony with his lover and two balloon-breasted women at Disney World. All four hold each other tightly at the waists, and look into the camera with eagerness and excitement: one platinum blonde who looks thirty or older, Tony with his Mediterranean features, one African-American woman who appears Lauren's age, and Tony's lover, who is Asian like herself. They wear skimpy and inappropriate clothing for the location but they are clearly happy and oblivious.

She paces as she talks to Ben, five short steps back and forth in the narrow space between wall and bed, toward the picture and away.

"I said a few things I didn't mean to Angel," she says.

Ben knows how to handle these moments, and quickly says, "Don't worry about it, babe!

It's only our photographer. She keeps our secrets, no one will ever hear about it." "That's not what ..."

"I saw the shots, you'll be a star when those hit the press." "But ..."

"I especially like the sitting poses! You look great, mysterious and exotic, the perfect representation to modernize the Fairy, to make adults want to see it all anew, we may even get people without kids with pictures like those."

"You think ..."

"I'm joking! Kids always come, but with you as the centerpiece, the adults won't come so begrudgingly, it will be like seeing it for the first time! I'm super excited! Babe, you're gorgeous, it will be great this year!"

"Don't ..."

"And then think of the roles you'll be able to take in the coming seasons."

The door opens and her boyfriend enters, smiles and reaches for her. She holds a finger to her lips and pushes back, but he grabs her in a hug and stops her pacing. She continues to talk and her body relaxes. The fight is spent, and passively she says to both of them, "I hurt my ankle this afternoon."

Ben doesn't hear and only says, "I'm telling you, it's going to be a great season for all of us."

"Are you okay?" says her boyfriend, and he sits her down, lifts her leg and takes a close look at the foot.

"I hurt my ankle this afternoon," she says again to the phone. "Seriously? Bad?" asks Ben.

She looks at the hair of her boyfriend, who is closely examining her ankle. He has removed the ice, he softly caresses the calf. He looks up with an expression of concern and questioning. There is no swelling. Does he care about her?

"Sorry, it's not bad," she says to both of them. "It'll be okay by tomorrow, but tell Mike I won't make it to evening rehearsal tonight."

"Sure, babe, anything you like, it's done."

"And I wanted to say sorry to Angel. I was off base."

Lauren waits then for a response, but after a few moments, the dial tone flicks in. Ben has hung up. She throws the phone to the bed.

Her boyfriend begins to peel off her clothes, and Lauren sees the picture again and she studies it while he kisses her neck. She has always suspected she should place it in a drawer. Staring at it is unseemly and feels vaguely like spying. But every time she has started to take it down, she has looked at it and felt the opposite, touching his belongings would be the intrusion on Tony's privacy and place. She does not have the right to move or touch his objects. And so it sits, and she never quite recognizes that the real reason she leaves it there is that the picture fills her with longing. The happiness of the four is something she wants and doesn't have in her life.

As her boyfriend pulls her toward him, she looks one more time at the photo, and then emulates the look of the African-American woman. She is joyous and happy in her moment and surroundings.

Bethpage Black

Jean Pfeffer

Return my father on a warm spring day,
Place him on the first tee box of Bethpage Black
Wearing his worn leather glove and his grass-stained spikes.
Remember his Callaway clubs and his gentle swing,
His handicap of five and his lucky tees.
Record every stroke on a scorecard for me.

Have him whistle as he sets my ball on a tee,
Wrap his warm hands around mine to guide my grip,
Make sure he grins when he says,
That was your longest drive yet.
Stay close after he points out the poison oak
And enters the woods alone to search for my lost ball.

THE CLOSET

Whitney Porter

(From *Metazen*)

She was always standing there. Always standing, with those long talon-like fingers pressed against her hips. Her withered look of disapproval, pulsing like a hemorrhage, a sleek green vein popping out the side of her neck. My mother, standing at the mouth of the walk-in utility closet, hovering over me, my pants half pulled down, with my best friend Bill pushing at my bare ass with an empty syringe he got from a toy doctor's kit. This was how we played doctor. It was our version of "I'll show you mine if you show me yours." But why oh why was I always the one that was showing mine? Why the fuck didn't Bill ever get caught showing his bare ass. Why wasn't he on his belly exposed, compromised and vulnerable, in front of his homicidal mother? Why was I the one caught time and time again, humiliated, with my ass hanging out of my pants? Why was it always me that was the patient and never the doctor?

As a little girl admittedly I was adorable, easily succumbing to the peer pressures of being desirable, a budding little "dyke to be" irresistible to the neighborhood boys, similar yet different enough for them to still be able to sexually objectify. With adorable round ballooning chubby cheeks, with greasy brown hair matted to my tiny peanut head that I steadfastly refused to wash, that stiffened under the weight of the Texas sun, a mix of my own oils and outside contaminants that smelled like something deep and satisfyingly gamey, coming from the very bowels of the ditches that I spent most of my days exploring with an exceptionally large twig that I ripped out of some dying tree. I was a tomboy. I climbed trees. I spit on sidewalks. I chased our dog. I rode our dog. In general I terrorized our dog. A poor pup if ever there was one. This wretched little runt my family picked up at some puppy farm with collie eye, an inferiority complex and a tenacious herding instinct that caused her to be often hit by cars. Repulsive little me, this butch oversexed five-year-old girl, assaulter of dead trees, abuser of helpless animals with collie blindness. Oh horny little me. I humped any sharp edge I could wrap my skinny little legs around. But me with my dirty knees and my crusty scabs, my little body as translucent, as pale as a ghost, and blistered by the sun, I was the object of desire for every nose-picking boy tyke that would eventually come out to be a preacher or a hairdresser. The congenital patient, locked in darkness, conspiring in closets, head dusted with unused overcoats, my stomach impaled on a bed of my mom's discarded shoes, their once sleek forms assaulted by my mother's raging bunions, and oh what bunions! Like a tiny rugged mountain range, a little flesh-covered slice of Appalachia mounted on each side of her foot, and there I was with my pants pulled down around my hips, my best friend Bill poking at my ass with a syringe. Which really begs the question, what kind of asshole packs an empty syringe into a kids' doctor's kit? How fucked up were the '70s? Who gives a child a syringe? What were they trying to do? Train us for heroin addiction when we finally realized how bankrupt our futures were going to be?

But I'll admit it was thrilling. The poking. The prodding. The syringing. My bare ass out in the open, the breeze from the central air blowing across it, like a gentle spring wind. We were five and this was sex. And my Mommy, for that's what I called her then, my long lumbering willowy Mommy, stood above me, my neck half turned up in abject terror. Bill already out the door, the bed-wetting little freak, running out the door, to be welcomed hopefully with a spanking from his own homicidal mother because that's what parents did back then. Thank you "spare the rod, spoil the child," and any of its proponents. There's a special place in hell for you. And I hope you're in it. And I hope it's an S&M club and that every safe word you utter gets the devil to hit you even harder. Left alone to face my fate. My shame. And my Mommy, my big long Mommy, who I loved more than anything in the world, probably because she was an excellent player of peek-a-boo in my infancy, whose crook of her arms I would during Sunday mass bury my face in, shielding myself from the boredom of it, reveling in her warmth, or maybe just to avoid the off-key utterances of bad Catholic chanting, she that I so desperately wanted to please, but couldn't help but continue to disappoint, would tear up upon seeing me splayed on the closet floor my pants pulled down past my pasty little rump. Her singsong East Texas twang unleashed like a dagger, fanged syllables unending. "Whuut rrrrrr youuuuu dooooooing?" What the fuck did it look like I was doing? Really? How is a five-year-old to explain this? What vocabulary did I have for this? I was humping toy chests at three fantasizing about Minnie Mouse. How the hell did I know what I was doing? It's doctor. It's natural. It's what little kids do. But bless her overly selective devout little Catholic heart, East Texas Catholic, a total oxymoron at that time, suspect, in a largely Protestant bucktoothed congregation, one of the few children in that town whose mother didn't marry her first cousin, little fuckers all of them. Mean as snakes. An unrelenting town, a stupid town, a small town, dry as desert much to my bourbon-drinking grandfather's chagrin. What was little Betty Blue to do? What would happen if she were caught satisfying a carnal urge, her lower body pressed purposefully into the occasional kitchen counter, the hard edge of a stiff-backed chair. Such a good Catholic girl caught hoisting herself on anything that had a point. Little girls aren't supposed to do this. Little girls weren't supposed to do a lot of things that I did.

Ship Out on the Sea

Máire T. Robinson

(From *The Chattahoochee Review*)

Sure any eejit could tell you that to win the Tidy Towns Contest you need to get yourself a boat, fill it with geraniums, and moor it beneath the town's welcome sign. Old water pumps are good too. They hint at the history of the place when *cailíní* in long skirts lined up with tin pails, before the water got contaminated with effluent or fertilizer runoff, or the well dried up altogether.

It's a strange reward for a town—not the most beautiful, not the biggest, not containing the most impressive architecture or decorous residents—but tidy, clean, manicured. Our town never did win that contest. Were you and I the reason why? The rogue elements on that wrought-iron bench beside the boat. Two teenage girls chain-smoking, stomping about in heavy boots, observing it all from behind dark eyes: miscreant weeds that had taken root.

Do you remember that night we emancipated the boat? And as we carried it down the narrow path to the sea, reeds bowed in greeting and the hawthorn blushed. The moon was shining just for us, illuminating a course across the dark sea. As we reached the water's edge, you turned to me and let out a whoop and your hair whipped about your head. We waded out and didn't care that our jeans got soaked. It was worth it to feel that boat cast off from our hands, to watch it set sail. We sat on the sand, smoking cigarettes until its outline was swallowed by the black horizon. But the next day, there it was, back under the welcome sign. No mark of the journey it had been on, apart from one tiny periwinkle shell stuck to its hull. We thought we'd done enough, but we were wrong. We should have captained that boat ourselves. That was our mistake.

I sat on the bench that day with fists clenched and talked about getting away from this place. You shook your head and told me it's impossible to be in the middle of nowhere. Every place is home to someone, so you are always in the middle of somewhere. I had never thought of it that way, but then you were always saying things like that: stupidly profound or profoundly stupid—I could never figure out which. And after all that, you were the one who left and I'm still here.

Sometimes we'd sit on that bench for hours, talking about nothing much and blowing smoke rings into the air, and we'd see them teetering past, stumble-drunk after closing time with their brown paper bags and late-night vinegar running down their arms and the lack of kindness everywhere. And the girls, panda-eyed and lonely, hitching their bravado to their short skirts, were telling themselves that this was living. We said we would never be them. But there was one boy who had kind eyes. His hair was the color of the sand and his smile promised everything. I told you he wasn't like the rest, but you didn't want to hear it.

I have a little girl now. She stares out to sea the way you used to, and tells me the places she will go. I swore I wouldn't get stuck in this town. Even as my belly swelled and he sat with his arm around me, I was filling his ears with the places we would go when she arrived, the three of us. It was a beautiful song I was singing and I believed it too at the time. But this place is home. It is somewhere, and like you said, every place is home to someone.

I wonder if you can see the sea from where you are, and if it smells the same. They're entering the contest again this year. I see them out in their high-viz vests with their plastic bin bags and their brooms. Sometimes I think it's a terrible affliction to yearn for disorder and chaos amid all this cleanliness. I wonder how anyone can hope to leave a mark when everyone keeps tidying everything away. That spot on the bench that was home to our scrawled initials has long been painted over.

The boat is still there. I passed it the other day and I thought of you and I found myself laughing. I've traveled a bit since you left, not abroad, mostly to coastal towns that are much like this one—always to the edge but never past it. It's not just this place. Those boats are in every town: vessels manned by daffodils on a static voyage to nowhere. I would like to gather them in a fleet, then captain a pirate ship—the Gráinne Mhaol head on me—and lead them to where you are. We could sit together for a time and blow smoke rings and talk about nothing much in particular.

GRIEF

Joyce Roschinger

The connection between a casserole and the bereaved person is understandable. The casserole is brought by a woman who is a good cook or does not know how to cook but feels she must. She assumes that the bereaved person is too distraught to eat during her period of mourning, assumes that the bereaved person wants to eat during her period of mourning, that nothing has changed except that the bereaved person is bereaved. Numerous casseroles are brought to Ruth's home and left on her doorstep, in the hedges, and on the kitchen counter after her husband's funeral. There are numerous casseroles frozen and dated in Ruth's refrigerator: tuna, cheese, quinoa, and tofu.

The connection between a casserole and the bereaved person is understandable so Ruth makes a creamy tuna noodle casserole in the middle of the night. She ties the strings of her husband's apron around her waist and places all the ingredients side by side on the counter from left to right with enough space in between each ingredient so that she does not break the eggs, spill the garlic powder, drop the peas, and she skips the blending of all ingredients, and mixes, whips, fluffs the cream cheese, milk, garlic powder, noodles, tuna, peas, mushrooms in a bowl and spoons, and layers, and packs the whole thing into a casserole dish left behind by a neighbor or a friend or someone with no name and covers the casserole and bakes it for twenty minutes or thirty minutes, or sixty minutes or however long her period of mourning takes.

THE LEGACY

Desiree Rucker

The last time I saw you
I thought you needed new clothes
and that you stood very tall for an old man
no bend in your back, defiance still
in your eyes

I have always seen you
as a proud son of the south
with every right to claim Greenville, South Carolina
with pride
and every right to look back at Greenville, South Carolina
with rage
You were a seaman's son, a farmer's grandson, and a slave's great-grandson
you were a boy and a nigger and a coon,
and when you claimed your manhood and a bus ticket
to the north
you carried that legacy
like patches on a world traveler's suitcase

I picture you flailing in the spray of the hoses,
taunting the barking dogs,
bowing your head for the expected blow
But you were not there
You were with me in front of our black and white TV
and I felt safe because you were there with me

Was that fear I saw on your face
the September morning
I took the school bus to where
"Eyetalians"
as you called them lived?

The yellow bus full of black children
off to learn the white man words
tethered to a road of tears, tar, blood and feathers
You hugged me so tight that morning.

I saw your confusion when you drove me to college in Connecticut
It did look like a plantation,
and everyone was white
except me and my roommate
That look before you drove off that asked "You sure?"
that I waved off,
tearing up as your brown Olds pulled away.

At my graduation you stood proudly amid all them hundreds of white folks
Yeah you were right there with them,
and nobody calling us names, or getting a rope
You were watching your daughter,
waving her scroll,
proof she was smart and proof
she we you were equal are equal.

Last time I saw you, we passed the hours in the sunroom while you chattered
I distracted by my own reverie of regret and anger,
could not tell you
how I had lost sight of the North Star
How I had names for myself that tore at my flesh and left my heart bruised
You need some new clothes I thought.
When I waved good-bye, I noticed that you stood very tall for an old man
with no bend in your back and defiance still in your eyes.

PIECE OF MY HEART

Elliot Satsky

(From *North American Review*)

Admitting the truth about a relationship can be life saving. Even if the pain rips your guts it may not hurt as much if you let yourself experience it. I used to have a photo on the wall above the towel bar in my bathroom, opposite the toilet. I hung it there to look at while taking a shit, to remind myself at least twice a day of what happened between my ex-wife Emma and ex-best friend Adler. As if I could forget! I shot the photo on a nude beach in Anguilla when Emma and I were still a couple. Adler's wife, Judith, was off getting her hair braided or pissing in the ocean for all I know. The photo seems innocent, Emma and Adler naked from the waist up. A couple of months later they were screwing. Now, Emma calls the police if I come near her. If she said the word, any word, I'd take her back in a heartbeat.

The women I've dated since Emma share her librarian expression and bad girl bed manners. They love the flowers I send on Fridays, peonies when I can get them. They role-play in sexy lingerie and let me lick their breasts in public bathrooms. They respect my temper. They don't hide my glasses or bother me about my cough or tease me when I cross my leg driving. They stay over when I want, and don't mention the photo of Emma and Adler.

They never seem to last. I wouldn't kiss Elise when she cleaned her face with a bitter antibiotic solution. She stopped using it but her cheeks flared with acne. Robyn is a botanist. She took on the smell of decaying plants whenever discussing her age and marital status. Jan's Shih Tzu marked its territory by puking on my pillows. Maggie baked pastries with imported chocolate. I lost my taste for croissants when her reminder lists started looking like recipes, you know, mix two phone calls to the travel agent with one heaping withdrawal from Joel's bank. Jennifer is an Egyptologist. Her lips sealed tight as the Sphinx when we kissed. I don't know if she has a tongue. Sex was best with Carol, as if her plumbing had been custom designed for me. Her summer home is next to a pond full of mosquitoes. She insists on sleeping with the windows open. I bought a pair of toy poodles, a black boy and white girl. The male peed all over my carpets; the bitch chewed a slipper I had stolen from Emma. I gave them back to the breeder.

Is it me? I want someone to overlook my scheming, someone to love me, someone to put up with my throat clearing and inappropriate cursing, someone to bathe me, talk dirty to me, sear me with hot wax, dine alfresco along the water with her toes in my crotch. Emma never questioned our love until after Adler met her nipples on the beach. Shouldn't I have expected better from them? Emma took me to court and claimed I was obsessive. Her brief included phone records thick as an almanac and a valise filled with love notes I'd written on Post-its. I thought the evidence proved my love for her and showed how much I wanted my family back. The judge stripped me of phones with redial buttons and banned me from buying office supplies.

I showed up at her house July 4. We'd always seen the fireworks together. So what if she had a restraining order against me? She wasn't home when I got there, so I climbed the trellis and waited for her on the balcony outside her bedroom. We'd built the trellis together. She wrapped it with wild roses after marrying Adler. I didn't mind the thorns stuck in my hands. I felt so warm and good in the sunshine, waiting for her blonde bob and flowery sundress, remembering the raised bumps of a birthmark blushing like a fresh-picked strawberry above her vagina. She tried to hide it when we first became intimate, turning off the lights or covering it with a Band-Aid as if a shameful mole instead of a sacrament I came to worship.

*

SHE HAD ME ARRESTED July 4 for illegal entry. The judge agreed to suspend jail time if I attended ten consecutive meetings of a self-help group known as HAMMER. It met Tuesday evenings at PS 183 on East Sixty-Eighth Street. I wore a wife-beater and camouflage shorts to the first meeting. A removable henna tattoo of a bloody skull dwarfed my bicep. To hell with being short and ignored! A Hispanic guard gripped his gun when I entered the school. His left eye gave me the once-over. The right eye crossed and stared at a mop in front of a trophy case. He reeked of cleaning fluid. I wondered if he doubled as the late night janitor. I mentioned a study linking industrial strength Mr. Clean to severe eye problems. He shoved me to the wall and frisked me.

"Metal detector's out," he said, "you fit the profile."

I wondered which profile. "Is it the tattoo?" I asked.

His breath yellowed my shirt. I coughed, cleared my throat, and coughed again. He aggressively patted my groin. His nightstick pressed my buttocks. He called me his bitch. I said I wanted his mother. He said his mother was dead and squeezed my balls. I scanned for video cameras, tapes for evidence in a suit against Emma and Adler, the judge, the guard, the school board, the City, the Feds, *anyone*, for the emotional damage I had suffered.

"I'm here for the HAMMER meeting," I said.

"Figures," he replied, "stairs to the basement, second door on the right."

The door was marked by a crooked oaktag sign with "HAMMER — Husband Anger Management Mental Evaluation Review" spelled out in blue Sharpie bubble letters. Way to go, Your Honor, just what I needed to cleanse the sins you let Adler and Emma pin on me in court while letting theirs go unpunished! The room had the sour smell, curdled walls, and waxy ceiling of a milk carton well past its expiration date. A morbidly obese man sat on an old Parsons table surrounded by kiddy desks. Fat stretched the wrinkles out of his skin. I guessed he was fiftyish, a few years younger than me. He ambled in my direction with the slow gait of a heifer plumped up to show at a county fair, each leg of his khaki shorts big as a farm silo. His sweat-soaked thighs matched a stain on the table's worn wood surface; an oxcart full of hay would have made a better seat.

"You must be Joel," he said. I was expected! His nametag read "Bob, Moderator" in the same bubble letters as the door sign. He smiled and reached out his hand. I cursed myself for leaving home without Purell sanitizing wipes and offered a fist bump. He didn't appear offended.

"I don't belong here," I said. "I'm not angry." Lonely and miserable, yes, abused and misunderstood, yes, angry, no, Goddammit! I made small talk with a bartender before the meeting but the margaritas left me with a hangover. I'd taken my last Percocet and the doctor refused me a refill. Even my son had turned on me. He won't let me see my new granddaughter because I shoved him at the hospital the night she was born. Didn't the little prick know I'd react when he let Emma bring Adler into the maternity waiting room?

The three regulars in the group introduced themselves. Brad spoke with a twang. He met his wife at a rodeo in Madison Square Garden. He walked with a gimp and claimed he'd been thrown by a bronco. He wore earmuffs if his wife made requests, chased her with a cattle prod if she made demands. Rick was a chain-smoking welder who married his pulmonologist. He insisted panache, not anger, led him to blowtorch his wife's stethoscope after she tossed his Joe Camel lighter.

And there was Rita. Braless nipples stabbed at her sheer blouse and jolted me. She arranged flowers in Brooklyn and raced motorcycles in Watkins Glen. Curls from her platinum Mohawk spilled over the close-cropped sides of her head. Her hands were disturbingly thin, nails down to the fingertips. The tattoo of a bloody dagger on one forearm aimed at a smiling Buddha on the other. I imagined her serving me tea and stroking my belly then beating me senseless.

*

THE "I DON'T BELONG HERE" attitude I maintained for the first few weeks didn't seem to faze Bob. His smile never diminished, as if the meetings were the bright spot in his life. I wondered what life would be like as a three- or four-hundred pounder, if Bob's huge belly sagged over his penis, if women ridiculed him. The thought appalled me.

Things heated up the night Brad limped agitatedly around the room. He blamed his wife for his bad disposition, said his bum leg was killing him but all she cared about was a nail fungus that forced her to cancel a pedicure. "Bought me a bus ticket to Montana," he said, "goin' back to the ranch where I was thrown. Gonna kill me a bronco."

Rita charged Brad before he could free himself from his desk; when he stood, it wrapped around his thick waist like a four-legged saddle. "Dump the dialect," she said, "you're from Staten Island, for Christ sake." She pointed a stubby fingertip as if provoking a fight. "Hurt a horse and you'll answer to me." Rita had balls. I looked away and rubbed a few wrinkles out of my shirt.

Brad found his New York voice. "Shut up, bitch," he said, "you got no right to be here."

Bob threatened to sit on Brad's lap. He seemed to know a lot about Rita and protected her, in a fatherly way I thought at the time. He explained that Rita's judge, a same-sex marriage advocate, had ordered her to attend HAMMER meetings. Rita returned to her desk and spoke again, this time about Phyllis, a Manhattan endodontist she referred to as her "ex-wife."

"I went to her for an emergency root canal," she said of their first meeting. "She got me loaded on nitrous, pinched my cheek and romanced a syringe of novocaine into my jaw. She flashed her shiny little files like she was tuning my Harley, humming and painless. I felt like a songbird. Then she probed my mouth with her tongue and licked the tooth exposed in the oral dam. I unbuttoned her lab coat right there in the chair, the nitrous mask still over my nose, the tooth hollow and nerveless. My crown was ready the following week; we were together the next four years."

Rita's story touched and excited me. An erection growing below my belt pointed to my obsession with Emma and Adler's first sexual encounter and the troubling reality that I couldn't get hard without visualizing it. I pictured Emma and Adler's chance meeting at a car wash when Elise unbuttoned my button-fly jeans. I smelled Emma's perfume when Robyn pinched my nipples. I saw Emma step into Adler's car when Jan drove her tongue into my ear. Adler's hand floated over the gear box and under the hem of Emma's sundress when Jennifer reached into my boxers. Emma guided Adler's hand up her thigh when Maggie took me into her mouth. I heard Emma groan when I climaxed with Carol. And when I masturbated, I was a lonely junky grooving on an erotic fix of Emma and Adler until shame found me and I cried.

"I came home early from the flower shop one afternoon," Rita continued, "with a dozen pink peonies, a surprise for Phyllis. Found her in bed with Butch, lead rider of the Avengers, my biker club. She said his name attracted her. Her smell was on him. My nails were long and black back then. I went out of my head, scratched most of the skin from her face. Then I turned the sidewalk in front of our apartment into a giant emery board and took my nails down to the skin. I would have filed 'em to the knuckles if the goddamn cops hadn't stopped me!" You could feel Rita's spirit sparking in the tips of her fingers. She had brought me to the heart of things.

I stopped in the bathroom after the meeting. The door lock was busted and I worried the guard might walk in; I can't pee with a nightstick watching. The light switch didn't work but enough light seeped under the door for me to recognize familiar shapes. I leaned against the tile wall above the urinal. I dug my nails into a layer of crud covering the tiles and scraped the filthy skin off. I unhooked my belt. My jeans dropped to the floor. I wasn't wearing boxers. The drain may have been clogged. Piss splashed my sandals when I peed and when I flushed, the coolness of whatever flowed onto my feet felt so good I didn't care what it was or that it might soak my jeans.

*

A FLY WOKE ME THE NEXT MORNING. My snoring must have distracted it from the pissy sandals and damp jeans I'd dumped on my bedroom floor the night before. I tripped on an empty shipping carton on the way to the kitchen and landed on a mound of T-shirts returned by a surf shop in Montauk. I'd started a T-shirt business after Emma kicked me out. I bought an appliqué machine and one hundred gross blank T-shirts on eBay. The New York Widows and Orphans Society agreed to endorse the shirts for a percentage of the profits. I trademarked "Black Widow," a brand name I thought would be well received in minority communities. The designs were hourglass-shaped scenes of black widow spiders eating their male spouses. The tagline read, "Deep down in your heart you know it ain't right," homage to Janis Joplin's "Piece of My Heart." A *Daily News* editorial called the designs "racially targeted, misogynist and frightening," and demanded my indictment on hate crime charges. The New York Widows and Orphans Society claimed irreparable damage to their reputation. Pickets from PETA and the National Organization for Women hung my effigy from a gargoyle over the front door of my building. The Janis Joplin Estate threatened copyright infringement litigation. I sold seventeen shirts at full retail; fourteen thousand four hundred twenty-three shirts choked my apartment. Disaster relief agencies wouldn't even take them.

I needed to get away from all that cotton. All I could think of was Rita. I wanted to see her somewhere other than the basement of PS 183. I went looking for her, for the heat signature of her footprints, the shine of her motorcycle seat, the fog of her breath on the rearview mirror, a plant stem cut by her scissor. I pictured what she did during the day and followed the trail. I started at the Harley dealer in Long Island City and found something unexpected. It wasn't Rita. Each Sportster and Nightster, Street Bob and Low Rider, Fat Bob and Soft Tail, Road King and Electra Glide was saddled with the presence of Woody Hughes, a guy who worked a wire-twisting machine at my family's metal alloy business back in the seventies. I recalled his visit to our factory a few weeks after he'd been bounced from his motorcycle by a county highway pothole, and his reverence for the utility pole guide wire that severed his leg below the hip so cleanly he didn't feel a thing. He may have taken too many pain meds, but

Woody seemed genuinely proud the guide wire was made in our factory, maybe even on his own machine. The thought propelled me from the showroom.

Rita had mentioned living in Park Slope. I went there next and searched florists. Blooms on Fifth and Rootstock & Quade, Zuzu's Petals and Opalia Flowers, Jasmine's Floral Designs and Picazo Buds: lots of vases, no Rita. The same result in Prospect Heights and Carroll Gardens, RAMBO and DUMBO, Flatbush and Bushwick, at Passion Florist and Flowers by Florence, Shalom Florals and Tehran Tulips, Mother Earth's Miracles and Belle Fleur: lots of sidewalks, no Rita.

I wandered and wondered. I convinced myself Rita could be for me. So what if we had never actually spoken? So what if she was dangerously damaged, displayed a destructive temper and preferred vaginas to penises? She moved and excited me. I wanted to kiss the nubs of her fingers and make them safe from bad things. I wanted her to reach for me, caress me, help me feel new, help me feel good. I was sure she could love me. If only I had a Percocet refill to tide me over!

*

MS. JOPLIN OF AT&T called the morning of the next HAMMER meeting. She demanded payment of Emma's old cell phone bills. "Why call me?" I said, "I'm not responsible."

"It's clear you're not responsible," said Ms. Joplin, "but that doesn't mean Emma *Adler* should pay. *You* signed the credit application. The debt will be disclosed to the credit agencies unless *you* pay the bills immediately. *Your* ability to receive credit may be adversely affected."

How dare she use the name Joplin, how dare she hassle me at 6:35 AM over cell phone bills, how dare she twist my words and say I'm not responsible. I bristled at her emphasis on "You" and "Your" and was convinced her otherwise robotic voice turned absolutely giddy enunciating "Adler." She e-mailed copies of the unpaid statements while I held on. The months corresponded to the start of my suspicions about Emma and Adler. Most of the calls were to or from Adler. The sons of bitches expected me to pay for their love calls!

"Take another little piece of my heart," I said to Ms. Joplin. I hung up the phone and crossed over to the bathroom. I ripped the photo of Emma and Adler from the wall opposite the toilet and dropped it out the window. I watched it fall twenty-seven stories, to the awning of Lee's Wash & Fold, the place that cleans my dirty laundry. To my horror the picture appeared undamaged, rescued by the awning like a baby thrown from a burning building to an NYFD safety net. Mr. Lee recognized Emma's likeness and personally delivered the photo to me before 7:00 AM, complete with its cheap frame in mint condition and his grin of moral superiority. His wash-and-fold service should only be that good. His lips pursed when I shut the door; the bastard expected a reward! Can you imagine my impotence? How could I kill the memory of Emma and Adler if I couldn't kill their damn photo by dropping it from a skyscraper!

Excuse me Your Honor, excuse me Emma and Adler, excuse me Hispanic guard, Bob, Brad, Rick and Rita, my problem wasn't anger. I lived in cuckold hell. I'd do anything to stay connected to Emma, even if it meant thinking of her and Adler screwing, even if picturing them screwing was the only way I could get off with other women, even if my viewing position looked up at Adler's six feet two inches and size thirteen shoes, even if Adler laughed at my five feet six inches and size eights.

Something had to give. I switched from Froot Loops and Capt'n Crunch to oatmeal, brown sugar and raisins. I ditched mac and cheese casseroles for orange roughy and salad. I replaced the bloody skull tattoo with a jade pagoda surrounded by lotus blossoms. I dressed in a seersucker blazer, collared shirt and khakis, my boxers fresh and my sneakers clean. I wanted Rita's attention.

"How was everyone's week?" Bob asked to begin the meeting that night. I spoke up for the first time and gave my version of July 4. I wanted the group to know the court misinterpreted the facts. I wanted Rita to know I wasn't a lunatic crossing her path.

"I'm waiting for Emma on her bedroom balcony," I began. I left out climbing the trellis.

"Was it OK for you to be there?" Bob asked. He must have read the police report.

"He wants to know how much of what you say is bullshit," said Rick the welder.

"Like your blowtorch story?" I asked, careful to control myself. "I see Adler carry a food platter from his car. I lean over the railing and ask what he wants. He starts pacing and gets nasty."

"Did you expect a dinner invitation?" Rita asked. I hadn't expected her sarcasm. "You were breaking and entering," she said. "You wanted to jump his wife's bones. You provoked him."

"I was having fun. I told him Emma was in the shower, hinted we'd had sex. He lost it, smashed the platter against the front door, salmon all over the place. He saw my car in the driveway and dumped marinade over the seats. He ruined my sourball stash! He's the angry one, not me."

"You were cruel to him," said Brad. He'd been working on his soft side since the exchange with Rita over killing broncos. I liked him better as a short-fused brute.

"Then he drops his pants and pisses in my car," I continued. "Do I get mad? No, I cheer him on. I'm thinking, 'The jerk's killing himself. Too bad Emma's not here.' Then her car pulls up while he's holding his penis. I'm thinking, 'Perfect! She finally gets to see who this guy really is.'"

"Did you see who you really were?" asked Rita.

"What don't you get?" I asked. "The prick was my best friend. He stole my wife."

"Maybe your marriage sucked to begin with. Maybe you were a bad husband, as much to blame as them."

"Maybe you and Phyllis were on the rocks," I wanted to say. "Maybe you did to Phyllis's face what you wanted to do to yours. Maybe Emma and I are none of your business." I kept my mouth shut. Rita had finally spoken to me. I liked this side of her, the honest and feeling side.

I followed Rita up the stairs after the meeting but the guard cut me off. He said he admired the Black Widow T-shirt I'd worn the week before and asked where I'd bought it. I offered to bring him one but didn't admit to warehousing fourteen thousand four hundred twenty-three of them. By the time I exited PS 183, the only trace of Rita was the fading heat shimmer of her Harley's exhaust. I would have battled the specter of Woody Hughes for the opportunity to ride off with her.

I felt a new urgency. It wasn't about sex, jealousy or rage. I felt frenzied, certain I'd made the wrong impression on Rita, frantic I wouldn't make it through the night without straightening things out. I debriefed myself about the meeting. I hadn't behaved angrily. Rita had finally spoken to me. She pushed me to admit things I'd never considered; I took it as a sign she cared about me. I needed a plan but couldn't put one together in front of the school. Instead, I wondered which of the chewing gum remnants on the sidewalk had come from Rita's mouth and whether drops of oil where her Harley had been parked indicated engine trouble and whether she'd make it home safely without hitting a pothole.

*

I WANTED RITA'S ADDRESS or information to locate her and thought Bob might be a source. I sat on a shipping carton at my computer desk and went to HAMMER's website, husbandanger.com. I scrolled through "Locations and Schedules" to find my group. The moderator was identified as Bob Biggz. I searched whitepages.com for the Bob Biggz, Robert Biggz, B. Biggz or R. Biggz closest to my 10021 zip code. The only noncommercial listing in the five boroughs was on Ninth Street in Brooklyn, a street I remembered from my Park Slope florist excursion. If the Brooklyn listing was for *my* Bob, it meant he and Rita lived in the same neighborhood. I left immediately, drawn to 215 Ninth Street without knowing where it would lead.

What I knew about Bob's connection to HAMMER came out the night of my first meeting. He'd been goaded by Ben, a Hasidic militant who later quit the group for fear of assassination by the guard, who, Ben believed, was Palestinian, not Hispanic. Ben incessantly bitched about size of the kiddy desks, size of the toilets, and absence of kosher products in the vending machines. Bob tried to quiet him by relating his own story about HAMMER and its benefits.

"I weighed 229 when I met my girlfriend Janine, 347 when she left me. The angrier I got, the more I ate; the more I ate, the angrier I got; the fatter I got, the sicker my thoughts. She threatened to start buying low fat ice cream. Instead of thanking her, I brought the argument to bed with us. When she fell asleep her nasal whistle kicked in and I rolled on top of her, not for sex, to smother her. Neighbors intervened and I passed it off as 'sleep-rolling.' The court ordered me to HAMMER meetings." Bob eventually became a moderator, the title given to counselors without master's degrees.

I got to Ninth Street at 9:30 PM I pictured Bob living in a full-service building with elevators and hallways large enough for his bulk. Such was not the case at 215, a two-story row house with a single, standard-sized front door. Nothing bloated the block, each home's gable roof, red brick walls and large windows duplicated the ones next door. Twelve-step stoops rose from clean slate sidewalks. The neighborhood was everything family, not what I expected for Bob. I was convinced some other R. Biggz lived there, perhaps Roberta or Ronald, Rachel or Ricardo.

I gazed at 215's entrance and second story from the sidewalk. Light shined through each first-floor window and one of three on the second floor. The twelve steps looked as steep as Mount Everest, a terraced slope of nerves, expectations and fear of disappointment that froze me. I felt childish, as if unable to stop myself from doing something I thought I shouldn't do without understanding why I shouldn't do it. Silly innocence took over and I recited, "She loves me, she loves me not," as I climbed each tread to the top. I peeked through the full-length window alongside the front door and saw Bob in a white T-shirt and massive plaid boxers. He may have been on his way to the kitchen. He wasn't expecting company. I rang the bell anyway.

Rita opened the door. Bob's bulk had hidden her; it could have hidden a squad of Ritas.

She shook her head. "Joel? Are you OK?"

The reindeer and red-cheeked Santas prancing on Rita's pajamas didn't seem to care it was only September. Long sleeves covered her tattoos, hands exposed and steady, Mohawk relaxed, hair flowing over her ears. Her beauty had become simpler, no longer the mirage I created to distance myself from Emma. The allure had vanished. I wore a look of surprise but mostly felt relief. She was Bob's and wouldn't be mine. If they found love, couldn't I?

I floated peacefully in a clear stream of honesty, sensing the current and flowing with it. I thought of Mr. Lee's awning and the rescue of Emma and Adler's photo. Would the awning have broken my fall? You can't see me in the photo but I'm embedded there, as much a part of it as Emma and Adler, an unchangeable scene blinding me to the stuff orbiting my present. I scammed myself by hanging the photo in the bathroom. Viewing it twice a day made the past my here, now and future. Rita's shattered pieces mirrored my vulnerability. I didn't see her putting the pieces back together, very big and very fat pieces it turned out. I had made Rita into a fiction, a story fitting what I wanted: an end to pain, an end to being alone, an end I wouldn't find in an old photo.

"I came here to see Bob," I said, "to ask him about you."

"Cup of coffee?" Bob asked.

A Lesson in Colors, Parts 1 & 2

Rosalia Scalia

There was a fourteen-year-old Black Boy. There was a twenty-one-year-old White Woman. There was a Whistle. There were two White Men. There was a Crow named Jim. There was Kidnapping. There was a seventy-five-pound Cotton Gin Fan. There was a Lesson in Colors, meaning that there were two White Men who thought they'd teach the Black Boy about a Lesson in Colors in Money, Mississippi. There was a Shed. There were Cries in the Shed over a Lesson in Colors, meaning the Black Boy who Whistled, who probably never, ever kissed any girl, who called for his mama, learned a hard Lesson in Colors. You just learned how to Whistle to call your dog Champ, but you don't want to call Champ anymore because the Crow might come instead.

There was Blue. There were Black and Blue. There was Purple mixed with Red. There was Number 45 stuck inside a shiny Silver pistol. There was that Crow who helped a fast-flying Bullet go into a tender head. A few days later, there was the Pop of the Bullet exploding in the North, in Chicago, where they learned that a Lesson in Colors in Mississippi includes topics like a Beating, a Lynching, a Shooting, a Killing, and a Sinking with a seventy-five-pound Cotton Gin Fan.

The talking White Man on TV said there was Emmett Till at the bottom of the Tallahatchie River, but your Black Father picked you up and held you in his arms when he yelled at the White TV Man about a damned rainbow puddled around Emmett Till, the Boy who Whistled. There were Blood Red, Purple, and Yellow Bruised Arms of the fourteen-year-old Black Boy in the Blue waters under a baking Yellow sun in the Azure sky in Green Money, Mississippi, where horseflies with iridescent wings and the Crow named Jim buzzed like electricity. There was the Pain. There was the Crow that caused the Pain that leaked out of the Black Boy but made him bigger and larger than before and oozed into his Chicago mama and into your Baltimore mama, who held you so tight you couldn't breathe and sang into your eight-year-old Black Boy ears Precious-Lord-Take-My-Hand, begging for the same Lord to keep you in the palm of His. There was Fear in your mama that leaked into you, wondering what if you fall out of the giant, invisible palm of His Hand or if it drops you like it dropped the Whistling Boy in Money, Mississippi.

There was a Lesson in Colors at school where Sister Ursula caught Darlene Parklee's big sister in the rear of the cloakroom, sitting on the stomach of a different fourteen-year-old Black Boy, her Yellow hair falling over them while she tried to smear her Pink Lips all over his Brown ones, as he yelled Stop It! and Get Off of Me! You wanted to stay home to avoid the Crow coming to teach you about colors at your school after you learned how to Whistle and after Darlene Parklee's big sister got sent home. The Chicago mama wanted everyone to learn about that Lesson in Colors taught by the Crow and two White Men in Money, Mississippi, but just like at school, no one paid attention for long.

Alcolu, South Carolina, and the Search for Purple Passionflowers: A Lesson in Colors, Part 2

THERE WAS A DITCH on the Black Side of town. There was Murder. There were two White Girls, ages eleven and eight, searching for Purple Passionflowers, which they called "maypops," before they went missing overnight in Alcolu, South Carolina. There was one fourteen-year-old, ninety-pound Black Boy. There was a Crow named Jim. There were Horseflies following the Crow, their iridescent wings buzzing with electricity. There was an Invisible Line in the center of the Gray railroad tracks that kept Black People on one side and White People on the other. There was an absence of Red, no blood in the muddy Ditch where the two missing White Girls who'd been searching for Purple Passionflowers now lay dead with bashed-in heads on the wrong side of town.

There were three White Deputies, including the Arresting Deputy, who said the fourteen-year-old, ninety-pound Black Boy named George Junius Stinney Jr. confessed to killing the two White Girls. There was no mention of a Beating that brought the confession or the Black and Blue, Purple and Yellow, a Rainbow of Colors on the fourteen-year-old, ninety-pound Black Boy's body that accompanied the confession. There was Stinney's sister Aime, who'd been playing with George at the time the two White Girls searched for Purple passionflowers on the Black side of town. There was Cold White Disbelief when little Aime said she and her brother spent the day in their father's meadow watching their Brown horse. There was the White Arresting Deputy who collected the fourteen-year-old, ninety-pound Black Boy at his house to arrest him when his parents weren't home. There was little Aime hiding in the barn when her brother was taken away without their parents being home, puzzling about a confession that couldn't be true when she knew the Truth.

There were eighty-one long days when this fourteen-year-old, ninety-pound Black Boy sat confined in a jail fifty miles away from his family, the first time he'd been away from home, away from his mama, away from his daddy. There were Gray walls and Black bars in the jail cell that felt like forever, despite the candy bar and Bible the Arresting Deputy brought him. There was a River of Tears at the Stinney home and at the jail where the fourteen-year-old Black Boy was given Black-and-White-striped clothes to wear. There were Gold letters on that Black cover and Gold-edged pages on that Black Bible he held with trembling hands, the thick book almost as big as his torso, his thin, short arms hugging it like a fairy tale. There were No Visitors allowed. No mama or daddy. No brothers or sisters. No aunties or uncles. No grandparents. No friends.

There was Fear. There was Terror. There was the Stinney family run out of town, out of Alcolu, away from their farm, away from daddy's job, which fired him. There was no lawyer present when the White Arresting Deputy said the fourteen-year-old, ninety-pound Black Boy named George Stinney confessed. There was no talk of the Rainbow of Colors that accompanied the confession. There was no White paper with Black Ink signed by the fourteen-year-old, ninety-pound Black Boy with Blue and Black, Purple and Yellow under his Zebra-striped clothes that accompanied a Confession.

At the same time the fourteen-year-old, ninety-pound Black Boy sat quivering in a jail cell in South Carolina, missing his mama, longing for the safety of the arms of his daddy, clutching his Black Bible with Gold-edged pages, there was your big brother Clarence arrested in Baltimore for protesting police brutality when he and other Black Teachers rallied in the streets to be represented on the School Board. There was your Baltimore mama crying in the kitchen, wringing her hands, clutching her own Green-Covered Bible to her heart, afraid her oldest child with his Silver wire-rimmed glasses, soft voice, and head full of idealistic notions would end up dead in the Baltimore City Jail, despite his hard-earned Beige University Sheepskin.

There was the Trial of the fourteen-year-old, ninety-pound Black Boy in South Carolina that lasted two and a half hours, including the minutes it took to select the All-White Jury because Black People were not allowed. There was a White Judge. There was a White Prosecutor. There was a White Defense Attorney who specialized in taxes and dreamed about political ambitions and his desire for votes. There were more than a thousand White Attendees in the court-room — Potential Voters — wanting revenge for two Dead White Girls. There was no Cross-Examination. There were Three Versions of the fourteen-year-old, ninety-pound Black Boy's confession, none on paper. There was no Evidence. There was no Request for evidence. There were just the White Deputies and the White Words falling out of their Pink Lips. There was no Transcript.

There were Ten Hours that Uncle Clarence and Baltimore's other Black Teachers sat in the Baltimore jail without being charged with any crime before they were released. There were Ten Minutes for the All-White Jury to convict the fourteen-year-old, ninety-pound Black Boy of killing two White Girls. There was the White Judge who pronounced the Sentence: Death by Electrocution. There was no Appeal. There were letters sent by citizens across South Caro-lina to the Governor, pleading for Mercy, pleading to Halt the Execution of the fourteen-year-old, ninety-pound boy, letters that were ignored.

There were Eighty-Three days from the moment the White Deputy collected the fourteen-year-old, ninety-pound Black Boy named George Stinney to the moment he was thrust into the arms of Ol' Sparky, the White People's name for the Red electric chair with Brown Straps. There was June 16, 1944, at 7:30 PM when the five-foot, one-inch, fourteen-year-old, ninety-pound Black Boy, too small for the man-sized chair, was forced to sit on his Gold-rimmed Black Bible as a booster seat because he otherwise couldn't be secured to the chair for being too small, making it clear that Ol' Sparky didn't want him. There was the state's Too-Big Man-Sized Mask that did not fit the fourteen-year-old, nine-ty-pound Black Boy's face. There were the Boy's Trembling Hands. There was Terror. There was Fear. There was No Mercy. There was the First Jolt, a 2,400-volt electrical surge that failed to kill the fourteen-year-old, ninety-pound Black Boy, but it knocked the Too-Big Mask off his face, showing everyone watching his tearful eyes, filled with questions, his frightened Child's Face, his Pink Tongue drooping out of his Red Mouth, his Brown Lips dripping saliva. There were Two More Jolts and the Four Long Minutes it took to teach George Junius Spinney Jr., a fourteen-year-old, ninety-pound Black Boy, a Lesson in Colors.

There was a Lesson in Colors at Clarence's job, where he was fired for being arrested, the White School Superintendent saying Clarence would be a bad influence on his ninth-grade Black Students at a school where the superintendent never visited. There was Clarence's Last Day, the same day the newspaper came carrying the headline about the nation's youngest murderer electrocuted in South Carolina, complete with a photo of the fourteen-year-old, ninety-pound Black Boy. Your mama sucked air, squeezed your fourteen-year-old Black Boy body into hers, her sweet perfume invading your nostrils, her tears falling into your Black Boy ears as she cried, "Please, Lord, please, Lord Jesus, tell me it ain't so." Clarence, proud of his University teaching degree that filled his head with notions of how things ought to be, punched the kitchen table with his fists, the table vibrating, until your daddy held him still. There was the Flap of Jim the Crow's Wings, nearly imperceptible, but enough to hear them beating the air around us.

The Red Bird

J.D. Serling

(From *New Ohio Review*)

We resigned to our bosses. Said farewell to our colleagues. Tried to explain exactly why we were leaving. The baby. Our workload. Our priorities changing. All of it some cliché of an answer that had nothing to do with anything. We felt thrilled. We felt pressured. We felt scared. But we were leaving. We stared at the slender remains of all those years working. Award certificates. Power Point presentations. The funny cartoons we'd cut out of old magazines. And we tried not to feel embarrassed by the looks certain colleagues shot us. The committed ones. The childless ones. The working moms who judged us. We pushed through the revolving doors, through the security booths and subway turnstiles, eyes wide, teeth clenched—terrified, relieved, anxious, confident, clueless—and woke up in a house in New Jersey, separated by a river, separated by a stratosphere, separated from our old selves by a time and place and expectation that stunned us. Motherhood. It overtook us.

FALL

WE ATE ALONE AT THE BAGEL HUTCH, alone at the deli, alone at the Target, surrounded by yellow popcorn we gulped by the handful. Not alone. Never alone. Never without our baby. Our baby. Growing, sprouting, molting into an almost toddler. We had Thomas. We had Sonia. We had Lucas. We had Clarissa and baby Jakey. We told ourselves we were happy. We told ourselves we'd done the right thing. We told ourselves it was okay to eat popcorn in the Target staring at the parking lot, surrounded by abandoned shopping carts, surrounded by other mothers.

Other mothers! They were nothing like us. Other mothers were weird, gooberish, cloying, annoying. They spoke, always and forever, in that singsongy voice to their kids. *I'm tying your shoes now; we're going to the bank now.* Where were the women we used to know, the ones with jobs and energy and verve? We stared at the other mothers from behind veiled eyes, from behind plastic soup spoons and stroller hoods. We stared and considered and were afraid we saw ourselves reflected back in their bored and vacant eyes.

*

AND THEN. AND THEN. . . .

We met. At the Bagel Hutch. At the swimming pool. At the music class where the teacher was nuts and we secretly whispered about her. We were funny. We were smart. We knew things and had a good education. We talked about careers and vacations and of course, old boyfriends and old neighborhoods. We talked and we laughed and we felt ourselves lifted — into something different, into something familiar, into something that carried us away from this strange holding pattern. And so we jumped right in. Best friendship! Saved.

*

TUESDAYS. PLAYGROUP DAY. We all loved Tuesdays. We wore makeup for Tuesdays, our favorite shoes that cost too much and weren't as comfortable as we thought they should be. We stood by the playground equipment, coffees in hand, pretending to watch our particular kid, half watching, listening at best, talking about nothing, competing for everything: popularity, status, best dressed, best mother, calmest voice, best-packed snacks, something, anything to ensure we'd fit in, be admired.

"Jamaican dirty water," Lorraine was shouting to us from the top of the slide, where she was forcing Jakey down it. "They sell it at the old-fashioned drugstore over on Main. It calms gas — and I don't know what else."

We all laughed. "What else" was what ailed us. What made us desperate to give the kids back. They were adorable with their eyes closed, the lids heavy with sleep, but the minute you thought you liked this job, liked this constantly being with them, they let out a wail or flung themselves on the ground and you couldn't for the life of you figure out how to make them stop.

"I think it's all chemicals," protested Wallis. She knew about these things—medicines and crèmes—even if it was just bits and pieces cobbled together from the *New York Times* Science section.

Lorraine didn't like this. Being questioned. Being criticized! She glowered at Wallis. Wallis pretended not to notice. We all pretended not to notice. It was important to maintain the easy camaraderie and false intimacy that none of us had earned and all of us craved so deeply. Lorraine bent down to sniff Jakey's diaper.

Wallis wanted to know, Did we or did we not like Katie Couric?

"I never put on the TV in front of Sonia," Deanne answered in her superior, college professor voice, the one she reserved for all things related to child-rearing. Our children, their dimpled legs tottering, were pushing each other down a giant woodchip pile that had been dumped in the middle of the playground. We stared at them. We shouted words of caution. But mainly we ignored them, eager to submit our qualifications for best friendship.

"It's so annoying," Jeanne whined. "Jason watches it all the time!" Then she giggled and covered her mouth with her hair, in case we didn't agree, in case our husbands were more perfect.

We agreed. We agreed. We hated that! We hated TV! But we secretly watched it all of the time, from morning till night, for company, for connection, for belief that even if the outside world had forgotten us, we hadn't forgotten it—its drumbeat and intonation, its riots and upheavals, the stock prices and mergers, the announcements and sudden conflagrations.

"I never even knew who Katie Couric was before kids!" shouted Mindy from the swing set, revealing her green plaid underwear as she bent down to pick up a snack bag. "But now that I've seen her, I have to admit, she is sort of fabulous."

She said this like she was cute. She said this like she was original. As if we all hadn't seen Katie's thousand-watt smile a million times before. As if we didn't all wait for Katie's appearance on TV to signal the awakening of the rest of the world! Before Katie, it was Teletubbies and Barney, the windowpanes glossy with lamplight, the world behind still swollen with darkness.

"My brother says Katie appeals to housewives." Wallis grinned, revealing her giant, too pink gums. She'd been waiting for this moment, to guilt us, to make us all see what we'd become. We cringed. We were self-righteous. Why were we housewives just because we weren't in offices?

"Who cares about Katie Couric?" Bethany asked, her voice flat, her tone judgmental. Oh how we hated Bethany. The way she'd pushed her way into our playgroup. Her low energy. Her poor parenting! Even now her daughter Clarissa was banging her head against the wire fence, Bethany shrugging, Bethany too exhausted to do anything about it.

"Is Clarissa okay?" Lorraine asked, rejoining us, pointing, hoping Bethany would take the hint, go away, do something about it. Bethany shrugged. Bethany wasn't moving. Bethany was a fortress of forced friendship. "Why are you talking about Katie Couric anyway?" she wanted to know.

We all ignored her. We always ignored her.

Deanne said: "I'm proud to be home full time. I don't care what you call it."

Of course we were proud! Of course we were pleased! Of course we thought motherhood more important than anything. Didn't we? Did we?

"I like *The View*," Jeanne giggled, playing with her hair in front of her face.

"*The View*!" we all echoed, incredulous, relieved, embarrassed by our shared and guilty secret. Joy Behar. Barbara Walters. The celebrity guests. All of them smart and well dressed, and right there in our living room, willing to spend time with us. It was different when we didn't have to watch. When we could interact with live people in offices who had jokes to tell and smiles to greet us. But alone in our kitchens, alone in our family rooms, alone with our wobbling children, we needed Joy and Barbara to care about us, to remember us, even if we knew it was an illusion, even if our approval ratings could never mean as much to them as they did to us, even if we felt pathetic.

WINTER

WE CALLED EACH OTHER on Wednesdays. We called each other on Thursdays. We called each other every day and every night and sometimes just for five minutes, to ask a question, to hang up, to call back again an hour later. Was it okay to have a birthday party without entertainment? Did we have to put out bagels if everyone was coming over at 10:30? Did anyone have a Saturday night babysitter we could borrow? A black clutch? The name of a decent hair colorist? And what should we do with all those old work clothes hanging in the backs of our closets? We said, *give them away*. We said, *keep them*. We said, *give them away and buy new ones if you ever go back!*

Going back? We couldn't imagine it. Not yet. We had only just arrived at this new destination, delivered from loneliness and uncertainty to the land of hang out and forever talking opportunity. Together we roamed the aisles of the giant big-box stores, staring. Cotton blue camisoles for $9.99. Cases of Pellegrino for under twenty bucks! Giant piles of bad DVDs. Exotic plants. Pretty towels and bathroom rugs. All of it beckoning to us, luring us in, promising us something we could only barely remember. Free time. A home. The chance to just stare and imagine. And then, the swarm of it as we unloaded the stuff from our trunks to our houses: New pillowcases. Down comforters. Wastebaskets. Hampers. And of course, sofa covers and trays for serving things down in the basement.

The basements. That below-ground place to which we'd been relegated. In the basement, the kids threw blocks at each other, chewed books, sucked on batteries. In the basement, the children were fine for five minutes, maybe ten, till they swarmed us again, whining, agitating, asking for more. More cheese sticks. Another juice box. Lunch even though it was only eleven o'clock. At times like these we would try to keep talking, one person's jaw moving fast, hurrying, with spittle near the corner of her mouth while stretching to reach for the snack that had rolled under the couch. *Is it too dirty to offer?* we'd ask. And in between bites of mini muffins and sliced apple snacks we'd say, *yes*, we'd say, *no*, we'd say, *I haven't finished telling you my story yet!*

It was always like this. Sometimes stories would take whole weeks to finish. Sometimes you left the wrong impression, like when Jeanne implied she didn't like her mother-in-law, who was dying. "It's not that I don't like her," she explained now, nearly two weeks later. "It's that I don't think she gave Charlie a very good childhood."

We told her we didn't remember. We told her not to worry. We told her dying had nothing to do with liking. But we were worried. What if we were doing the thing that Jeanne claimed she didn't accuse her mother-in-law of doing? What if we were failing?

"My mother meditates three hours a day," Wallis was saying apropos of nothing. Or maybe it was directly related to this thing?

"My mom couldn't go anywhere alone," Lorraine half shouted, always eager to be the loudest in any conversation, as if this could insure her authority, her popularity among us. "She did every single thing, and I mean *everything*, with her sister. Then her sister died and she couldn't go to the grocery store without me! It was ridiculous."

Was this the same Lorraine who was forever calling us up during the afternoon nap, obsessively making plans, afraid of being left out? We ourselves had been invited to go grocery shopping with her many a time, and, despite thinking it weird, had gone along with it, for the novelty, just to see how it would feel. Now it creeped us out. The psychology of it. Lorraine's failure to see it!

"I wish I had a sister," Bethany said, angrily, accusing us.

"I'm nothing like my mother," Deanne pointed out.

Of course she wasn't. Of course we weren't. We were stylish. We wore faded jeans. Graphic T-shirts. But alone in our kitchens, alone in our bedrooms, alone with our voices and bodies and identical personalities, we knew differently. We knew we were exactly like them! We had veined hands, shrill voices, a growing muffin top and no patience for our husbands! How had this happened? We couldn't let this happen!

"My parents are both dead," Bethany announced, her eyes dead, her eyes robotic. "They died when I was eleven."

We looked down. We looked away from her. Had she seen us hating our mothers, feeling sorry for ourselves? We made small clucking and sorry noises. We said, *oh, how terrible.* We felt badly for Bethany. But we mainly we wanted to get away from her. In case we were tempted to compete with her—in martyrdom, in victimhood—or worse, to bathe in the jellied malaise that she was spreading all over us.

Spring

TIME COLLAPSED ON US. Time was an accordion. It was warm and our children could run freely, their bodies swinging from monkey bars, their legs wrapped around twirling poles. Our life in the sunshine was like a reawakening, a rebirth to the seasons, to the daytime and the movements of shadow and light. Had we really spent all those years working? Inside conference rooms and offices? It was marvelous. It was freeing. We were so grateful for our new lives!

And yet. In the spring, when the birds were beginning to chirp and buds were starting to bloom in our gardens, the ones we'd supervised or planted or inherited from previous owners, we felt it still, that old familiar longing, that lost limb we couldn't help but remember having: our youth, our ambition, our feelings that we were going to take a great, big, giant bite out of something, stamp ourselves on the world.

"I never felt that," Bethany said, rolling her eyes at whatever it was Mindy had been saying. About work. About yearning. We were in the café with the chipped blue china cups and the ugly mismatched couches. It was raining. Our kids loved the beat-up toys for about twenty minutes, long enough to have a real conversation, long enough to know things about each other that we'd been trying to forget. Like that Bethany hated Mindy now. Or that Mindy disliked Lorraine. Or that Lorraine now liked Bethany but was mean to the rest of us. All of this for reasons we couldn't quite fathom, tried not to imagine, didn't want to get drawn into and latched on to, the way we had for the rest of the winter

"Now is when your kids need you more," Deanne said to Mindy. She was eating the crust of her scone. The rest of us were picking at the inside. This way we were all still on our diet and no one felt guilty.

"I'm not saying I want to go back to work," Mindy protested, sweeping her hair off her face, blushing, then leaning forward to accidentally reveal her thong beneath her too low jeans. She was always revealing it. "I'm just saying, is this all there is? Twenty years of driving carpool and setting up playdates?"

"I want to start having lunch with people," Bethany offered. "This summer. When the kids are at mini-camp."

We cringed. We pretended not to hear her. Mini-camp was supposed to be our alone time. The hours when we turned back into our real selves.

"I'm joining a gym." Deanne laughed, pushing the scone away from her. We stared at the crumbled remains, willing ourselves not to reach out and eat it.

Wallis looked down at her orange loafers, not smiling, not happy. We all knew she was trying. For a second. And failing. And her failing made us nervous and guilty and angry. We wished she could be happy with what God had given her!

"I'm going to send out an e-mail to everyone," Bethany continued, undeterred by our ignoring her. "To suggest dates for lunches."

We nodded. We shifted and acted noncommittal. But when the e-mails came, we knew that we'd go. To say no would be dangerous. To say no would upset the carefully laid balance of our pretend friendship arrangement. But oh, why couldn't pretending be enough for her? Why couldn't it be enough for us?

SUMMER

WE WENT ON TUESDAYS. We went on Thursdays. We went reluctantly and only after canceling and rescheduling. Never together. Never as a group. Alone. That's how Bethany wanted us. She was testing us, interviewing us, hoping we'd jump in. Be her one best friend. We didn't want this. We did want this! But not with her. We wanted someone with energy, enthusiasm. Ideas!

She hated work, she confided. So dull. Boring. She never felt a passion for it. She was passionless! There! She'd said it. There was nothing we could do about it. And yet, when she described it, her loneliness, her at-sea-ness, we knew just what she meant, that feeling of being lost, of hoping to be found. And we couldn't let her see this. Couldn't let her latch on to us, pull us down into the endless, needy, lost abyss that was her!

*

MINDY TOOK HER SHOPPING. Shopping! To Loehmann's.

"She needed a dress for a wedding," Mindy told us at Mexican lunch. Bethany was home waiting for a plumber. The strange balloon man was at our table paying too much attention to our kids.

"I must have picked out fourteen different outfits!" Mindy said, exasperated, her bangs bouncing around her face in perfect, symmetrical alignment.

Why? we all shouted.

"Because I thought it would be weirdly fun," Mindy said and shrugged. "She always spends too much at Neiman's and then it looks bad anyway."

"She likes to do that!" insisted Deanne, petulant, angry, as if Mindy had broken the rules that Deanne had set for her, for all of us. About ignoring Bethany. About mothers not shopping.

"I see that now," admitted Mindy, playing with her hair, fluffing it up for us. *You do?* we shouted.

She did.

What happened after the fourteen outfits? we asked.

Mindy told us. About how Bethany didn't even try to like anything. How she seemed uninterested, and by the end, as if it was *she* who was doing *Mindy* the favor.

"Some stuff honestly looked good on her," Mindy complained, incredulous. "It's like she was planning on buying something lousy at Neiman's all along!"

Poor Mindy. She was so deflated. That she couldn't even share a spark of Loehmann's magic with Bethany. As if changing Bethany could have reassured her. Could have convinced her that clothes really were that important. With every season, Mindy herself had become better dressed, more fashionable. Wedge heels when everyone else wore Keds or flip-flops. Expensive purses. Designer swimsuits. As if she expected that with the right shoes and handbag and body, she was suddenly going to be bigger, more worthwhile, more special. Oh how we teased her. How we sniped behind her back. But we secretly envied her. Her style. Her boldness! Her belief that she could be noticed, that she could be more than just a mother.

Fall

"I'm going to take creative writing classes," Mindy announced on a Thursday. We were at the Great Swamp, taking a "spontaneous nature walk." Our preschools encouraged this. They believed it made us good parents. We hated the mud and the effort, but we did it anyway, if nothing else so that we could brag about it to the other mothers who refused to do it.

"Why writing?" asked Lorraine, eager as always to have the first and final word on everything.

"I used to be a writer you know," said Mindy, and we all stopped for a minute, embarrassed, angry, confused. A writer? Was that what she was claiming to be? Some sort of intellectual who didn't live in suburban New Jersey, didn't shop at Target, didn't worry about how much to tip the babysitter?

"In the very beginning of my career," she explained, blushing despite the cool air, looking down and away from us.

"You never told us that," Deanne said, nodding imperiously, as if it were impossible that she hadn't known everything, about Mindy, about all of us.

"I was a magazine writer," Mindy said. "I actually wrote a sex column. And horoscopes, if you can believe it."

"I always knew those things were made up!" shouted Lorraine.

"Were you actually published?" demanded Deanne.

"Yes and yes," Mindy said, skipping along now with faux joie de vivre, pointing out how far the children had progressed without us, trying to change the subject.

"Where were you published?" asked Deanne, struggling to sound careless in her questioning, as if it wasn't all that mattered to her now.

"A magazine that folded. You probably never heard of it," Mindy said, still walking ahead.

Deanne didn't press. We let it go. A no-name magazine didn't bother us.

We walked on, the dense brush all around us now, forcing us to concentrate, to steer clear of the broken branches, the odd piles of leaves and muck. Ahead of us, the children were doing as they'd been told by the welcome center lady, tiptoeing quietly like little squirrels, their hands curled like paws in front of them. We struggled en masse to keep up with them, thinning to single file when the trail became a planked walkway leading through the dense forest. We were silent, only our rubber-soled shoes squeaking and clonking. And then all at once, we were out of the trees, high up on a deck, out in the open. The Great Swamp. Still water. Blue sky. The birds and frogs calling to one another in their strange, asynchronous chorus. It was fantastic. It was surprising. The greenery. The otherness. The fact that we were still in New Jersey!

Our children were squealing, anxious to see over the high wooden railing that blocked their view. We lifted and pointed, squinted and explained until they begged to be lowered and left to their own imaginings. The welcome center lady had given us a gray-white Xerox with pictures and descriptions of indigenous birds. We'd taken it to be polite, to burnish our image that we were nature-loving, good mothers. But now, with nothing else to preoccupy us, we felt compelled to look upward, to search the dense canopy of trees leaves for those tiny chirruping creatures. We felt their presence all around us, in tree-tops and in shady groves, but with or without the bird sheet, were completely unprepared to identify them, to suddenly penetrate this strange and mysterious world. It was beyond us. It was not important to us. And yet we scanned and scanned, feeling like biddies, feeling like adventurers, prepared to discover the impossible, to suddenly see something wonderful and know what to say about it.

"We should have brought binoculars," Wallis said, sighing.

"If we were going to be serious, which we are not," Deanne said, laughing.

We agreed. We disagreed. Why weren't we serious? Who said we couldn't be?

"Birds are stupid," Bethany informed us, her whole body slumping.

"They poop all over the place!" Lorraine screamed in agreement.

We thought this was gross. We thought this was true. But why did everything have to come back to the house or the kids or cleaning up from pets!

"Shh," said Wallis. "You'll scare away all the good birds!"

"I think the kids are bored," insisted Bethany, filling her plump cheeks with air and blowing them out again.

"Will you be a professor? Deanne asked Mindy, as if they'd been in one, single conversation since leaving the woods.

"What? Me? No. I mean, maybe," Mindy said, still scanning the treetops.

"Well, if you're not going to teach, what is it, a hobby?" Lorraine pressed, rolling the word "hobby" around on her tongue like some strange and dusty memory. We thought of Girl Scout badges and comic book collections, of wacky packs and miniature doll sets. Was that what we had been reduced to now? Hobbies? Was that what Mindy was going to admit to wanting?

Mindy continued scanning, her face turned toward the sunlight. And then, amid the chirruping, thumping dialog of birds and frogs and children, Mindy said, "I want to write. I told you, I want to be a writer."

"You should try writing children's books," Jeanne suggested, giggling in case someone thought this was dumb. We did think it was dumb. To be so uninspired. To be so predictable! But we thought maybe it was a good idea. To aim lower. To save yourself from having to explain to everyone when you couldn't do the thing you'd set out to. Why you'd failed.

Mindy sighed, her neck arched all the way back. And then, pointing toward a speck of red in the sunlit treetop, she said: "Look, right there, I see something cool!"

We squinted. We arched. We moved back and forth from shade to sunlight, trying to get a better look at it. Wallis consulted her sheet. Lorraine let out an aggravated sigh.

"It's either a really rare American redstart," said Wallis, frowning in concentration, turning the bird paper sideways and back to study it, "or just a robin."

"It's just a stupid robin!" shouted Lorraine, and we saw the bird's brilliant red wings lifting up, taking the bird away from us.

The sun went behind a cloud. The children started to bicker. We said it probably wasn't the rare thing, the special bird. But still, we planned to come back and try to see it again. Another day. Not with each other, but by ourselves, when we could imagine what we chose to believe about the bird, about ourselves.

Astronauts

Christopher X. Shade

(From *Steel Toe Review*)

I'm as Catholic as the next guy, but it's beyond me what possesses my wife to spend all her time at church. I guess that's what Faith is, knowing that loved ones are being looked after. Meanwhile I'm doing what I can. I bring snacks in little plastic tubs and eat next to her in the pew. Most of the time we're alone and she watches nothing happening up at the altar. It's like a movie screen has fallen in front of the big crucifix on the back wall and rolling down it is one of her all-time favorite flicks. But that's not what's happening. We're alone, I glance at the altar, and I ask what's so interesting up there. She shushes me. I munch on pretzels. She says I make too much noise when I eat so I'm working on that. As exhausted as I am, I get clumsy with the little tub and accidently lose half the pretzels, and when I'm picking them up I go into a pretzel-like shape to reach far under the pews and I accidently lose the other half. I do this on purpose to make her laugh. She laughs when I do things like this. Her laughter echoes along with a gentle cooing of finches or doves or some kind of delicate bird in a nest on the other side of one of the glorious windows. Their occasional flutter and flap, their shadows on the colored glass, are the only real activity happening here.

I don't know why Father Kelly doesn't lock up anymore. Probably because she's here now. Here in this small church, St. Charles. Not an interesting name. We're a small parish in a small town. We compete with a church named Sacred Heart of Jesus, over in Anniston. Now that's a name. Sacred Heart of Jesus. Wow, just listen to that. Who the hell is Charles, anyway? She shushes me. She says you make too much noise, it doesn't matter who he was, it's just a name. She won't turn all the way to look at me. It's like she doesn't want me to see the other side of her.

Father Kelly stops by the pew and asks me if I have any carrots. I tell him that no one was a fan of carrots so I had to stop bringing them. I hold out a tub of pretzels and he piles a bunch in one hand. He comes back for more. He's got so much weight on him, it's like he rolls around church. He probably should be eating carrots instead. She shushes me. I say, What a fatso. It's just a name for him, but she'll have none of it.

She's always been better at putting food in little containers to go. That's because she was always the one to do it. I'm not so good at it but I do my best. In the cabinet where we pile all the plastic tubs of all sizes and all the lids for these, we still have the smaller ones with race car stickers on them. Of course I haven't thrown anything away. The little guy loved everything about race cars. He was going to drive one. He was five and always saying that he'd be a race car driver. He practiced all the time, careening around the house with those tiny metal cars up in the air, bashing them together. It's like he knew that his mother was going to drive them into a car crash. Cars and trucks and every-thing. Our Subaru ricocheting like a bullet, breaking through the bridge rails and then turning slowly in zero gravity, but it wasn't zero, all the way down to a csx freight train passing under the bridge, our Subaru knocking a tanker car right off the tracks and the whole train with it, the tanker detonating in what must've been a mushroom cloud, while the Subaru pinballed off into the trees and killed a deer. I wanted him to be a pilot like his great grandfather. I figured there was time to convince him. She wanted him to be a priest, but that was when we expected to have more. We wanted like a hundred kids. That seems centuries ago now. Thousands of years. But I guess it wasn't.

Didn't we, baby? That's my pet name for her. It's nothing fancy but it's always felt right.

I keep looking back at the cry room. That's the room in the back where people take their wailing kids during Mass. I've actually never been in there. She always took him. An empty little room with some folding chairs. Looks like a bleak place. She says, Well why don't you go see it instead of sitting here going on about it? I take her up on it. I leave the food in the pew and do just that. From behind that window, I see Father Kelly coming down the aisle like a big bear sniffing for the food. At the pew he helps himself to more pretzels. Behind the good father, she floats right up into the air. Like, suddenly, she weighs less than air. That's about the best physics I can do. I know a lighter thing rises. Fatso doesn't seem to see what's happening behind him. I wave like mad from the window but it's no good. I rush out to the pew. He's walking away, and she's floating up higher. He's not alarmed at all. He must see this kind of thing all the time.

She's about ten feet up. She's turning slowly in the air, and she seems very relaxed about it. There's no fear in her. I've never seen her at peace like this. I say, You're an astronaut, baby. With that peaceful look about her she turns toward me in that zero gravity way of hers, and she says, What's up? I say, *You* are, baby, you're up. I say, You can't leave me, baby. She shushes me.

A PRICE FOR LITERACY

R. A. Shockley

(From *Loose Change*)

Herman knew who'd done it—Fatnose Morehouse and the two jerks who ran with him. As a trio they defined the epitome of brainlessness at Blythe Middle—at least that's what Herman had thought yesterday. Now he wasn't so sure.

Knowing his enemies didn't help, though. It was *cold* down here. His breath had turned visible only in the last hour, but he could swear that each cloud he exhaled swelled thicker than the last before dissolving into the growing darkness.

He was the one who'd been stupid, he realized. Liking a story they'd read in Mrs. Lamsky's lit class was one thing, but saying so, especially saying it so enthusiastically, had been a fatal move. Fatnose had seen his chance, and Herman could still hear him snickering in the back corner. It'd been an evil snicker, punctuated with one quick snort through his namesake.

As hard as it was to believe, he'd underestimated Fatnose. He'd always judged the bully's intellectual capacity as microscopic, but even Fatnose had responded in his own perverted way to Stockton's "The Lady or the Tiger?" Herman wasn't about to offer him any new respect given his current situation, but he couldn't deny the evidence that Fatnose had actually been listening.

Herman watched the dust drifting up toward the cellar's filthy joists, each speck luminous in the sunlight that streamed, nearly horizontal now, through the lone, barred vent just below the ceiling. That dust had been invisible two hours ago, before the sun had sunk so close to the horizon.

He'd never been in Blythe's cellar before—hadn't even known that the school had one. He wasn't, in fact, certain that that's where he was. The walls had the same brick as the school, though, the same messy, community-volunteer mortar in its joints. That was the first thing he'd noticed when he'd finally squirmed out of the burlap sack they'd stuffed him into. There wasn't much else to look at—just an empty cellar without even a furnace.

He shivered and decided not to think about the missing furnace.

For the hundredth time he almost yelled for help, and for the hundredth time he stifled himself. The embarrassment would be too much. There were the two doors, after all, right in front of him, side by side in the far wall—at least one of them had to be a way out.

Also for the hundredth time, Herman asked himself, *Why?* Why would any cellar have two doors, side by side? He worked at piecing together the school's layout, trying to imagine what room configuration would account for such a need. But he couldn't even remember how many halls and rooms the ancient building had.

Quiet. It was so quiet now. Everyone would have gone home hours ago. He doubted that even Fatnose would have waited this long to play the game out.

He was alone, alone with a choice. Again Herman marveled at Fatnose's ingenuity. In fact, he almost damn admired it. It was that realization, he supposed, more than anything else, that kept him sitting on the floor, leaning against the far corner in the growing cold. If Fatnose could invent this predicament, what could he have imagined to leave behind the frigging doors? Not a tiger, but something *bad*, of that Herman was certain.

"Fatnose!"

He'd screamed without thinking, startling himself with the loudness of it. He steeled himself against whatever would come next, whether nothing or embarrassing rescue.

Only silence.

He nestled back into the corner, thinking the walls' closeness might help him conserve heat, then moved away again, thinking they might absorb it from him instead. That had to do with the second law of thermodynamics, he recalled. They'd covered that in science last week, but Mr. Ragsdale's explanation wasn't helping much.

An hour ago he'd managed to touch the handle of the first door, but only the once. His hand had fallen from its tarnished steel, commanded by a brain far wimpier than he had ever imagined his own to be. He hadn't even approached the second door, more afraid of repeating his first pitiful performance, perhaps, than whatever Fatnose had left behind it.

He tucked himself further into the corner, shivering constantly now, and slept. When he awoke, there was only darkness, cold, and quiet.

He tried to rise, managing it on his second attempt after first falling from the stiffness in his joints. He knew the direction of the doors, or at least knew he could find them by feel if he had to. He had to get to them — the cold had become a physical pain that seemed worse in the deadly quiet. He could no longer hear even the occasional car on the highway that he knew lay only a hundred yards across the athletic field.

He made two steps, three, then four, but the fifth wouldn't come, no matter how hard he tried to force it. The fifth would bring the doors closer, *too* close. He might touch one again, might even open one, but then what? If he chose right, he might still be locked in the school until dawn. If he chose wrong . . . *what?*

From outside the cellar walls he began to hear loud, cracking noises, some followed by muffled crashes. He welcomed it, this break in the awful silence, until he realized its source.

Ice.

There was ice in the oaks, breaking limbs to splinters and dropping hundreds of pounds of wood and water to the ground.

Ice.

For a moment the realization hid another, even scarier awareness. He could no longer tell where he was, could not decipher the direction to the corner, doors, or vent. He dropped to his knees, then lay on the freezing floor, reaching out with his long legs and shuffling on his belly until he kicked a wall. He crawled to it, then along it, praying. He wept when he realized that the prayer was only to once again find his corner.

Along the joint between the brick wall and floor he felt wetness, a cold, hard, slick wetness.

Desperate, he reached along the wall into the darkness. Nothing. He reached further still, willing his arm to stretch beyond anything it should have been able to reach until, finally, his fingers touched a wall perpendicular to the first.

His corner.

He crawled to it, cowered into it. He could feel the border of ice along the joint, could feel where the ice yielded to water, and, through the night, where the border moved farther across the floor.

He felt the ice, the cold, the darkness, the aloneness, far into the morning hours, felt it all until he could feel nothing more at all.

How You Learn Your Ex Is Dating an Apple Retail Specialist Also the DJ Also a Transman & How You Learn to Pray, Realizing You Want Her Back

Tristan Silverman

The summer dug her nails into the sky. Giant gobs of yellow
rushed out through the holes so we left the windows open but

closed the blinds &she is saying something about the place
feeling like a cave &I'm saying something about the heat &it is

the crushed currant sound of sirens, bicyclist music or the
metronome of cops pulling cars blasting hip hop; there is

a maniac screaming at our bus stop, a dark barking, a tire peeling
out in front of a light, her asking me for some water—

a catastrophe flash of breaking glass when two vehicles meet;
there was the smell of every kind of urine drifting through our

window from the street, the dust of dry pollen, our dog &the
neighbor's dog &weed, there was something baking in the oven,

again the whiff of scream and peel &light, &when the wind blew
north, I swallowed a piece of the bay, fish&earth&war,

&it is Sunday &three months later when I remember this &am
staring at her online calendar, which she forgot to stop sharing

on my online calendar. It had just popped up on my screen. Her
every day flashing like Vegas' many tiny lights &seeing her

schedule held to mine, a no-man's-land where appointments
sit like shy girls in prom dresses, I hear her in my ear

the night she tore through my phone, my journal, my life
looking for any crime she could. Saying through clenched

    teeth, eyes like hands with thirty
    beaks: *where is it? where is it?*   *give it to me.*

ACROBAT

Patricia Solari

On the golf course, a leaf
large as a baseball mitt
tumbled to the green we
were putting, twirled
and spun on its stem
like a ballerina, flipped
on its teeth to cartwheel
the circle of green—
then like a defiant teen
turned handsprings
head over heels in
love with the wind.
I tried to save it, but it
vanished among swirls
of unrequited others.

STILL. LIFE.

Mara Sonnenschein

(From *Liars' League* NYC)

Gus wheels me from my prepartum room on the 7th Floor North to my OB/GYN office, 4th floor South. "What you doing today, Susan?" he asks. "The usual excitement." I try to breathe in some sunshine as we pass through the glass lobby at NYU-Langone Hospital. "Wheelchair rides. Sonograms. Bed rest."

*

"HOW'S THE BABY?" Irina asks me, after Gus drops me off in the waiting room. I want to get up and walk, but Irina maneuvers the wheelchair to just outside her exam room.

I shrug. "We'll see."

I get out of the chair and walk to the exam table. I slide on and wait.

That was twelve steps.

I used to try to do 10,000 steps a day.

*

THE CLEAR GOO IS ON MY STOMACH. Irina's wand does its magic. We look at the monitor together. Gray pixels show a spine, a balloon of head. Hands and feet and minuscule fingers and toes.

A shadow in the upper left corner. "What's that?"

Irina pauses. "Reduction sac," she says in her thick Russian accent.

*

"THE DIASTOLIC IS HIGH FOR a twenty-six-week fetus," Dr. Griffith says, after Irina wheels me to his office. "I'd hoped the reduction would bring down both your blood pressures, but unfortunately it seems you have the start of preeclampsia. You should start preparing yourself for a premature delivery."

He passes me a printout. Black spikes on white paper. Triangles of my remaining girl's heart rate.

His face is smooth and rabbity, his fingers pink and plastic-looking. Sixteen days ago, his hands reduced me from two babies to one.

*

BACK IN MY WHITE SLAB of a hospital room. Small kicks inside me could be a foot, could be an elbow.

Do mothers know which twin is kicking as they get bigger?

"It's not like you have a choice. They said the one is already compromised," my sister had insisted over the phone.

"This is probably life or death for you and the other baby," Dr. Griffith had said. "Probably."

Jason's strangled words as we lay in bed at home, crying and deliberating what we should do: "I want them both."

*

THE HOSPITAL'S AUTOMATED blood pressure cuff tightens around my arm.

Lisa's the nurse on duty.

"I've got some gossip for you," she tells me. "But first, let's talk about your blood pressure? Your numbers went way up an hour ago."

"My sister called."

Lisa looks at my chart, then at her wrist.

"Time for your blood thinner. And Dr. Griffith wants you to get a steroid shot, too, for her lungs."

"What's the gossip?" I ask, but Lisa's on her way out to get my drugs.

Jason calls. "Let's make this quick," I tell him. "Gordon Ramsey just found rat shit in a Lancashire pub and I don't want to miss the meltdown."

"I'll be over after work," he says.

*

LISA RETURNS TWO HOURS LATER.

"Sorry about that. I don't like to keep people waiting?" she uptalks. "But there was an emergency?" Her blond hair is spilling out of her ponytail and there's the sheen of sweat on her upper lip.

"You look like you've been at the gym," I say.

She barks out a laugh. "I wish," she says, and produces two syringes.

I point to my right side. "Lovenox is here today."

She administers the blood thinner, then rips open a wipe.

"Steroids hurt," she says. "It's in the thigh. Sorry."

A rap on the door, then a yarmulked man looks through the wedge of glass into my room. "I thought I'd see ..." he yells in, but Lisa cuts him off, shaking her head at him.

"Rabbi, not a good time."

He puts up his hands like we're police after he's dropped his weapon. He lingers a moment, then leaves.

"I keep telling him I'm Jewish by birth only," I inform Lisa as she rubs my leg with the alcoholic wipe. "You know what he says? He says, 'It's Yahweh or the highway.'"

Lisa jabs the needle into me. My thigh muscle screams and curdles around the dose. I think of a tiny heart and a needle of potassium chloride, of weeping in doctors' offices, of baby bones disintegrating in a dried-up amniotic sac.

*

DAYS BLEED OUT. I am a human Crock-Pot, attempting to give this baby a slow cook of forty weeks.

Jason visits me after work, occasionally before. On weekends he spends the day by my bedside while I watch TV.

"Good times," I tell him, after a nurse comes in and sticks my arm for the latest blood work.

"Whatever it takes," he replies.

And then one Wednesday night, start of my twenty-ninth week, Dr. Griffith comes in to my room around 9:30. Jason is just packing up to go home.

"Your liver enzymes have doubled," he says, like we know what that means. "So we are going to deliver."

Jason asks, "When?" and Dr. Griffith says, "Now," and next thing I know I'm in an operating room getting a nerve block in my spine.

*

CHARLOTTE, MY FAVORITE NURSE: "Are you in pain?"

I shake my head but mutter, "Heart hurts." I can't say more. Did I even say that?

I think I'm awake with cotton mouth? No water—or visiting my baby—until the magnesium sulfate drip is dripped dry.

*

THE DOCTORS CAME BEFORE the C-section and told me, "Premature babies can look ... shriveled."

A flash of her after they pulled her out of me and washed her: slice of forehead between hat and blanket. Forehead sandwich.

Then they whisked her away from me and shoved a tube down her throat to inflate and deflate her minuscule lungs. They took her to the Neonatal Intensive Care Unit: the NICU.

I don't know what she looks like. Reptilian? A little lizard?

Jason tells me, "She's beautiful." But was he here? Did I make that up?

This drip drips dreams into me. Percocet every four hours adds some luster.

*

JASON WALKS IN WITH a lizard in his hands. A two-pound lizard isn't that tiny. A two-pound human is tiny.

How is it possible that the two-pounder is in his arms? She should be upstairs in the NICU? In her little fake womb-bed?

"This is for you," Jason says and puts down the baby: A cup of ice chips. Not my daughter but something I want almost as much. My mouth is suddenly cold and wet again. Thirst isn't quenched but there are other things to worry about.

*

MAGNESIUM SULFATE, commonly known as Epsom salt.

My veins are getting a salt bath. Salt stops seizures. Preeclampsia causes preemies.

Preemie. Pre-me. Prehistoric-looking, maybe?

Or maybe perfect but miniature?

*

MAGNESIUM.

Sulfate. Sulfa? Sulf...

I'm focusing more on what my baby looks like than on her medical problems. Is that sulfish?

It was very sulfish of me to have a baby at forty.

Because of my sulfishness, my daughter was born eleven weeks early.

*

THEY ARE HERE TO CHECK MY SCAR. I feel hands pushing away my hospital robe, pulling my underwear low.

"Healing nicely," my OB says. I love my OB right now. He delivered my baby and she is alive.

Then he says, "Your daughter is no longer intubated and is using a CPAP, but I'm concerned about brain bleeds. She is not in the clear yet and she may never be."

I don't understand. CPAP? What?

Is that Jason standing there, crying? I hear a noise like the one I made when my mother died. A roar ripped from deep inside, like the sound of the ground grinding in an earthquake.

Who's making that noise?

The nurses avert their eyes. From me.

*

I'VE BEEN DECLARED post-preeclampsia. The magnesium sulfate did its work; now that my blood pressure is hovering around normal, I've been moved from the prepartum hospital room to a shared room on the maternity ward.

The hospital is showing its attention to detail and concern about every patient's well-being with this room share. I'm sharing a room with a woman whose baby is full-term and healthy. I get to hear her nurse while I struggle with a mechanical pump to extract the almost nonexistent milk in my breasts. I get to wake up every time her baby cries at night. I get the vicarious experience of family and friends arriving in droves to congratulate her and coo over her baby.

Nobody asks me about my baby.

*

She lives in a house of glass. Sometimes a blanket is dropped over the roof like a tarp placed over an unfinished project.

"We do our best to mimic the womb," a nurse tells me. "We're keeping her in darkness."

I can't hold her. I'm not supposed to even stick my finger through the tiny window of her incubator to touch her. My germs could kill her.

There's not much to do in the NICU. It's an alien world full of tiny bodies hooked up to wires and machines. I sing to her and read her books. I am a crazy woman, reading to a box shrouded with a blanket.

*

Jason was right: She's beautiful. Except. Except she's the size of a squirrel.

Except she has a hose pumping oxygen through her mouth.

Except her right temple looks like a fender that's been dented.

In the midst of all the medical concerns, I am focused on her forehead. Will it grow out? Is that just how it is in babies this early? Or will she always have to wear long bangs to cover it?

These don't seem like appropriate questions to ask the doctors and nurses.

*

We have been trying to come up with a name for her.

"What about Hope?" Jason asks. I look at him to make sure he's serious.

"Can't do that. Hope is the thing with feathers. She looks like a plucked chicken."

Jason leafs through the name book.

"How about Avian?" he says. It's the first laugh we've had since my delivery.

*

I HAVEN'T BEEN OUTSIDE in thirty-two days.

The best thing about still being in the hospital is my constant access to the NICU.

The worst thing? The constant access to the NICU.

The rubbing alcohol smell of that sterile room. The dim lighting, the pods of isolettes (incubators). Thin blankets and IV drips. The alarm bells, the blood draws, the spinal taps. The quiet mumblings of parents cooing to their babies. The soft voices of nurses and doctors intoning the best and the worst.

And my baby, the acorn I dropped early, sleeps away the days and nights in an enclosed box that's not a coffin.

*

HORNS AND SWEAT AND pore-clogging dirt and I start to cry. Fresh Manhattan air! Thirty-six days in the hospital and I'm finally released, a rat leaving its cage.

But Amelia's still inside. That's the part the doctors and social workers don't even mention: If you have a premature baby, you will go home first, and come back to see your baby as often as you can.

Visiting hours with my own baby.

*

THE HASIDIC MAN IS ARGUING with the head doctor, and I overhear Dr. Berg tell him, "If you take your son home today for his first Sabbath, it will also be his last Sabbath."

Two hours later, the man and his wife leave the NICU. With their son.

*

MARIAN IS A SMALL WOMAN with a large body. She often comes into the NICU with grease stains on her shirt from the egg sandwich she wolfs down on the PATH train to the hospital. She will say, "Can you believe I fucking started lactating just thinking of Hamish on the way over?" as if the stains are milk spots, but the smell of the egg and cheese and bacon give away her lie.

*

SOME PARENTS BARELY visit their babies. They don't hold them. It's hard not to be judgmental about this but I'm reminded of the advice my grandmother told me her mother told her: Don't fall in love with your child until they turn one. They're less likely to die after that.

I spend hours now doing Kangaroo Care with Amelia. The nurses pick her up, wires attached to her with minuscule leads, and they place her on my bare chest, then drape her with a blanket. Amelia wears only a diaper, the tiniest triangle of white. After ten or twenty minutes, she sticks to my chest with the heat we make. She stays tucked against me like this for three, four hours, until I'm stiff from staying in one position and hoarse from singing: "Scarborough Fair." "Dream a Little Dream." "In My Life."

Those are the best days.

*

THE BLOOD INFECTION SHOWS UP six weeks in. One of the nurses notices that Amelia isn't as feisty as usual and that her color is off. The doctors agree and start treating her with antibiotics, even though it will take ten days to get the results from the cultures.

Jason and I hear lots of talk about fungal balls that could lodge in her liver or brain or kidneys, hiding from the antibiotics and destroying Amelia's future. We sit together, glazed in shock.

We call our family members scattered around the country, a few overseas, and we tell them about the infection. What's left unsaid: "You may never have a chance to meet her."

We don't leave the hospital for seventy-two hours.

Amelia has a spinal, two blood transfusions, and who knows how many doses of antibiotics that may cause her to have drug resistance in the future.

Whatever it takes, we tell the doctors.

*

THIS IS NEW YORK CITY; even the NICU is competitive.

Who pumps the most milk.

Who pumps the least. I win the title for Least Productive Breasts.

Whose baby was born the earliest.

Whose baby had the most blood transfusions. Whose baby took the most antibiotics to kill an infection.

Whose baby is most likely to leave next.

*

"HOW'S AMELIA TODAY?" Marian of the egg sandwich stains asks me.

Her baby, Hamish, is scheduled to have a feeding tube inserted in his stomach tomorrow, and it hurts to look at him.

I shrug my shoulders and say, "She's doing well. No apnea episodes. They think we can take her home in a few days." The NICU version of the humble brag.

*

THE DOCTORS AND NURSES HUG US. The most exciting day of our lives is routine for them. "Please send photos," they say, and, "Have a wonderful life, Amelia!"

We are outside the NICU now, in the fluorescent lighting and dingy green hallway. In the heavier air, the warmer air, the dirtier air outside the NICU. I am standing outside the NICU with our girl.

We are about to plunge into the afternoon, into the sunlight, into the grime and noise of Amelia's hometown. The city skyline, the Empire State Building, the stretches of sky above—all are inconsequential compared to the four pounds of baby asleep in my arms.

SKIN

Douglas Sovern

(From *The Madison Review*)

Honoring the Earth was the tribal way. Grandfather taught us that meant the grass, the trees, the sky, and especially the animals: the elk, the bear, the wildcat. He would kneel and weep over a great bull elk after he brought it down. He would sit, legs crossed, and cradle its head, resting in a bed of wild mint, the scent mixing with the smell of the dying animal. He would sing to the Sun spirit, eyes tight, his tears washing elk blood across his lips as he rocked back and forth. Then he would take his great knife and cut the elk apart, from the bottom to the top, wasting nothing, the way his grandfather had shown him. Sometimes it would be hours before he would emerge, dragging the dark carcass in quarters from the forest. We would eat for a whole winter from that one elk.

"When will you show me how to hunt?" I asked him.

"Such a thing is not for children." It wasn't sport, he said. It was worship. I would learn when I was older.

I was different from the moment I was born. I was dark as blackstrap. Blacker than a cormorant against the winter sky. I was like a hole in the universe. Sunlight would disappear beneath my skin and never get out. The first smoke from a summer lightning fire wished it were as dark as I was. I didn't know it at first. Not the way I do now that I'm fifteen. Babies are born colorblind. You can be purple or orange or green, and it won't matter one whit. It takes a few years before the other kids learn enough to let you know.

*

WHEN SISTER AND I WERE FIVE, we went on our first real hike, through the Bob Marshall Wilderness, with Grandfather and my best friend Kyle. Kyle was a big, husky kid with hair as pale as the early corn. I nearly stepped in a pile of fresh bear scat. Grandfather showed us the huckleberry bits and cherry pits. There was a smaller pile nearby, with whole berries and cherries the bear didn't even digest. It was like a steaming patty of fresh jam.

"Two bears," said Grandfather. "Mother and cub."

And just ahead, around a bend, there they were, two black bears snuffling along our trail. Grandfather put up a hand to stop us. Sister and Kyle and I watched the bears.

"That baby looks like you," Kyle said to me. I didn't think so. He looked like a black bear. I looked like a boy. The spruce above us still looked like a spruce. The meadowlark in its branch didn't look like the nighthawk.

Grandfather smiled. "There are worse things to be like than a black bear."

Kyle told the story at school. Kids started calling me Black Bear. I didn't like it. Sister shortened it to BB.

Kyle's older brother and his friends would snicker at me when I played at Kyle's house. One day, wading in Mission Creek, I caught Kyle gazing at my bare chest.

"Hey, BB, what are you, anyway?"

I didn't understand the question.

"I mean—where do you come from?"

"You know where I'm from. Missoula. Same as you."

"But you don't look like Missoula."

I wasn't sure what that meant. Missoula looked like many things. I was dark, like the river. I was smooth, like the stones below the falls. I had black hair, like the young bison grazing on the range.

"My papa says our family came from Norway," Kyle said. "Where did you come from?"

I shrugged. "America. I'm American," I said, although I didn't really know what that meant either.

I could have come out so many colors. Grandfather was pure Kootenai: a tribal leader, an elder of the Flathead Valley. His skin was like glazed clay, the color of a crayon you use to finish off a Big Sky sunset. His bride was a Jew from Ukraine. She was a pale olive, the blade of grass that didn't get quite enough sun. Their daughter married an exchange student from Senegal. He would have been a prince back home. My father. I came out looking just like him. I would have been the only African Jewish Indian in all of Montana, if not for my twin sister. She was born with blond hair and butterscotch skin. We were like salt and pepper spilling from the same bowl.

The sun didn't disappear inside Sister. It seemed like it came *from* her. When she cut herself, glitter poured out. When she walked through the woods, it was a wonder she didn't spark a fire just by brushing up against the trees. Her hair was long, like mine, but where mine was straight and crow black, she had soft, golden curls. Grandfather used to say that at night, when the sun lay down tired and out of energy, it would rest until dawn in Sister's bed, drawing from her the fire it would need to light the new day.

It was good to be Sister's shadow. No one ever asked where *she* came from. It's not a bad thing to have the sun walk around with you all day. And she didn't mind. I was the dark space in the galaxy that made her shimmer even brighter. When I was with her, matter went through me, around me—it just didn't see me. When we were apart, it was as if people noticed me for the first time. They didn't realize I was there before.

We couldn't always be together. They split us up for gym class. The girls on one field, the boys on another. I was taller than the other kids, so the coach thought I was strong. I was the only black boy, and the only native, too. I guess he figured he'd won a prize.

"Hey kid," he said to me. "You're going to be my pitcher."

I shrugged. I was eight. I wasn't much for baseball.

He tossed me a ball. I bounced it well short of the plate.

"No, no," he said. "Like this." He showed me how to throw. I skipped the ball like a flat stone from the lake, the way I was used to. It crashed into one of my smaller classmates, raising a welt on his arm like a rotting spot on a white August peach.

"What's the matter with you?" snapped the coach. "You should be good at this."

"Why?" I asked.

"Because. Look at you."

I looked down at my disappointing hands. I saw blue veins coursing between sinew and bone. I saw my pale palms, their rough geometry of creases and lines tracing toward the black of my wrists.

My eyes lifted to the dark hills beyond our school, thick with lodgepoles and larch. I wondered how many bears were rooting for huckleberries on the trail to the creek. How many grizzlies, and how many black?

"Here. Try again," he said. "Don't let the ball go until your arm comes all the way forward. OK?"

I flung the hardball into the dirt, nowhere near the dusty boy squatting behind home. The other kids started to laugh. The coach let out a long breath. He looked as dismayed as Kyle the year the harvest didn't happen in time for the cherry festival.

"Maybe you're a hitter. I bet you've got some power."

He thrust a bat into my hands and positioned me at the plate. I swung and missed at his easy pitch. Then another. And another.

"Jesus, kid," the coach muttered.

"Can I go now?"

The coach clenched the ball and sized me up again.

"How come I never see you people in church?"

"Which people?" I asked.

"You. Your family."

"My mom goes on Saturdays. We're Jewish."

The coach snorted. "Just my luck. The only black kid in town and he's a damn hymie."

I didn't want to be that, whatever it was. I didn't want to be anything. I missed Sister.

"Can I be done now?"

"Yeah, go. You're no use."

*

I PREFERRED SPENDING TIME with Sister in the woods behind our house to playing sports on the fields. The trail wound through the tamarack, up and down the emerald slope of the foothills. We collected tufts of fur and bits of hide from the broken branches. Rabbit fleece left by a wolf. Reddish-gray coyote hair snagged on a limb. A whole deer leg, black hoof and all, snapped by somebody's jaws, probably a grizzly. Once, the soft, feathered wing of a brown owl. The feathers were like the teeth of a comb. We brought it to Grandfather, and he told us that was so the owl could glide silently, and sneak up on its prey. No one could hear the owl coming.

We found nests of black beetles and golden bees and sat and waited for the bears to come. The black ones liked to root them out and eat them, a paw full at a time. When the bugs were gone, they would graze on the grasses and flowers, hoping for berries, settling for seeds. Osprey would glide over from the lake and settle on a limb above Sister, watching her closely with their moon yellow eyes. A pale blue moth would land on her shoulder and whisper in her ear. When she got up to leave, salamanders the color of bark would slither along the trail behind her. The trees would wave their arms in protest over her departure. She would tell the wind to stop making such a fuss, and it would listen, and the woods would fall quiet.

*

I PRACTICED BEING THAT QUIET. I would sit still and see who could make less noise, me or the silent sky when the air was resting. I learned how to walk so softly that the leaves did not complain beneath my feet. I would give my weight to the sky to hold, so that my steps did not disturb the soil.

It took a little longer, until I was almost eleven, to learn how to become invisible.

We were in the western store in Ronan. Mother was buying a new tent, and summer clothes for Sister. I wandered off, unnoticed. It was easy to slip through the rambling maze of rooms and disappear among the hats and vests and saddles and rods.

I was drawn to the Stetsons, the leather ones. I liked the pebble of the hide between my fingers. Dirt brown, Palomino yellow, black like the night of the new moon. I chose one that matched my hair. It had silver buckles and lariats stitched in the band. In the mirror, I thought I made a pretty fine cowboy.

"Hey, look at the nigger cowboy in the black hat! I can't tell where his head ends and the hat starts." The voice came from behind me.

"That ain't no cowboy. It's a cow*girl*. Look at that hair. It's a long-haired, nigger cowgirl."

That was another word I had never heard before. It was jagged and mean, like the snarl of a wolf ripping meat from a rival. I could see them in the mirror but didn't understand that they were talking about me. Until one of them grabbed my shoulder and spun me around.

"Hey, kid—whoa, this ain't no normal nigger. What are you, part Injun or somethin'?"

They were nineteen. Twenty, maybe. Real cowboys, I thought. The one who grabbed me had cashew hair, startled, sky-blue eyes, and some wishful scruff on his chin. The other one wore a mahogany felt hat, hiding close-cropped hair above his sunburned neck. His eyes were dark and cold and scary. They looked cool and tough in their worn blue Carhartts, flannel shirts, and scuffed dark chocolate boots.

I put my silence into practice. I willed my body into taking up as little space as possible. I could feel the brim of the hat slip down over my eyes as my head contracted. The whole world turned to black leather.

"I'm talking to you, boy. How 'bout it?"

"Maybe he's stupid or somethin'."

I had seen small animals do this: disappear into the landscape around them and escape the wrath of the wolf or the bear. Turn the same color as the leaves or the ground, or curl into a ball and play dead. I stepped back into the rack of western wear behind me as my body continued to shrink.

"Billy, are these the bullets you're wanting?"

The woman whose husband owned the store came around the corner behind the cowboys, holding two boxes of ammo. Somehow, she saw me.

"Billy Butts, what are you up to there? Leave that child alone!"

"We were just havin' us some fun. It's nothin'."

"Nothing is what you have between your ears. Scoot now and let's be done with it."

Billy's friend glared in my direction and they backed away. Billy snatched the boxes from the woman's hand and they went into the next room. The woman pulled me gently out from the black gunfighter shirts and the embroidered crimson Pendletons.

"Do you need some help, hon? You okay?"

I could feel my body return to its normal size. The hat pushed back on my head.

"Don't you mind that Billy Butts," she said. "He's just a crazy simpleton who doesn't know any better."

I nodded.

"I need to go finish up at the gun counter. I can come right back if you want some help with these hats."

I shook my head.

"I'm not sure this one is quite your size."

"Ma'am?"

"Yes, hon?"

"You could see me?"

She smiled and adjusted the hat on my head. "I have special powers," she said.

*

I REMAINED DETERMINED. If the glaciers could learn to disappear, then so could I. Grandfather had taught us about the glaciers, how the ice turned the deepest, darkest blue from the weight of time. When we were six, Sister and I dug our boots into the snow atop Grinnell Glacier and peered down into the crevasses. Only the narrowest band of cobalt light could escape the layers of compressed snow. It was bluer than the eyes of a hungry puma. Grandfather passed the day we turned twelve. After he went to the spirit of the Sun, Sister led me back to Grinnell, just us, for a sunset snow hike. The glacier was tired. The world had pressed down for centuries and centuries, and it had had enough. The place where we had stared into the blue eyes of the ice was now a rocky moraine. All that snow had gone to hide, taking refuge in the mercy of the heavens. And the stars held out their arms in welcome. I had never seen so many. Fleck after snowy fleck, blanketing the sky, like tiny flakes escaping distant frozen worlds to come to the rescue of the forsaken sheets of blue ice. If they had all fallen to the ground, they would have been a blizzard thick enough to form another century of glacier. Instead, they hung together in the sky, holding the dark ice to their brilliant hearts. There were so many stars, so close together, that I could feel their weight press down on me. If I lay there long enough, I would become compressed like the snow. I would be the new streak of blue growing deep within the earth. Some of the stars winked at Sister. They joked about who shined more brightly. We wondered which two were Grandfather's eyes. The indigo sky darkened and turned black. I was the invisible ice, the black between the stars, clever enough to vanish into the sky.

*

THERE WAS NO SKY THE DAY IT HAPPENED. The air was gray December cotton. I stayed even closer to Sister so that my fleece pullover would be enough. We climbed the trail in silence. She nodded along the way to the animals and trees she knew best. I focused on my pale breath.

There were signs of bear. There hadn't been much snow yet and Sister said many of the bears were not sleeping well. I slowed to collect some rocks. She drifted ahead on the trail.

I heard the heavy feet of someone who didn't know how to walk in our woods. I felt the click of the gun even more than I heard it. I looked up to see the hunter step out of the trees and aim his rifle at a black bear, an adolescent. Sister screamed "No!" and ran in front of him, raising her arms. The startled bear scampered up the nearest tree, behind Sister.

"Get the fuck out of my way!" The hunter pointed his gun at Sister.

"It's December," she said, calmer now. "You can't hunt in December!"

"What are you, a fucking ranger? Move!"

The bark of the trees seemed to shudder. The bear scrabbled higher, seeking refuge in thinner sky.

"I am Kootenai!" Sister said. "And this is tribal land." She spread her arms, a radiant shield between the hunter and the whimpering cub. "This bear is a member of *my* family."

"Get out of my way, you little brown bitch. Before you get yourself hurt." He leveled the gun at Sister. The trees and the birds drew their breath. All the yellow and orange drained from the leaves.

That's when I felt myself start to disappear. I could have shrunk into the trees. But the hunter seemed blind to Sister's dazzle. To me, and so many, she was a golden goddess. To him—just another brown person. She needed me.

He couldn't see me. He didn't hear me. I moved quickly but silently, my feet barely skimming the ground. An owl, with comb-toothed wings, descending on unsuspecting prey.

I jumped him from behind. He let out a surprised yelp. The gun jerked toward the sky. I held him so close I could feel the thunder through my chest as his rifle went off. A clutch of birds scattered through the colorless canopy into the white beyond. We fell backward. I swiped the gun from his loosening grip and flung it into the brush. Before he could land on top of me, I rolled to the side, so that he hit the ground, hard. His head bounced on the frozen dirt. I heard a cracking sound. I jumped on his chest and held a rock over him. He moaned and was still.

Sister ran to my side. "BB! Don't!"

She couldn't see that I was invisible to the hunter, that white people couldn't see me when I didn't want them to, like the lizard who changes the color of his skin to hide from his enemies, or the brown rabbit who turns white in winter, and back again in spring.

She had been fearless in front of the hunter's gun. Now, as I told her, she looked afraid.

"You're not a lizard, BB. You're a boy! Boys can't change colors. Or become invisible."

"Are you sure?" I asked, looking down at the pale, bleeding man, unconscious beneath me.

"BB —is he dead?"

"I don't think so." I caught a whiff of wild mint, mixing with the scent of the fallen hunter. I dropped the rock and got off him.

The bear climbed down slowly from his perch and padded over with a soft whimper. There was a rush through the trees as the animals stopped holding their breath.

"Let's just get out of here!" Sister said. She turned to run. I didn't follow.

"Come on!" she shouted, and took off down the trail.

I took my time, striding slowly out of the woods. The color flushed back into the leaves behind me as I passed. The gray that had invaded the forest receded to the brightening sky. A whistling marmot and a pocket gopher fell in behind me as honor guard. The trees seemed to murmur their acclaim. I pushed my way through their branches toward home. Where I touched the outstretched limbs, I could see sparks, and the smell of kindling catching fire warmed the brittle winter air.

FOUR DECKHANDS

Sean Sutherland

(From *The Maine Review*)

Twenty minutes to dress. Wool socks, long underwear, wool shirt,
hooded sweatshirt, rubber boots, union suit, oilskins, cotton gloves
under neoprene gloves, wool toque, hard hat, and compressed life jacket.
Then one of us would open the bulkhead of the deck locker
and a sea sprite of snow would dervish on deck,
and the high whine of hydraulics would stand in for our adrenaline,
and the twin Detroit Diesels would hum under our feet,
and the wind shear was like tearing metal, while waves loomed
out of the whiteout, twenty, thirty, forty feet;
"maker of the weather for the world" the Aleuts call the Bering Sea.
And we would go out on deck to bring in one hundred tons
of pollack every five hours. Four lines of three-inch cable spooling in;
that would lift and fall with crest and trough;
their binding sound like a crack of thick ice, tightening louder;
able to snap off a foot at the ankle with one hard list.
And maybe a nine-pound jay hook would come loose,
and one of us would push the other out of the way,
or we would smash with baseball bats salt ice off the sides
that froze deeper with every swell, and someone would slip,
and one of us would shove him away from the side. Or the fish would
pour fast, then faster the way a flash flood of rain around the bend
of a street does, and carry one of us down into the hatch
until three pairs of hands were there to pull him up.
Until finally after the shift, one of us would bluff and lose at cards,
all of us cupping a filterless Camel in hand, eyelids swollen,
and laugh at him as if he had just told the greatest joke of all time.

THE SWANS

Anamyn Turowski

(From *New Ohio Review*)

S he bought the swans because of the empty pond. Lonely; that's why, really. She saw two swans in profile in a poultry magazine she'd picked up at the dentist's. She paid $1,500 for a pair. As if swans could change anything. Her husband says she needs birds like she needs a hole in her head. A lobotomy, she thinks, that's what I need. Every time she stares out the window toward the pond, the empty water makes her cry. She charged the pair on a new credit card that came in the mail that day. What's the interest on that card? You never read the fine print.

She isn't the sexiest wife. She's aware of this. Since the operation he hasn't touched her. That was three years ago. They've the house and the dog and their two grown children who call on birthdays, Christmas.

The swans arrive in a box with holes in it but no instructions on how to care for them. Her husband's the one to bring the swan box home from the post office. He's thinking she's going into the poultry business; perhaps she's going to sell eggs. Do something with her life. He opens the box and one swan — the male? — bites him on his lip. They'll make a good stew, he yells. Can you eat swan, she wonders. Would he do that? She's sitting on the floor with the swans flapping about; white, with speckles of pink where the blood dripped. Why not ducks, he says. Ducks cost $20 for a pair. What was she thinking? She's so impulsive. Water fowl, what the fuck? Return them.

A strict no fowl return policy, says the operator. Unless they're sick. Are they sick? They're mean. No returns. Is she smirking through the phone? What have I done? I'm just after some beauty. You're a pain in the ass, he says when she's off the phone. Get these birds back in the box, back to the post office, and call the credit card company.

Do you still want me, she'd asked three months after the mastectomy. He looked surprised. Those days are over, don't ya think, he'd said. Let's just go forward. He pats her like she's their terrier. He goes out of the room. The shower turns on upstairs.

It's pointless to have an empty pond. Got to get these swans in the pond. They're in the living room. How to get them out of her living room?

She'd thought this a good project. She imagines the swans in the pond. No! She sees herself standing at her window looking over at the swans on the pond. But they are devilishly mean. She tries grabbing one by its wings but it squawks and almost bites her. She runs and gets a towel, two towels. Then four more; she throws towels at the swans trying to catch them. Their wings whoosh as they dodge past her, darting from the towels. They can't fly, that's something. But they can run fast. All around the sofa she runs, around and around trying to catch first one, then the other. White feathers and swan shit all over the living room. Bits of cloudy down on the walls even. And straw from the shipping box. Strings of straw everywhere. Who knew two swans could make such a mess in so little time? And the male, it's got to be the male. Obviously. On top of the female. His beak is holding down the female's head and he's going at her. She's lying under him passively. Looking at the male atop the female makes her angry, and isn't her husband coming back to help her? She hears his footsteps at the back of the house. Maybe he's brought a net? That old butterfly net in the boys' old bedroom. He's coming back. He opens the door, looks in. There's a Band-Aid across his lip. He's showered and changed. Shakes his head. What a mess! He slams the front door on his way out.

The female swan lets out a scream. Heartbreaking. She puts her hands over her ears. Jesus, what have I done? She stands up and gets a broom. They squawk and flutter and she's stepping in excrement and it's imbedding in the hardwood floor cracks. And the smell. She's nauseated. God damn it, you swans, get yourselves into the box—now! But the male's on top of the female again. She gets a towel and throws it over both. In one fell swoop she has them, grabs them up. They weigh a lot, she almost drops them, feels her lower back stab with pain. She drops the towel and swans in the box and closes the box flaps. But she needs him to come lift this box. The box is ungainly. She's out of breath. Sweat is pouring down her scarred front; pooling around the elastic of her panties. She grabs two encyclopedias and puts them on top of the box.

She checks the swans hourly. Her husband comes back after midnight. He smells of gin, tangy and ripe. Familiar. She asks, Please take the box out to the pond.

Those stupid swans still here? I thought you were shipping them back. Can't. Have to keep them. They're a couple, you know. He owns her.

He takes her whenever he wants.

The house stinks, her husband says. So take the swans to the pond and it won't stink anymore. He frowns at her but picks up the box. She goes to the window and watches. She sees him making his way across the bridge to the pond. He's struggling with the box. He gets to the pond and kicks the box over — huge wings span out. He jumps away. The swans waddle to the pond. She can just make out the ghostly outline of them in the water. Tomorrow morning, she thinks, I'll have a cup of coffee and watch the swans.

THE FATE OF ANTON K—

Santian Vataj

Anton knows karate and last week threatened to paralyze me. I haven't left the apartment ever since. He haunts the front of the building, chatting and performing pull-ups on a low-hanging fire escape. He catcalls pretty girls and meets any negative response by grabbing his crotch and making a kissing sound. Since this occupies much of his time I can't go outside without seeing him. If by chance he isn't there, then I run the risk of encountering him on my return.

In the meantime, I watch Van Damme films and carefully study Jean-Claude's moves. My brother Gezim's portrait hangs in our living room and his monochrome face watches me helplessly. The movies (I have seen them all at this point) have done little to improve my skills or physique but they sometimes make me feel brave enough to venture into the hallway. The other day I made it to the lobby before taking the elevator back upstairs.

A heat wave has paralyzed the Bronx. The streets are empty and those who can manage make their way to Orchard Beach while everyone else waits until dusk before emerging like nocturnal animals to mingle with neighbors over cheap beer, cigarettes and ices. I am stranded inside of course.

My cousin Nitty, who is also my best friend, lives on the second floor. I seldom go to his house though, it is dark — even in midsummer — and my uncle is usually there sitting in the foyer smoking a chain of cigarettes, which fills the apartment with clouds of smoke. He is dying and his eyes have turned slightly yellow from either the tobacco or diminished health, no one knows. His mustache has grown larger but is unkempt and has begun taking on the same shade of yellow as his eyes. The last time we spoke I asked him how he was doing.

"Soon ... Soon I'm going to be with Gezim." He pointed to the ceiling. Nitty listened from the living room, staring at an unspecified point on the ground. We sat in silence. At my place at least the folks are always at work and we can play Sega Genesis, watch films and listen to Wu-Tang tracks.

"So you called him a *retard*?"

"He is one."

Nitty shakes his head, "You brought this on yourself, cuz, were you drunk?"

"Don't worry about it," I say. "Listen, I need you to go to the library and pick up these books, will ya?" I hand him a small piece of paper (*Karate in 10 Days; The Way of the Dragon; Street Fighting Explained; My Life as a Paraplegic*).

Nitty, God bless him, returns with the books in the afternoon and a message from Anton, who asks: "Where is that fag cousin of yours?" Nitty ignored Anton but that is no guarantee against a savage beating. I tell him to be more careful, he shrugs his shoulders. He is covered in sweat, dark parabolas of moisture have formed under his arms, chest and upper back.

"You know you can't go on like this," Nitty says, wiping beads of sweat from his forehead.

"What do you want me to do, Nit?" I say while still holding the books.

"Talk to him — apologize maybe?" But he says this with little confidence.

"No way, not this time, I've really done it."

Nitty lifts his head, "You know there is a woman on the third floor who reads fortunes — my mom thinks she's the real deal. Give it a shot."

"Why would I do that?"

"See how this all ends.... She charges ten bucks."

Nitty leads me to the third-floor apartment and knocks hard on the door. We hear the shuffling of feet before a woman in her thirties appears. Surprised to see us she kisses Nitty on his cheek and asks after his mother.

"You brought a friend I see."

"Yes, my cousin. Can you help him? You aren't busy are you?"

She looks me over with a smile and invites us in. The apartment has the identical sunken living room as ours but with less furniture. We sit on the couch, which is incredibly soft and threatens to swallow us.

"I'll prepare the coffees. You boys make yourself at home."

I begin to chuckle under my breath, Nitty mumbles something to me, his expression is severe. The fortune teller has returned; she is carefully balancing two tiny cups filled to the brim with black Turkish coffee. She sets them on the table while explaining that you mustn't spill even a drop. One of the cups is hers. The coffee is thick and bitter I take small sips and roll tiny grains of coffee around my mouth.

After finishing her coffee, the fortune teller presses her right thumb into the bottom of the cup where a rich deposit of grounds has settled, then proceeds to flip the cup onto the saucer.

"Do exactly what I just did" she says.

I stare at the black circle of coffee sloshing around the tiny cup, drink the last sip and do exactly as the woman instructed.

"All done."

"Now we wait a moment," she says, crossing her legs.

Without warning she takes my cup and holds it to the light while turning it in her hand, carefully discerning the black canals of sludge. "Look how it is fractured here like a tree," she says, not taking her eyes off the cup but tilting it so I can see. I nod, confirming the tree-like appearance of my future.

"What are you afraid of?" she asks, not looking at me.

"Anton."

"The boy downstairs? Uka's son?"

"Yes, him."

"Mhm ..."

The fortune teller suddenly places the cup down and without looking at me says, "You must be careful in the coming weeks; it is worse than you imagine." She is staring at my hands, which are resting on my knees. "Another man will settle this for you. I see also a girl, maybe a future wife. Should Anton strike you in front of her the two of you will never be. This is all I can tell you."

I nonchalantly place ten dollars on the table and quietly say good-bye without shaking the woman's hand. In the hallway Nitty asks what I think.

"I think I want to take a walk."

Nitty says something but I have already begun descending the staircase toward the lobby. I haven't been outside in days and from the lobby the outside world appears to be splashed in an unrelenting sunlight whose glare bounces off the long rows of parked cars. The heat is overwhelming and so I do my best to walk only in the shadows of buildings whenever possible.

I follow the long rectangles of shade all the way to the entrance of Bronx Park East where families picnic after visiting the zoo. Today it is empty like all the surrounding streets. When I was a kid, Gezim and I would hang out and explore what seemed then like a vast forest but now under the harsh sun it is only a desperate patch of trees and an outcrop of rocks. I walk through the grove, an island surrounded by an army of buildings. Between the trees I see someone furiously digging a hole. *A body? Treasure? A dead pet? What is he up to? Maybe a lunatic.* I approach like a curious animal.

The man is immersed to his shoulders, he is shirtless, sweating madly. The veins in his temple resemble tiny snakes preparing to hatch, I think he may die of exhaustion at any moment.

"Buddy," I say, "what are you doing?"

He removes two more shovels of earth. "Looking for diamonds, what does it look like I'm doing?"

"Digging a hole ... You really lookin' for diamonds?"

"Nah." He is panting, breathing in the hot Bronx air. "Be honest, I'm just working out kid. I can't stand the gym, ya know?" He smiles, flashing a gold tooth. "Why the hell would I pay the gym to work out? — This is free."

"Good point, that's smart," I say without actually meaning it.

So we get to talking and for some reason I tell the guy about Anton and the fortune teller and I even talk about Gezim and I couldn't shut up so I tell him that Gezim would never have let this happen to me; that he must be ashamed of me, but that's assuming there is an afterlife, I tell the man I'm not sure there is one. The complete stranger has stopped digging and is leaning against a wall of earth in silence.

"You know, a while ago some guy was messing with my sister real bad," he says, jabbing his fist into the palm of his other hand. "A nasty guy kid, a real nasty guy."

"What did you do?'

"So my boy gives me a card with a number on it, says call the number."

" —And?"

"So, I call the number and, couple weeks go by, and these people take care of this dude for me. Never messed with my sister again and, come to think of it, no one has seen him ever since."

"Just like that?"

"Yup ... Just like that." The man snaps dirty fingers.

The stranger is going through his wallet; he finds a business card and lifts his hand outside the hole, "Here, give it a shot." The card is completely white with a glossy surface and it contains nothing except for a phone number in bold black characters: **931–9482.**

"What have you got to lose? Just ask for Delph."

"Delph? That's it?"

"Yea, maybe they can help you out with this Anton punk."

I place the card in my back pocket and thank the man, who immediately has begun shoveling again.

"How deep do you go?"

"Deep."

The sun hung low in the sky, obscured by the legion of buildings; it occasionally poked through but I walk home much more comfortably. The streets have slowly been returning to life: old ladies occupy lawn chairs along building fronts, children chase each other on bicycles while miserable grown-ups shake off the day's work. Two blocks from my building I catch a glimpse of what look like three men standing by its entrance. One of these men has long arms and an otherwise lanky frame; he is wearing a red tracksuit. His hair is slicked back and reflects a little sunlight; it is Anton. I circle the block but each time I come into view of my building there they are. I could be here all night.

I find myself walking toward them, imagining Van Damme kicking the shit out of some thug; I am sleepwalking toward fate.

Two guys I recognize say something to red tracksuit who takes a final pull of his cigarette before letting it fall to the ground. There is muffled laughter. I look down and make for the building's entrance. *Almost there.* My name is called, laughter, red tracksuit has blocked my path; I am only feet away from the door. I lift my head to say something but I hear the crack of the slap before I even feel it. My ears are ringing and I stumble, surprised by the viciousness of the blow. Anton tells me I am lucky; that I had better watch my pussy mouth next time.

I stand up, shaken but not paralyzed. In the vestibule I struggle for my keys. A girl lets me in, it is Sonya. *"Are you okay?"* I am bleeding from my ear but say nothing to the pretty girl with auburn hair. I walk the six flights to my apartment. It is over.

*

THE NEXT MORNING IS a Saturday and my parents have the day off. My mother makes me a breakfast, which I eat in silence.

"Everything alright?" my father asks.

"Yes, everything is good, Dad."

"Want to come to Uncle Kol's?"

"No, I can't; have school stuff." I lie.

"But school is out."

"They give us summer readings, Dad, keep us sharp, you know?"

"Do you see," he says to my mother. "Do you see why America will never lose? Imagine they did that back home?"

"You would be a genius." She says.

"Damn right. Instead, look at what has become of us." He opens his arms and curses Yugoslavia.

When they leave for my uncle's I fetch the business card and carefully dial the number. After four rings a voice answers. "You are not calling from a payphone, please call from a payphone." The voice hangs up. I go outside and cross the street to where I know there is a working phone, I slide a quarter into the slot and again dial the number. Again the voice answers after the fourth ring.

"Who referred you?"

"Delph."

"Delph you say?"

"Yes."

"Would you like to stop by for an interview?"

"An interview?"

"To discuss your situation, sir." The man is perturbed.

"Yes, I would."

"Do you know Lydig Avenue?"

"I do."

"On the corner of Lydig and Barnes is a produce shop. Toward the back, on the right-hand side you will find a staircase. Walk up and ring the bell—someone will let you in."

The call is over. It is another hot day and by noon the birds have eaten whatever bread crumbs were left to them. The old ladies are holed up in air-conditioned apartments. The major streets are choked with traffic, which has the effect of making it seem hotter and more miserable. The noon sun bores down on me as I make my way toward Lydig Avenue. I walk for another three blocks until I arrive at what I think is the produce market.

The place is more crowded than I expect. A man with a large mustache carefully assembles a mound of tomatoes. I pretend to be interested in an eggplant. Looking over rows of dark green, red and yellow produce, I scan the back of the large shop for what looks like a staircase. On the far right, beside a tall shelf there is an entrance. I drop the eggplant and walk toward it. A long narrow staircase meets me. It is too dark to see where it leads, I hold the railing and ascend the stairs. Eventually there is a door and I almost knock before I remember that I must ring a bell. In the pitch blackness I feel out the frame of the door and the side of the walls until I discover what feels like the outline of a button, I press it. The door swings open and a well-dressed man invites me into the fluorescent light. It looks like an accountant's office, there is a waiting room.

"Delph, right?"

"Yes."

"Have a seat please." He motions toward the waiting area where there is already what looks to be an Italian woman with rollers in her hair filling out a form.

"Fill out this application before you are called in." He hands me a clipboard with an attached form.

First name: Driton

Age: 18

Gender: (Male)

Birthplace: Yugoslavia

Name of Violator: Anton K—

Ethnicity/Race: Albanian/(White?)

Last Known Location: 2040 Bronxdale Avenue, Apt. 1T, 10461, Bronx NY

Reason for Claim: Anton is a lowlife who lives in my building. He has beaten me publicly for no reason and threatened to paralyze me on a number of different occasions. He calls me names and makes threatening gestures. When my brother was alive no one bothered me but now life has become unbearable.

Annual Family Income: $35,000–$40,000

Address: Same as above (Apt 6D)

THE MAN TAKES MY APPLICATION and I follow him into a windowless office where there is a simple desk, behind which are dozens of tile-sized black-and-white photos of men. "Have a seat please." He looks over my application in silence and nods occasionally.

"So this Anton guy is bad news, huh?"

"Sure is"

"Does he bother anyone else you know of? Is he involved in any criminal activity? Drugs? Organized crime maybe?"

"He bothers plenty of people, especially my cousin Nitty, who is a quiet kid, like me. As far as crime, I don't know of any but it wouldn't surprise me."

"I see …" The man is taking notes on my application.

I finally ask, "So what are you going to do to him?"

The man hesitates. "Of course we will investigate Anton to make sure your claims check out. If they are true and we can link him to other criminal activity, even better, we will eliminate him."

"—Is that legal?"

"Technically not but our organization operates with the tacit approval of law enforcement."

"What does *tacit* mean?"

The man shuffles in his chair and sighs. "We target the bad seeds who would otherwise go on to be drug dealers, robbers, rapists. There is evidence to suggest that our efforts have produced stunning decreases in crime throughout the city." He gestures toward the pictures assembled behind him. I say nothing and imagine the police bursting through the door at any moment.

The man continues, "The authorities don't interfere because they recognize we are engaging in what's known as Preemptive Justice Protocol (PJP). The city was brought to its knees by crime two decades ago, no one wants to see that again and we are the main reason for the turnaround."

"I understand."

"Great, you don't need to do anything else. In two weeks you will receive a letter in the mail. It will inform you that you have been preapproved for a credit card. This will serve as the signal that our investigation has found Anton to be a menace deserving of PJP. Within five to ten days Anton will be eliminated, gone from this world." I nod.

"Am I free to go?"

"Yes, but one more thing, this is irreversible. Never attempt to contact us again, do you understand?"

"Yea, that makes sense" I say, standing to leave but experiencing weakness in my knees.

*

THE DAY I DREADED ARRIVED on a Saturday. My father is holding a torn envelope in one hand and a letter in the other.

"Looks like some kind of credit card offer, can you imagine them giving a kid like you credit?" He hands me the materials. "Throw it in the garbage, my son, this is how they ruin the world with their debt." I tear the letter and envelope without examining either. I tear them into tiny pieces, which I crumble and immediately toss in the trash. *It cannot be.* I cross myself twice. In the hallway I walk the trash to the chute where it descends down the shaft with a muffled swoosh.

July turned into August and brought with it news of Anton's disappearance. The men, including my father, held an informal vigil outside the building, passing out cigarettes to one another while consoling Anton's father, who occasionally made an appearance. The talk never shifted from the missing bully: *Where could he have gone, the rascal? He was a tough kid but thick,* said another man tapping his temple. *God have mercy on him. How could he do this to his folks,* asked a desolate face. No one could say where he was and anyone with information was urged to call the local station, which did little besides fill out forms and offer the family assurances. Everyone waits.

I wonder what they will say about me when I die: *He was a quiet little creature; could really hold a grudge that Driton; nothing like his brother (God rest his soul).* Nitty would have kind words but no one would listen, we are made of the same shit he and I.

I can't bear it any longer, I walk until the street names become unfamiliar: Stedman, Barksdale, Bronxwood, Taylor, Rochambeau. Someone leaves a fire hydrant on, it bleeds a stream of water onto the street. I cup my hands and drink.

It is past ten, I make it home to find my father asleep with the TV on. A nature program is playing, narrated by a solemn British voice (*The Javan rhino is disappearing from the wild, the species is headed for oblivion.*) I turn off the television and find my bed in the pitch darkness.

Thugs

Iromie Weeramantry

(From *Green Hills Literary Lantern*)

Husband and wife have just turned off the TV set for the evening when they hear cars screeching to a halt outside their locked gate, doors slamming, and the clink clink clank of chains smashing against metal. They've come, oh my God they've come, and the lights are on and we are here, says the wife to the husband as he rushes from the exposed living room to the office, which fortunately has its windows shut, and she follows and they feel the cool tiled floor through their slippers. Just then the leader starts shouting in a gruff voice: Open the gate, we've come for the money, open up open up. But I didn't do it this time, I only lost one tenth of what they are claiming, says the husband. Shut up, says the wife, now's not the time for debate. The gruff voice continues: Open up I say or we will break down the gate. Then other voices join in. Wait, wait, maybe they are not in, the car is not in the driveway. What do you mean they are not in, don't you see all those lights, you idiot.

Both husband and wife, crouching, their aged bodies hovering over the floor, are listening and thinking how fortunate that the husband once again miraculously escaped from an accident and that the car is being fixed at the mechanic's. Clink clink clank and the wife sucks in her breath as the husband gets on all fours and crawls out of the office and toward the darkened back of the house, almost like a retreat to childhood. Alone, she thinks, I am alone, and then the phone cuts through the silence, loud and clear, but she cannot answer it. It rings and rings and rings. Outside the leader is holding a cell phone and muttering, I cannot believe this, they are not picking up, they must not be home, let's come back tomorrow. The engines rev up.

But the next day, the leader cannot bear the thought of further loss of face. Should he have broken in? Could they simply have been hiding? The truth is that he hates having to be violent, but that is something he can never reveal to his men. Here—get them on the line, he says roughly, handing the cell phone to one of them. And the incessant ringing resumes, the ancient yellow phone in the office vibrating wildly while husband and wife argue and scream above the din. Don't pull the cord out, the husband pleads nervously, and again, Darling, I didn't do it. Don't "darling" me, the wife glares back, the phone and everything else conspiring to make her blood rage, but despite the spinning of her head and her inward cursing at the foolishness of this man she is bound to and despite her strong desire to enter that seductively satisfying mode in which the self is permitted to wallow in layers of comforting self-pity, she realizes that she must keep her wits about her and summon up functions customarily denied those caught in perilous situations such as these, functions such as clear thinking, the wisdom of gut and heart, and faith in a higher power—she must summon these up and decide for herself, and she does, so that when she finally picks up the phone, it is with a ferocity that temporarily disarms the caller on the other end.

You don't understand, madam, he spent X, and she responds, You are lying and you know it, you will have to prove it to me, do you hear? You must pay up, the gruff voice gets louder, and you must pay up today or we will be forced to ... Yes yes, I know you have your methods, and she did know, for they were living in turbulent political times conducive to even more extreme methods than usual. Madam, there is no need for all this. Your husband is one of our regulars, we can work with you, work out a payment plan, we mean you no harm. You are not listening to me, she interjects, and we will not be intimidated, do you hear? I can't stand this woman, thinks the leader, never having expected such a fight. We are coming to get the money today, he yells, and the wife, despite her fear, despite the terror in the husband's face, continues. We will pay you Y and no more—you are PIGS—at which a portent silence ensues, for the caller, despite his shady activities, likes to consider himself well bred. We will be coming over this evening, he insists, and you will be ready. Fine, fine, the wife shrieks, come on over, come on over and kill us. We are Catholics. We are not afraid to die. CLICK.

The receiver is returned to its cradle and the husband looks at the wife, mouth open, thinking back to the timid nineteen-year-old girl he married so many years ago. What's going to happen? he asks, knowing that they simply have not got X in the bank. Leave me alone. Her voice is shaking. Several towns away, the caller feels angry and confused, knowing in his heart of hearts that he himself is afraid to die. How dare she!

An hour later, the phone rings again. We'll lower the amount and pick it up at the house at 4 PM. Don't be ridiculous, says the wife, we don't keep that kind of money in the house, we will need to go to our bank in the city and withdraw it, so it will have to be tomorrow, she continues, and there is whispering on the line. All right tomorrow then, we will be there at 8 AM. No, it must be in a neutral place, she adds, and there is more whispering. Fine, meet us at 8:30 at the police station in Town B, and although she is trying to think clearly, it is not until she arrives at the location the next morning with her husband and their younger trusted friend that she realizes her naïveté and the probable complicity of the local authorities who can be heard talking through the torn mosquito screen of a window of the long police bungalow veranda, where the transaction is to be conducted.

It is a beautiful breezy morning, the sun playing hide and seek with the palm trees. The leader, who is the casino owner's son, and the casino manager are on the veranda, wearing cheap smiles and expensive open-neck bright-colored sport shirts. Good morning, they say jovially, and shake the husband's hand, and the wife cringes as she watches the husband smile back. God be with you, interjects the friend. Who is this creep, they wonder, and eye him with distaste, while the wife, with her petite frame and white hair, remains at a distance and grudgingly nods at them. Oh God, thinks the leader, she looks like Mom. He had expected someone larger and stronger, based on her phone voice. Did you bring the money? he asks her. We've brought what we owe you. Good, he responds, business-like now. We will take this for now, but you will owe us the rest later. And at this the wife's eyes flash, anger bubbling up inside her, anger at these despicable men and a greater anger at herself for having been duped, for having allowed herself to be brought to this place full of enemies. You are liars. We had an agreement, she says, her voice cracking. And she points to the leader. You are a thug! I am not the thug, he bellows—YOU are! At this, a strange wave of satisfaction runs through her. The leader now thrusts a piece of paper at her—look at this—your husband signed it himself, he owes us X.

A wail breaks out from the husband—I didn't! The manager suddenly grabs the old man by the elbow and steers him out of sight. Don't touch him, the wife screams, but something collapses inside her and the friend senses this and reaches out and lays his hand on her arm. The document is shown to her and through her tears, she sees the signature and feels totally defeated. You see, madam, he's been lying to you, it's common behavior, very common. I'm sorry, madam, and part of him actually is, but then slowly, ever so slowly, the old woman puffs up, like a tiny cartoon character who's been squashed flat only to come back larger than life. This is not my husband's signature, she says quietly. What! says the leader, and one has to wonder what his role is in all this, does he know, was he also duped, does the truth really matter, aren't good people destroyed all the time anyway? As the husband calls her name from some distant corner of the bungalow, the wife hears herself repeating, this time in a booming voice: This is NOT my husband's signature, I will give you what we owe you and not a cent more, and then the friend, who has been silent, reaches inside his shirt and extracts a three-inch silver crucifix, which he rests silently on top of the pure white cotton of his shirt. The metal crucified Christ gleams in the sunlight and the leader suddenly feels cold despite the morning heat. I can't believe this. What is going on? Are the old woman and her monkish friend casting some kind of spell on me? The leader shudders and shouts to someone. A skinny policeman emerges from the bungalow, nods to the leader, and leans against the wall, arms akimbo, watching the wife and friend while the leader rushes down the veranda steps into the lush tropical garden below, takes out a cell phone, calls his young wife and begins speaking in hushed and rushed tones. Shortly afterward, the old husband, looking ashen, but otherwise unharmed, is brought back onto the veranda and they all wait together—the wife, the husband, the friend, the manager, the policeman.

Fifteen minutes later, the leader ascends the steps with a strange calmness and walks right up to the wife. Madam, I will take the lower amount and nothing else. The manager glares at him incredulously, while the wife nods to the friend, who pulls out of his pants pocket a folded envelope containing the allotted sum. The leader continues, I am doing this for my new bride ... she is Catholic and though I myself am not, I respect her and do not want to bring sorrow down upon us. The wife nods, exhausted. Praise be to God. A coconut drops with a thud at the far end of the veranda, a monkey screeches overhead.

BOYFRIENDS

Cynthia Weiner

(From *Ploughshares*)

Give or take a day or two, I've had a boyfriend for the past twenty-five years, starting with Nicky Braun when I was ten and up to Eddie now, and when I say *boyfriend*, I really do mean the *boy* part: I'm not a big fan of men, if you want to know the truth. There have been a couple of what I guess you could call manfriends (bow ties, pension plans, some Winston Churchill biography on the nightstand), but it's really boys I like best. I like the way they hang tacky souvenirs off the rearview mirror in their cars, the way they shave their head when they're going bald, the way they stare at your mouth when they want to kiss you, the way they buy you silly presents like kazoos and Flintstones vitamins. Boys like to hold hands and they like to watch porn and they like to fix things around the house. Men'll say "your breasts are lovely in the moonlight" or "candlelight" (they've always got moonlight or candles around; what's that about?), whereas a boy will say "you have great tits," and maybe it's me, but I can't think of a more honest phrase in the English language. Show me the hunger in "your breasts are lovely." Show me the passion, the conviction, the need. That's the thing about boys: they need you in a way that a man never will.

Nineteen boyfriends in twenty-five years, and I had to break up with each and every one of them. You can probably guess what happened: they became men. Tony got a promotion at work and suddenly wanted to be called Anthony. I admit, I wasn't as enthusiastic as I might have been. I said, "Anthony's not even your real name." (He kept a framed copy of his birth announcement on the coffee table, Tony Brian Miller, next to—what else?—a picture of his mother. Boys worship their mothers.) He said, "They're giving Anthony an office with two Ficus trees." I put my arms around his neck, rubbed myself against his jacket. I said, "How come you never call me kitten anymore?" His eyes were shining. "One Ficus tree is de rigueur," he said, "but two is a genuine coup." Where had he learned to talk like that? He wouldn't even take off his tie until I examined his upgraded stock options.

With Jerry, it started when his best friend's wife got pregnant. One night I woke up to a thermometer wedged under my tongue—he'd begun secretly charting my ovulation cycle.

I'm not sure what exactly got into Ritchie, but one day he began referring to me as a woman, as in "what a challenging woman you are." I cringed every time I heard it. *Woman* makes me think of chapped lips and public television. Women are earnest in that self-congratulatory, beige-pantyhose way, and they always have a lot of plants in their apartments. Women make *me* nervous and I (at least in chromosome, if not spirit) *am* one.

Next came Bob, who on his thirtieth birthday stopped shaving his head, and then went out and bought a pair of crepe-soled shoes like his grandfather's.

Danny picked me up a box of tampons on the way to my apartment, without a word of protest.

Rudy gave up meat and started watching tennis on TV. Soon he was asking permission to kiss me.

See what I mean? Even Nicky Braun, my first true love, my wild, skateboarding delinquent, joined the math club in junior high, spending every afternoon in heated debate over fractions vs. decimals. Fractions and tennis and *woman* and tampons: maybe these all seem like little things, but put enough little things together and what do you get? You get "Not tonight, honey—my ulcer's acting up." You get "Isn't that skirt a little on the short side?" You get "What do you mean, you don't know what OPEC stands for?" You get a pear-shaped diamond and a stack of monogrammed towels with your husband's initial in the center, no matter what you told everyone about not changing your name. You get a kitchen with too many appliances and a couple of kids who truly believe you're the biggest moron they've ever met. You get an oncologist who thinks you've got a fifty-fifty chance, sixty-forty with radiation. Am I the only one who understands this?

*

MY FRIEND KAREN ASKED ME to spend a few hours at her daughter's kindergarten for what was being billed as Grandparents and Special Friends

Day. Grandparents are evidently a rare quantity these days, what with most of these kids' parents in their forties and fifties—someone must have figured the "special friends" would fill out the house a little. But when I got there, it was just a bunch of kids fooling around with tissue paper and pipe cleaners, and about a half dozen elderly people nearly toppling off those tiny school chairs. The two teachers were huddled by the gerbil cage, arguing about whose turn it was to clean it. "Last time I looked," one of them whispered, "*somebody* did nothing but dump a pound of shavings over the old poop"; the other one made a face and said, "*Somebody* better watch their tone of voice unless they want the kids to find out what really happened to Twinkle's brother." I could've listened all day, the two of them in their plaid kilts and Peter Pan-collared blouses, but they spotted me and put on big, sunny smiles. "You must be Allie's special friend," one of them chirped. "She was petrified you wouldn't show up!"

Actually I was only about fifteen minutes late, but I've noticed that people who spend all their time with children get a little snotty when it comes to adults. Maybe they've gotten used to bossing everyone around, or maybe they just started out like that, but either way it's one of the reasons I'm a little wary about having kids of my own. When you've got kids, you're at the mercy of all their teachers, and their principals and pediatricians, not to mention the various toy store managers, shoe store salesmen, and zookeepers you encounter throughout the day. It's bad enough when you're by yourself in the world—everyone I know seems to feel perfectly free to make pronouncements on my job (or lack thereof), my wardrobe (or lack thereof), my maturity (do I need to say "or lack thereof" again?), but once you've got children, forget it: you're *really* public property. It's apparently everyone's duty to remark on how you're raising them, and the worst part is that a lot of the time you have to listen, or at least look like you're listening. If your son bites another kid's ankle, you can't tell the principal to mind her own business when she asks what's going on at home. You can't voice much opposition when the guy manning the Ape House suggests you read Dr. Spock, not if your daughter's just pulled up her dress to try to entice a chimpanzee.

I told the teachers I'd been at an important conference and was lucky to have gotten away at all (I thought "conference" had an impressive ring to it, with its vaguely medical implications), and then I went over to Allie, who didn't look especially petrified, just a little befuddled as she tried to bend a pipe cleaner into the shape of a flower stem. She's a smart kid, not the most dexterous, maybe, but good at card games and knock-knock jokes, which is why we get along so well. Next to her was a boy with black hair and that milky white skin that's nearly translucent. He was looking down at the table, his head cocked to the side like he was contemplating the properties of linoleum. He glanced up when Allie called my name, and I saw that his eyes were blue, steel blue verging on gray, with a look of absolute gravity as he regarded me.

He said, "Hello, Fiona."

Something came over me. I still can't explain it. That hot-cold feeling like when you're in the grip of the flu, or when you've just gotten caught in a whopper of a lie. He had a vertical crease over the bridge of his nose, faint circles under his eyes that spoke of restless nights, of raising the window to stare out at the constellations. I thought about my boyfriend Eddie—his sailboat pajamas with the buoys on the sleeves, Lucky Charms for breakfast. Suddenly they seemed to have lost some of their luster. Over the course of a lifetime, how many of those yellow marshmallows are you really meant to ingest?

"James doesn't like making flowers," Allie informed me. "But he does like to sing songs, though."

She smiled at him. Was she flirting? I was having trouble catching my breath. I thought: when he's my age, I'll be sixty-five. A mouthful of bridgework, but half price at the movies—not such a bad deal, right? if you look at it that way? "Flowers can be very attractive," I said, inanely, "but music is, you know, the food of love and everything."

Had I really said that? He appeared to consider my words. "That's true," he said finally. His voice was husky, judicious. No one had ever taken anything I'd said so seriously.

*

THERE WAS A MESSAGE from Karen on my answering machine when I got home, saying she hoped no one at Allie's school had tried to hit me up for a donation, and also that she'd spotted Eddie on the subway that morning reading the newspaper and was I aware that *Family Circus* made him laugh so hard his eyes teared? She hung up abruptly: she's got another kid besides Allie, a two-year-old son who starts chewing paperclips when he thinks she's been on the telephone too long. For a moment I considered calling back and telling her about James, the jigsaw puzzle we'd worked on close to an hour, and how as the picture gradually came clear—a zebra's eye here, then a flank, then a hoof; the mane of a lion, its ear and then its tail—we named each animal together, like some twenty-first-century Adam and Eve. But I wasn't sure what she might do with that anecdote (for instance, ban me from her apartment, considering she's got Charlie running around day and night in nothing but a diaper), and if I tried to explain that it was James I found so compelling, James specifically, the James who'd shaken my hand when it was time for me to leave and said, "I hope you'll visit us again," I wouldn't even put it past her to get a little competitive, like, what—Charlie can't shake your hand and exchange a few pleasantries? Charlie's not *specific* enough for you?

And for a different reason, I didn't tell Eddie either. Although once in a while we explored the possibility of having a baby—"Want to maybe do it without a condom?" he'd ask; I'd say, "I don't know, do you?" and he'd say, "Maybe in a couple of weeks?"—I think it's fair to say that we were both somewhat ambivalent. But I think it's also fair to say that of the two of us he was the less ambivalent (I *was* aware that *Family Circus* makes him laugh so hard his eyes tear). I didn't want him getting the idea that my affinity with a child might mean I was ready for one of my own. I'm not so sure I'm cut out to be a mother. I get along really well with kids unless I happen to be related to them, and then I'm struck with self-consciousness, the kind that gives you clammy hands and a stutter, the kind that usually overcomes you in the middle of a job interview when you recognize how flagrantly unqualified you are for the position. I get so flustered around my nieces and nephews that I mispronounce their names; I babble nostalgically about movies they've never seen, and ask them age-inappropriate questions like *Can you believe how much a tank of gas costs these days?* or, *Does my butt look bigger since the last time you saw me?* Maybe I'm just one of those people whose DNA gets uneasy when it senses itself nearby.

So I didn't tell anyone about James, but it was days before I stopped shivering whenever I thought about him—when I thought about the way he'd held the door for me as I left the classroom; when I thought about his solemn eyes on mine, in the moment before it swung shut.

*

THAT SUNDAY I WOKE UP WITH only half an hour to get ready for the baby shower I had to go to at noon. I'd stayed awake way too late the night before watching a movie on one of those obscure cable channels, a science-fiction-y thing where some microbe got into the water and reversed the aging process.

Everyone was born old and got younger and younger, so that people who started off at eighty turned seventy-nine twelve months later, and then seventy-eight, and by the time they were thirty they had enough old-age wisdom to truly appreciate their stamina and their youthful good looks. It wasn't the kind of movie you could switch off in the middle, plus I had Eddie asleep next to me making his familiar, but still somehow always alarming, grunts and mumbles, plus I wasn't exactly overjoyed about going to a baby shower anyway, my tenth this year. Look: I understand what it is about babies that gets people worked up—the tiny fingers and toes, the hope for a new generation, etc.—but at most showers the baby isn't due for at least a couple of months, so why are the women already so *giddy*? Today, for instance, there were pink and blue streamers hanging from every doorway in such profusion it felt like walking through a car wash, and the hostess had filled several of those infant bathtubs with fruit punch which she was encouraging guests to drink out of baby bottles *with* the nipples still attached. She'd also fallen prey to the newest trend of serving only the foods that the mother-to-be has been craving the past few months, though is anyone really meant to eat anchovies sprinkled with cinnamon, or peanut butter and turkey sandwiches?

Still, all that was bearable for an hour—I was able to scrape clean a couple of bites of turkey, and I even managed to smile politely through the usual chitchat about episiotomies and rectal lacerations and placental discharge—but the minute the plates were cleared, a woman in a Gymboree T-shirt announced that it was game time. Someone always wants to play games at a baby shower, and that *someone* invariably turns out to be a mother. Then the other mothers started cheering and rushing to move the chairs into a circle; it makes you wonder if the games aren't a way to even things up a little with the non-mothers, a kind of subconscious retaliation for every tactless remark and impatient shake of the head. It's not that I'm unsympathetic. Honestly, if I had to endure one too many hints about the wonders of Ritalin, or if I got reproachful looks in restaurants no matter how discreetly I unhooked the clasp on my nursing bra and lifted my child to my breast, it might be me proposing a diaper-sniffing contest, urging the non-mothers in particular to don blindfolds and guess if the smear in the crotch is mustard or soy sauce. I suppose I might even get a kick out of the game where everyone has thirty seconds to safety-pin a cloth diaper on a balloon, or a doll, or the person sitting beside her. And although I do hope I'd draw the line at passing out ice cubes with little plastic babies frozen inside, insisting that the first guest whose ice cube melts shout "My water broke!"—well, if I had to hear "It must be so relaxing, being out of the rat race" even once, I can't swear that isn't a line I wouldn't cross.

I slipped out as this last game was getting under way. I was still carrying the paper cup with the ice cube inside, but it seemed somehow churlish, I guess, or at least a little improvident, to just drop it in one of the garbage cans along the sidewalk. The air had that electric feeling to it, the type of day that swivels back and forth between sunshine and rain, but I decided to walk home through the park anyway. I passed the entrance to one of those spooky old tunnels my friends and I used to hang out in after school, the kind that's damp and echoey inside with a million cigarette butts on the ground that no one ever seems to clean up, and it occurred to me that that's where I'd want my own baby shower to take place, if the day ever came to pass. Seriously: no chocolate-covered sardines, and no molding babies out of clay or soap or chewing gum, just a lot of dopey trash-talk about boys, and maybe a séance for old times' sake as the sun went down, and then we could all go back to one of our parents' apartments and raid the liquor cabinet and search the phonebook for people with the same names as celebrities so we could crank-call them.

The air got even mistier as I walked past the baseball diamonds, and by the time I got to the playground a few yards away from the park's exit, it had started drizzling. Parents were packing up shovels and juice boxes while the kids took a last ride down the slide. I was thinking about the scene in the science-fiction movie that I'd liked best: a middle-aged woman planting roses in her garden for the first time, her eyes lighting up as she pats the soil into place with once-arthritic fingers. In the playground there was one boy left on the jungle gym, hanging from a set of bars a few feet above the ground. It was his watch I recognized first, a clunky block of steel on a leather band that he'd told me was a gift from his uncle, and I recognized his wrist, too, pale and slender with a small scar alongside the vein. (A dying dog'll bite if you pet her, he'd explained when we were putting together the jigsaw puzzle. That's the only way she knows how to say good-bye.) I leaned against the entrance gate to watch him—there were a few adults still collecting toys and zipping jackets, but I didn't hear anyone call his name and it seemed entirely possible that he was here in the park by himself.

He saw me and dropped to the ground, then took a couple of steps in my direction. "Your cup has flowers on it," he said. "Did you go to a party?"

"A baby shower," I said. I tilted the cup so he couldn't see the plastic baby inside. It seemed suddenly kind of obscene, especially since the ice cube had melted off everything but its backside.

He was looking at me in that pensive way I remembered, his eyes bluish-gray like the sky, but steady. "Babies aren't supposed to take showers. They can drown."

"Tell me about it," I said, glancing again into the cup.

"I think it's because babies aren't very good at holding themselves up, so the water would hit their heads too hard and knock them over," he said. I was studying his face, his black hair falling into his eyes, and it took me a moment to get that he hadn't recognized my "tell me about it" as rhetorical. "Plants and radios don't go in the shower either," he added, "but that's for completely different reasons."

He emphasized "completely" in a way that reminded me of a friend I once had, a very tall girl who'd fallen for a guy who barely reached her shoulder. "I'd completely marry him," she liked to say, "if we could sit down at the altar." As I watched James push his hair out of his eyes, I was thinking about this friend, who wound up marrying not the guy who reached her shoulder but an even shorter one who hardly reached her bicep, and I was also thinking about the rose-planting lady in the movie and how her knuckles had gone from swollen to smooth in a picturesque, time-lapse-y way, and then I thought that I ought to start coming to the park every Sunday afternoon. Why not? It was just a short walk from my apartment, and there were certainly a number of things I knew that James could benefit from knowing, too, such as about baby showers and rhetorical statements, for starters, and also other things like how to wrap a comic book in Mylar so the pages don't yellow, and how to help a girl out of a taxi so that her legs won't get tangled in her skirt. I could come every Sunday for, say, a year or two, and if that year or two went smoothly then for another year or two, and after another year or two and then another—well, sooner or later he'd be old enough for us to spend time together in a venue other than a playground.

The rain was starting to fall a little harder. He pointed to a girl sitting on a bench who was holding an umbrella over her head and talking on a cell phone, and said she was his babysitter and that her favorite color was purple. The wind began to pick up, enough so that the swings were twisting and swaying on their own, but we stood there a while longer, not saying much, just watching the rain and listening to the creak of the swings. Toward the end of that science-fiction movie, the rose-planting lady, now a little girl in a velvet dress with lace at the hem, approaches an old man on the deck of an ocean liner. There's some talk about canasta, how she used to play it with his grandmother; then he says,

"So, how old are you these days?" and she laughs and says, "The funny thing is, I've lost track." That's the closest I can get to what it felt like, standing with James in the rain.

*

EDDIE'S PARENTS WERE DRIVING DOWN from Hartford on Saturday, and much of the next week was devoted to helping him choose a restaurant for dinner. I was generally fond of them, though they could be a bit exhausting what with their dogged pursuit of fun. (Or at least their idea of what constituted fun, their tastes being of the high-school-kids-on-spring-break variety: comedy clubs, theme restaurants, margaritas with extra salt and little umbrellas. The last time they visited, as we gallivanted from video arcade to bowling alley to Times Square to trawl for defunct peep show houses, I thought I overheard Eddie's father tell Eddie that he wasn't sure I was "plucky" enough for him, though Eddie later insisted he'd said "plucking" — something to do with the width of my eyebrows.) In the midst of our investigations, Eddie suggested I move in with him. I suggested we discuss it after the weekend. He suggested we discuss it during the weekend, since after all it was his father's name on the apartment lease and it might not be a bad idea to consult him. I suggested we see how dinner went before bringing it up, considering my lack of either pluckiness or tidy eyebrows. All these suggestions gave a kind of portentous undertone to our debates about the WWF Café vs. Sir Gawain's Bar and Grill, though I tried to lighten the mood by renting his favorite X-rated videos three nights in a row. They restored a measure of harmony between us, enough so that we were able to settle on a haunted-house cum Mexican restaurant for Saturday night, but by the time we got there Eddie's mood had plummeted again, since really porn can only go so far when cohabitation issues are at stake.

"All this," he said sourly, frowning at a display of what looked like bloody fingers on a shelf above the bar, "for the price of a burrito."

It was another half hour before Eddie's parents arrived, their faces flushed and their hair windblown as if maybe they'd veered off I-84 for a quick stroll by the Housatonic. His father was wearing a wide tie the color of toast with a scatter of yellow, melted-butter-looking squiggles, and his mother had on a yellow, squiggle-matching dress. Her name was Priscilla, which was what she'd told me to call her, though she referred to herself as "Silly," as in "My friends say, Silly, you're insane to keep a ferret as a pet." They complimented Eddie on his choice of restaurant. His mother called it "moody." His father said, "We could be in Vincent Price's living room." They peered around, chuckling over a display case in which a werewolf knelt beside the prone body of a bride, blood and gore at her throat and down the front of her wedding dress. Eddie grinned, vastly enlivened by the presence of his parents, and pointed out a shark by the waiters' station, one sandaled foot with pink-painted toenails sticking out of its mouth. From a couple of speakers embedded in the ceiling came the creepy-cello notes of Verdi's Requiem. I was starting to feel a little jittery, like when you get an overseas call and for the first few seconds all you hear is that windy, moaning sound over the line; I was starting to feel the kind of thirst I'd felt the day after my favorite aunt died, when her name was printed in the newspaper not as Bess Kagan but as Boss Keegan. I drank a glass of water in one gulp. Body parts were swinging from the rafters on long stretches of rope. A waiter came to our table holding a pad in one hand and a scythe in the other, and Eddie's father ordered refried beans for all of us. He said he thought we should drive out to Coney Island after dinner. Eddie's mother said that the week before she'd forgotten the word for "carousel." Eddie's father said the week before that, she'd forgotten the word for "stethoscope."

They all roared with laughter. I thought about how Eddie'd said Boss sounded cooler than Bess, like a mafiosa. I thought about how he'd told me that the day after he was born, his father reserved a burial plot for himself, Eddie and Eddie's mother in a Las Vegas cemetery. I downed another glass of water. How do I describe what I was feeling? There was static in my ears. There was a pain in both my ankles, as if I had my shoes on the wrong feet. There was sweat collecting at the back of my neck, behind my knees, in my palms. The bones in our coffin were glowing like they'd been coated in radioactive waste. Eddie's mother unfolded her napkin and placed it on her husband's lap. She said, "My friends say, Silly, you're losing your marbles." Eddie grabbed my hand and told his parents he had something to discuss. A kidney swung so close to my head I thought it might smack me in the face.

I said, "Eddie, I'm sorry, but this isn't going to work."

It wasn't what I'd meant to say. I'd meant to say something about refried beans — how I'd heard that an oddly high number of death-row inmates requested them for their final meal; how if no one minded, I thought I'd get an order of nachos — but now the words were out and I can't say I wasn't relieved. Eddie was staring at me, looking confused and then hurt and then confused again, and I figured the least I could do was help him make up his mind. If I told him the truth, he'd from now on get to brand me as the wayward one in our relationship, the one who'd flipped and broken his heart instead of the other way around, thus ensuring future girlfriends' sympathy. So I started at the beginning, Grandparents and Special Friends Day, the pipe-cleaner flowers and the scar on James's wrist. The static in my ears faded. The bride with the gore got to her feet and the werewolf brushed some dust off her dress. Eddie's mother said, "I didn't know that's why dying dogs bite." His father said, "Son, I'm not saying I'm pleased with what I'm hearing, but you have to admit there's some pluck involved." I told them about the jigsaw puzzle and the baby in the paper cup. I mentioned the word "incorporeal," though I was kind of winding down by that point, plus the waiter had set the beans on the table but was nevertheless lingering. Eddie's father asked for three Coronas, and a Shirley Temple for me. His mother said, "Oh, are we allowed to joke?" His father spooned beans onto his plate. "Fiona's kidding," he said. He smiled at me with more warmth than I'd ever felt from him. He said, "You're kidding, right?"

I shook my head and glanced at Eddie. He was fiddling with the rubber spider he'd found under his napkin, but his shoulders sagged and his face had that gloomy last-game-of-the-season look that made my heart break a little.

"Kidding," he said, pronouncing it like two separate words. "Sort of the way I'd go sledding or canoeing."

"Sort of," I agreed, not exactly sure what I was agreeing with but happy to let him have the last word. Although I did add that I guessed I ought to be going, and all of them, including the waiter, said that would probably be best.

*

A FRIEND OF MINE, the one who married the guy who hardly reached her bicep, once calculated how many days of her life the average woman has her period. Five days a month for thirty-seven years—that's 2,220 days and somewhere in the neighborhood of eleven thousand tampons; that's over fifty thousand hours worth of cramps and crankiness and a greater-than-usual awareness of the reproductive mechanism lodged inside your body, the same body that you feed Devil Dogs and cram into too-tight jeans and settle on various, and often suspiciously sticky, barstools. This is what I was thinking about when I left my apartment Sunday afternoon, premenstrual spasms like darts below my rib cage. And as I got closer to the park, I was also thinking about James, and what I was going to say when I saw him. It was the first really sunny day in weeks, the sky one of those mild blues that makes it seem like nothing bad can possibly happen, but I was still nervous.

The playground was overrun with kids in shorts and T-shirts. I sat down at the end of a bench beneath a cluster of trees, occupied by a row of sleepy-looking women with tiny babies strapped to their chests. I had on a billowy shirt so I could pass for pregnant-and-therefore-here-to-observe-and-anticipate in case anyone questioned me, and I was carrying a roll of Tums and a box of Raisinets in my handbag as my mother had through three pregnancies, but the women hardly glanced my way after a couple of quick, weary smiles. It occurred to me that James might be here with one or both of his parents, a potential encounter it seemed a good idea to avoid, although after a minute I spotted his babysitter on a bench by the sandbox. Her eyes were closed and her head was tipped back to face the sun. James was sitting a few feet away on the edge of the sandbox with a book on his lap, observing an argument a group of kids were having over who'd brought which shovel to the park today. My nervousness subsided a little as I watched him watch them. All the boys I've ever liked have been fidgety, the gum-chomping leg-shaking knuckle-cracking type, whereas James was so still he seemed almost like an element of the park instead of the crowd that would leave at the end of the day, like the water in the water fountain or a branch on the tree behind the seesaws. I think I could have sat there all afternoon watching him, but then he turned his head and saw me. He said something to his babysitter and she smiled vaguely in my direction before pushing her sleeves above her elbows and leaning her head back again.

I guess I must have looked to her like just another tired mother on a bench, though I certainly didn't *feel* like a tired mother, the violent jump in my heart as James walked toward me. There was a cut on his knee I hadn't noticed from a distance, a smudge of dirt and a tiny speck of blood. He carried the book in one hand, his finger inside I guess to mark the page he'd read up to. The pedagogic chatter I'd rehearsed (rhetorical statements, comic books, etc.) deserted me: he sat down and the only thing I could think to say was, "Fancy meeting you here," a phrase I not only detest but that was barely audible anyway, my throat was so dry.

He squinted at me, holding his hand over his eyes to shield them from the sun. "Fancy?"

"It's a way of saying hello," I stammered. "Kind of like, oh, we're both in the park—what a coincidence." I cleared my throat and added, "I'm usually more of a hi kind of person, but I guess today felt like a fancy day." He looked a bit bewildered. How much longer was I going to stay with this topic? A little longer, apparently; I said, "If I were you, I'd just stick with hello. Or hey. Or hi."

"Okay," he said. "Hi."

"Right back at you," I replied. I wasn't sure where to go from there, but I figured I'd better stop talking for a few minutes. I rummaged through my handbag until I found a Band-Aid, and he thanked me as I set it over his cut. Then we sat quietly, watching a couple of toddlers chase after a squirrel, listening to the chirps and murmurs of the babies and mothers beside us. After a while he held his book out to me.

I said, encouragingly, "It looks likes a very soulful story."

He nodded. "Yes, I think the little bear is about to get lost on the mountain trail." As he turned to look at me, a piece of hair fell in his eyes. He said, "Do you have this book in your house?"

Outsmarting the Female Fat Cell, Meditation for Dummies—that's the type of book that was in my house, but I didn't think this was the appropriate time to divulge my shoddy taste in literature. "Please don't take this the wrong way," I said, "but a little bear on a mountain trail—well, that's sort of for children, isn't it?"

His hair was still in his eyes and I brushed it away, my heart jumping again when I saw that his gaze was one of those searching ones, the kind a boy gives a girl when he wants to ask her something personal, or tell her something he's never told anyone, something that she senses will change everything between them. The kind of look a boy gives a girl when he's about to kiss her for the very first time.

His gaze fell to the Band-Aid on his knee, then he glanced back up at me and said, "But aren't you somebody's mother?"

It's funny how certain moments you remember only pieces of. You try to fix the full force of your memory on the whole, but different parts keep slipping just out of grasp. You can see the silver span of the first plane you ever flew on, but you can't hear the roar of its takeoff; you can feel the slide of your grandmother's iced tea down your throat but the taste is permanently gone. Except that this wasn't one of those moments. James placed his hand on the book and even now I can picture it next to mine, less than half the size and his nails smooth and small as a doll's. I could describe the chalky remains of the Tums I was sucking on, though I'll spare you that, and I'll also spare you the ache in my side as my period began, and the scent of azaleas in the air. I'll just tell you that there was something grave but also kind in his eyes as he moved a little closer, that he pressed his shoulder to mine and said, "Could you read to me for a little while?" And with the most perfect clarity I can still recall the wail that went up from our bench, because I swear I'm not making it up when I tell you that every last baby chose that moment to start crying, first one and then a second and then all eight or nine, like some miniature Greek chorus.

HOMECOMING

Abigail Wender

(From AP *English Literature & Composition for Dummies*)

A Dutch armoire opens:
Rush of mildew.
"It's the sea," my husband says.
Hair plump as a watered bush,
He paces the house he was born in
As if a part of him
Unsuitable for a cold immigrant's life
Were stored alongside his batik shirts
In the sandalwood cabinet.

An orange and black sarong tied
Around his waist, he struts the garden,
Returns to the veranda.
He's the son of kings.
Baby Hamu,
The servants call, Baby Master.
A sari halves my stride.
Suddah Hamu, they call me,
Ghost Mistress.

His aunties and uncles arrive,
Wishing us a long, happy marriage.
They bring packages of tea
And hammered ashtrays in the teardrop
Shape of the island, etched:
Love from Ceylon!
When I tell them we don't smoke
They shake their heads *no,*
Meaning *yes.*

It's three AM jetlag: he's reading
His father's faded letters in the near-dark office.
On the desk there's a typewriter,
No fingerprints on its keys,
And a black and white photo, one arm raised,
His father seems to wave.
A son could do so much
For his country.
Yes, I say, meaning *no*.

KNITTING AIR

Carol White

And with whispers he soothes her, brings grape
Popsicles to her mouth, props get well cards
On the table of the hospital room.
No drip of chemo in her veins, no
Stream of classmates or doctors through the day,
Can staunch the blood that ebbs from her bones.
Each night she knits that same scarf
Without needles or yarn,
She chatters at nothing and nods at the air,
Pearl one, knit two.
In the kingdom of cancer,
She permits radiation with a regal thumbs-up.
Surrounded by roses and her stuffed dog, he
Turns her himself, like when she was new
Covered in ointment and powder.
Pearl one, knit two. She's
A body
Unraveling
Now he grasps the needles,
Like when they knit
Scarves—all those winters ago.
And she whimpers protest as he holds her hands
Between his own trembling palms
Until the morphine slips in.
And with the monitor as metronome,
Pearl one,
Knit two,
He kisses   his daughter
And   untangles
Her   hair

Lou Gehrig's Army

Catherine Wolf

(From *Bellevue Literary Review*)

Some of us limped, and some drove motorized wheelchairs
in the graveyard, and those who had still had voices sang
"Amazing Grace," and we were the graveyard army
searching for our tombstones, and one had a frog who kept rhythm
and one of us had an orange sneaker which she played like a saxophone.
We were slogging through mud because the sky was a wet sponge
squeezed over the earth, and some of us got to sloganeering: "Crips are
hip," and "Not dead yet!" From the nearby highway our song must
have sounded slurred, and the orange sneaker brayed, but we were
thrilled just to breathe, and some of us wore diapers and pissed
with abandon when we found our namesake disease memorial,
and we gathered together, and some prayed, which is often reckless
for cripples and frogs.

Contributors

The Writers Studio
Founder and Director

PHILIP SCHULTZ has been teaching creative writing for almost five decades. He founded The Writers Studio in 1987, after spending four years as the director of New York University's graduate creative writing program, which he also founded. Mr. Schultz has taught undergraduate and graduate fiction, poetry, literature, and craft classes at a variety of universities, including Tufts University, the University of Massachusetts Boston, and Columbia University. He won the 2008 Pulitzer Prize for Poetry for *Failure* (Harcourt, 2007). His most recent book, *The Wherewithal*, a novel in verse, was released in February 2014 by W.W. Norton, which will publish his new collection, *Luxury*, in January 2018. He is also the author of the influential memoir *My Dyslexia*, published by W.W. Norton in 2011. His six other poetry collections are *The God of Loneliness* (Harcourt, 2010), *Living in the Past* (Harcourt, 2004), *The Holy Worm of Praise* (Harcourt, 2002), the chapbook *My Guardian Angel Stein* (1986), *Deep Within the Ravine* (Viking, 1984, recipient of the Academy of American Poets' Lamont Prize), and *Like Wings* (Viking, 1978, winner of an American Academy and Institute of Arts and Letters Award and a National Book Award nominee). His work has been published in *The New Yorker*, *Poetry*, *The New Republic*, *Five Points*, *The Gettysburg Review*, *The Paris Review*, and *Slate*, among other magazines, and he is the recipient of a 2005 Guggenheim Fellowship in Poetry. He has also received awards from the American Academy of Arts and Letters and the the Levinson Prize from *Poetry* magazine.

The Writers Studio
Advisory Board and Friends

JILL BIALOSKY was born in Cleveland, Ohio. She studied for her undergraduate degree at Ohio University and received a Master of Arts degree from the Writing Seminars at The Johns Hopkins University and a Master of Fine Arts degree from University of Iowa Writers' Workshop.

Her collections of poems are *The Players* (2015), *Intruder,* (2008), *Subterranean* (2001), and *The End of Desire* (1997). Bialosky is also the author of the novels *The Prize* (2015), *House Under Snow* (2002) and *The Life Room* (2007). Her memoir, *History of a Suicide,* was a *New York Times* Bestseller and finalist for the Books for a Better Life Award and the Ohioana Award. She is the co-editor, with Helen Schulman, of the anthology *Wanting A Child* (1998).

Her poems and essays appear in *The New Yorker, O Magazine, Paris Review, The Nation, The New Republic, Kenyon Review,* and *American Poetry Review,* among other publications. She is currently an editor at W. W. Norton & Company and lives in New York City.

CARL DENNIS attended Oberlin College and the University of Chicago before receiving his bachelor's degree from the University of Minnesota in 1961. In 1966, Dennis received his Ph.D. in English literature from the University of California, Berkeley. That same year he became an assistant professor of English at University at Buffalo, where he has spent most of his career; in 2002, he became an artist-in-residence there. Dennis has also served on the faculty of the graduate program at Warren Wilson College.

Dennis has received several prizes for his poetry in addition to the Pulitzer Prize for Poetry, including a Fellowship at the Rockefeller Study Center in Bellagio, Italy, a Guggenheim Fellowship (1984), a National Endowment for the Arts Fellowship in Poetry (1988), and the Ruth Lilly Poetry Prize (2000).

His books include *A House of My Own, Climbing Down, Signs and Wonders, The Near World, The Outskirts of Troy, Meetings with Time, Ranking the Wishes, Practical Gods, Poetry as Persuasion, New and Selected Poems 1974–2004, Unknown Friends, Callings,* and *Another Reason.*

CORNELIUS EADY is the author of *Hardheaded Weather* (2008); *Brutal Imagination* (2001), which was a finalist for the 2001 National Book Award in Poetry; *the autobiography of a jukebox* (1997); *You Don't Miss Your Water* (1995); *The Gathering of My Name* (1991), which was nominated for the Pulitzer Prize; *BOOM BOOM BOOM* (1988); *Victims of the Latest Dance Craze* (1985), which was chosen by Louise Glück, Charles Simic, and Philip Booth for the 1985 Lamont Poetry Selection of The Academy of American Poets; and *Kartunes* (1980).

In 1996, Eady and the poet Toi Derricote founded Cave Canem, a nonprofit organization serving black poets of various backgrounds and acting as a safe space for intellectual engagement and critical debate. Along with Derricote, he also edited *Gathering Ground* (University of Michigan Press, 2006). In 2016, she and Eady accepted the National Book Foundation's Literarian Award for Outstanding Service to the American Literary Community on behalf of Cave Canem.

He currently lives in Columbia, MO, where he holds the Miller Chair in Poetry at University of Missouri.

JENNIFER EGAN was born in Chicago and raised in San Francisco. She is the author of *The Invisible Circus*, a novel which became a feature film starring Cameron Diaz in 2001, *Look at Me*, a finalist for the National Book Award in fiction in 2001, *Emerald City and Other Stories*, and the bestselling *The Keep*. Her most recent novel, *A Visit From the Goon Squad*, won the 2011 Pulitzer Prize, the National Book Critics Circle Award for Fiction, and the LA Times Book Prize. Her short stories have appeared in *The New Yorker, Harpers, Granta, McSweeney's* and other magazines. She is a recipient of a Guggenheim Fellowship, a National Endowment for the Arts Fellowship in Fiction, and a Dorothy and Lewis B. Cullman Fellowship at the New York Public Library. Her non-fiction articles appear frequently in the *New York Times Magazine*. Her 2002 cover story on homeless children received the Carroll Kowal Journalism Award, and "The Bipolar Kid" received a 2009 NAMI Outstanding Media Award for Science and Health Reporting from the National Alliance on Mental Illness.

JULIA GLASS is the author of six books of fiction: the National Book Award–winning *Three Junes; I See You Everywhere*, a collection of linked stories that won the Binghamton University John Gardner Fiction Book Award; as well as the novels *A House Among the Trees, And the Dark Sacred Night, The Widower's Tale*, and *The Whole World Over*. Other published works include the Kindle Single *Chairs in the Rafters*, essays in several anthologies, and, most recently, two poems in *The Golden Shovel Anthology: New Poems Honoring Gwendolyn Brooks*. Glass has won fellowships from the National Endowment for the Arts, the New York Foundation for the Arts, and the Radcliffe Institute for Advanced Study. In 2005, after 24 years in New York City, she moved to Marblehead, Massachusetts, where she now lives with her family. She is a Distinguished Writer in Residence at Emerson College and a cofounder of Twenty Summers, a nonprofit arts and culture program in Provincetown.

EDWARD HIRSCH's first collection of poems, *For the Sleepwalkers* (1981), received the Delmore Schwartz Memorial Award from New York University and the Lavan Younger Poets Award from the Academy of American Poets. His second collection, *Wild Gratitude* (1986), won the National Book Critics Award. He has published six additional books of poems: *The Night Parade, Earthly Measures, On Love, Lay Back the Darkness, Special Orders,* and *The Living Fire: New and Selected Poems.*

Hirsch is the author of five prose books, including *A Poet's Glossary, Poet's Choice,* and *How to Read a Poem and Fall in Love with Poetry.* He is the editor of Theodore Roethke's *Selected Poems,* and co-editor of *The Making of a Sonnet: A Norton Anthology.* He also edits the series "The Writer's World."

Hirsch has received a MacArthur Fellowship, a Guggenheim Fellowship, an Ingram Merrill Foundation Award, a Pablo Neruda Presidential Medal of Honor, the Prix de Rome, and an Academy of Arts and Letters Award. In 2008, he was elected a Chancellor of the Academy of American Poets.

He taught in the English Department at Wayne State University and in the Creative Writing Program at the University of Houston. He is now president of the John Simon Guggenheim Memorial Foundation.

MATTHEW KLAM was named one of the twenty best fiction writers in America under forty by *The New Yorker.* He's a recipient of a Guggenheim Fellowship, a Robert Bingham/PEN Award, a Whiting Writer's Award, and an O. Henry Award. His first book, *Sam The Cat and Other Stories,* a finalist for the *Los Angeles Times* Book of the Year in the category of first fiction, was selected as a Notable Book of the Year by *The New York Times, Esquire Magazine, The Los Angeles Times, The Kansas City Star,* and by Borders for their New Voices series. His work has been featured in *The New Yorker, Harper's Magazine, Esquire, GQ Magazine,* and *The New York Times Magazine.* He is a graduate of the University of New Hampshire and Hollins College, and has taught creative writing in many places, including Johns Hopkins University, St. Albans School, American University, and Stockholm University in Sweden. His novel, *Who Is Rich?,* will be published in 2017.

JAMES LASDUN was born in London in 1958 and now lives in the U.S. He has published three novels, four collections of poetry and four books of short stories, including the selection *The Siege,* the title story of which was made into a film by Bernardo Bertolucci (*Besieged*). His most recent books are *Bluestone: New and Selected Poems* and *The Fall Guy,* a novel. With Jonathan Nossiter he co-wrote the films *Sunday,* which won Best Feature and Best Screenplay awards at Sundance, and *Signs and Wonders*, starring Charlotte Rampling and Stellan Skarsgaard. With Michael Hofmann he edited the anthology *After Ovid: New Metamorphoses*. With his wife Pia Davis he has written two guidebooks, *Walking and Eating in Tuscany and Umbria*, and *Walking and Eating in Provence*. His essays and reviews have appeared in *Harper's, Granta, The London Review of Books, The New York Times, The Guardian* and *The New Yorker*.

His work has been widely translated and won numerous awards, including the inaugural BBC National Short Story Award. He has been a finalist for the T.S. Eliot Prize, the Forward Prize and the LA Times Book Prize. His first novel, *The Horned Man*, was a New York Times Notable Book, and his second, *Seven Lies*, was longlisted for the Man Booker Prize.

ROBERT PINSKY is a poet, essayist, translator, teacher, and speaker. His first two terms as United States Poet Laureate were marked by such visible dynamism—and such national enthusiasm in response—that the Library of Congress appointed him to an unprecedented third term. Throughout his career, Pinsky has been dedicated to identifying and invigorating poetry's place in the world.

Pinsky's work has earned him the PEN/Voelcker Award, the William Carlos Williams Prize, the Lenore Marshall Prize, Italy's Premio Capri, the Korean Manhae Award, and the Harold Washington Award from the City of Chicago.

He is the author of nineteen books, most of which are collections of his poetry. His published work also includes critically acclaimed translations, including *The Inferno* of Dante Alighieri and *The Separate Notebooks* by Czesław Miłosz. He teaches at Boston University, where he is a professor of English and creative writing in the graduate writing program. In 2015 the university named him a William Fairfield Warren Distinguished Professor, the highest honor bestowed on senior faculty members who are actively involved in teaching, research, scholarship, and university civic life.

GRACE SCHULMAN was awarded the 2016 Frost Medal for Distinguished Lifetime Achievement in Poetry. Her seventh collection of poems, *Without a Claim*, appeared in 2013. She is the author of *The Broken String, Days of Wonder: New and Selected Poems, The Paintings of Our Lives*. Her book of essays, *First Loves and Other Adventures*, came out in 2010. Among her honors are the Aiken Taylor Award for poetry, the Delmore Schwartz Memorial Award, a Guggenheim Fellowship, New York University's Distinguished Alumni Award, and a Fellowship from the New York Council on the Arts. Her poems have won five Pushcart Prizes, and have appeared in *The Best American Poetry*. Editor of *The Poems of Marianne Moore*, she is translator from the Hebrew of T. Carmi's *At the Stone of Losses* and co-translator from the Spanish of Pablo Antonio Cuadra's *Songs of Cifar*. Schulman is former director of the Poetry Center, 92nd Street Y, 1974–84, and former poetry editor of *The Nation*, 1971–2006.

Schulman, who received her Ph.D. from New York University, has taught poetry writing at Princeton, Columbia, Bennington, and Warren Wilson. Her poems have been published in the *New Yorker*, the *New Republic*, *Paris Review*, the *Hudson Review*, the *Kenyon Review*, and the *Atlantic*. Schulman was married to the scientist Jerome L. Schulman before his death in 2016. She lives in New York City and East Hampton.

PATRICIA SMITH (born 1955 in Chicago, Illinois) is an American poet, spoken-word performer, playwright, author, writing teacher, and former journalist. She has published poems in literary magazines and journals including *TriQuarterly*, *Poetry*, *The Paris Review*, *Tin House*, and *Epiphany* and in anthologies including *American Voices* and *The Oxford Anthology of African-American Poetry*.

Smith's poetry books include *Incendiary Art*, *Shoulda Been Jimi Savannah*, *Blood Dazzler*, *Teahouse of the Almighty*, *Close to Death*, *Big Towns, Big Talk*, *Life According to Motown*. Her nonfiction book, *Africans in America*, was co-authored with Charles Johnson.

She is on the faculties of the Stonecoast MFA Program in Creative Writing and the low-residency MFA program in Creative Writing at Sierra Nevada College.

Smith is a four-time individual National Poetry Slam champion and appeared in the 1996 documentary *SlamNation*, which followed various poetry slam teams as they competed at the 1996 National Poetry Slam in Portland, Oregon.

ROSANNA WARREN'S second collection of poetry, *Stained Glass*, received a Lamont Poetry Selection award from the American Academy of Poets in 1993. Her most recent book of poems is *Ghost in a Red Hat*, published in 2011. She is also the author of a book of literary criticism, *Fables of the Self: Studies in Lyric Poetry*, published in 2008.

Warren is a member of the American Academy of Arts and Letters and the American Academy of Arts and Sciences, and has served as chancellor of the Academy of American Poets. Among her numerous honors are a Pushcart Prize, the Witter Byner Poetry Prize, the Sara Teasdale Award in Poetry, and a Guggenheim Fellowship. Warren was a fellow of the Dorothy and Lewis B. Cullman Center for Scholars and Writers at the New York Public Library.

She graduated from Yale University in 1976 with a bachelor's degree in painting and received an MA from the Writing Seminars at the Johns Hopkins University in 1980. She is a contributing editor of *Seneca Review* and the former poetry editor of *Daedalus*. She was the Emma MacLachlan Metcalf Professor of the Humanities at Boston University. She is a professor at the Committee of Social Thought at the University of Chicago and lives in Chicago, Illinois.

THE WRITERS STUDIO TEACHERS

L.L. BABB has been a student and a teacher at The Writers Studio San Francisco since 2007, encouraging and mentoring over 300 students. Lorraine's short stories and personal essays have appeared in *The MacGuffin, Dos Passos Review, Rosebud,* the *San Francisco Chronicle,* and elsewhere. She is currently at work on a novel about friendship, motherhood, and a long con.

LISA BADNER'S poems and other writing have appeared in print and online publications including *TriQuarterly, Mudlark, The Satirist, Five to One, Fourteen Hills* and most recently *Rattle* and the *New Ohio Review.* Without The Writers Studio, Lisa would never have had the nerve or the skills to become a writer/poet and she is incredibly grateful to Phil, The Writers Studio, and this amazing community of writers. Lisa directs The Writers Studio's tutorial program and is a student in Philip Schultz's Master Class.

LISA BELLAMY teaches New York City Advanced Poetry and New York City Level III and is on the tutorial staff. She graduated from Princeton and joined The Writers Studio as a Level I student. Her poetry chapbook, *Nectar,* won the Aurorean-Encircle Publications Chapbook Prize in 2012. Her poetry and prose have appeared in *TriQuarterly, Massachusetts Review, New Ohio Review, The Sun, Hotel Amerika, Asimov's Science Fiction, The Southampton Review, Cimarron Review, Chiron Review, Harpur Palate,* and *Calyx,* among other publications. She won the 2008 *Fugue* Poetry Prize and received special mention from *The Year's Best Fantasy and Horror 2007.* She is working on a new poetry collection and a children's book.

RENEÉ BIBBY is the director of The Writers Studio Tucson, where she teaches advanced and beginner creative writing workshops. Her work has appeared or is forthcoming in *PRISM international, Thin Air, Third Point Press, The Worcester Review,* and *Wildness.* She is a contributing editor at *The Wilds.*

SARAH CARRIGER was a teacher at The Writers Studio Amsterdam. Although fiction is her main interest and passion, she has spent most of her professional life as a science writer—working with international research organizations to communicate findings to policy makers and stakeholders via print, web and social media. She holds Bachelor's and Master's degrees in English Literature from Stanford University and joined The Writers Studio in 2010 when the Amsterdam branch opened. She draws inspiration from her southern U.S. roots as well as her experiences traveling and living abroad.

DORIS CHENG received an MA in English literature from Columbia University. She is a fiction writer whose work has appeared in *Calyx* and *Apeiron Review.* She is working on a novel.

JENNAFER D'ALVIA holds a BA in creative writing from Sarah Lawrence College and an MA in applied linguistics from Columbia University. Her story "Then One Day You Give a Guy Your Legs" was previously published in *34th Parallel* and nominated for a Pushcart Prize. Her work has also appeared in *Hanging Loose,* and in 2012, her story "Waiting for Hercules" was named a finalist for *Glimmer Train*'s Short Story Award for New Writers. She lives in New York City, where she's currently at work on a collection of stories.

ISABELLE DECONINCK is a fiction writer whose work has been published in *Five Points, Epiphany,* and *KGB Lit.* She has received several fellowships in fiction from the Helene Wurlitzer Foundation (Taos, NM), and a 2015 Honorable Mention from the Pushcart Prize. An independent public relations consultant for the arts in New York City, she is also the reading coordinator for The Writers Studio.

LESLEY DORMEN is the author of *The Best Place to Be: A Novel in Stories* (Simon & Schuster, 2007). Her short stories and essays have appeared in *The Atlantic, Ploughshares, Five Points, Open City, Glimmer Train, Elle, Epiphany,* the *New York Times, The Washington Post, Playboy, Seventeen, O the Oprah Magazine,*

Vanityfair.com, Mirabella, and *Unholy Ghost: Writers on Depression,* among other publications and anthologies. Several of her short stories have been shortlisted for *Best American Short Stories.* She is associate director of The Writers Studio in New York City, a fellow of the MacDowell Colony and Yaddo, and a recipient of a Fellowship in Fiction from the New York Foundation for the Arts.

THERESE EIBEN's publishing credits include a story in the *Alaska Quarterly Review,* a radio play produced by the BBC Channel 4, *The Practical Writer: From Inspiration to Publication* (co-editor, Penguin 2004), and a *Glimmer Train* contest finalist. Formerly the editor of *Poets & Writers* magazine, she teaches both beginning and advanced workshops for The Writers Studio.

ELIZABETH ENGLAND, a recipient of a 1998 New York Foundation of the Arts Fiction Fellowship, has published stories in the *Nebraska Review, North Atlantic Review, Berkshire Review,* and the *Connecticut Review.* She won Ohio State University's *The Journal*'s 2007 short story contest as well as *Inkwell Magazine*'s 2001 short fiction competition, where the winning story was nominated for a Pushcart Prize. An excerpt from a longer piece appeared in the 2011 issue of *FictionNow.* Most recently, Elizabeth's story "Bruised People" was shortlisted for New Rivers Press's American Fiction Short Story Award and will be published in its *New and Emerging Writers Anthology* due out October 2017.

GAIL FORD is a poet and graduate of Stanford University. She happily teaches poetry and prose for The Writers Studio San Francisco. Her work has appeared in *Minotaur,* the *Carquinez Review,* and *Northern Contours* and has been anthologized in *An Eye for an Eye Makes the Whole World Blind* and *A Ghost at Heart's Edge: Stories and Poems of Adoption.*

CHRISTINA FREI grew up in Nova Scotia, Canada, and since 2001 has lived in Senegal and currently in the Netherlands, where she taught for The Writers Studio. Her poetry has appeared in numerous journals including *Red River Review, Apple Valley Review,* the *Inflectionist Review, Kansas City Voices, Hollins Critic, The MacGuffin, Freshwater, New Millenium Writings, RE:AL, Gravel, Animal, Potomac Review, Apeiron Review,* and *Into the Void.* She has been nominated for Best of the Net 2013, two Pushcart Prizes, and a Best New Poets Award.

REBECCA GEE is cofounder and director of Kids Write, a nonprofit branch of The Writers Studio, where she teaches creative writing to youth in Brooklyn and students with dyslexia in online workshops. Gee received her MFA in poetry and fiction from the Bennington Writing Seminars at Bennington College. Her poems have appeared in *The End of the World* and the *Madison Review*. She is currently working on a collection of poetry.

SHERINE ELISE GILMOUR graduated with an MFA in poetry from New York University. She was recently nominated for a Pushcart Prize, and her poems have appeared or are forthcoming from *Green Mountains Review, Public Pool, River Styx, So to Speak, Tinderbox*, and other publications.

MICHELE HERMAN'S stories and essays have appeared in the *The New York Times, The Sun, Lilith, Diagram, Outside In Literary & Travel Magazine*, and many other magazines and journals. She is recipient of the 2015 Willis Barnstone Translation Prize, was a finalist for the 2015 Robert and Adele Schiff Award in fiction and the 2016 Bass River Press Poetry Competition, and a semifinalist for the 2016 Raymond Carver Short Fiction Prize. In addition to being a long-time teacher in The Writers Studio online program, she is a columnist for *The Villager*, and sometimes performs her own work in theatrical and cabaret settings in New York City.

JOEL HINMAN is an editor-at-large at *Epiphany* magazine, one of the curators of Writers Read NY, and has taught at The Writers Studio for fourteen years. His fiction has appeared in *Epiphany, Fiction Now*, and the *Brooklyn Review* and is forthcoming at the *North Atlantic Review*. He lives in New York City with his wife and son. His story "Persons in Need of Supervision" grew out of his work as a mediator where PINS is the designation used for family cases involving young adults.

LUCINDA HOLT is the director of The Writers Studio Online Program. She also edits *Sex, Etc.*, a national sexual health magazine and website written by teens for teens. Her work has appeared in the anthology *What Your Mama Never Told You*. Lucinda grew up in Fort Worth, Texas, and now lives in New Jersey. She is at work on a novel.

SCOTT HUNTER graduated from New York University. He worked on Madison Avenue developing brand strategies and ran workshops to improve writing in business. Scott is on the faculty of The Writers Studio and studies in Philip Schultz's Master Class. "Wilding" is his first published story.

PHILIP IVORY graduated from Columbia University with a BA in English literature and spent a year at Cambridge University reading Shakespeare and Chaucer. His fiction has appeared in *The Airgonaut, Literally Stories, Devolution Z, Bewildering Stories,* and *Dali's Lovechild.* He's a winner of the 2015 Writers Studio "Write-to-Read" contest for his story "Most of Us Are from Someplace Else" as well as *Bewildering Stories'* 2016 Mariner Awards for his eerie novelette, *The Yellow Man.* In 2017, he was nominated for the Pushcart Prize. Philip is proud to teach creative writing at The Writers Studio and is working on a novel that explores the dreams, darkness, and danger of childhood. He lives in Tucson, Arizona.

KATHIE JACOBSON's work has appeared in *Crack the Spine, Driftwood Press, Pithead Chapel, Necessary Fiction, Twisted Vine,* and other literary journals, and has been featured as a *Longform* Fiction Pick-of-the-Week. She teaches at the San Francisco Writers Studio and is a student in the Master Class.

ELEANOR KEDNEY is the author of the chapbook *The Offering* (Liquid Light Press, 2016). Her poems have appeared in a number of U.S. and international periodicals, including *Connecticut River Review, Cumberland River Review, Cutthroat, Many Mountains Moving, Miramar, Mslexia, Mudfish, The New York Quarterly, San Pedro River Review, Skidrow Penthouse, The Maynard,* and *Turtle Island Quarterly.* She has contributed to the anthologies *No Achilles: War Poetry* (WaterWood Press, 2015) and *Write to Meow* (Grey Wolfe Publishing, 2015). Eleanor is the founder of The Writers Studio Tucson, where she served as the director and the advanced workshop teacher for ten years. She lives with her husband, Peter, their dog, Charlie, and their cat, Ivy, in Tucson, Arizona and Stonington, Connecticut.

LIZ KINGSLEY is the administrative director of The Writers Studio, where she studies with Philip Schultz. Liz is a graduate of Mount Holyoke College and New York University. Her poetry has appeared in *New Ohio Review,* the *McNeese Review,* and *The Round;* her fiction has appeared in the *William and*

Mary Review; her essay appears in the collection *Blended: Writers on the Stepfamily Experience* (Seal Press, 2015); and the poem that appears in this anthology was nominated for a 2013 Pushcart Prize. When not writing poetry, she works as an elementary school special education teacher. She lives with her partner and their five children and two dogs in Westfield, New Jersey.

PETER KRASS teaches poetry and fiction writing at The Writers Studio, and he's a former member of the school's Master Class. Peter's poetry has appeared in venues that include *Rattle,* the *New Verse News,* and *Atlanta Review.* By day he works as a freelance writer and editor, and by night he sleeps in Brooklyn.

ANDRÉE LOCKWOOD is a New York City-based writer. Her fiction has appeared in *Epiphany* and has been nominated for a Pushcart Prize. She is one of the producers of the Writers Read NYC reading series.

NANCY MATSUNAGA has been a teacher with The Writers Studio since 2007. In 2010 she founded the Amsterdam branch of the school, which she continued to direct until 2014. She now lives with her family in Munich, Germany, where she teaches writing tutorials via Skype and also works as a freelance editor and writer of English-language learning textbooks. Nancy's fiction has been published in the journal *Calyx* and has received a Pushcart Prize nomination.

SARAH MCELWAIN is a stress management trainer and teaches yoga to the blind and visually impaired at the Lighthouse Guild in New York City. She is also one of the hosts of Writers Read NYC, which provides performance venues for fiction writers, memoirists, and poets in downtown Manhattan. Her nonfiction has been published by Chronicle Books, and recent fiction in *Skidrow Penthouse* and *Fiction Now.*

JOANNE NAIMAN is a tutorial teacher at The Writers Studio. Using The Writers Studio method, she has been privileged to assist novelists, memoirists, and short story writers find their voice as writers and develop as artists. She is also a divorce mediator who writes on divorce for national audiences. She won a Clarion Award for writing on the subject and regularly blogs about divorce mediation for the *Huffington Post.* Joanne explains that being a writer and a divorce mediator are similar; they're both about managing fears and drama, and connecting to the hope of resolving conflict. Joanne is currently working on a book of short stories.

RACHAEL NEVINS is a Brooklyn-based freelance writer and editor. "The World Outside My Belly" first appeared in *The Mom Egg*, and her other poetry and prose has appeared in *Rattle, Literary Mama, Comstock Review, Hazlitt*, and elsewhere. She teaches online poetry workshops with The Writers Studio.

MARK FENLON PETERSON opened The Writers Studio San Francisco in 2007 after studying with Philip Schultz in New York for ten years. As director and teacher of the San Francisco Advanced Workshop, Mark enjoys helping many great writers develop their craft and is proud of their many successes. Mark has published his fiction and poetry in the *Milo Review* and *Santa Barbara Review*, and is currently working on a novel.

WHITNEY PORTER is a teacher at The Writers Studio. Her work has appeared in *Ping Pong Literary Magazine, Battered Suitcase,* and *Metazen*. In 2016 she received a fellowship from Lambda Literary. She has a degree in journalism from SUNY Empire State, and currently resides in Brooklyn, New York.

ELLIOT SATSKY sensed a lack of creative fulfillment during a successful career in which he conceived and operated various businesses. Though unaffected by personal loss, he felt redirected by 9/11 onto a path focused on quality of life and artistic expression. In 2003, he came to The Writers Studio and found a community of teachers and students working together to examine, and unlock, the protective barriers blocking their individual expressive cores. He was a student in Philip Schultz's Master Class for several years before joining The Writers Studio faculty. His short stories have appeared in *North American Review, Our Stories,* and other magazines. He lives in Manhattan with his Bedlington Terriers, Holden and Monte Cristo.

LELA SCOTT MACNEIL was born in Los Alamos, same as the atomic bomb. She has an MFA in creative writing from the University of Arizona, and her work has been published in *Gertrude, Essay Daily,* and the noir anthology *Trouble in the Heartland*.

ANAMYN TUROWSKI is a graduate of UCLA. She teaches creative writing at The Writers Studio and recently, with Therese Eiben, opened The Writers Studio Hudson Valley, a branch of the school in Hudson, NY. She is assistant editor for *Narrative Magazine* with Tom Jenks. Her publishing credits include

New Ohio Review (Pushcart nomination). She lives in upstate New York with her husband, two sons, and numerous farm animals.

CYNTHIA WEINER is the assistant director of The Writers Studio. Her work has appeared in *Ploughshares, The Sun,* and *Open City,* among others, and was awarded a Pushcart Prize. She is working on a novel.

ABIGAIL WENDER'S poems have appeared in the *Cortland Review, Epiphany, Kenyon Review Online,* the *Massachusetts Review, New Orleans Review,* and other journals and anthologies. Her poems have been nominated for a Pushcart Prize and a Best of the Web Award in 2016. Her translations of the German poet Sarah Kirsch appear in *Tupelo Quarterly 1* and the *New Haven Review.* Currently she is at work completing a poetry manuscript and translating a contemporary German novel, *The Essential.*

THE WRITERS STUDIO STUDENTS

LAUREL INGRAHAM AQUADRO has been writing poetry since her poet father visited her third-grade classroom and taught her class how to write a haiku. She followed a love for poetry to college, where she majored in creative writing and published pieces in various Cornell literary magazines. Since graduating, she's taught English in New York City for a decade and has continued to seek homes for her poems, being published most recently in *Chantarelle's Notebook* and *Bluestem.* When not writing or teaching, she runs a photography business with her husband and loves weekend walks through Prospect Park with her dog, Gatsby.

J. N. BANERJEE is writer who lives in Washington, DC.

CÉCILE BARLIER was born in France and has lived in the United States for over a decade, raising a family and working as an entrepreneur. Cécile traveled extensively and lived in Mexico, Spain, and England. She has been a regular student at The Writers Studio San Francisco for many years. Her short stories, "A Gypsy's Book of Revelations" and "Forgetting," have been nominated for the Pushcart Prize. Her work is featured in *Amarillo Bay, Bacopa Literary Review* (first place for fiction, 2012), *Clare Literary Journal, Crack the Spine, Cerise Press,*

Delmarva Review, the *Emerson Review, Gold Man Review, Knee-Jerk,* the *Lindenwood Review, New Delta Review, Penmen Review, The Saint Ann's Review, Serving House Journal, Sou'wester, The Tower Journal,* and *Valparaiso Fiction Review.*

SYLVIE BERTRAND writes short stories and is working on her first novel. Her short story, "One of Them," was published in the Fall 2016 issue of *Epiphany.* The story was nominated for the 2017 PEN/Robert J. Dau Short Story Prize for Emerging Writers and for a Pushcart Prize. A native French speaker, she was born and grew up in Montreal. She received a BA in Political Sciences from Hunter College and an MA in anthropology from Princeton University. She is a student of Philip Schultz's Master Class at The Writers Studio and the lead fiction reader for *Epiphany.* She lives in Brooklyn, where she moonlights as a restaurant owner.

JULIANNE BOND is a Master Class student at The Writers Studio. Her poem "Why I Fly-fish" will appear in *Sport Literate* in Summer 2017.

ROBLEY BROWNE is a student in the San Francisco Writers Studio Master Class. He received his AA in film studies from De Anza College and has worked as a bookseller, cartoonist, and clerk at Kayo Books in San Francisco. He has also served as a volunteer reader for the Zoetrope All-Story contest. His most recent work can be found in *Midway Journal* and *Knee-Jerk magazine.*

CHRISTINA PEREZ BRUBAKER is a fellow recipient at Chapman University, in Southern California, where she is pursuing an MFA. She lives and writes in Costa Mesa and teaches creative writing at Orange County School of the Arts.

ERICA BRYANT is a reader, writer, cartoon enthusiast, and serial craft project starter. She graduated from the University of California, Irvine, and received her teaching credential from Mills College. She currently teaches eleventh- and twelfth-grade English in Oakland, California. Erica is a radical feminist with great hair and an untold love for stepping on crunchy leaves.

ROSS BRYANT grew up in Colorado and lives in Tucson, Arizona. He has developed an affinity with saguaros but still misses trees. He received a geology degree from Colorado College and subsequently traveled the U.S. and the South Pacific for ten months. Then he worked in the social services, landscaping, and international consulting in Burlington, Vermont. In 1988 he moved with his new family to Tucson to get a degree in soil and water science. In Tucson he has worked in climate modeling, remote sensing, and micro-meteorology. He has two grown children and three growing grandchildren. He currently lives with his girlfriend. They have no pets. A long time ago he built a porch.

KIM FARRAR lives in Astoria, Queens. She is the author of two chapbooks, *The Brief Clear* and *The Familiar*. Her work has been published in *Alaska Quarterly Review, Chicago Quarterly Review, Rhino,* and *Salamander*. She was nominated for the Pushcart Prize in 2017 and 2015. She teaches at LaGuardia Community College.

PATRICIA FOLLERT is a former book publicist, short story writer, journalist and photographer. She received her MFA from Stony Brook/ Southampton. Pat is a member of the League of Professional Theatre Women and serves on the advisory council of Keen Company, an award-winning off-Broadway theatre company. She is an avid fly fisherman, shooter and field dog-handler who makes her home on the East End of Long Island.

JANET FRANKLIN studies law at the University of Baltimore, where she is a staff editor for the *University of Baltimore Law Review*. Her poetry has appeared in the *Cider Press Review, Thrush Poetry Journal, Atticus Review, Common Ground Review,* and *Potomac Review*. She has studied at the Tucson Writers Studio under the instruction of Reneé Bibby and Eleanor Kedney.

ANNETTE FROST is a poet, educator, and traveler. She was born in Boston and currently resides in Istanbul, where she fights from afar against bans and walls. Annette recently completed her MFA in poetry at Boston University and then received the Robert Pinsky Global Fellowship in Greece. Annette's poetry can be found in *Nature Inspired Anthologies* and *Strange Horizons,* among other publications. She believes in the importance of acknowledging both feelings and climate change.

JUDY GERBIN grew up in Syracuse, New York. She is a Master Class student in New York City, and her work has appeared in the online journal *Ozone Park*. Judy lives with her husband in Yonkers, New York, where they are only temporarily cat-less.

JAMES GIBBS is a writer and company dramaturg with The Builders Association, a NYC-based multimedia performance company. He cowrote its most recent large-scale productions: *The Elements of Oz* and *House/Divided*, featured at BAM in Brooklyn. He is at work on his first novel. In a previous life, he founded DBOX, a company that makes stories about buildings (advertising, branding, media) and won an Emmy in 2012 for *Rising: Rebuilding Ground Zero*.

NANCY GREEN has been a member of The Writers Studio community for over fifteen years. She was a student in Philip Schultz's Master Class. Her work has appeared in *Bellevue Literary Review*, *Fiction Now*, and *Practice, a Journal of Politics, Psychology, and Culture*. She is a clinical social worker practicing at an outpatient mental health clinic in Queens, New York.

PATRICK CABELLO HANSEL was part of Philip Schultz's Master Class while living in the Bronx and Philadelphia. He has published poems, short stories, and essays in over thirty-five anthologies and journals, including *Painted Bride Quarterly*, *Ilanot Review*, *Lunch Ticket*, *subprimal*, and *Hawai'i Pacific Review*. He was a 2008–2009 Loft Literary Center (Minnesota) mentee, and a 2011 grantee of the Minnesota State Art Board. His novella *Searching* was serialized in thirty-three issues of *The Alley News*. He is the editor of *The Phoenix of Phillips*, a new literary magazine for and by people of Phillips, the most diverse neighborhood in Minneapolis. He and his wife pastor a bilingual church in Minneapolis.

CAREY ANN HUNT is a writer, artist, designer, and personal consultant inspired by humanity in its vast array of idiosyncratic splendor. She spends much of her life working creatively with people of all ages and abilities. She is full of desire to expand upon any existing beauty and joy there is. She finds comfort and awe in words, and has from a very young age. She is thrilled to have found The Writers Studio right around the corner from her Hudson Valley home. Carey Ann has recently relocated to the west coast and is looking forward to further developing her writing with The Writers Studio.

ELIZABETH KANDALL is an advanced poetry student at The Writers Studio. She works as a psychologist and psychoanalyst in private practice in Manhattan. "The Boat and the Water" was based on and inspired by Ada Limón's "State Bird," a poem studied in The Writers Studio Craft Class.

TIMUR JONATHAN KARACA'S stories have appeared or are forthcoming in the *Baltimore Review, Indiana Review, Narrative, Potomac Review, Redivider, Willow Review,* and other journals. He is a practicing anesthesiologist, and has been a student at The Writers Studio San Francisco since 2010. He is currently a student at the MFA Program for Writers at Warren Wilson College. He lives in Oakland.

JENNIFER KEARNS is an Irish citizen, currently resident in Vienna, Austria, where she works as a simultaneous interpreter. From 2004 through 2014 she lived in New York and was an online student of The Writers Studio between 2012 and 2015. Her poems have appeared in *Edge, Freshwater* magazine, *Broken Plate,* and the 2015 Outrider Press anthology. Her chapbook, *The Hungry Gap,* was published in 2014 by Toadlily Press as part of a quartet.

ROBERT LEE KENDRICK lives in Clemson, South Carolina. He has previously published, or has work forthcoming, in *Tar River Poetry, Xavier Review, Louisiana Literature, South Carolina Review,* the *James Dickey Review,* and a chapbook, *Winter Skin* (Main Street Rag Publishing, 2016). He was a student in Peter Krass's online Intermediate Poetry class.

MAGGIE KENNEDY'S poems have appeared in *Meat for Tea, Cloudbank, Zone 3,* and other publications. In between writing poems and enjoying online classes at The Writers Studio, Maggie works as a freelance writer and lives with her family in a Chicago suburb.

HANI OMAR KHALIL is a lawyer, writer, and photographer living in Park Slope, Brooklyn. Born in Texas, and raised outside Chicago, he received his BA from the University of Wisconsin-Madison and his JD from Rutgers Law School. He has been a contributing writer for *CultureBot,* where he has written extensively on cultural and theatrical works connected to the Egyptian Revolution of 2011. "Satellite" is his first published work of fiction, and grew out of an exercise he wrote for Level IV of The Writers Studio with Lesley Dormen.

JAY KIDD'S poetry has appeared in a number of publications including the *Bellevue Literary Review, Burningword Literary Journal, Ruminate Magazine,* the *Florida Review,* and *Atlanta Review.* His work will also be appearing in upcoming issues of *Crosswinds Poetry Journal* and *Appalachian Heritage*. Jay was the 2013 winner of *Ruminate Magazine*'s Janet B. McCabe Prize for Poetry. In 2015 his poem, "I watch him, my husband," which appears here, was one of the winners of *Atlanta Review*'s International Poetry Competition. Additionally, he is a four-time Pushcart Prize nominee. Jay lives in New York City and is a Master Class student at The Writers Studio.

CORI KRESGE is a freelance dancer, teacher, and writer based in New York City. She performs with various artists in works for stage and film. This is Kresge's first published piece of writing. She would like to thank The Writers Studio for making this possible.

IRIS LEE, a Master Class student at The Writers Studio, is a poet and editor living in Brooklyn. Her book of poems, *Urban Bird Life*, is published by New York Quarterly Books. Her work has appeared in *Haibun Today, OccuPoetry,* and the *Marsh Hawk Review*, among others. She runs a writing workshop for theater professionals at the Actors Fund in New York City.

ANN LOVETT lives in Ashland, Oregon, where she maintains an active practice in both poetry and visual art.

MARNIE MAGUIRE took the inspirational course "Teaching Creative Writing to Dyslexics" with Rebecca Gee in 2016. A lifetime ago, she studied creative writing at Brooklyn College when Allan Ginsberg still walked its halls. She now lives with her husband, two sons, and a husky in Aurora, Ontario, where she writes, teaches, and frequents a lot of hockey rinks. "Graffiti Dreams" has become part of a novel called *A Lick of Fire*.

ANDREA MARCUSA'S literary fiction and essays have appeared in *River Styx, Ontario Review, New South, Star 82,* and others. She's received recognition for her writing in a range of competitions, including those from *New Letters, Ontario Review, and Ruminate Magazine,* and she has been nominated several times for a Pushcart Prize. Andrea began her career as a writer for *Glamour* and *Mademoiselle* magazines, where, fresh out of college, she received her first national byline for a piece chronicling the ups and downs of a long-distance romance. Her writings have appeared in national newspapers including *The New York Times, The Christian Science Monitor, Newsday,* and others. Andrea lives in New York City with her husband and cockatiel, L.B., where she divides her time between creating literary works and writing articles on medical, scientific, and educational topics.

JEAN PFEFFER writes fiction and poetry. When she's not writing, she can be found wandering through used bookstores and historic graveyards. She divides her time between New York and New Jersey. She is currently working on a novel. She is indebted to The Writers Studio, and to the teachers and community for their inspiration and support.

MÁIRE T. ROBINSON lives in Dublin, Ireland. She is the author of the short story collection *Your Mixtape Unravels My Heart* (Doire Press, 2013) and the novel *Skin, Paper, Stone* (New Island, 2015).

JOYCE ROSCHINGER was born in Heidelberg, Germany, and grew up in San Antonio, Texas. She received her undergraduate degree in creative writing from San Francisco State University. She lives in San Francisco with her husband and is currently working on a novel set in San Francisco.

DESIREE RUCKER recently earned an MFA in creative writing from Long Island University, Brooklyn, and has a BS in marketing from Fairfield University. She attended The Writers Studio from 2008 through 2009. Her short stories have been published in literary journals such as *Brooklyn Paramount, Downtown Brooklyn,* and *Under the Overpass.* "The Legacy" is from her long-awaited memoir, *Relativity: A Memoir in Prose and Poetry,* which will be published in March 2017. She lives in Brooklyn with her fur-baby, Lady Addison.

ROSALIA SCALIA's fiction has appeared or is forthcoming in the *Oklahoma Review, North Atlantic Review, Notre Dame Review,* the *Portland Review, and Quercus Review,* among many others. She holds an MA in writing from Johns Hopkins University and is a Maryland State Arts Council Independent Artist's Award recipient. She won the Editor's Select Award from *Willow Review,* and her short story in *Pebble Lake* was nominated for a Pushcart Prize. She lives in Baltimore with her family.

J.D. SERLING's debut novel, *Good Neighbors,* will be published in February by Twelve. Her short stories have appeared in *New Ohio Review* and *North American*

Review. She currently lives in New Jersey with her husband and children and is at work on her second book.

CHRISTOPHER X. SHADE is a writer, book reviewer, and editor based in New York City. He's had over twenty stories appear in publications, and has won story awards including a Writers @ Work Fellowship Competition and a Pushcart nomination. A member of the National Book Critics Circle, his book reviews have been widely published. He's a BA graduate of The New School's creative writing program, and now studies at The Writers Studio as a member of the Master Class led by Philip Schultz. With two novels in agent circulation, Christopher is now working on a new novel based loosely on his experiences being raised in the South.

R. A. SHOCKLEY is a novelist and short story writer from Athens, Georgia. His fiction has appeared in a variety of journals, mainly in the Southeast. His grandfather, also a writer, claimed Stockton's "The Lady or the Tiger" as a favorite story. He read it to his grandchildren for the first time in the mountains, on a cool California night in 1956. Unfortunately, experience with bullies is something that few children entirely escape. Whether good or bad, some memories we never forget. For this author, both varieties seem to have found their way into the same story.

TRISTAN SILVERMAN began writing poetry in Chicago's poetry community and has been living in San Francisco for the last three years. Tristan is a recent alum of the Community of Writers at Squaw Valley (2016), and is published in numerous journals including *Boxcar Poetry, decomP, Pedestal Magazine, Up the Staircase Quarterly,* and *November 3rd Club.*

PATRICIA SOLARI is a retired English teacher who has written poetry for a very long time. She learned so much from Lisa Bellamy's poetry courses and Joel Hinman's short story courses.

MARA SONNENSCHEIN has an MFA in screenwriting from the University of Southern California. In 2013, she started classes at The Writers Studio and now focuses on fiction writing. She has written a novel and is at work on a second book. She lives in New York City with her family.

DOUGLAS SOVERN wrote the first-of-its-kind Twitter novel "TweetHeart" in 2011. Since then, his short stories have appeared in *Narrative, Sand Hill Review,* the *Madison Review,* and over a dozen other magazines, have been honored by *Narrative* and Zoetrope: All-Story, and have been nominated for four Pushcart Prizes. A graduate of Brown University, he is a reporter at KCBS Radio in San Francisco and has won more than 200 journalism awards, including the duPont-Columbia, Edward R. Murrow, Sigma Delta Chi, and National Headliner awards. He is also a bassist and songwriter and performs with three rock bands. He was born in New York City and lives in Oakland, California, with his wife and children.

SEAN SUTHERLAND is currently studying with Philip Schultz at The Writers Studio in New York City. His poems have appeared in *Prick of the Spindle, Gravel, Lime Hawk, Blast Furnace, The Meadow,* and the *Maine Review,* for which he was a finalist for its 2014 poetry award. He is the director of the reading series Verbal Supply Company in Brooklyn, New York. He is also a MacDowell Colony fellow. He has enjoyed productions of his plays from the Stonington Opera House in Maine, to Los Angeles, to New York City at the Ensemble Studio Theatre. He self-published a chapbook of haikus and short poems in 2009 entitled *Forever in the City, Forever Arriving.*

SANTIAN VATAJ was born in the former Yugoslavia to Albanian parents. In 1987 his family moved to the Bronx, where he spent the next twenty-five years. He attended public schools in the borough before studying history at Lehman College. He is thirty-one years old and currently lives in Westchester. For the past nine years he has taught history at the high school level in the Bronx. Several years ago he took a class at The Writers Studio on a whim and it marked the beginning of his interest in writing stories; those Monday night classes remain very vivid in his memory. "The Fate of Anton K." is his first published work. He continues to write in his spare time.

IROMIE WEERAMANTRY is a Sri Lankan-born American fiction writer who splits her time between the Catskill Mountains and New York City, where she was fortunate to be a longtime member of The Writers Studio. Her short stories have appeared in *The Alembic, Green Hills Literary Lantern, The Saint Ann's Review,* and *Hamilton Stone Review.* Her story "Thugs" first appeared in *Green Hills Literary Lantern*. Iromie is honored to have it included in this special anthology and deeply grateful to Philip Schultz and The Writers Studio community for their support.

CAROL WHITE is a nurse practitioner living in Chattanooga, Tennessee. She works at a large inner city hospital, where she receives inspiration for her writing. She is relatively new to this writing business, and greatly appreciates The Writers Studio for its fabulous curriculum, supportive teachers, and inspiring community. Her short story "Pedicure" was published in the journal *Southern Women's Review*. This is her second publication. Carol is unused to writing about herself in the third person.

CATHERINE G. WOLF studied language development in graduate school, and was fascinated by this unique human ability. In 1997, when she was stricken with ALS, also known as Lou Gehrig's disease, her ability to speak was taken away by this disease. She found poetry had a special ability to express her innermost feelings. By losing her physical voice, Catherine found her poetic voice. Catherine has published in the 2016 *Rat's Ass Review* edition of *Love & Ensuing Madness*, *Rat's Ass Review*, *Front Porch Review*, *Verse-Virtual*, *Cacti Fur*, and *Bellevue Literary Review*. She uses assistive technology to communicate, and raises her right eyebrow to type.

PREVIOUS PUBLICATION CREDITS

"Harvest" by L.L. Babb from *The MacGuffin*, Fall 2014.

"Macaroons: The Last Days" by Lisa Badner from *The Cape Rock*, Fall 2009.

"Forgetting" by Cécile Barlier from *The Lindenwold Review*, Issue #4, 2014.

"Monkey Spinning a Prayer Wheel" by Lisa Bellamy from *Nectar* (Encircle Publications, 2011) and *Massachusetts Review*, Vol. 51, No. 3, Autumn 2010.

"One of Them" by Sylvie Bertrand from *Epiphany*, Fall 2016.

"The Lucky Ones" by Jill Bialosky from *The Players* (Alfred A. Knopf, 2015).

"Best of the Boy Stuff" by Reneé Bibby from *Third Point Press*, Issue #5, Summer 2016.

"Overboard" by Robley Browne from *Knee-Jerk*, July 2015.

"Hellion" by Doris Cheng from *Calyx Journal*, Vol. 29, No. 3, Winter/Spring 2017.

"Then One Day You Give A Guy Your Legs" by Jennafer D'Alvia from *The 34thParallel Magazine*, Issue #32, November 2015.

"Road Trip with a Dead Therapist" by Isabelle Deconinck from *Five Points*, Vol. 15, No. 3, Fall 2013.

"The God Who Loves You" by Carl Dennis from *Practical Gods* (Penguin Books, 2001).

"The Old Economy Husband" by Lesley Dormen from *The Best Place To Be* (Simon & Schuster, 2007) and *The Atlantic*, December Issue, 2001.

"Bad Dream" by Cornelius Eady from "Transition: Poems in the Aftermath," an online series by *Indolent Books*, December 2016.

"One Piece" by Jennifer Egan from *Emerald City and Other Stories* (Anchor, 1993) and *North American Review*, Vol. 274, No. 2, June 1989.

"First Girl" by Elizabeth England from *The Journal*, 2007.

"She-Monster Gets Fired" by Kim Farrar from *New Ohio Review*, Fall 2016.

"Thank You for Making Today Beautiful" by Patricia Follert from *Epiphany*, Fall 2015.

"First Kill" by Janet Franklin from *Cider Press Review*, Vol. 18, No. 1, 2016.

"Judy Garland Gets Dressed" by Christina Frei from *Third Wednesday*, Vol. IX, No. 1, 2015/2016.

"Attainable Felicity" by Julia Glass from *The Washington Post Magazine* (The Fiction Issue), November 2011. (The version of the story appearing in this anthology differs from the original).

"Patrimony" by Nancy Green from *The Bellevue Literary Review*, Vol. 13, No. 2, 2013.

"Keep Moving" by Patrick Hansel from *Perfume River Poetry Review*, Vol. 1, 2013.

"A Room That Has Lizzy in It" by Michele Herman from *Outside In Literary & Travel Magazine*, Issue #11, March 2013.

"The Watch" by Edward Hirsch from *American Poetry Review*, Vol. 45, No. 4, Jul/Aug 2016.

"Probably Last Meeting of Bluebell Ridge II Homeowners Association" by Philip Ivory from *The Airgonaut*, March 2017.

"Cleaved" by Kathie Jacobson from *Twisted Vine*, Summer 2015.

"Echo Lake" by Timur Karaca from *Narrative* magazine, September 2013.

"Eve" by Jennifer Kearns from *EDGE*, Vol. 10, 2016.

"Apple Pie" by Eleanor Kedney from *The Offering* (Liquid Light Press, 2016) and *Connecticut River Review*, 2015.

"El Camino" by Robert Kendrick from *Concho River Review*, Vol. 29, No. 1, 2015.

"Uprising" by Maggie Kennedy from *Meat For Tea*, Vol. 10, Issue 1, March 2016.

"I watch him, my husband" by Jay Kidd from *Atlanta Review*, Fall 2015.

"Trust" by Liz Kingsley from *New Ohio Review*, Issue #11, 2012.

"Issues I Dealt With In Therapy" by Matthew Klam from *Sam the Cat and Other Stories* (Vintage, 2001) and *The New Yorker*, July 12, 1992 Issue; © Condé Nast.

"All Dressed in Green" by Peter Krass from *Rattle*, Issue #33, Summer 2010.

"The Incalculable Life Gesture" by James Lasdun from *It's Beginning to Hurt* (Picador, 2010).

"Implausible" by Iris Lee from *Urban Bird Life* (NYQ Books, 2010).

"Anyone Crazier Than You" by Andrée Lockwood from *Epiphany*, Spring/ Summer 2011.

"Playboy" by Lela Scott MacNiel from *Gertrude Press*, Issue #21, Summer 2014.

"Back" by Andrea Marcusa from *In The Words of Womyn International 2016 Anthology* (Yellow Chair Press, 2016).

"Etchings" by Nancy Matsunaga from *Calyx*, Vol. 28, No. 1, Winter/Spring 2016.

"Purple Head" by Sarah McElwain from *FictionNow*, Winter 2013.

"The World Outside My Belly" by Rachael Lynn Nevins from *Mom Egg Review*, Vol. 9, 2011.

"Dancers" by Mark Fenlon Peterson from *The Milo Review*, Vol. 2, Issue 4, Winter 2014.

"In the Coma" by Robert Pinsky from *At the Foundling Hospital: Poems* (Farrar, Straus and Giroux, 2016) and *Poetry*, February 2016.

"The Closet" by Whitney Porter from *Metazen*, November 2011.

"Ship Out to Sea" by Máire T. Robinson from *The Chattahoochee Review*, Vol. 32, No. 2 & 3, Fall/Winter 2012.

"Piece of My Heart" by Elliot Satsky from *North American Review*, Vol. 300, No. 1, Winter 2015.

"Prayer" by Grace Schulman from *The Paintings of Our Lives* (Houghton Mifflin Harcourt, 2001) and *Poetry*, Eighty-Fifth Anniversary Issue, October-November 1997.

"The Adventures of 78 Charles Street" by Philip Schultz from *Failure* (Harcourt, 2007) and *The New Yorker*, April 24, 2006 Issue; © Condé Nast.

"The Red Bird" by J. D. Serling from *New Ohio Review*, Fall 2010.

"Astronauts" by Christopher Shade from *Steel Toe Review*, Issue #19, May 2014.

"A Price for Literacy" by R. A. Shockley from *Loose Change*, Issue #5.2, 2015.

"The Sweet Red Awakening of Bruce Allen DeSilva" by Patricia Smith from *Able Muse Review*, Issue #13, Summer 2012.

"Still. Life." by Mara Sonnenschein from *Liars' League NYC* (online), February 2015.

"Skin" by Douglas Sovern from *The Madison Review*, Spring 2016.

"Four Deckhands" by Sean Sutherland from *The Maine Review*, 2014.

"The Swans" by Anamyn Turowski from *New Ohio Review*, Spring 2012.

"Cotillion Photo" by Rosanna Warren from *The New Yorker*, February 1, 2016 Issue; © Condé Nast.

"Thugs" by Iromie Weeramantry from *Green Hills Literary Lantern*, Issue #25, 2014.

"Boyfriends" by Cynthia Weiner from *Ploughshares*, Spring 2004.

"Homecoming" by Abigail Wender from *AP English Literature & Composition for Dummies* by Geraldine Woods (Wiley Publishing Co., 2008).

"Lou Gehrig's Army" by Catherine Wolf from *Bellevue Literary Review*, Spring 2015.